MW01629055

Odyssey of Hope

Odyssey of Hope

The Story of a Lithuanian Immigrant's Escape from Communism to Freedom in America and the Return to his Beloved Homeland

By JOSEPH KAZICKAS
with VALDAS BARTASEVIČIUS

translated by VIJOLĖ ARBAS
edited by JURATE KAZICKAS

VILNIUS 2006

UDK 888.2-94
Ka677

Photograph illustrations from the family archive
of Alexandra and Joseph Kazickas
Design by Vida Kuraitė

Printed in Lithuania
ISBN 9986-16-505-9

CONTENTS

FOREWORD

Esteemed readers,

These memoirs are not merely the story about the road in the lives of Alexandra and Joseph Kazickas. Here readers will experience the dramatic and tragic breaking points in the history of 20th century Lithuania, right along with the remembrances of the authors.

The life of Joseph Kazickas, a distinguished Lithuanian businessman, public activist and philanthropist, perfectly reflects the historical fate of the Lithuanian nation.

That Kazickas was born on the steppes of Russia in a village of Lithuanian exiles rather than in the homeland of his ancestors was due to the fierce fate of Lithuanian history. Czarist rule banished the Kazickas family to one of the most remote and rough backwoods area of the Russian empire for participating in the 1863 Insurrection which had been an effort to re-establish the statehood of Lithuania and Poland.

Neither repressions nor bitter exiles quenched the thirst of the Lithuanian nation for its freedom. Just as many others, the banished Kazickas family preserved their native language, religion and customs over the long decades. Plus they fostered a passionate longing to return to their homeland. Such an opportunity did not present itself until more than a half a century had passed when the Russian empire collapsed and the independence of Lithuania was reinstated in 1918. Kazickas is a member of the third generation in exile. Despite the distance of vast Russian steppes where Lithuanians had been forced to settle, Lithuania was their dreamland. Thus, as soon as they were able, they returned to the historical land of their ancestors.

Kazickas was only four years old when he first saw Lithuania. A few decades passed and, once again, he, like thousands of other Lithuanians, was forced to leave his country. To save the lives of his wife, Alexandra, and his year and a half old daughter, Jurate, he had to flee west to escape the forces of the Soviet occupation.

The people of Western countries can barely imagine the difficult road taken by Lithuanians and those from other enslaved nations towards freedom. This book helps readers, especially Americans, to better comprehend the feelings of Lithuanian émigrés. Even though they had barely a few dollars in their pockets, they were smitten with an unconquerable hope for a better life as their ship approached the shores of New York and the Statue of Liberty.

Homeland lost, Lithuanian émigrés still managed to create new, productive lives in the United States. The Kazickas family, here again, is a perfect example of Lithuanian perseverance, determination and diligence. After earning his doctorate at Yale University, Kazickas made a successful career in business. The story of his success testifies to the tolerance and democracy of the people of the United States.

Joseph and Alexandra Kazickas made tremendous accomplishments in the United States, but they never forgot the country of their origin. They actively participated with the American -Lithuanian Community in the United States and constantly backed organizations that were struggling for the liberation of Lithuania and protesting against Soviet occupation in the international arena.

Lithuania finally re-established independence on March 11th of 1990, after five decades of occupation. This opened new opportunities for American Lithuanians to assist their homeland. Kazickas accomplished an especially great deal by supporting the efforts of the newly created government of Lithuania in overcoming diplomatic isolation and cracking the Soviet blockade. He was one of the first émigrés to begin investing in the homeland by creating a business in modern technology. Due to his efforts, several multinational enterprises entered the Lithuanian market.

With the tremendous experience and accumulated capital he had gained in the United States, Joseph Kazickas again returned to the Lithuania, which had re-established its independence, with his works and public actions.

The road traveled by Kazickas and so many other émigrés is well known to me as well. We all sought the same goal in different ways – re-creating a flourishing state of Lithuania.

The forming of nationhood is a never-ending process. The expansion of democracy and the formation of public welfare are of key importance. Even today Kazickas is enthusiastically engaged in this important work.

My generation knows the price of freedom only too well. Freedom must be constantly defended and guarded. It is of utmost importance that the younger generation learns the values of democracy and cherishes its own homeland not only with words but also with tireless efforts. The life of the Kazickas family is an excellent example for young people to utilize their abilities and experiences to build lives that are beneficial not only for themselves but for their countrymen as well.

I am convinced of the value for people from abroad to read this story about the perseverance and endurance involved in cherishing and loving one's homeland. This book reveals the true spirit of the Lithuanian people. It is also an optimistic story about the need to preserve hope and faith during the most trying times.

Such is the eternal odyssey of hope.

VALDAS ADAMKUS
President of the Republic of Lithuania
December, 2005

INTRODUCTION

My Father, My Country

When my father was born on April 16, 1918, his face was covered in a caul, a thin membrane that throughout many cultures over the centuries has been seen as a sign of greatness, promising a life of good luck and accomplishment. Several gifted people in history have come into the world this unusual way, wrapped as if in a magical second skin.

Joseph Kazickas' life story did become one of great luck and success. He was a refugee from Lithuania who came to America with nothing but his quick wits and prospered. But throughout the 50 years of Soviet occupation of the Baltic countries, he never lost his love for his homeland and the dream that one day his country would be free again. At this writing, he is now in his 88th year, still launching new business ventures, helping his beloved Lithuania and continuing, as always, to dream the impossible and make it a reality.

As Soviet troops advanced in 1944, my father made the painful decision to leave Lithuania. I was then just a baby in my mother's arms but, over the years, I have heard that story a thousand times. We were a little caravan of anxious souls, twenty-one men, women and children on horse-drawn wagons followed by a cow, plodding through the dark forests, fleeing west as the artillery thundered in the distance.

We found safety in the displaced person camps of Germany but lived through years of uncertainty and confusion. My father parlayed his modest English language skills to work as a translator for the American military, who introduced us famished refugees to the delights of white bread and peanut butter.

But everything comes into focus for me when we crossed the stormy Atlantic on the freighter, SS Ernie Pyle, in February 1947. Sailing into New York harbor, I had my first glimpse of skyscrapers and that iconic symbol of freedom, the Statue of Liberty. It was my fourth birthday and the chef on board baked me a cake. My excitement was bittersweet because the pathetic rag doll I had always carried with me lost her head in the crush of people rushing to get their first look at the Promised Land. My mother told me to throw her overboard. I did as I was told but, through my tears, I can still see the headless bundle of cloth floating on the murky waters. I was devastated. My mother assured me that I would have many more great big dolls in America.

Our Lithuanian host family in Brooklyn who took us into their home did indeed give me an American doll. It was hard, stiff and cuddle proof with an unpleasant chemical smell. But it was the biggest doll I had ever seen.

My father sold insurance door-to-door in Wilkes Barre, Pennsylvania before we settled in New Haven where my father began his studies at Yale for his doctorate in economics. I shared the bedroom with my parents in a big house on Chapel Street with several boarders. I liked to slide down the shiny mahogany banister and poke around the other people's rooms that my mother cleaned. She had a university degree but never once complained that here she was, scrubbing other people's toilets.

My parents were great music lovers, especially opera. Saturday afternoons I would lie on the floor coloring while Milton Cross narrated the plot of some magnificent opera on the radio. My mother had a beautiful voice and would often join in the arias. I felt loved and protected. The war years were far behind us.

At St. Mary's School, a kindly nun named Sister Wilfrida made a decision that has impacted my life in so many ways. When we enrolled at the school, my mother suggested that perhaps I should be called by my middle name, Catherine, since Jurate was not so simple to pronounce. Sister Wilfrida was adamant. "Jurate is her name and that's what everybody will learn to call her." It has not been easy throughout my life being burdened with a foreign name but, then again, it has always given me the opportunity to talk about Lithuania. During the dismal years of the Cold War, I welcomed the chance to acquaint anyone who asked the origins of my name with the sad plight of my homeland.

When my father cast his fate as an entrepreneurial businessman instead of becoming a college professor, we moved to New Rochelle, and our family expanded rapidly. Four boys were born in six years. My teenage Saturdays were spent helping my mother care for my brothers. She always said with pride that she never had to hire a baby-sitter.

Our house on Lyncroft Road, which my father built, had a large finished basement with a ping-pong table and a fancy train set for the boys. There was a magnificent seascape on one wall painted by a Lithuanian artist, Česlovas Januša. Hidden in the foam of the tumbling waves was my mother's nickname, Alė. When we had visitors, it was always fun to see who could spot the letters first.

The basement was the scene of many parties. My parents were gregarious and generous with the champagne. Their Lithuanian friends came often to dance and sing. Inevitably, as the night wore on, their songs changed from cheery folk tunes to the saddest of ballads ending with our dolorous national anthem. Everyone would cry. They wept for the loss of their homeland, fearing that they would never again walk along the shores of the Baltic or smell the fragrant pine trees or make wreaths from the clover in the summer fields.

Upstairs in my room, I would hear the singing, and it made me sad. I felt that these poor immigrants were clinging to a faded dream. The communist system was so powerful. Nothing would ever change. Lithuania was not even on the map anymore. It did not exist.

But my father always tried to end the evening with a more spirited song. He believed in the deepest part of his soul that Lithuania would be free one day. He never doubted it for a minute. He knew the communist system was doomed because nothing was more powerful than people's yearning to be free. He thought that perhaps the Soviet Union would collapse internally like some hideous giant dragon whose heart gets crushed from its own weight. During the tense years of the Cold War, he speculated that a third world war might break out between the super powers and, in the chaos of the struggle, the captive nations would rise against their oppressors and break their chains. But in his wildest dreams, I don't think he ever imagined that his tiny homeland would initiate the break-up of the Soviet Union.

But long before that most dramatic event, my father occupied himself with business affairs, learning very early on a fundamental secret of how to succeed. Today we call it networking but, for him, it was nothing more than a genuine passion for meeting new people. Through his dynamic personality, charm and warmth of character, individuals from all walks of life were drawn to him.

My father always made a point of learning the name of a limousine driver or a waiter or a chambermaid. He always spoke to them as if they were long-lost friends, inquiring about their work and their families. He was genuinely interested in what they had to say, and it showed. His easy rapport with waiters had an unexpected bonanza when many of them went on to become maitre d's and owners of exclusive restaurants like Le Pavillon, La Cote Basque and Club 21. Thus, when he showed up, he was always assured of the very best table. I loved going to those fancy places with my father. Surrounded by New York's famous elite, there we were nobodies but treated like royalty.

And then there were the true royals that my father in his many travels befriended like the Indian maharajahs. A chance encounter at the Olympic Games in Helsinki with a member of India's shooting team resulted in an invitation to hunt with the Maharajah of Bikaner in Rhajastan. Years later I was the guest of the Maharana of Udaipur and spent a night in the most magnificent palace with dozens of servants hovering outside my door. Everywhere I looked, on the walls, the shelves and tables, artifacts covered with rubies and emeralds dazzled my eyes. My first taste of curry came with a spinach casserole covered in edible silver leaf.

I know that my father had business reversals many times when deals dried up, and suddenly there was no money coming in. But it was a point of pride with him that his lifestyle would not change and that his family would never have to compromise our quality of life for a mere inconvenience like an empty bank account. Even during the early years in America, my father was determined that we enjoy the good things in life. One of the pleasures for the three of us, when we lived in New Haven, was a weekly visit to the movies. He budgeted carefully for that special treat. When *Gone with the Wind* came to the theaters and cost double our weekly allowance for entertainment, the other Lithuanians went home dejectedly, but we marched right in. "This is our movie night and no matter what it costs, we're going," said my dad.

So I never knew whether his business fortunes were up or down. He always insisted on going first class, staying at the best hotels and dining at the finest restaurants. My father traveled so much during those early years of his business ventures. Sometimes he would be gone four or five weeks at a time, drumming up new business opportunities in Europe. But I knew that when he came home, my mother and I would be lavished with gifts. What he loved more than anything was to buy clothes for us by the most fashionable designers in Italy and France. I barely gave him a welcome home kiss before tearing into boxes filled with luxurious sweaters from the house of Dior, Hermes scarves and Gucci bags. The presents did not make up for the long, lonely weeks without him, but I think they made him feel less guilty for being gone.

I learned to love to travel from my father. As a high school graduation present, he gave me a first class tour of Europe. In 1960 we left my mother home with the four boys, and he and I took off for a six-week trip through the major European countries from England on to the chateaus of the Loire Valley and the castles of Bavaria to the treasures of glorious Italy. My father was the best companion, knowledgeable, boundlessly enthusiastic about every tourist site and indefatigable. A long day of sight-seeing was capped by dinner at some fancy restaurant where, of course, the head waiter knew him by name.

I was dazzled by the number of influential people that my father somehow managed to meet. Corporate titans, international diplomats and millionaires were drawn to him because of his charisma, delightful sense of humor and dazzling conversational skills. He was humble enough to know that sometimes one of these luminaries would look over at him and wonder, "Joe who? Who the hell is that guy? How did he get here?"

He always used these connections that seemed to materialize in total serendipity to press the cause of freedom for communist occupied Lithuania. His life story is replete with chance encounters that became friendships that resulted in meetings with the powers that be to lobby for Lithuanian independence. One of the more remarkable examples of this was his inspired idea to call an old friend in Washington on behalf of Prime Minister Kazimiera Prunskienė in 1990. Lithuania had just declared independence in a bold move that would precipitate the total collapse of the Soviet Union but, at that moment, the world was not paying attention. His phone call initiated not only an appointment with the President of the United States but meetings with the heads of state of England, Germany and France that, I believe, were instrumental in Lithuania's eventual acceptance into the international community.

His sole motivation was to do all he could to help his beloved homeland. And that profound love for his country has been the underlying theme of my father's life. Whether giving fiery anti-communist speeches during those early years in America, or lobbying Senators and Congressmen to uphold non-recognition of Lithuania's forcible occupation or building a business to bolster the Lithuanian economy, all he wanted was to see his country become a successful member of the free world.

His guiding force has always been his deep faith. Nothing could shake it even in the darkest days. It was a beacon that summoned him to do his very best, to be honest, kind and generous. He always felt that freedom is one of God's most precious gifts that must be protected and cherished. I know he is eternally grateful for his many blessings.

And the greatest of these is his wife and my mother, Alexandra. Throughout my father's long, interesting life, his constant companion was my mother. His story, I think, would have been very different without this extraordinary, selfless woman who helped him achieve his dreams. She could have been an opera star but put aside her own dreams to raise a family and support her husband. Sometimes she endorsed his wild ambitions and sometimes she scoffed that they were preposterous. Whatever her reaction, my father was fiercely motivated to prove her right – or wrong.

Their enduring marriage, now more than 65 years, is an inspiration. Through the best of times and worst of times, they held on to each other. Together they created a wonderful family that delights my father so much. Nothing makes him happier than to be surrounded by his children and grandchildren.

To all of us, my parents have passed on their passionate commitment to Lithuania. My first trip there was in 1968. I spent five days in Vilnius, meeting with old friends of my parents. I could see the despair in their faces. They were plodding through life with no joy or hope. We couldn't really talk openly because there were microphones everywhere, under the bed in my hotel room, in the plastic flowers on the table in the restaurant. I breathed a sigh of relief when my plane took off but felt so sad for the desperate plight of my country, seemingly forever in the clutches of the Soviets.

So it was with the greatest happiness that, on March 11, 1990, I sat with my father in the Parliament Hall in Vilnius when Lithuania declared its independence once again. I watched in tears as the yellow, green and red national flag that had been banned for decades rose from the floor to obliterate the huge bronze hammer and sickle, the loathed communist symbol, once and for all.

My father and I embraced, hardly able to believe what we had seen. I was never more proud of my tiny homeland and thrilled for my father who had so yearned for this day. Even at that moment I could sense he was already thinking of all the work ahead and what he could do to help.

As we sang with fervor that once forbidden national anthem, the words resonated with me in a new way. Now, whenever I hear *Lietuva, Tėvyne Mūsų*, I can't help but think of my father – his long life, his many good deeds and above all his dedication to that beautiful country we hold so dear…

"Lithuania, our fatherland
Home of heroes grand….
May your children forward stride
Always on the path of virtue.
May their service be in your name
For the betterment of all people…
May the love of Lithuania
Burn forever in our hearts…"

JURATE KAZICKAS
February, 2006

A Note to the Reader

Alexandra and I initially decided to put these memories of ours down on paper, thinking about our grandchildren. Born into a comfortable way of life in the United States, they have never experienced poverty or the loss of freedom. They cannot imagine the way we, their grandparents, lived and the complicated road of life we have traveled.

So, we embarked on the sea of our memories. At first we thought we would only write about our past in Lithuania, the terrible years of war and the difficulties we faced as refugees in Germany before coming to America. But we had so many adventures and fantastic experiences later on, after those hard early years of settlement in the United States that we decided we wanted to share the bountiful times as well. The end result is a book that encompasses our entire lives.

I was in a quandary for a long time, wondering if someone who read these pages would get the impression that this book was no more than the vainglorious musings of a lucky old man, flaunting an exciting and happy life. But Valdas Bartasevičius, who came to me with the idea for this book and interviewed me for many, many hours, convinced me that my story would be of interest to people even outside our family circle.

Beyond all my adventures, my experiences and relationships along the way with successful and prominent people helped me understand many things. Economic success and fairy-tale wealth do not bring joy. A person can only feel true happiness in creating a more beautiful life for others – not only for oneself.

Another truth came to me while I was observing life in various countries of the world. No matter how rich one is, the pleasures money can provide cannot be freely enjoyed if tremendous poverty exists. Wealth then becomes a challenge, a sore splinter in the eyes of society.

The worth of a person is not measured by how much he or she has but by how much one is able to give. Life only has meaning when one is sharing good fortune with others and contributing to a better life for everyone. I believe good works start in the home for the family and then must extend to friends, countrymen and, ideally, the world at large.

Anytime that something beneficial for others is being done, a sort of magnetic field develops between people – creative energy is transmitted from one to another. All energy, expended for the sake of others, returns again to motivate and eventually enhance the self.

These are the simple truths of daily existence which I inherited from my own parents. They never discussed the meaning of life, certainly not in any philosophical terms. They simply lived naturally by the Ten Commandments of God, loving the persons close to them, their community and their own country. I am thankful for all that they taught me by their example.

I think many people would say that, despite many hardships, my life has been successful. I learned early on that small goals often demand as much effort as grandiose ones. That has convinced me never to fear pursuing even the most impossible dreams.

But success goes hand-in-hand with responsibility. Whoever receives the most from life also holds the greatest responsibility. As a businessman for many years, I know how important that is. I have always felt that a businessperson must have a hard head and a soft heart. By relying on a hard head, it is possible to create new enterprises and accumulate wealth. The danger is that a sense of meaningfulness can be lost. Purely selfish goals deplete the soul and get in the way of true happiness.

A soft heart alone is also not the best advisor in business. The ability to say "no" is necessary. Otherwise failure threatens. Only a balance between head and heart can help develop the sort of business ventures that benefit the community and eventually the entire country.

Essentially this is the link between business and morality. World experience has shown that when the creation of the economic life of an individual or a country does not rest on a firm foundation of morality, any material advancement is merely temporary or even illusionary in the best case.

After fifty years of isolation from the world, Lithuania will have a tough time overcoming all that it lost. As values change, it is not easy to find the right road and the foundations of morality sometimes weaken.

Nevertheless I have been an optimist all my life. During all the years of the occupation, I never doubted that the Soviet Empire would ultimately self-destruct, and Lithuania would regain its independence. Now in my very old age, I am an even greater optimist.

There is not a doubt in my mind that Lithuania will catch up with Western countries at social and economic levels. I further know that this will not take as much time as the movement for independence took. Advancement is already obvious today. It only remains unnoticed to those who are too weary from all the hardships and deprivations they've suffered to open up their eyes.

No matter how hard it was for me, no matter how much a situation seemed hopeless, I still never lost hope. I always saw a recourse rushing head on to my assistance. This is the reason for entitling these memoirs, *Odyssey of Hope*.

At present I think too many of my country folk are pessimistic and lack faith. This motivated me to publish these memoirs first in Lithuanian for an audience beyond my grandchildren. Should any person – especially a young one – solidify his or her hope at least a little bit by reading this book, my telling of the story will not be in vain. This is a tale about a child born to Siberia-doomed exiles, inheriting nothing more than the moral principles of his parents, and the long road traveled, all the way from the ravages of war to the most prestigious places of American life.

I want to thank Valdas Bartasevičius for helping me to recall the most significant moments of my life through his long, probing interviews. Though I was at first reluctant to do so, he encouraged me to make my story public. He shaped my many musings and memories into the original Lithuanian text with great skill and style. At the urging of my children, I then agreed to have the book translated into English. My deepest thanks go to Vijolė Arbas, who undertook this massive assignment with grace and patience. A Lithuanian, she was raised in America. She has a linguist's gift of finding just the right word. No one could have done it better.

We decided to use the Lithuanian alphabet with its thirty-three letters and distinctive markings for the proper names in the book. After the 1863 Insurrection (causing the exile of my grandfather), this alphabet was prohibited for forty years. Then, for all those years under the Soviets, Russian was forced upon us as the official language. This is just a small way to pay tribute to our distinctive culture.

But I must hasten to add that while the words here are indeed all mine, they were recorded strictly from my memory without any access to notes or documents or interviews with colleagues, relatives or friends. Thus I take full responsibility for any errors or discrepancies with actual facts and apologize in advance if my recollection of events may differ with those of other participants.

But I do hope that that even more people will learn about Lithuania through the experience of one fortunate refugee. I am a patriotic American and grateful for all that this country has given me but I have never lost my love for my homeland.

This book is also meant to show gratitude to God for life. It is a thank you to all our relatives and friends. It is for all those who bring me happiness by their very being with no one more dear to my heart than my beautiful, devoted, fabulous wife, Alexandra, whom I love with the same passion and intensity I felt more than sixty-five years ago.

This book is also for my ancestors who have moved on to eternity leaving behind their priceless gift – all the unforgettable moments of life together.

JOSEPH KAZICKAS
February, 2006

PART I

Six Decades in Exile

Prologue:

Recollections of Grasilija Sereičikaitė-Meiluvienė, Joseph Kazickas' Aunt

I was born near Kazakhstan, in the Russian steppes which range over the Ural Mountains between the Caspian Sea and the Volga River.

My parents were exiled from Lithuania when they were just children. My mother, Natalija Bugaitė, was seven years old and my father, Jonas Sereičikas, was nine. My mother used to tell us the story of how our family had been driven so far from home:

"It was *Kūčios*, the Lithuanian Christmas Eve. After fasting all day, we'd just sat down to our festive supper. Suddenly there was a crash and the door burst open. It was a Cossack. He ordered us all to get ready for a journey right away. 'What journey? What for?' He didn't give a word of explanation; he just barked orders. 'Quick! Throw your furs over your shoulders and get out of the house!' A one-horse sleigh stood in the yard. Only the very young and the very old were allowed to get in. Grandmother brought out some bedding to cover us up. 'No! That's not allowed!' the Cossack shouted.

"The winter was bitterly cold; there had been deep snowfalls. We saw more sleighs around us, with more children. The families plodded alongside, people from our village and other villages. This was Russian vengeance – and our sentence – for the Insurrection of 1863 which the Cossacks were then violently crushing."

Horrifying scenes from that journey into exile stayed with my mother to her last breath. During the daytime, people struggled through the snow on foot to keep up with the sleighs; there were only a few pauses for rest, and those were brief. At night they were all herded into makeshift jails. Starved and freezing, one traveler after another fell exhausted by the roadside and died. By the time the caravan reached its final destination, in the steppes near Kazakhstan, my mother was an orphan. She hadn't really understood what was happening: Father simply disappeared and then, suddenly, Mother was gone too. Five children, three girls and two boys, were left without parents to face an incomprehensible world. They wound up in the care of a Ukrainian family who had been exiled to the area some time earlier.

Once the weather turned warmer, the Lithuanians began building huts – *zemlianka*s – on the land they'd been assigned. They made their bricks by molding clay with hay. That was the origin of Chornaya Padina – Black Hollow. About three hundred families settled the village.

Mama told us that at first people would beg and beg the Russian officials to let them go back home. All they would get in reply was a threat of worse punishment. Sometimes the officials would deliver a beating the minute a person started to plead. The Lithuanians finally understood that they were doomed to exile there for a long, long time. And, at that point, they began to worry about holding on to their Catholic faith and their native tongue. One elderly man – everyone called him Grandpa Gudas – carved a huge wooden cross and put it up. People would gather around it, kneel and pray, and every prayer carried the same entreaty: "Lord, bring us back to our homeland."

Meanwhile the Lithuanians watered the rich soil of the steppes with their dusty sweat, gradually improving their lives. By the time I was a child, we lived on a large and well-ordered farm. A tall fence surrounded our yard with a gate that could be locked. At night people took turns guarding the village from robbers and arsonists with the help of trained dogs loosed from their chains. The Lithuanians now lived so much more comfortably than the people did in the surrounding villages that they had stirred up angry jealousy. All kinds of lowlifes and thieves did their best to loot Chornaya Padina. Horses, cows, sheep, chickens, tools, even little household items – in other words, anything they could get their hands on – were all stolen. The danger was worse during the summer when the men and some of the women had to leave to work in the far outlying fields.

I was the youngest child – the runt – of the family. I was still a little girl when my older sister, Katerina, married Mykolas Kazickas. She gave birth to their daughter, Viktorija (Victoria) – Viktutė – not long afterward. I was only a few years older than Viktutė, and she and I became good friends. When we got older, we went to school together. The school was a few kilometers from Chornaya Padina. During the winter we didn't try to get back home after classes – we rented a room from a Ukrainian family. Since I was a bit older, I felt responsible for Viktutė. Several times I had to defend her from the Russian louts who would accost us. At night we never set foot outside the door without an adult at our side.

But we had our fun after we got back to Chornaya Padina. We would play and swim in the river. If my parents gave me some sweets, I would immediately run to Viktutė's to share them. We were as inseparable at home as we'd been at school.

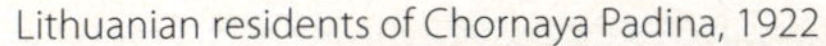
Lithuanian residents of Chornaya Padina, 1922

World War I broke out. The Russian Army drafted all three of my brothers. Then my father got sick, and my mother had to devote all her time to caring for him. Though I was still a child, much of the farm work fell to me. What a blessing it was that Katerina's husband, Mykolas Kazickas, was there to help us out. He'd been injured so he was excused from military service. You might say that he became the farm administrator, and I was his assistant. I cooked for the family in gigantic kettles. It was also my job to take care of the camels, and it was a horror trying to get them under control so I could harness them to the reapers.

The war ended but, with the Russian Revolution, the times got even worse. One after another, Red Army units and gangs of armed thieves terrorized the villages. Estate owners, military officers and administrators were massacred. Only by a miracle did my brother, Juozas, who had risen to the rank of lieutenant while serving on the front with the Czar's army, escape with his life. He and a group of army officers were put in front of a firing squad, but the bullet that hit him only injured him. He fell into the corpse-filled pit, unconscious. After a while, he came to and clawed his way out from under the shallow layer of earth that was covering the bodies and ran away. He found people who were good enough to hide him and feed him, but then someone informed on him. Juozas couldn't return to our farm; he had to stay hidden to evade arrest. Bolsheviks searched our house many a time, looking not just for Juozas but for my other brothers as well. After the revolution and the civil war, they couldn't come home either. My mother, my wretchedly ill father and I were only able to survive with the help of our relatives. Katerina and Mykolas lived right across the road and, whenever they noticed any armed men in the village, they would rush over to warn my mother and me to hide.

One time I very nearly was shot. Thieves broke into our farm and plundered the whole house. They took all the food they could find and all sorts of other things. Suddenly one of them walked over to me, aimed his rifle at me and asked if I happened to know him. I did know him – he was a hired hand from a neighboring village – but instinctively I sensed that I had to pretend I'd never laid eyes on him. I answered, "No, I've never met you before in my life."

"Lucky for you," he snorted. "I would have shot you if you'd recognized me." He turned around and walked out of the house.

It was during those terrible times, on an April day in 1918, that I got the news that Viktutė had a brother. Katerina had given birth to her second child, a little boy. He was christened Juozas (Joseph); affectionately we called him Juozukas. I loved to watch him bouncing around in his diapers like a little ball. Viktutė and I were only sorry that he was too small for us to take everywhere. Time sped on at a furious pace. Our little Juozukas grew up into Juozas Kazickas.

Conversation recorded in 1977

The End of Exile: First Recollections of Joseph Kazickas

My parents bequeathed me a joy in living that I've never lost. They lived their lives according to four principles: love and support inside the family, hard work every day, a thirst for knowledge and the relentless pursuit of freedom. They never put these principles into words; they simply lived by them, and the example they gave me was their greatest legacy. Our family was poor, but our hardships never became a source of hopelessness. We were happy with what we had. We shared our daily bread and our love.

I was one of two children – my sister, Victoria, is ten years older. We loved and respected our parents. Every evening at bedtime, we would kiss our father's hand and our mother's cheek. And then Mother would put us to bed with a kiss, and Father would stroke our heads. We always knew they would do anything for us.

When my grandparents were children, following the Insurrection of 1863, they were exiled from their home in the village of Užpaliai, in the Utena District of Lithuania, to the Pavolga Steppes, far away in Russia, along with a large group of other Lithuanians. Cossacks had forced their way into their parents' home on a peaceful *Kūčios* (Christmas Eve) evening, ordering them to gather up food and clothing and be ready to leave in a few minutes. Most of the people had to travel by foot; only children and the very old were allowed to sit in sleighs. One Cossack told my grandfather's grandmother – a very old woman at the time – "You, granny, are going to eat, sleep and die in this sleigh."

And that's what happened. She and many others died over the long year it took to move the families of the insurgents nearly two thousand miles east to Pavolga. When they finally reached the steppes, the Cossacks pushed the survivors, with their belongings, straight out into a stretch of wide-open fields. That first night they actually had to dig a trench out of the snow to lie down in, and they huddled together to sleep. The name of the new village may well have come from their memory of that first night in the place of their exile. They called it Chornaya Padina – Black Hollow. "This is the black pit of our fate," the people would say.

At daybreak the men took off to inspect their new surroundings. A few kilometers away, they came across some unusual looking farms. The residents were a race of people they had never seen before: the Tartars. The Tartars were friendly enough but couldn't really help them, because they were living in wretched poverty themselves. As though it had been planned that way, their first winter in exile was bitterly cold. Food was scarce. The freezing weather picked off one after another of the near-starved settlers; children and the elderly especially buckled under the hardships. Only the strongest managed to survive until spring.

The first year of farming was pure misery. The exiles had no idea when the best time was to plant grain in this unfamiliar land or what method was the best. They hadn't been allowed to bring even the simplest farm implements, so they had no choice but to make everything they needed with their own hands. Fortunately Pavolga's lands were very rich, even though the summers were short. After a year or two, the Lithuanians were living no less poorly than their neighbors. By the time the Russian Revolution began in 1917, they had managed to create a life for themselves far better than the lives of the nearby Tartars, Ukrainians and Russians. The Lithuanians were considered wealthy in that part of the world. They were growing grain for export to the West; they had developed solid herds of farm animals. Some had moved beyond agriculture into other fields to earn their livings.

But, during the unbearably difficult early years of exile, they knew that God alone could help them through. They associated hope with prayer. As soon as they managed to improve their lot a little, they built a church in Chornaya Padina. As things got better still, they even brought out a priest from Lithuania. An elementary school was built so that the children could learn to write in Lithuanian (which, unlike Russian, uses the Roman alphabet), and a teacher traveled out from Lithuania. In this tiny Lithuanian enclave, all but lost on the vast Russian plains, the people managed to nurture their own language for six decades. (In fact, when we were finally able to return to our homeland after the government of Lithuania had been reinstated, we settled in Vilkaviškis, which is a town of the Suvalkija region, where Lithuanians speak a fairly distinct dialect. When we arrived, the local folk could hardly understand our speech: we had retained, virtually unchanged, a mid-nineteenth-century dialect that had been spoken only in areas around Utena, quite a distance northeast of us.)

My grandparents had been very religious since their early childhoods, and they raised their children with the same devout Catholicism. Every single one of our days in Chornaya Padina ended with our kneeling together in prayer. On every night in May, the month of Mary, we would pray through all the beads of the rosary. And each morning began with all of us gathered to pray again. My parents kept up these strict traditions when we returned to Lithuania. Of course today such piety may seem excessive. But back then this constantly reaffirmed a relationship with God, nourished our faith that our lives would improve, gave us confidence in our strength and bound us together into a tightly knit family. My mother – Katerina Sereičikaitė was her maiden name – had an especially strong and openhearted faith. She would concentrate all her thoughts into her prayers so intently that it seemed as though she had a direct relationship with God. Her religion gave her peace; her prayers were her way of letting go of the pain that gnawed at her so deeply and so often, through her life.

As the end of World War I drew near, my father, Mykolas Kazickas, was seriously wounded. Back in those times, you could get killed for the pettiest reasons. I never did learn all the circumstances, but apparently he'd wound up in some sort of shootout with some thieves. A bullet hit him in the lungs, and it was never removed. I remember him later, after our return to Lithuania, often choking and gasping for air.

I was born on April 16, 1918, in a dark time. Russia was ablaze with civil war. A scene from my infancy has stuck in my memory: in a haze I can see the Chornaya Padina Church and the square before it; some kind of shooting has broken out. I can feel the warmth of my mother as she presses me tight against her chest.

Kazickas family, Chornaya Padina, 1912

I remember my father better from later times. I think of him as a tall, lean man of about 40, always happy and always reading. He loved to read. He also had beautiful handwriting – it was virtually calligraphy. I used to watch him write, amazed it was possible to form letters so smoothly and artistically.

I was barely three, in 1921, when starvation hit Russia. Earlier, during the revolution and the civil war, people had looked for ways to get around the constant expropriations of property. They had slaughtered their animals and taken their grain out of the granaries and hidden it in the fields under a thin layer of earth. But the rains rotted the grain, and then nothing was left but to dump the putrid seeds into the Volga. Hungry men and women stood sorrowfully along the banks, watching their bread float off toward the Caspian Sea. And, to make matters worse, a drought followed. There was no harvest. The granaries were bare; the barns were empty. All around, people were going mad from starvation.

I remember how, when a package of food arrived in Chornaya Padina from Lithuania, people would gather in the church square and take packets of rice and bread out of the bundle. These must have been for the children, because the packets were handed out to mothers who had come with their children.

But while the Lithuanians at Chornaya Padina were having a difficult time, they weren't starving like the Tartars and Kirghiz who flooded into our village, sometimes at the edge of death, begging for food. Units of Bolshevik soldiers constantly passed through, taking whatever food they could find. Our people were somehow clever enough to hide their stocks, and not a single person died of hunger. Yet, all around us, anything that was alive would get eaten. The dogs and cats disappeared from Chornaya Padina; hungry gangs who wandered into the village caught them all. Later Father told us that even shoe leather had been used for food – it was chopped up in small pieces and boiled. We would lock ourselves in our homes, bolting the doors and windows. Even if you dearly wanted to give someone a crust of bread, it was extremely dangerous to open the door. If you let someone in, more were likely to force their way. The torture of hunger and hopelessness clouded their minds. There were robberies, even murders.

I remember one event as vividly as though it just happened. Dusk is falling, and someone – probably a Tartar – rattles our window, his face swollen from starving. "I have to eat. Give me something to eat!" he begs in Russian. My mother slices a hunk of bread, and my grandfather leaps forward angrily: "Just what are you planning to do? The minute you open that door a whole mob of them will push their way in. Think what can happen!" But my mother does not obey him. She cracks open the door, thrusts the bread outside and quickly shuts it again.

This wordless lesson in Christian charity sank into my child's mind and stayed with me for the rest of my life.

There's not a lot else I can still recall of our life at Chornaya Padina – just splinters of visions, afloat like little islands on the sea of my memories. I remember riding with my parents out to the far outlying fields. Every summer the people of Chornaya Padina would leave the village to work in the steppes where they lived in tents for almost the whole season. Only the old stayed behind to watch over the homes. Once, when I was riding with my family in a camel-drawn wagon, I fell out and nobody noticed. I must have frozen up in fear, failing to utter so much as a yelp as I tumbled out. As soon as I came to, I took off, wailing, after the wagon, but it only rolled farther and farther away. A terrible sense of loneliness swept over me, as though I had been abandoned in the big world. Finally my sister shrieked, "Where's Juozukas?" and they realized that I had fallen out somewhere behind.

My clearest memory is of our long trip from our Chornaya Padina home to Lithuania. Our reinstated government had negotiated with Russia for the repatriation of Lithuanian exiles, and our family had decided to return to the land of our ancestors. Most of the others had too, though some families couldn't bring themselves to leave the large and beautifully running farms they had built up with the sweat of their brows in Russia. They tried to convince the rest of us to stay. Nobody in Lithuania, they said, was awaiting the return of the 1863 exiles; but here in Russia, civil unrest would slowly dissipate, and the way would open up again to a life of hearty farming. They were wrong, of course.

The rich harvests of Chornaya Padina had brought affluence to my parents. Our family sold grain for export; we had cattle and camels. Although we lived in the village, before the revolution we had bought a house in Saratov. By the Bolsheviks' measure, we were thoroughly bourgeois and, if we hadn't returned to Lithuania when we did, we would have found ourselves, as did so many other affluent families under Bolshevik rule, exiled to Siberia – or worse.

But getting back to the homeland was far from easy. Anyone emigrating had to acquire all sorts of documents to prove that he or she, or at least his or her parents or grandparents, had been born in Lithuania. Someone from the family had to travel all the way to Moscow to search for birth certificates. It took months of preparation, but we set out for our journey at long last early in the summer of 1922. We had never laid eyes on the land of our grandparents' birth but we had heard countless stories of its beauty. As it turned out, we wouldn't see it until autumn was well underway: the trip was to take a good three months.

I was only four, but I clearly remember crossing the Volga with our huge pile of belongings. The Soviet government prohibited repatriates from taking out any gold but, after my family's many years of hard work, of course, we had acquired some gold. My parents cleverly hid it in the bedding, and no one discovered it during any of the property searches along the way. But the Soviets did permit us to take our furniture, carpets and all manner of utensils and appliances, and so it was that we were lugging a big bundle of goods. I remember in particular a large carpet that my father had a hard time selling when we got to Lithuania. No one had rooms big enough for a carpet like that. It eventually wound up in Vilkaviškis Church.

We had to wait on the riverbank for a long time – it may have been several days – before someone could be found to ferry us across. I was awed by the vast width of the Volga. I see myself in my mother's arms. I see the boat cutting across the dark waves of roiling water. I see the opposite shore and on it, the Pavolga Railway Station. Again it was a long wait for the train. We ate and slept on the bags and boxes where all of our accumulated wealth was packed.

Finally the train arrived. Four families of Lithuanians clambered aboard into each waiting freight wagon. Slowly we started moving forward, praying for God to bless our journey to the mystical birthplace of our grandparents. After that, the trip seemed to go on forever. We became numb to the noise of the rolling wheels, ceaseless, monotonous, day after day – or not quite ceaseless, since the train also took long stops. Sometimes those stops seemed endless when as much as a week went by without our moving an inch.

We ate mostly food we had brought from Chornaya Padina, potatoes and slabs of smoked bacon. The horrendous starvation of 1921 had ebbed to some degree, and bread and a few other items were available for a small price at the towns where the train stopped. Since we had no (visible) money with us, Father would sell or trade items from our load to buy food. We could drink tea or have soup on the train. Our relatives had brought along a big samovar-like teakettle; we would break up firewood into tiny pieces and light a fire under it. The smoke went up a small chimney and out the window of the wagon.

When, after what seemed like forever, we reached Moscow; the train stopped for several days. All of our documents and baggage were thoroughly checked. The adults would leave for long stretches to explore the city but, since I was a child, I got left behind, stuck mostly in the freight wagon or the large waiting room of the railway station.

Eventually the train left Moscow and dragged laboriously toward Latvia. There we were stuck in the capital, Riga, for three days; no one was allowed to venture into town. I gathered from what I overheard that the Latvians were afraid we might decide to stay. But no one, in our family at least, had the slightest desire to settle in Latvia. We were on our way to the Promised Land. We might never have seen Lithuania but we had been there many a time in our dreams. Nearly six decades had passed since soldiers forced the caravan of sleighs into a distant exile after the Insurrection of 1863. Not a single member of that entourage still walked this earth. It was we, their children and grandchildren, who were returning to the land of their birth, the country we considered our own homeland. No matter if we were the descendants of exiles who had been dragged away while they were mere children. Our grandparents had retained some recollections of Lithuania, and the more time passed, the more beautiful the stories of their cherished homeland grew. And then their children – our parents – embroidered the stories even more. To us children, Lithuania had become a fairy tale land.

When the tiniest breeze floated in over the fields during those relentlessly hot summers in Chornaya Padina, people would wipe their brows in relief and say, "Ahh, it's coming from Lithuania." At night the old people would stare up at the star-filled sky and say, "The stars shine brighter in Lithuania." Many was the time I heard that, in the distant land of my grandparents, fruits and berries grew that could never have been imagined on the steppes. During that eternal journey across the vast Russian plains, I grew more and more impatient for the wondrous place named Lithuania. In my mind's eye I saw wide stretches of a beautiful sun-drenched land with gardens full of apples.

At last my parents began saying we were about to cross into Lithuania. By that time it was October, and the sun was no longer shining. The sky filled up with dark clouds, and it started to pour. But that meant nothing to me: we hadn't reached Lithuania yet, and there everything would be very different.

On October 14, 1922, we arrived at Obeliai Station. "Here we are!" my parents declared. "This is Lithuania."

Before these momentous words could register, we first had to undergo a sanitation check. The large group of arrivals from Russia was taken into showers that had been erected in a lean-to. Next we had to go through a period of quarantine: we were all placed in barracks for several weeks. There we ate soup and potatoes that had been cooked in a huge common kettle. Flavored with a bit of butter, the food was delicious.

But still the rain fell ceaselessly, soaking all of Lithuania.

Finally the quarantine ended. Our family received permission to leave Obeliai for the village of Vailiuškiai, in the Žalioji – 'green' – rural area of Vilkaviškis district. I had lost faith that the rain would ever stop falling. The roads and pathways over which our horse-drawn wagon bumped were pocked with holes. All around were vast expanses of muddy fields filled with great gray puddles. Even at midday the dark clouds held back any ray of sunshine to dissipate the gloom.

This Lithuania looked completely different from what I had imagined – and yet I could feel the joy that enveloped my parents. "Life will be good for us here," they told each other. And so I felt happy too. I believed what they said as we approached Vailiuškiai, shaking and rattling in our carriage.

PART II

Return to the Promised Land – Independent Lithuania

Childhood

My mother's three Sereičikas brothers, with their wives and children, joined us in the village of Vailiuškiai, but not all of our returning relatives headed for the southwestern Suvalkija region. My father's parents, his younger brother and his sisters decided to take their families to the Pasvalys district, in the northeastern area of Saločiai. The Lithuanian government was granting eight hectares – about twenty acres – to every family of exiles returning from Russia. (It had provided a similar land grant to the veterans who fought for independence in 1918.)

Vailiuškiai had a once-grand estate, whose owner had decamped to Poland when Lithuania declared independence. The returning exiles settled on this property, though the war had left its buildings in a state of crumbling disrepair. Our new residence was the former caretaker's brick house. It had been a spacious facility when it was inhabited by a single family, but now our entire extended family – my parents and my sister and me; my maternal grandmother and her unmarried daughter, Grasilija Sereičikaitė, and my three uncles and their wives and families – had to squeeze in. We numbered about twenty in all.

There was no stove, no windows and no doors. During our first nights there, we had to heat bricks over an open fire to warm up our makeshift beds. We snuggled together, wrapped tightly in our blankets to keep from freezing. The men wasted no time in getting to work. The first order of business was putting in a door and windows. Next they laid the bricks to build a stove. We'd brought enough potatoes from Obeliai to last us several months. And that was how we survived our first winter in Lithuania.

It wasn't easy getting used to this kind of poverty. In Chornaya Padina we were affluent; now here we were sleeping on a dirt floor. It took a while for the men to build beds for us – two to each family, one for the parents and one for the children. It was winter and the house was unheated; a thick, enveloping snowfall made it all the colder. There was no running water, so we had nowhere to wash up. It was a daily struggle for the women just to cook the meals.

All in all, our first winter in Lithuania was dauntingly hard. I have no idea now how we kept from freezing, but somehow we managed to warm up a little bit – mostly, I suspect, by clinging together. Food was scarce. We didn't starve but we had just enough to keep our stomachs from growling all the time.

Yet, for all those hardships, I can still remember our joy when our first Christmas in Lithuania arrived. Gifts were out of the question – we children didn't dare dream about them. Our usual potatoes still appeared on the table but with a dollop of butter spooned on top to turn them into a holiday feast. And we were thrilled with the treat. The whole family sat huddled together, singing Christmas hymns and other songs. Singing was our primary entertainment for any special occasion. (On ordinary evenings, the men would play cards, the women would knit or sew and chat and we children, who were learning to read, would stick our noses into a book.) It was a beautiful and blessed holiday.

This place didn't have the vaguest resemblance to the storybook land of our dreams. Yet the harsh reality did not give rise to the least bit of disillusionment or bitterness on the part of the adults. I never heard any of them complain about Lithuania or utter a word of regret about leaving Russia. They bore every burden patiently, bolstering one another's spirits by repeating, "This is nothing – it's just the beginning. It'll take some time to settle in, but later on our lives will be completely different."

Soon after Christmas, exactly as promised, we received land from the government: eight hectares for each of our families. And then one job piled on top of another. We must have lived at that time much as our great-grandparents had when they were first exiled to the Pavolga Steppes – life had to be started from scratch. We acquired a flock of chickens and a few cows. Father would ride to the open-air market in the town of Vilkaviškis to sell eggs and the butter Mother had churned, and that was how they made their living for about three years.

At the end of 1925, however, we decided to move to the village of Geltonpamūšis, not far from Saločiai where my father's family was living. His health had begun to break down, and he wanted to be near his parents and his brother and sisters. He transferred our land to my mother's brother, Feliksas, and he and my mother and I left for the Pasvalys district. My sister, Victoria, stayed behind in Vilkaviškis. She and my Aunt Grasilija, who was nearly the same age, had both started high school, and my parents thought it better not to interrupt her schooling.

Although we weren't really any better off in Geltonpamūšis than we had been in Vailiuškiai, Father felt more at ease in these new surroundings, near the loved ones he knew he could rely on in any misfortune. We moved into a small house – just two rooms and a hallway. (Many years later I returned to Lithuania with my children and showed them this old home of mine. They couldn't believe we had lived in it. "Where's the bathtub? Where's the toilet?" they asked naively. No, there were no such modern conveniences then; nonetheless, I explained, this truly had been our home, and here we had felt happy and content.)

The front door led straight into the front room which my parents converted into a shop. We lived in the room in the back, which served as bedroom, kitchen and bathroom (I remember being bathed there) all in one. The thing I liked best was our huge wood-burning stove. Since I was still little, in the wintertime my parents would lay me on the ledge behind it to sleep, so I no longer had to suffer the kind of cold I'd had to in Vailiuškiai. The floor was solidly pounded clay. A bed for my parents and one for me fit nicely upon it, as well as a chest for our things and a small table upon which stood the Singer sewing machine Mother had brought with her from Chornaya Padina – a valuable piece of property back in those days.

In the front-room shop stood a barrel of herring and a bag of salt. On the shelves along the walls were sugar, coffee, bags of different herbs and spices, nails and boxes of matches. The shop also became something of a post office. The state postal service delivered letters, newspapers and packages for Geltonpamūšis to a farm on the opposite bank of the

Mūša River. Every day my father or I would ferry across the river to retrieve the mail, and the villagers would come in to our store to pick it up. We weren't paid for this work but, of course, it drew people into the store. And my father, I sensed, had another reason for performing this service: it allowed him to read all the newspapers that came through. Then he would share the news with the neighboring farmers. Few of them subscribed to a newspaper back then; some couldn't even read. Over time our home became a kind of community center. I can still see Father, a tall, lean man in frail health but with a naturally happy disposition, talking with the neighbors as he loved to do. He would relate the latest goings-on in Russia and the newest developments in Lithuania. Ten villagers at a time might gather, some of them standing in the doorway or even outside because the room was too small to accommodate them all.

People were always asking us about our lives in Russia, particularly during the years of the revolution. Father would tell them about the terrible famine of 1921. He would recall the executions by gunfire, meted out without trials and on the flimsiest evidence – often out of nothing more than revenge or the exigency of getting rid of hostages. For Father these instances showed how little human life meant to the Bolsheviks. Our neighbors always included one or two communist sympathizers, who didn't want to believe that such things could really be happening in Russia. Father would get into heated arguments with them, warning what a disaster it would be if communism came to Lithuania.

My parents had only attended the Lithuanian elementary school in Chornaya Padina; but illiteracy was then still widespread in the backwaters of the country, and elementary schooling was considered a lot of education. In Russia some of our relatives had gone much further. One had graduated from military school in Saratov, and another was studying at a university. These were unusually high accomplishments for stateless exiles with no legal rights.

By the age of seven, I could decipher writing. My elementary school was about a kilometer from our home. Three years later, in 1928, my parents sent me off to study at the Pasvalys Gymnasium (High School) – my very first separation from my family. They didn't have to pay for my education since poor families were exempted from tuition. They did have to pay for my room in Pasvalys. (Food was no problem: they brought me produce from their farm.) The townsfolk would rent rooms to students for very reasonable sums. My father placed me with the Ogintas family – truly tender-hearted people, as it turned out. They had a sizable house. One room was rented out as a shoemaker's shop. The two shoemakers lived in another room which had three beds. The third bed was for me. The shoemakers were men in their twenties; I was only ten and I could have had a lot of trouble getting my homework done in the evenings with those men in the room. But the Ogintas couple prevented any problem by setting up a desk for me in their own room.

On the day Father first brought me, it was already twilight when we arrived. Mr. and Mrs. Ogintas invited him to spend the night, and he accepted. They were also returned exiles, so the dinner conversation revolved around their former lives in Russia. When it was time for bed, Father called me to him and said, "Juozukas, let us say our prayers." We knelt together and prayed, and then I went in to sleep with the shoemakers. Father slept on a cot in the Ogintas family room.

I didn't give much thought to the fact that Mr. and Mrs. Ogintas hadn't knelt down with us. Some time later, I was amazed to learn that they didn't believe in God! I had been raised a believer from the cradle and I had no idea there might be any other way. There were few freethinkers like the Ogintas family back in those times, particularly in the small towns. But they were very tolerant – never did they try to convince me that there was no God. Quite the opposite in fact: they were the ones who were always reminding me on Sunday, "Juozukas, hurry up! It's time for you to get to church." It didn't matter that they didn't go to church themselves. They helped me to understand, for the first time, how varied the world is. The mere fact that other people held different views was no reason for looking down on their principles.

High School Years

Now came a carefree, happy period in my life – more carefree, as it turned out, than it should have been. I had to repeat the fourth grade. All my friends went on to the fifth grade, and I had to sit in class with the little kids a full year younger than I was. It was terrible delivering the shameful news to my mother. She didn't scold me but she hardly needed to, with all the blame I was casting on myself: *Poor Mother works from sunup late into the night so that I can get my schooling, and I was having so much fun I didn't even pass!* And so on.

To make matters worse, by this time Father had passed on. The tragedy had hit us in 1929, when I was eleven and in my first year at the gymnasium. He knew that he was dying and he remained fully conscious up to the moment of his death. He managed to say his farewells to all of his loved ones – except me.

One Sunday my uncle Feliksas showed up unexpectedly at the Ogintas' house and told me, without any explanation, "Juozukas, we have to ride home right now." At first I was excited. I thought he'd just happened to be in Pasvalys and was offering me a chance for a nice visit home. But then we stopped at a store, and he started to speak Russian with the owners. He bought black fabric, and a sense of unease began to descend on me. Why was he taking me home? Tomorrow, after all, was Monday, and I had to be in school. Why did he look so gloomy? We walked back to his wagon and silently rode out of Pasvalys. It was springtime, and the road was still soaked from the last ice thaw and early rains. The wagon wheels splattered through the mud. My heart was sinking lower and lower. By now I was certain that something was amiss but I dared not question my uncle. Then he turned to me and announced, "Juozukas, your father has died."

Instantly a frightening loneliness engulfed me. I wept silently all the way home. The realization of just how dear someone is to you may not become fully comprehensible until that moment of irreversible loss. More than seventy-five years have sped by since that day, but I need no piece of paper to remind me of the date: April 28, 1929.

All of our relatives came in for the funeral. A long procession followed the coffin on foot for the five kilometers to mass in Saločiai Church, and from there to the cemetery. Hymns resounded along the entire route. This funeral tradition is still observed in Lithuanian villages and occasionally in the cities. The deceased lies in state at home for three days. Then a wagon (or, in cities, a car) carries the coffin over long-familiar paths as a final farewell while relatives and friends, sometimes almost the whole village, follow. Hymns of grief – *raudos* – are sung at home and along the road to the final burial.

Our life became markedly harder after my father's death. Victoria was still in high school at Vilkaviškis, and Mother had to support the two of us by herself. She had to hire a horse, harness it to a wagon and ride into Pasvalys to pick up products. She had to load and unload the goods. And, of course, she had to handle running the store – all alone.

One day Mother dictated a letter for me to take down. Since I was at the gymnasium and she had only completed elementary school in Russia, by then I wrote much better than she did. It was a gloomy letter to her brother, Feliksas, complaining of her many hardships and asking if he might allow her some sort of support in exchange for the eight hectares our family had given him. In the intervening years, my mother's brothers had gotten on their feet. Uncle Feliksas held the highest position in the village of Žalioji. He managed his farm well and energetically; including the lot from us, it had grown to thirty-two hectares on which he produced dairy products and brought in fine harvests of sugar beets and grain.

I have no idea whether Uncle Feliksas responded to my mother's request with any aid. Although he lived comparatively well, he really didn't have much spare cash; his earnings were all earmarked for the further development of his farm. (One of his less successful projects had involved the construction of an electrical plant that was supposed to power the entire neighborhood. Unfortunately the stream he'd had dammed began flooding the fields of people outside the area of his domain, and there was no choice but to tear down the dam.)

Juozas, another of my mother's brothers, had been appointed head secretary to the notary public for the town of Vilkaviškis. He was able to earn a decent living from this job alone. My sister, Victoria, lived with his family and, some time later, I also began spending my summer vacations with them. Uncle Juozas would give me a summer job as a scribe, copying documents.

A couple of summers after Father's death, Victoria came to me with a piece of news. Carefully selecting her words, she said, "Mother is making plans to marry again." The announcement hit me like a blow. It seemed as though Mother was betraying the memory of Father, and I began to cry. Victoria soothed me as best she could. "Try to understand," she beseeched. "It's really hard for her to be alone. She needs a man in the house. Things will get easier for us, too – you'll see."

Only later in life did I understand that Mother had virtually no choice. She worked very hard, hauling heavy items back from Pasvalys – barrels of herring, bags of salt, sugar and flour. Since the store was open during the daytime, she also had to pick up these products after dark when the roads were not very safe. There was an especially dangerous intersection near the town of Raudondvaris where robberies were frequent. Mother used to tell us how frightened she was when she drove through that spot. Once her wagon got stuck in the mud there, and she had a horrendously difficult time getting the horse turned around to pull it out.

Juozas (Joseph) Kazickas, 1934

Mother married Kazimieras Jackūnas, a carpenter with a calm demeanor and high moral standards. He turned out to be a good stepfather. It was clear almost immediately after the wedding that life would now be easier. Kazimieras earned his living by working on home construction jobs but he also reduced Mother's workload by taking on the task of picking up products for the store. And, between the two of them, the household income increased considerably.

Up to then the profits from the store had been meager. After being in business for many years myself, I became convinced that the people who meet with the greatest success are those who find the right balance between a soft heart and a hard head. My father had had much too soft a heart. He handed out goods on credit too lightly. The IOUs often went unpaid; Mother inherited a whole stack of them upon his death. I've seen them. Some villagers owed ten or twenty *litas* (the *litas* was the official currency of Lithuania until the Soviet occupation and returned into circulation again in 1992.) Others owed as much as a hundred. She knew she would never be able to collect on them. During the 1930s, Lithuanian farmers were having a truly hard time eking out a living. They borrowed out of dire need, never intending to default on their loans. But they could never muster up enough money to pay them off.

Thus, some time after the wedding, my mother and stepfather decided to close the store in Geltonpamūšis and move to the town of Joniškėlis, where they opened a textiles store. The town was tiny but it had more people who could pay for their purchases than the village had. As the 1940s rolled in and the standard of living in Lithuania slowly bettered, people spent more money on clothing and sewing materials. In truth, the textiles store was just another little village shop though it was double the size of the previous one and certainly brought in more income. It took up two rooms in the house they rented, and they lived in the third room, the smallest in the house. All that fit was their bed, a small table and the old Singer sewing machine. There was hardly room for me to spend the night when I came home for a visit. That was when I started spending my summer vacations in Vilkaviškis with Uncle Juozas. After Victoria got married – I was fourteen at the time – I spent my vacations with her.

In my eyes, my sister had stepped right into the upper class. Her husband, Juozas (Joseph) Gruodis, was an officer in the military. At the time of their marriage, he had attained the rank of senior lieutenant and was serving as adjunct to the regiment commander. I was bursting with pride that my sister was the wife of an officer! I couldn't take my eyes off my brother-in-law's uniform, especially its trim of white braid set off by sparkling metal tips. That year the epitome of happiness for me was walking alongside him when a unit of soldiers was marching by. The military code required that a formation of soldiers display a ceremonial greeting not only to the commanding officer but also to his adjunct. The officer leading them would bark a command, and the marching soldiers would stretch their backs straight, with their hands at their hats in salute. I practically wallowed in the aura of high respect. Memories such as these later motivated me to enter military school.

Initially Joseph served in Vilkaviškis, but he was relocated from town to town each year, and so every summer I would travel to a different place to vacation with them.

Mother's small business was now a success. Another clothing-and-textiles store nearby, belonging to a local Jewish family, had been in operation for a long time, but my mother and stepfather kept up with the competition. Over time people came to prefer their shop. It's possible my parents were selling at lower prices; Mother would travel to Kaunas – then the capital of the country – to purchase materials directly from manufacturers' warehouses which, no doubt, helped them keep prices down. But, I believe, their character was the real factor in their success. Customers felt at home with them. My parents took the time to talk to people about their lives. They never rushed a sale. They would discuss the best and most economical means for sewing clothing and bedding. As the years passed, they expanded the store and became reasonably well-to-do. Unfortunately their comfort wasn't to last. When the Soviets occupied Lithuania, the store was nationalized, and they moved to Vilnius where, by that time, I was working for the city. All that, however, came much later.

I graduated from Pasvalys Gymnasium in 1937. My first and last school failure had been the fourth grade, which proved to be a crucial lesson in my life. From then on I studied so hard and earned such good grades that I reached the point of being able to tutor other students. (Six decades later I attended my high-school reunion. The organizers read my school records publicly. What a relief that I had nothing to be embarrassed about. My final grades were so good that I was surprised to hear them myself.)

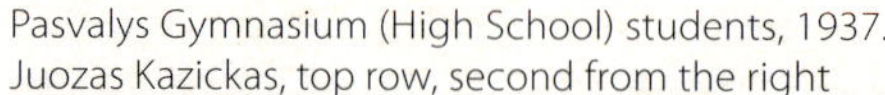

Pasvalys Gymnasium (High School) students, 1937.
Juozas Kazickas, top row, second from the right

My studies also prompted me to read a great deal, and not just fiction. The writings of St. Augustine led me to more philosophy. These books stimulated me to think deeply about the meaning of my own life. I remember once trying to flirt with a classmate I liked, but the only thing I could think of to talk about was the wisdom of those philosophical ideas. The young lady quickly ran out of patience with my intellectual musings.

Nearly all my school friends were members of the *Ateitininkai*, or Fedaration of the Future, a Catholic organization. (It was founded in my times, retained by Lithuanian expatriates and again active in post-communist Lithuania.) Sometimes I would attend their meetings. The government of President Antanas Smetona had banned the activities of the *Ateitininkai*, so the student members met only semi-officially, at a church or someone's apartment. I thought the prohibition unjust and I attended the meetings as a protest. Nonetheless, I joined the Lithuanian Scouts – mainly out of love for the English language since the main sponsor of the Scouts was Mr. Baravykas, our English teacher. I was intent on learning English. For some reason, Great Britain and the United States attracted me more than Germany did although Germany was much closer to Lithuania and had a much greater presence in the country. I earned the highest grade in my class and studied with such zeal that Mr. Baravykas used to let me correct the other students' assignments.

I didn't much like German but I loved my German teacher, Mrs. Hofmanienė (Hoffman). She was the daughter of a German family who owned an estate in Latvia and she had graduated from a Swiss university. I can still remember her noble, aristocratic face. Mrs. Hofmanienė was also my homeroom teacher. The duties of the homeroom teacher included instructing students coming in from the villages in personal hygiene. They sometimes had to be familiarized with basic cleanliness (and coaxed into washing regularly) as well as with rules for dress and behavior in public and at home. The school doctor also gave us lectures on hygiene, and every week the entire class was taken to a steam bath.

Mrs. Hofmanienė and I became good friends. She began to look out for me in special ways and often invited me to her home. This was one of her pedagogical methods. She would invite her students, one at a time, to her small but elegant apartment for tea or supper. The lesson started the moment you got to her door. An ornamental doorbell hung at the entrance; you would push it, it would ring, but the door wouldn't open immediately. Since we were impatient kids, we would knock. Mrs. Hofmanienė would then crack open the door and explain that you don't start knocking right after ringing the bell. Using such real life examples, she taught us the rules of good manners and she was a skilled teacher. She would make you feel as though you were having a conversation with her and not being lectured, even when she was explaining the right way to hold a knife and fork or how to eat an apple.

Mrs. Hofmanienė didn't limit the talk on these visits to etiquette lessons. She would always inquire about your parents and take an interest in your ideas about your future. Although I wasn't the most wholehearted student of German, Mrs. Hofmanienė never took offense and I became one of her favorite students. Later on, I came to regret that I hadn't made more of an effort to perfect my German. As things turned out, this was a skill I was going to need.

Reserve Officer and Student

Being so star-struck by my brother-in-law, the officer, upon graduating from Pasvalys Gymnasium in June 1937, I decided to enter Kaunas Military School. The school was in Panemunė, a district in the city of Kaunas. I wasn't sure, however, that I wanted to become a professional officer. The graduate studies program, as it was known there, required fifteen months of study and led to the rank of junior lieutenant in the reserve infantry. It could be completed in time to enter the university the following fall. Becoming a staff officer with the rank of lieutenant took three years.

I was nervous about being admitted. Although I was tall, I was skinny – just over six feet and a mere 122 pounds. I was afraid I'd be jeered at: "What kind of an officer can you become? You're a bag of bones!" But nothing came of my fears and I was accepted. By the time I completed the program, I weighed 165 pounds. I exercised diligently. I would always volunteer to drag the machine gun up the hill in Šančiai (a neighborhood in the city of Kaunas). Everybody thought I was crazy to keep doing this, but I would tell myself, "This will be tough; it'll take a lot of sweat, but I'll build up a few more muscles." Every morning we were all required to run five kilometers. I always ran the full course – I never held back.

Juozas Kazickas with his mother, Katerina, and Victoria and Joseph Gruodis and their sons, Romualdas and Algirdas

I completed the military graduate studies program so successfully that I was awarded a Gediminas Medal (named for the Grand Duke Gediminas who ruled Lithuania from 1316 to 1341). Immediately after the graduation and awards ceremony, I was approached by Captain Ramanauskas of the Staff Officer Department who said, "Lieutenant Kazickas, we're inviting you to join our staff officer corps." The school's board of directors had decided to recommend me for regular military service immediately. They were going to grant me the rank of staff lieutenant without my having to complete the full three years of studies. And that wasn't all – I could choose the division I wanted to serve in. I was a bit taken aback and I responded, "Captain, sir, please give me a day to consider."

My brother-in-law, Joseph, was now the commanding major of the infantry artillery battery regiment in Šančiai, and I went to him to talk over the offer. The generosity of it greatly impressed him, but he didn't try to pressure me into accepting. We discussed the benefits and drawbacks of military service. My mother and stepfather were now quite comfortable; nonetheless, they were not in a position to support my studies at the university to any significant degree. If I were to enter the service as a staff officer, I would be well off materially at once. In addition the military was highly respected now that General Stasys Raštikis was in full command of the Lithuanian Army. Its reputation had risen; there were no more of the old cases of corruption. Moreover the best officers were sent to Belgium, France and Germany to study, and that opportunity tempted me greatly.

Joseph mulled over the situation and concluded, "If they're offering you the rank of staff officer without requiring you to continue your education, it means that they've evaluated you above the rest. Later on they'll probably send you to study abroad. That would truly open up great career opportunities."

I tossed and turned all night long but I finally decided to reject the offer. I burned for a higher education, for study at the university. My father's lectures to me on the importance of education must have sunk deeply into my subconscious, and the university seemed to me the absolute peak of any educational pursuit.

I applied to the Economics Department of the School of Law at Vytautas Magnus University in Kaunas and, in the fall of 1937, I began my studies there. Initially I'd wanted to study medicine but I chose economics because the department offered evening courses, from 3 p.m. to 10 p m. – a schedule that allowed me to work since government office hours were 8 a.m. to 2 p.m. And I already had a job. Joseph's brother was working at the Ministry of Transportation and he had helped me get a post in the Statistics Department.

I loved the university. Most of the instructors were tremendously impressive people, far more brilliant than the average Lithuanian. Professor Vladas Jurgutis, for example, had a huge influence on my views on economic issues. Later our department relocated to Vilnius University, and he continued to lecture there. I still have a letter he wrote me informing me that the university, at his recommendation, was awarding me a scholarship to study at the renowned London School of Economics. By this time I spoke English quite well. But the Soviet occupation scotched that plan.

Among the other memorable personalities at the university was the keenly intelligent Mykolas Reimeris, a professor of law, who was rector during my years of study. I remember the lectures of Professors Krivickis and Šimkus as being exceptional. I developed a close relationship with Pranas Padalskis (he later changed his surname to Padalis), a professor of economics, who had finished his excellent education in the West. He became a friend for many years.

I was only starting the second year of my university studies when World War II broke out.

In Vilnius

I learned of the invasion of Poland on Sept. 1, 1939, when I reported for work at the Ministry of Transportation the next morning. None of us got much work done that day – we were too busy talking. How would the war affect Lithuania? What would the future hold for us now? No one had any doubt but that Poland would soon be crushed, probably within a month. Many believed that Germany would quickly win the war. But one of the employees, a man of German descent, named Bremeris, prophesied on that first day, "My dear friends, this is only the beginning. You'll see what kind of a stew gets cooked up from this. The present war, like the earlier one, is going to last no less than four years."

Poland capitulated in just a couple of weeks. The war rolled toward the Lithuanian border. Yet quite a few people were pleased that the Germans had crushed the Poles because they were focused only on Vilnius, and its return to Lithuanian jurisdiction. Poland had seized Vilnius in 1919, and independent Lithuania was never able to wrest the city back. Kaunas, the country's second-largest city, had become the interim capital but, from the time we were children, we were raised to believe that Vilnius was our true and ancient capital. That Vilnius might again become part of our country was perhaps the greatest aspiration of Lithuanians and one that unified the entire country.

As a reserve officer, I was called into service once the war began. I assisted in the handling of the defeated Polish army soldiers who were swarming into Lithuania. Historical grievances were set aside, and the Lithuanians treated these Poles with great respect. We tried to make their lives as comfortable as possible in the military barracks our government provided them.

8. Šeimynos padėtis: Nevedęs

Susituokė su Aleksandra Kalvėnaite
Vilniaus m. metr. apyl.
1941 m. VIII mėn. 12 d.
(metr. Nr. 1322)
Metrikų ved.

9 Dokumentai, kuriais remiantis pasas išduotas:

Asmens žymės:
Ūgis
Veldas
Plaukai
Ypat. žymės
Akys

Paso savininko(ės) parašas

Šiuo tikrinama,

LIETUVOS VALSTYBĖ

Passport of the Republic of Lithuania, 1936

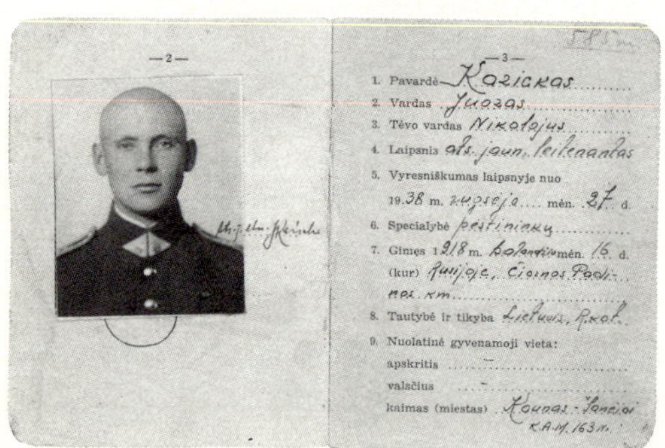
—2—

—3—

1. Pavardė Kazickas
2. Vardas Juozas
3. Tėvo vardas Nikolojus
4. Laipsnis ats. jaun. leitenantas
5. Vyresniškumas laipsnyje nuo 19.38 m. rugsėjo mėn. 27 d.
6. Specialybė pėstininkų
7. Gimęs 1918 m. mėn. 16 d. (kur)
8. Tautybė ir tikyba Lietuvis, R.kat.
9. Nuolatinė gyvenamoji vieta:
apskritis
valsčius
kaimas (miestas) Kaunas

Reserve officer identification, 1938

Galioja iki 1939 m. kovo mėn. 1 d.

Galioja iki 1940 m. kovo mėn. 1 d.

Galioja iki 1941 m. kovo mėn. 1 d.

Galioja iki 1941 m. lapkričio 1 d.

Vytautas Magnus University student identification, 1938

Of course the Poles were seriously debilitated. And the Lithuanian army had to disarm them, causing a number of heartbreaking scenes. My brother-in-law told us one very touching story. A Polish officer presented him with a revolver whose handle was adorned with coral shells. It was a family heirloom, he told Joseph, and he wanted to make a gift of it to a Lithuanian army officer in gratitude for the sanctuary the government of Lithuania had provided.

The news spread that Lithuania was about to regain Vilnius. The widespread joy overwhelmed any sense of threat that the Soviets might be on the verge of occupying the country. By October 10th, when Lithuanian soldiers were to ceremoniously march into Vilnius, I had been demobilized so I joined a group of students who had organized a railway trip to our ancient capital. We stood in Cathedral Square and greeted our incoming army, gleefully chanting our hurrahs. The military orchestra played; Lithuania's national anthem resounded everywhere. (Little did I then suspect that I would marry a girl in the crowd that day – my bride-to-be was a member of a student choir – or that we would return to Vilnius to celebrate our diamond anniversary sixty-two years later.)

It was a grand holiday. I had never been to Vilnius before but I knew a great deal about the city from books. I knew its churches and the Hill of Gediminas, named after the Grand Duke Gediminas, whose castle still stands atop the hill. These I had seen in photographs many times. And yet there was something cheerless about the capital that day. In comparison to Kaunas, the city looked sadly neglected. The day was overcast; it was sprinkling. I was unsettled by the presence of the Soviet Army; the Russian officers seemed to consider themselves our caretakers. And the gloom of the local Polish residents cast a pall over everything. At the time Lithuanians were only a minority in Vilnius. No skirmishes erupted, but the dark, disconsolate faces watching us were disconcerting. A mood of depression hung in the air.

We took a train back to Kaunas the same night. We may have been cold and tired and unsettled but we sang happily all the way back.

Within a couple of months, I would be moving to Vilnius – our department at the university was transferred to Vilnius University. Jonas Šimukonis, a Lithuanian resident of the city, and I rented a room on Basanavičius Street from the wife of a Polish officer who had been missing since the start of the war. She was a short, full-figured woman who lived with her two daughters. They were quite poor; our rent was their most important source of income, so they tried very hard to please us. The daughters – one was eighteen, the other twenty-two – eyed us with yearning and actually competed to serve at the table or bring us our tea, much to our amusement.

I got a job with the Vilnius Municipal Services Department as assistant to Colonel Gražulis, a director on the Roads Board whom I knew well from the Ministry of Transportation. First we had to take over the maintenance of the streets from the Polish administration; it had gone into total disarray since the start of the war. Another Lithuanian, an older man by the name of Daugirdas, worked in our office as the interim Technical Director, but all the other employees of the Roads Department, including the drivers, were Polish. There was a severe shortage of Lithuanian speaking employees at government offices. Polish was the dominant language everywhere in the city; you couldn't use Lithuanian in a single shop or office. My roommate, Jonas, being a local, could speak Polish fluently, so I hired him as my assistant.

Sometimes I encountered thinly disguised Polish opposition in the course of my work for the municipality. Sometimes it wasn't so thinly disguised. Once I attended a meeting of the bus drivers who made angry speeches in Polish. They were clearly tossing innuendos in my direction. Apparently I left in the nick of time – they were passing a resolution denouncing me.

Upon my arrival in Vilnius, I joined the Ramovė Reserve Officers Corporation. I had become a member of this group when I entered Vytautas Magnus University in Kaunas. In Vilnius I was elected Assistant to the President of Ramovė. When several Ramovė board members were invited to Kaunas to brief President Antanas Smetona, who had presided over the republic since 1926, on the situation in the recently reinstated capital, I had the honor of taking part.

The President received us in his private rooms. He listened to us deep in thought, questioning us in a low, quiet voice about conditions in Vilnius and the mood of the locals. General Julius Čaplikas, Commander of the Lithuanian Army, also met with us.

But our most memorable meeting that day was with General Stasys Raštikis, who had recently been relieved of his command of the Lithuanian army. He was a man held in the highest esteem in Lithuania. We sat in his living room; Mrs. Raštikis served us tea, interspersing her own questions between the general's. He was entirely open and frank with us. He complained that President Smetona had stripped him of his command as a result of intrigues and out of fear of his rising popularity.

The demotion, he told us, had hindered the upgrading of the Lithuanian defense forces, a task of vital and immediate importance.

I had seen Stasys Raštikis when I was still at the military school in Panemunė. He lived not far from the school. Often I took our unit out for guard duty. We would watch the road intently and, as soon as the general's automobile came into view, the cadet leading the column of soldiers would issue a command, and the entire column would salute. To me this duty seemed to carry a great responsibility. As I marched along the road and the general drove on, I always felt a certain tension.

And so when I went this time to visit Stasys Raštikis, I felt an inner quiver that probably had its source in my memories of military school. However, I left feeling disillusioned. I had hardly expected a man of his stature to start complaining to a group of students about his mistreatment at the hands of President Smetona.

The First Soviet Occupation

As the spring of 1940 arrived, the sense of threat from the east kept intensifying.

I became friends with Juozas Juodišius, a Ramovė reserve officer, whose uncle had been a general in the Lithuanian army. We grew so close that I decided to leave the widow's house on Basanavičiaus Street and move in with him. We found a more spacious room on Pylimo Street.

Juodišius had been working for the police. He gave them information about the Poles of Vilnius and their generally unfavorable attitude toward Lithuanians. A greater source of anxiety for us, though, was all the Soviet troops. The Russian soldiers weren't yet interfering in our lives directly. But, once in a while, we would notice them, driving somewhere in a truck with a portrait of Stalin painted on the cab, and Juozas would comment that there was increased movement at the Soviet bases – meetings of some sort were being held there. We figured that the Russians were probably beefing up in preparation to enter the war that was raging in Europe. At that time everyone in Lithuania thought that, once the war ended, the Soviets would remove their bases from our country.

One sunny Sunday morning in June, Juodišius and I drove out to a beach on the Neris River, in the Valakampiai district, to swim and sunbathe. The water was already warm, and we had a fine time. By midday we were already on our way back into town. As we walked along the slope of Gediminas Hill toward the library on Vrublevskio Street, suddenly we heard the roar of airplanes. We looked up and, as the roar got louder, spotted some thirty, perhaps forty planes flying in single file, all marked with Soviet stars.

Then we heard the din of tanks and realized that something terrible was happening. We ran down to Gedimino Prospect, Vilnius' main street. Columns of Soviet tanks were rolling by, the heads of soldiers protruding from the hatches and scanning the streets from side to side. Groups of unfamiliar people – some we recognized as Polish and Jewish – were cheering and waving at the Russians; some were actually tossing bouquets of flowers at the soldiers. We were stunned. All the Lithuanians with whom we associated believed that Russia was the greatest threat to our country, and we could not believe that anyone thought otherwise. Wordlessly we walked over to Ožeškienės Square and stopped, no longer able to hold back our tears.

We had another shock when some of those out welcoming the Soviet Army began shaking their fists at us and our tears. Some were already carrying red flags – heaven only knows where they'd dug them out from. They waved their flags and shouted and cheered at the seemingly endless line of tanks. Strains of the *Internationale* and Russian songs filled the air.

It was a while before we were able to come to our senses. And then what was happening slowly dawned on us. The end had come; Lithuania had perished, and so had our way of life. It was June 15, 1940. The day before the Russians had handed the government of Lithuania an ultimatum, but that was a Saturday, and we hadn't been listening to the radio. The scene on Gedimino Prospect was a completely unexpected horror. We felt as though we'd been hit by lightning on a sunny day.

At first the Russians said nothing about annexing Lithuania to their empire. Nonetheless, it was clear that the march of the Soviet Army through the streets of Vilnius meant one thing and one thing only: occupation. We soon heard that President Smetona had fled the country. We were facing the unknown. I still had a year left to complete my studies, but nobody had any idea whether the Soviets would shut down Vilnius University.

The morning after the Red Army march, rumors were rife that the NKVD (the Soviet secret police that were the predecessors to the KGB) was operating and that a lot of people had been arrested. At work, though, nobody spoke about what had happened. There was also silence at the university, even though the students and faculty were some of the most patriotic people in the country. Overnight, it seemed, everyone became cautious. Suddenly we all distrusted anyone we didn't know very, very well.

But of course that initial shock soon began to ebb. The Lithuanians of Vilnius, or at least the young ones with close friendships, began to meet and talk over the situation.

The official line was that Lithuania was still an independent country. The friendly Soviet Army had simply marched in at the invitation of the Lithuanian people. Stalin had intimidated several key politicians and artists into signing an agreement to this effect. The substance of his threat had been that the Red Army was going to occupy the country whether they signed or not; but if they signed, Vilnius would remain under Lithuanian jurisdiction. The Lithuanian army did not fire a single shot when the Red Army came in.

Soon afterward the Soviets also occupied Latvia and Estonia.

"Elections" were to be held for the so-called People's *Seimas,* but it was obvious that they were nothing more than a show being staged by the occupier. The *Seimas* had been the democratically elected body of government of independent Lithuania but, once the Soviets took over and named it the People's *Seimas,* it was no more than a puppet for their own tactics.

Another shock hit us when we heard some of our most influential writers on the radio, bubbling with enthusiasm for the triumph of Stalin, that great leader of the world proletariat, in "liberating" Lithuania from the "oppression of the fascistic Antanas Smetona regime." The writers included Justas Paleckis, a leftist journalist who had attained great authority in the country; Petras Cvirka, another leftist, a prose writer of high acclaim; Salomėja Neris, a talented and much beloved poet and the winner of the country's highest award for poetry and Liudas Gira, a political activist who had even served as a minister and was close to the Smetona government.

It was bizarre and very hard to hear these members of the intelligentsia spouting propaganda. How could they, after living so well and speaking so freely on whatever subject they wished in this purportedly fascistic Lithuania, have turned their political hides inside out so suddenly? How could they have become traitors? Traitor was the word we used when we talked about them. How could they sound so enthusiastic? They were practically bursting in their ardor for Stalin and the "liberating" Red Army. You couldn't explain their behavior simply as a cowering response to the NKVD's intimidation. Members of the intelligentsia who did not want to blacken their reputations by collaborating could still stand quietly on the sidelines in those early days. But those who craved seats in the People's *Seimas* had to demonstrate their loyalty to the occupying forces. The suspicion grew that these turncoats had been recruited by the Soviets much earlier.

Any remaining illusion we harbored that the Russians might at least allow Lithuania some trappings of independence was finally shattered when the People's *Seimas* produced an official request – purportedly in response to the passionate desire of the workers – to be "accepted" into the Soviet Union. And once our country was officially swallowed up, it didn't take long for our lives to unravel.

The Soviets nationalized my mother and stepfather's store, leaving them without a source of income. Since I was still working for the municipality of Vilnius, I was able to help them move there; we felt they would be safer in a city than in one of the small towns where shopkeepers were being harassed as capitalists. I managed to find work for my stepfather at the bus assembly plant. The city bought motors and transmissions for its buses from Germany, but the chasses were manufactured and the buses themselves assembled at this small plant.

By the fall we were hearing more and more frequently about arrests. Today we know from documents in the archives that not all that many people were apprehended during the initial weeks of the occupation but, of course, rumors tore through the city. Every ten people who were arrested were multiplied by rumors into hundreds. The atmosphere of fear was electric.

My job frequently required me to drive out in the very early morning hours and check on operations on the night bus routes. Once I heard screaming. I looked around and saw a couple of black cars in front of a house. Several men in leather coats of the kind favored by the NKVD rushed out, rapidly pushing a man forward as they held his arms twisted behind his back. They shoved him into one of the waiting cars and drove off.

One day my boss, Colonel Gražulis, the head of the Department, failed to show up for work. Later we learned that the NKVD had arrested him.

The other Lithuanians who had come from Kaunas were still working for the city. Quite a few of them were reserve officers like me. Whenever we met we would exchange a few thoughts about what we might be able to do in this miserable situation. We fully understood the danger of forming any sort of opposition group, but it was unbearable to sit around with our hands folded.

Juozas Juodišius and I decided to seek out contacts with the anti-Soviet underground, which we were certain was already operating. A man named Šimkus joined us. His cousin, Major Valerijonas Šimkus, was the chief of the Vilnius Fire Department; later I found out that he was a significant figure in the resistance. The underground was organized into little groups like our trio. The resistance movement forming in Vilnius was led by the Lithuanian Activist Front. The political wing included several people I knew well, among them Professors Pranas Padalskis and Zenonas Ivinskis. They were instrumental in contacting political leaders in the resistance in Kaunas – Professor Juozas Brazaitis (who went on to serve as Prime Minster of the Provisional Government at the beginning of the German occupation) and Adolfas Damušis (who served as his Minister of Industry). Both of them were instrumental in organizing and leading the Lithuanian Activist Front and later the uprising against Soviet rule in June of 1941. (These men also eventually fled west as I did and continued to pursue the mission of an independent Lithuania all their lives.)

Members of the military like soldiers below officer rank (who generally were not arrested) and reserve officers gathered in small groups to prepare for an armed uprising when the right moment presented itself. The Soviet Union, we knew, would sooner or later become entangled in the raging World War; if it were defeated, it would have to retreat from

Lithuania. Of course no one could have forecast at the time the way that events would play out. Who could possibly have guessed in the autumn of 1940 that Stalin – who was then calling Hitler a friend – would ally himself with the West and ultimately win the war? All we knew back then was that France had capitulated, but that England continued to battle Germany.

A small group of university instructors took part in the activities of the political headquarters of the Lithuanian Activist Front in Vilnius and, urged by Professor Padalskis, I joined them. I was the youngest member and the only student. We met at different apartments but usually at the home of a Vilnius attorney of long standing, named Jurgelionis, who lived near Lukiškių Square, in the center of the city. As a reserve officer, I was delegated to retain contact with the military wing of the Lithuanian Activist Front of which Juodišius was a member.

Our group made contact with Lithuanian officers and government officials who had fled to Germany. They informed us that the Germans seemed to be preparing for war with the Soviet Union; by the spring of 1941, they were certain that fighting would break out soon. Finally we heard that the Germans were going to attack the Russians on June 15th. As matters unfolded, the information was off by barely a week.

We started mimeographing proclamations urging the populace not to cooperate with the occupiers and to prepare for open conflict when war between the Russians and Germans erupted. That we felt would be the moment for Lithuania to reclaim its independence. We would leave leaflets in the streets. We made special efforts to get them to the Lithuanian units that had been swallowed up by the Red Army. These units had not been dismantled but simply incorporated into the structure of the Soviet Army with a change in commanders and the assignment of numerous commissars to oversee them.

Alexandra Kalvenaitė, the woman I would eventually marry, was also active in the underground. She would get copy paper from her friend, Stasė Daumantaitė, a typist at the university, and bring it to me; I used it for our proclamations. Once the leaflets were mimeographed, I would pass on stacks of them to a number of trusted military officers who, in turn, would make more copies and disseminate them among the soldiers. Proclamations and copies of resistance newspapers were also smuggled in from Kaunas; the risky job of transporting them usually fell to Vytautas Bitinas. (After the war, he enrolled in a seminary in Rome and became a priest.)

In addition to my other duties, I wrote several short articles for the underground press. My subject was the importance of adhering to strict rules in order to keep the NKVD from being able to track individuals in our organization. Maintaining secrecy was a key condition of our activities. There were a lot of stories going around of the brutal torture to which the NKVD subjected the people they arrested; anyone could break under torture and tell all he or she knew. And so information pertaining to our internal contacts had to be carefully safeguarded to lessen potential danger to the organization as a whole. We operated on the principle of threesomes: a member of the resistance generally knew only two other persons within the organization.

I knew more though. I had contact with two military officers because I was a dispatcher for the political headquarters of the Lithuanian Activist Front. One was Colonel Vitkus (who, during the postwar years, acting under the pseudonym Kazimieraitis, was in charge of a district of partisans). He and I would have brief meetings. Without naming any names, he would fill me in on the situation of soldiers serving in the Soviet Army, and I would pass this information on to headquarters.

Colonel Vitkus was a well-grounded expert on warfare; thus it fell to him to develop the plan for the uprising against the Soviets. During the first days after World War II hit Lithuania, he went into action, leading an operation to blow up a strategic bridge in Kaunas. He had perfectly calculated the points to place the explosives, and the bridge tumbled exactly as he had planned.

The other member of the armed underground I was in contact with was Major Valerijonas Šimkus, the Vilnius Fire Department Chief. He was an exceptionally brave and energetic man. He had figured out how to get weapons from the Lithuanian units of the Soviet Army and he stockpiled pistols, guns and even machine guns in a hideout in the Valakampiai area of the city. Being the fire chief, he could wander through all kinds of deserted buildings without raising any suspicion. Nonetheless, we did eventually receive information that the NKVD considered Šimkus a suspect and planned to apprehend him. We got the news in time, and

Šimkus had gone into hiding when the NKVD arrived. It was no easy matter for him to hide. Six feet five inches tall and weighing more than two hundred sixty pounds, he stood out in a crowd, especially in those days. But he eluded the NKVD.

One night he sneaked home to see his family; they lived on the bank of the Neris River. The NKVD had their dragnet in place. But while their henchmen were breaking down the door, Šimkus managed to leap out a window, run down to the river and jump in. It was late autumn and the water was bitingly cold, but he made it to the opposite shore and seemingly evaporated.

His disappearance lasted only a few months. In the spring of 1941, he was arrested. What saved his life was that not long afterward Germany went to war with the Soviets. The NKVD interrogations had lasted several months; so, when the war started, he had not yet been taken out of Lithuania. When we finally located him in a cell in Lukiškės Prison, at first we couldn't recognize him – he was a shadow of the man he had been. His body was covered with cigarette burns, and he had been beaten so severely that he could no longer walk on his own. As we led him away, we had to hold him under both arms to keep him from falling. But Šimkus slowly recovered. His solid health had helped him withstand his terrible trials. While his sphere of contacts in the underground organization extended beyond his own threesome, even under horrendous torture, he had not informed on a single person.

We only came to understand this as the Soviets were fleeing in retreat. When Šimkus was arrested, many of us had been extremely nervous. Soon afterward there was a wide sweep of arrests, all at the same time. Reserve Officer Aleksa, one of my coworkers, failed to arrive for work one morning. I had recruited him into our underground organization and I knew that he had been assigned to the military group in which several of my acquaintances – Lieutenants Rutelionis and Kavaliauskas and several other army officers – were also members. The suspicion crept over us that Soviet agents had managed to infiltrate our threesomes. But Šimkus had betrayed no one.

During the occupation, Juozas Juodišius was also arrested and tortured so viciously that his legs were broken. He later died in exile in Siberia.

Alexandra – My True Love

I had more than just myself to worry about during those stress-filled days. There was also Alexandra who was helping me with our underground activities.

The first time I saw Alexandra, I was sixteen or seventeen. Sporūta, our high-school athletic team, took part in games every spring with students from Pasvalys, Rokiškis, Panevėžys and other nearby towns. The games were generally held on weekends and lasted for two days. The school authorities would spread straw over the gym floor for us to sleep on though, naturally, we hardly slept at all. High school kids have plenty of energy – enough to compete in games for several days and still party all night long.

I had a spot on the Pasvalys Gymnasium's track team for one of the games being held in Panevėžys. My time on the hundred-meter dash wasn't bad, but it wasn't as good as that of my friend, Vytautas Kasiulis, who was the favorite at all the games. (Vytautas went on to become a renowned artist, and a number of his paintings now grace our homes in the United States and Vilnius.)

I found myself with some spare time on my hands. So I went over to watch the girls from Panevėžys play basketball against the girls from a Polish high school. The Polish girls ran onto the field first, outfitted in white shorts and white gloves. But the Lithuanian girls! I was practically on the edge of my seat with anticipation and when they appeared, even without white gloves, they looked every bit as stunning as the Polish girls. Most of the fans were Lithuanians and they gave the local girls a resounding round of applause.

The game was fierce, but the Lithuanians won, 12 to 8. I was clapping wildly when I stopped short at the sight of the prettiest player on the Panevėžys team. I didn't know her name, but her black hair and her dancing eyes made a deep impression on me. Later on I saw her again, running in a relay. She was fast. I could not forget the way the wind tossed her black hair.

The next time I saw her was a couple of years later when I was at military school at Panemunė. I remembered her immediately. Unfortunately she was there not to visit me but another soldier who was grinding away at his studies to become an officer. I saw her sitting in the canteen, enjoying some chocolate. What a delightful sight! But once again, I missed the chance to meet her.

Another year went by. Now I was attending Vytautas Magnus University. One day, as I was walking down Laisvės Alėja, a main pedestrian way in the center of Kaunas, I suddenly spotted that black-haired beauty from Panevėžys walking briskly ahead of me. But I was a coward. Instead of trying to strike up a conversation, I turned away, pretending she didn't mean a thing to me.

Alexandra Kalvėnaitė, 1937

But I checked around and learned that she was also studying at the university. And that wasn't all: the hand of fate had pointed her to the School of Law. She was even majoring in economics. Much to my surprise, she was a classmate!

And then I saw her many times walking down the hallways between classes. But no romance flared between us. I never even sought a pretext to talk to her. It wasn't just because I was shy or because of my work load. I was deep in my studies and also had my job at the Roads Bureau. It was because I was already going out with another young lady. We were dating seriously, in fact, and I never considered being unfaithful to her.

It was the same after the school transferred to Vilnius. We were both studying economics, but again we would sit in the same auditorium without talking. We might have both graduated without ever getting to know each other but for a chance occurrence that changed my life.

It was the winter of 1940. The war in Europe had left the city with a dire shortage of fuel. Vilnius University had hardly any heat. We often sat in the auditoriums wearing our coats and gloves. One morning we were waiting for the beginning of a finance lecture by Professor Vladas Jurgutis. Finance was one of our most difficult subjects, but we all held the professor's teaching in high regard. Professor Jurgutis had been a governor at the Bank of Lithuania for eight years and had written several indispensable text books in the field. He was generally held to be the highest authority on banking and finance in the country. Missing one of his lectures was virtually a mortal sin.

We sat shivering in the large room, waiting for him to arrive. He was very late. We all started to whisper and move about. The young woman in front of me was wearing a knit woolen hat. I leaned over and said, "Miss, your hat is lovely." She turned around – why, it was the brunette from Panevėžys! – and shot back at me, "The hat is just a hat. What can you say about the girl wearing it?"

"Oh, of course" – I quickly recovered myself – "the girl is much lovelier."

From the Diary of Alexandra Kazickas

December 12, 1940

We're waiting for Professor Jurgutis to begin his lecture. The guy sitting behind me strikes up a conversation by complimenting me on my hat. I retort, "What can you say about the girl wearing it?" He rises to the bait, tells me I'm much lovelier than my hat and, without another second's pause, invites me to go for a walk sometime. I tell him I have absolutely no free time. And that is true: I study, I work at the university, I attend music school and I sing in the choir.

He seems taken aback. "You have no time at all?"

I open my notebook to my daily schedule and show him. "There, you see? All my evenings are filled."

Just then the professor's secretary comes into the auditorium and announces, "Today's lecture is canceled."

"Well, you have time to go somewhere now," the fellow says, smiling.

And I figured that would be more interesting than going right home, so I agreed.

He suggested the restaurant in the Saint George Hotel on Gedimino Prospect. Well, I thought, that's classy. It's the most prestigious spot in all of Vilnius, and I've never been. So far I'd been only to two fancy restaurants, both of them in Kaunas – Metropolis and Versalis. So off we went.

The meal was wonderful. We sat there sipping wine and talking. This man has a way with conversation. He told me that he'd already known me for a long time – since the days of Panevėžys Gymnasium. He said he'd seen me many times both in Kaunas and here in Vilnius but hadn't been brave enough to talk to me. That was a little hard to believe. But for some reason, I did believe him. I was very impressed with his manners. We were at a fashionable restaurant, but he was completely at ease; he ordered with an air of self-confidence. He was nothing like the typical student with holes in his pockets.

Alexandra with her mother, Veronica, 1924

Actually he had caught my eye before. I'd noticed him back when we were studying in Kaunas – he was tall and very thin and, I thought, very pale. He always wore the uniform of the Ramovė reserve officers – army boots, gray pants, brown jacket. I'd see him walking with his friends, brisk and intent and very serious. Still I wouldn't say that he mattered to me back then – just that I noticed him.

When I went to Kaunas to study at Vytautas Magnus University, I was so happy to be on my own, free from the suffocating care that my relatives felt so obligated to give me – the poor orphan. I had a job; I had my studies but I always found time for fun. I had many friends, women and men. One guy got a little too persistent about "looking after me" and finally told me that he was madly in love with me. His ardor got annoying, but I couldn't find a good way to disentangle myself. It was a stroke of luck that our school moved to Vilnius. I'm finally free of him, free at last to enjoy myself with friends I actually care about.

Juozas Kazickas – I know his name, because we're in the same department. I see him at the university every day when I'm working and in classes. He's distinguished himself by being extraordinarily well versed in every subject.

Once, during the summer session of 1940 – the Russians had already occupied the country – we all had the nervous sweats waiting for our turn to take our oral exam with Professor Remeris. As always the professor asked for a volunteer

Alexandra with her mother, Veronica

to go first. This tall, pale, very skinny fellow stands up and booms, "I'd like to." And then he fires off his answers, complete with dates, numbers, facts and ideas, as though he were reading them from a sheet of paper. My friend Birutė, who was sitting next to me, whispered that he was from Pasvalys, a friend of her boyfriend's. I felt kind of irked at him. After he was given his A grade, he strode out of the auditorium, saying as he passed us, "Don't get too nervous while you're waiting!" I thought, "Well, isn't he full of himself? That's some arrogant guy."

Fall arrived, and the new semester started. Although he and I sat in the same auditorium, I didn't pay much attention to him. I had a boyfriend already – an army lieutenant who would go out of his way to do whatever he could for me. With him around, there was really no room in my thoughts for this scrawny student from Pasvalys.

After classes I have to run straight to work. Right after my shift, I'm off to music school for voice lessons and then back to the university for choir rehearsals. By then it's already evening. I go out walking with my lieutenant for an hour or so and, before you know it, the evening has turned into night.

That's how my days passed until Juozas invited me to dine with him at the Saint George Hotel. Afterward, naturally, he took me home. I walked alongside him, holding his arm. I wasn't ready to admit it yet, but his charm dazzled me. He talked and talked, told stories, joked around. And he asked me, "When can I see you again?"

"I just don't know. I really am busy."

"Well," he laughed, "I guess I'll have to wait until another professor gets sick." Then he added, "Maybe we could go somewhere on Christmas."

I took a second to mull it over. Well, why shouldn't I? I thought. We made a date to meet on Christmas at four in the afternoon at Šventų Jonų *[St. Johns'] Church.*

But my relationship with the lieutenant is getting serious. His name, Arkadijus, is Russian – his family is Lithuanian-Russian. But his nationality doesn't bother me. Soviet ideology hasn't affected him at all. He's a very pleasant and well brought-up young man, and I like him a lot.

But now Juozas has appeared in my life, and I'm in a bit of a dilemma. I don't feel right about breaking off with Arkadijus. But all the same, I notice that I'm thinking about Juozas more and more. I can't bring myself to say no to him either.

December 22, 1940

Lionė has come out from Kaunas to visit her sister, Stasė, over the Christmas holidays. Stasė is my best friend; she and I share an apartment on Didžioji Street. Lionė is studying medicine at Vytautas Magnus University. We were having tea and talking about our boyfriends, and I couldn't contain myself – I told them about Juozas and our approaching date.

"But he already has a girlfriend!" Lionė was so surprised she was shouting. "He's dating my classmate, Antutė. She talks about how much she loves him – she says she wants to marry him. It's really going to hurt her when she finds out about your romance!"

Stasė said, "If they're that serious about each other, you'd be better off not getting involved."

Why should I compete with Antutė? I have a fine boyfriend – Arkadijus is a gallant officer. Not to mention several more fellows who'd like to get to know me better. I think it would be best to break off this relationship with Juozas before any more feelings develop. I really think that's what I have to do.

Christmas 1940

My decision is final: it's just not worth it going out with Juozas anymore. Still, he's a man who's a cut above the rest. I couldn't bring myself to simply stand him up; I decided I had to at least have the courtesy to let him know. So I ran to the post office this morning and sent him a telegram: "I am sorry but, for various reasons, I will not be able to meet you."

Arkadijus has been particularly attentive lately, offering to do all sorts of things for me. It's almost as though he's sensed something in these past few days. We agreed to get together today for Christmas. In the morning we attended mass at Šventų Jonų Church and sang the hymn, Maria, Maria. *Arkadijus joined in the singing with all the gusto he had – which is rather risky for an officer in a Lithuanian unit of the Soviet Army.* Maria, Maria *has become our unofficial national anthem since the Russians banned our official one.*

After mass we went for a walk in the woods of Žvėrynas district. The weather was gorgeous. It had snowed; now the sun was out and the new snow sparkled in its rays. We jumped in the snowdrifts and had a snowball fight. Arkadijus let me shoot his pistol at the trees on the edge of the woods. Then we parted, agreeing to get back together again at four on the corner of Vrublevskio Street, by the library.

That was when I was supposed to have my date with Juozas. But our meeting place is different – I was supposed to join Juozas at Šventų Jonų Church on Pilies Street. As four approached, I felt uneasy. What had Juozas thought when he read my telegram?

I decided to go home and talk it over with Stasė. At a few minutes to four we left together, because she had a date at the same time.

I was visiting my sister, who lived on Treniotos Street, close to my apartment. My neighbors knew where I was. One of them rushed over with the telegram. In those days telegrams were rare; usually they announced a death or, at the very least, a piece of urgent news. I tore it open and read: "I am sorry but, for various reasons, I will not be able to meet you. Alexandra."

My sister immediately started in on me. "What happened? Who sent that telegram?"

"Oh, it's just a message," I told her. "Nothing's wrong." I had no idea what had happened, only that something had gotten in the way of my relationship with Alexandra – something that was not good.

I came home and wrote in my diary, "I won't give up. I'm going to the center of town. I'll meet her one way or another."

Making use of my position, I called the driver for our office and asked him to take me to the Old Town in the Volkswagen that belonged to City Hall. The car was small but, back in those days, any kind of a car was a luxury and a sign of status.

I've always been punctual and this time I got to the Church well before four. I had a feeling Alexandra would be somewhere nearby. Although she had canceled our date, she might want to see if I'd shown up anyway.

I paced back and forth. I looked at my watch – a few minutes past four, and Alexandra was nowhere to be seen. I still hoped, at least a little, that she might come by after all. A few more minutes passed. And then I saw Alexandra and Stasė walking up Pilies Street.

I turned and walked toward them. As we were just about to meet, I tipped my hat and continued on without saying a word. But, of course, I looked back over my shoulder. Alexandra had stopped in the middle of the street and was whispering with her friend.

Christmas 1940

(continued)

Stasė punched me in the ribs. "Go over there and at least talk to him! He must have been waiting for you a long time." I glanced back and saw that he was looking at me. I left my pushy friend standing there and walked up to Juozas. "Didn't you get my telegram?"

"What telegram?" he asked without so much as the blink of an eye.

"I sent you a telegram this morning informing you that I wouldn't be meeting you. And there are some very serious reasons."

In a cold but calm voice he replied, "I think I know what those reasons might be. Please don't pay attention to idle talk. Believe me; there's nothing between that girl and me anymore."

"How can I believe you? I know what people are saying about the two of you. I truly don't want to interfere. I have no intention of breaking up your relationship."

He told me he could explain everything and asked me only to hear him out. I said I had no time to listen, because someone was already waiting for me by the library.

"That doesn't matter. Your lieutenant can wait a little while since he'll get to spend the entire evening with you. In the meantime, I'm the person you had a date with originally. I'm only asking for a few moments of your time."

We paced back and forth in front of the church, Juozas doing his best to convince me that there was nothing between him and Antutė. He said that for the thirteen days since our meal at the Saint George, he'd been doing nothing but waiting for the hour when he would see me again.

It started to snow lightly, then harder. The wind whipped up; it looked like a blizzard was on the way. Finally I said, "I simply can't walk around here with you any longer. Arkadijus has been waiting for me by the library for a good half hour by now, and that's all the way over on Vrublevskio Street." The snow was sticking to my eyelids and falling down the back of my neck.

"He'll have left a long time ago. But if you want – I came here by car, and we can drive over and take a look."

And indeed an automobile was waiting for him. We got in and drove off toward the library. The streets of Vilnius looked incredibly beautiful in the freshly fallen snow. We reached the library; the driver slowed down. It was obvious that Arkadijus was nowhere to be seen. By now it was five o'clock.

Apparently Arkadijus waited for a little more than half an hour and then rushed over to my apartment to find out why I hadn't shown up. By then Stasė was back. "Where's Alytė*?" he demanded.*

"I don't know," Stasė told him. "She went out somewhere an hour ago."

By then Juozas and I were driving toward Verkiai, a park that used to be a private estate. We stopped and got out of the car. Dusk was slowly enveloping us. The storm had calmed. The pine trees glistened white with the new snow, which crackled under our feet as we walked. The ruins of the manor, which had once housed the bishops of Vilnius, loomed mysteriously before us as we walked across the park. Suddenly Juozas wrapped his arms around my shoulders, pressed his face against my snowy cap and told me he'd fallen in love with me long ago and was happy just to be able finally to say that to me. I stood silently, listening to him tell me we were fated to be together. He confessed that he'd received my telegram but had been convinced I would show all the same. He repeated that we were fated never to part.

We decided to have supper at Valgio Svetainė, the cafe on Gedimino Prospect that's the most popular meeting spot in Vilnius. On certain evenings – known, for some reason as "five o'clock" evenings (in English), though we have no idea why – there's live music and dancing on the second floor. The only drawback is that, since the occupation, Russian soldiers have taken a shine to these functions. They stomp onto the dance floor in their army boots; often they've already had too much to drink by the time they arrive. And indeed, when we pulled up to Valgio Svetainė, there were a bunch of Russians whooping it up. This evening, though, we barely noticed them.

We sat down and ordered drinks. Juozas talked nonstop. The music began, and I swayed to its rhythm. When the orchestra played a song I liked, I suggested we dance. "I don't know how to," Juozas demurred.

"You don't know how to dance? How can anyone not know how to dance?" I was incredulous. I took him by the hand and walked him out onto the floor. It was true! He hopped in place from one foot to the other, holding me away from him as though he were afraid he might step on my feet. The Russians were stomping in a circle, pushing one another around in what they presumably considered a dance. They weren't paying attention to anybody else. It was as though we were alone on the floor. I pulled Juozas close to me. This was his first dancing lesson.

Day after Christmas 1940

I realized right away that I had to call things off with Arkadijus. I did it today. When he asked why I hadn't shown up for our date, I answered him directly: "My heart belongs to someone else." He began reprimanding me – I had no right to act like that with him! I probably just wanted to test his love, but there was no reason for that. His love was strong. "No," I told him. "It's really not that. I'm sorry it has to be this way, but everything between us is over. I can only be happy with someone else."

January 1941

Christmas Day was fateful. Since then Juozas and I have gone everywhere together – even to work. We sit next to each other in class. I've moved out of my apartment on Didžioji Street and rented a place in the Žvėrynas neighborhood so I can be closer to him. Now he can walk me home in the evenings and not have so far to go home himself. Every morning he taps on my window. I always wait for his tap with a little anxiety – I worry about the chance he might be arrested without warning. So far, every morning, to my relief, he's knocked on my window again. We walk to his office on Gedimino Prospect together. From there I go on to the university by myself. We always try to leave work together.

January 25, 1941

Today Juozas proposed to me – it only took a month. Early in the day, he sent me a bunch of roses. Later he came in person.

*His proposal was simple and to the point. "*Alytė*, will you marry me?"*

My answer was also simple. "Yes, I will."

I know how to live independently. I had to learn because I lost my parents when I was still very young. Until I met Juozas, taking care of my own needs and handling my own affairs was no more than a long-familiar matter of course. But things have changed since Juozas came into my life. I've been living in an entirely different world. There doesn't seem to be anything he can't do. He takes all our common concerns firmly into his own hands.

By now he and I have become inseparable; all that we possibly can, we do together. I feel entirely secure in my heart that my life with Juozas will be wonderful.

[A later insert in the diary: And indeed it has been. We forged our lives together during these early days of our relationship. The day we said "I do" was blessed by fortune – like all the days we've been together since.]

February 26, 1941

Today is my name's day. [Lithuanians celebrate the date of the saint's day with the same name more often than birthdays.] As usual, in the morning, I hear a rap on my door. I open it. There stands Juozas holding out – I can't believe my eyes! – a bouquet of blossoming white lilacs, a winter miracle. And there's more – a present for me: a bottle of Coty perfume. What luxuries these have become since the Soviets took over!

Spring 1941

We've been talking about setting a date for our wedding. Juozas' brother-in-law urges us not to delay. He thinks that should my husband be arrested, I, as his wife, would be permitted to look after him – at least, I'd be allowed to take him food in jail.

[Much later we realized how very naive such notions were.]

If we were to be exiled, it would be easier to be shipped out together. Juozas says that the possibility of exile frightens him. He thinks we should wait a while for the wedding, until the future becomes clearer. We're still very young – Juozas is twenty-three and I'm twenty-one. There's no reason to rush into marriage right now when we have no idea what even the next day might bring. Besides Juozas' mother has become very ill.

As the summer approaches, the anxiety level in Vilnius and throughout Lithuania is rising higher and higher. People everywhere are whispering that war is about to erupt. Juozas is wrapped up in his underground activities. We've noticed that he's being followed. We've often seen the same man wandering about near Juozas' apartment. He wears a black coat with a black hat, just like a spy out of a movie. He's short and always peculiarly hunched over. Once we caught him trying to look in Juozas' window. It was raining hard, and we tried to talk to him, but he just turned and walked away.

A wave of arrests has hit. Masses of people have been shipped out in boxcars to exile in Russia. There's tremendous tension hovering in the air at the university. People have stopped showing up at work. There have been instances when employees who were called into their superior's office ran out of the building and disappeared. We think they're hiding out with relatives or friends.

Work Under the Soviets

With the occupation, the Municipal Services Department got a new head: Lėmanas, a Vilnius native of German descent, who had previously been an ordinary driver (I never even knew his first name). He was an honest, hardworking man and a terrific chauffer but he was hopeless at administrative work. Our department was in charge of city services – hospitals, laundries, steam baths, the gas utility plant and public transportation. We had some three hundred employees. With no experience and no aptitude for managing such an array of services, Lėmanas was happy to delegate all the administrative work to me. I had been promoted to assistant head just before the Soviet invasion and, when he asked me to continue in that capacity, I consented. After all I had to have a job.

Lėmanas trusted me. He would tell me candidly about the discussions at the Vilnius Communist Party Committee meetings. Once he alerted me that this governing body had, for some reason, expressed a particular interest in me. Lėmanas warned me to behave very carefully.

Soon thereafter a Communist, a commissar from Russia showed up to work in our department. This man had lost his left arm in the Spanish Civil War and was very proud of it. His job was indoctrinating employees in communist ideology and identifying possible "enemies of the people" among us. The commissar distrusted me from the first day he set eyes on me. The truth is that he simply didn't like me. Needless to say, the feeling was mutual. Although neither of us ever publicly expressed our animosity, I could tell that he was watching my every move. I suspected he was waiting for the chance to censure me, perhaps even declare me an enemy of the people.

Despite his disability, he managed to captivate a young woman in our office. We assumed that she passed on anything she happened to hear at work.

Naturally the commissar did not know the Lithuanian language and had no desire to learn it. We had to deal with him in Russian. Our senior bookkeeper knew Russian quite well and, whenever anything complicated had to be related, he would act as our translator. Another employee also spoke Russian; later on we found out he was an NKVD agent. Lėmanas also managed to make himself understood in Russian.

I had very limited skills in the language. In time I could more or less understand what was being discussed but I never actually spoke Russian with anyone – partly, no doubt, out of my antipathy toward the occupying force and its language.

Most longtime employees of the city retained their jobs. Besides the commissar, our department got only one other new employee from Russia – an engineer named Vlasov, who came from St. Petersburg, by then already renamed Leningrad. He was completely different from the commissar: intelligent, calm and tactful. Maybe that's the reason I can still remember his first name after so many years. (I have no idea how we addressed the commissar, even though I dealt with him far more.) I could appreciate Vlasov. He just did his job and didn't harass us Lithuanians about the proper communist spirit.

We worked in a well-maintained building on Gedimino Prospect. Jonas Šimukonis, my former roommate from the widow's house on Basanavičius Street, was my assistant. Jonas' desk was in a small room through which it was necessary to pass to reach my office.

Upon arriving one morning, I noticed Jonas looking unusually weary and worried. He had recently gotten married, and I thought perhaps he'd had a spat with his wife. But since he didn't volunteer a word of explanation, I simply said good morning and continued into my office. I did bring up the subject at the end of the day, but he shrugged and assured me, "It's nothing. Everything is fine."

One morning, a couple of weeks later, he looked so crestfallen that I thought, he's simply not himself. Something is really amiss. I invited him in for a talk. "Are you sick? Did you get into a fight with your wife?" I was trying to sound lighthearted, but he squirmed in his seat, clearly uncomfortable. "It just seems that way to you," he said. "Nothing's wrong. Nothing's happened." Well, I thought to myself, if you don't want to talk about it, then we won't talk about it.

A few more days went by. One morning I got to work first. When Jonas showed up, he cracked open my door and hung a hat on the handle on my side. I understood immediately that he was giving me a signal. I walked over, and he whispered that he needed to talk to me.

We pretended to be reviewing some papers. I asked him into my office and closed the door. Jonas whispered, "I was arrested. They interrogated me. They demanded that I sign a promise to work with the NKVD. At first I refused, but they threatened me. They said they would hold me and arrest my wife. I gave in and signed. I have to inform them about everything that goes on in our office which means, primarily, I have to report on you – what you talk about, whom you meet with and what you do at night if you come into the office."

In fact I sometimes had to drop into the office late at night to make sure the public transportation system was running as scheduled.

Jonas told me that he had to submit a handwritten report every Friday to a certain apartment in a building on Lukiškių Square, containing what he had observed in our office and naming any employee he'd heard talking in a way that was contrary to the spirit of communism.

"The situation really is ugly. In no way do I blame you," I told him. "I thank you from the bottom of my heart for letting me know. Maybe someday there will be some way I can help you."

I realized now that a trap was being laid for me. Jonas had told me I was the employee of greatest interest to the NKVD. I suspected that the commissar had passed on negative information about me.

Approximately two weeks went by. Then, one day, the commissar ordered me to show up at nine that evening at the municipal building next to the Archdiocese to report on the work of Municipal Services. I asked him to whom I would be reporting. He barked back that this was not my concern – I would learn all I needed to know when I got there.

Lėmanas and Vlasov were already seated when I arrived. I sat down next to them. Apparently they had no idea why we had been called in either. We waited. An hour went by, but no one else showed up. The next time I looked at my watch, it was nearly eleven. This wasn't funny. Lėmanas kept getting stiffer and stiffer, but Vlasov remained calm. He tried to kid around a bit and tell us some jokes. What was going on? I had no idea.

The time approached one. We'd now been waiting for four hours. The door finally opened; a man in a leather jacket walked in and told Lėmanas to follow him into another office. I was left sitting with Vlasov who now grew very quiet – but then we had no one to translate for us anymore. Another hour went by. At two Lėmanas emerged, and the man in the leather jacket ordered me in.

I walked into a huge office in which two men were sitting. One of them was a Lithuanian; he was the translator. At first they asked me biographical questions. "When and where were you born?" "Where did you study?" "How did you come to be in Vilnius?" "Who helped you get a job with the city?" "With whom have you worked?" I answered all their questions.

Next they switched to questions of a political nature. "Do you understand how fortunate it was that the Soviet Union adopted Lithuania into its family of nations?"

Well, how could I not understand that? I told them that this was entirely clear to me.

"Are you helping the other employees to better understand the advantages of the Soviet order?"

"Certainly. I talk to them about how good life has become. All the people in our office agree."

But they kept badgering me: "Haven't you noticed certain people who don't favor the Soviet government? Aren't there some workers who, you can tell by their conversations, don't respect Stalin, the great leader of all nations?"

I tried to convince them that I had never encountered any such persons.

"But do you ever have heart-to-heart discussions with the employees in order to learn their real feelings?" This was a question they kept pummeling me with in various forms.

The questions came at me like blows, one after another. They would ask the same thing over and over again. It seemed as though it would never end. Time was passing slowly. The clock showed nearly five a.m. The Russian questioning me kept making notes on a pad. Sometimes he flipped through a file full of clipped-in papers, appearing to read something in them. I assumed that this was the file on me. At last he told me, "Thank you. You may leave now."

I had been in that office for three hours; before that I had waited from nine to two. I was dead tired. Although I had been sitting the entire time, as I walked home, my legs felt as though they were folding up under me. After this meeting, I could well imagine how the NKVD broke people down in interrogations without ever using physical violence. I was very nervous over the next several days.

Aleksa, my coworker and friend in the underground, had disappeared two or three weeks earlier. All the office knew was that the NKVD had arrested him. By now I was well aware of the will and strength a person would have to have to keep from informing on someone during security police interrogations. But Aleksa never betrayed me or anyone else. It wasn't until after I had moved west that I learned his fate: he, along with a group of prisoners, was shot to death at the start of the war between Germany and Russia.

Fear of Arrest

The summer of 1941 approached. In May a typhoid epidemic struck Vilnius. There was a shortage of medication, and a lot of people died. However, the epidemic was under control by June.

The members of the resistance had received word from Germany that the Germans would attack the Soviet Union on June 15th (but that didn't happen until June 22nd). By now I carried a revolver around with me. I had several motorcycles hidden at a farm in the suburb of Pavilnys. We were preparing to stage an uprising in Vilnius as soon as the order reached us from Kaunas. Though there were comparatively few Russian soldiers actually stationed in the city, we couldn't fight a head-on military conflict because there were too few Lithuanians in Vilnius. Our percentage of the population had dropped after the occupation, partly as a result of all the arrests and partly as a result of the large number of immigrants of different nationalities who had streamed in from Russia. Consequently we planned only to take possession of the bridges and thwart the Russian crossings as the German Army approached the city.

I had another hardship to face during those days: my mother's terminal cancer. She was in the hospital for a long time. We couldn't visit her there since the hospital had been quarantined due to the epidemic. I could only see her at the window of her hospital room, looking ever weaker, paler and thinner. Eventually she lapsed into a coma, and we took her to my sister's apartment, where she and my stepfather had been living since their move from Joniškėlis. On her last night, Victoria and I stayed at her bedside; she died on the morning of June 13th without regaining consciousness.

It was draining, amid everything else, to have to plan the funeral. But we made all the arrangements and walked in great sadness behind the coffin to the cemetery. And then, during the meal afterward, I was appalled to learn of a new misfortune: a great sweep of arrests. People were being herded to the railway stations, shoved into boxcars and hauled off to Russia. Many members of the underground had disappeared.

I had a nice apartment on Treniota Street but, as soon as I heard about the arrests, I decided to stop spending the night at home. Vladas Kulbokas, my former teacher at Pasvalys High School, who lived with me, also decided to stay away that night. We found an empty shed behind the Russian Orthodox Church at Žvėrynas Bridge in our neighborhood, packed our vital belongings and moved in that evening. I didn't go to work the next morning.

But, as fate would have it, I had a final exam with Professor Mykolas Remeris that day. I mulled it over and decided to go to the university. Luckily no one was looking for me there. I'd had no time to study, but the professor knew how well I had done in the seminar discussions, so he helped me along by asking questions he knew I could answer. I passed with a B but I still felt bad about it – up to then I had made As in all my subjects.

We spent a second night in the shed. The next morning was a Sunday, and Alexandra and I decided to attend mass at the Cathedral.

Sunday, June 22, 1941

Juozas came over very early, and we left for the Cathedral. We were strolling down Gedimino Prospect when suddenly we heard a roar of airplanes overhead. I'd hardly had time to notice where they were heading when there was an explosion, then another. The air-alert sirens went off, and we realized: it was war! Hitler had finally started his battle with Stalin. Our country had been waiting for the day when the Germans would lock horns with the Russians for a very long time. And now the day was upon us.

We turned and ran immediately for the nearest courtyard. The German planes seemed to be right over our heads. We stopped at a gateway into a building and pressed ourselves against the brick wall, waiting for the planes to pass. They flew onward.

The airport was bombed. It appeared that a few bombs had been dropped over Žvėrynas as well. Apparently the German pilots noticed Russian trucks in the area. Much distressed we rushed back to our neighborhood, but neither Juozas' apartment nor mine had been hit. Someone told us that several bombs had dropped near the street where Victoria and her children live. We rushed over. There were two huge craters in the courtyard of her building. All the windows had been shattered, but the building itself was intact.

Victoria met us at the door, trembling with fear. She was alone with the children. No one knew where her husband, Joseph, was or the fate of his Lithuanian unit in the Soviet Army. Victoria was in a state of shock over him, terrified that he might have been killed. We did our best to comfort her, assuring her that there hadn't yet been any battles in the area where Joseph was stationed. He and the other Lithuanians will probably manage to run away from the Russian army in time.

After we had calmed her a little, we went back to Juozas' place. The air-alert sirens started screaming again. It wasn't safe inside the apartment, and the building didn't have a cellar for us to take refuge in, so we decided our best course was to run out into the yard under the cover of trees.

The German attack subsided in the afternoon. I suggested that we have supper at the cafe, Valgio Svetainė. "There's probably going to be a food shortage very soon," I said. "At least we can have a good meal this one last time."

And we did. There were a lot of people there – we had a hard time getting a table. The state of tension was high, and the room was loud; everyone was talking about the turn of events. People had lost their fear of talking openly because the Russians were evacuating their offices and fleeing Lithuania in panic. Someone reported that an uprising had started in Kaunas and some other areas. Partisans were releasing prisoners from the jails. Others said their relatives had managed to escape from the trains that were supposed to carry them into exile in Russia.

Spirits were high. The news arrived that the rebels in Kaunas had captured the radio station and broadcast an announcement that Lithuania was once again independent, and a provisional government was being formed. Everyone was relieved that the terror of communism, the arrests and torture, had finally come to an end. "Germany is a civilized nation," we agreed. "They won't act like the Russians. They'll let us have our own government."

[How could we all have been so incredibly naive?]

Juozas was in a hurry to get back into town and join his compatriots in the underground against the Russians. I cried and begged him not to leave me alone. I pleaded with him to think of his sister and her little children since God only knows where her husband might be. "The Soviets are in a panic. They'll shoot anybody who gets in their way! Please wait till tomorrow at least," I implored him.

[I was right. A number of people fell under Soviet bullets on that first day of the war on the basis of the slightest suspicion.]

We couldn't just spend the whole day sitting in the parlor. We had to think what we were going to do under wartime conditions. Even though it was a Sunday, we found all the stores open. People were rushing in to buy whatever they could; everything was being swept off the shelves. Nobody knows what tomorrow might bring. Will the withdrawing Russians rob all the stores? Will the Germans take all the food for their own army? Will the supply system break down entirely? Long lines quickly formed in front of every store. And then the German planes appeared again in another bombing raid. The sirens screamed, but this time no one dispersed. They watched the sky in fear but they were no less afraid to lose their places in line.

End of June 1941

Just days before war broke out between the Russians and Germans, the NKVD arrested Stasė. She had been giving me sheets of paper to pass on to Juozas for proclamations. She was called in before an officer and never returned. As the German Army approached Vilnius, the Russians took her and a group of other prisoners from Lukiškės Prison to the railway station and shoved them into a boxcar to ship to Russia. The war kept the train from leaving. Stasė was freed.

I have been horribly anxious these days since the war started and Stasė disappeared. I am very afraid that Juozas or I could be arrested.

July 1941

War has indeed flared. The Russians have been running as fast as they can out of Vilnius and out of the country. Matters have stabilized here a little. Juozas and I have decided to set a mid-August date for our wedding.

The Germans Arrive

On the second day of the war, we learned that the Germans had marched into Kaunas. The Russians couldn't muster enough forces to defend Vilnius and they were fleeing in a panic. Some of the higher-ups tried to take their spoils with them, lugging out huge bags and stuffing them onto trucks. Others abandoned everything but the pants they were wearing and dashed to the railway station. Short columns of military trucks sped out of the city. Quite a number of soldiers banded together in Žvėrynas, raising serious fears of a clash with the approaching German units in our neighborhood. But they, too, soon got out of town.

I reported to work. The municipality was trying to keep things from dissolving into chaos. I took on the job of making sure that our drivers didn't walk off their jobs and that the city buses continued running on schedule. The commissar, of course, had disappeared and so had Vlasov, the engineer. We went into the commissar's office. He had fled without bothering to return for his documents. I found the report about my interrogation among his papers. It substantiated my suspicion that he was the one who had filed the complaint with the NKVD, claiming that my loyalty was highly suspect. But we found documents of far greater importance. There was a list of employees from our office earmarked for deportation to Russia with my name at the top. All of us were described as untrustworthy workers, harboring opinions in opposition to the Soviet government.

There was another surprise. Among the documents was a report handwritten by one of our colleagues, a musician by education who knew the Russian language quite well, reviewing the morale of his coworkers. My name also appeared in his report several times. He had not fled Vilnius. When we caught up with him, he tried to lie, insisting that he had never spied on anyone; he only fell silent when we placed the proof before his eyes. But we didn't hand him over to the Germans who would probably have shot him on the spot. We simply fired him.

On the third day of the war, the German Army appeared on the outskirts of Vilnius. Motorcycles led the column. Light armored tanks followed not far behind. Next came the trucks, filled with ground troops. Last were the tanks, rolling on their clattering caterpillar tracks and raising a terrible noise.

The motorcycles rode to Savanorių Street (known today as Savanorių Prospect). I happened to be there and saw an officer step out of his car with a map in his hands. I walked up and introduced myself as a member of the Municipal Services staff in charge of transportation. My German was still weak at the time, but I was proficient enough to understand what he was asking: he wanted to know what streets would take them across Vilnius quickly, without having to go through the center of town. I knew enough to say, "Follow me." I led the Germans to the edge of Vilnius, pointing the column in the direction of Minsk. As I was leading them, the thought crossed my mind that, while the German Army performed like a well-oiled machine, the soldiers were no more than cogs in that machine, devoid of souls.

The Germans suffered no losses on their march across Vilnius. A few random shots were fired, but that was all. There were some rather large Soviet military formations not far away in the woods around Varėna, but the Russians were so demoralized that they didn't attempt a serious confrontation even from such a nearby position.

The Soviet-incorporated Lithuanian military units were also ordered east. Most Lithuanian soldiers disobeyed these orders, and battles ensued as they tried to escape. Not all of them did; any captured Lithuanian soldier was shot on the spot as a deserter. But fortune smiled on my sister's family. Joseph Gruodis returned home alive and fit. His regiment in the Soviet Army had been engaged in maneuvers in Varėna when the war erupted. Joseph immediately fled and thus evaded the perils of deportation or arrest.

As soon as the Russians were out of Vilnius, I went to Lukiškės Prison with Major Šimkus' cousin. The prison guards had run away and the gates were open. Some of the prisoners had managed to break out of their cells on their own. We walked up and down the gloomy prison hallways, looking for Šimkus. We finally found him collapsed in his cell and unable to walk on his own. Somehow we got him to the car and drove him home. Even though Šimkus was in poor shape, we were all relieved. We felt confident that he would recover and that these horrendous times were over, never to return.

Happiness Becomes Horror

When the Germans first took over Vilnius, they didn't interfere in municipal operations. Their military commanders never so much as appeared at our office. They had not yet developed a civil administration for Lithuania. All the same, the residents of the city at once felt the hard hand of the Germans. Threatening announcements appeared on posts and bulletin boards warning that any opposition to the Reich's Army or infraction of the orders issued by the military command was punishable by firing squad.

Despite such ominous signs, the Lithuanians of Vilnius were euphoric that the Russians had been run out of the country. We eagerly waited for the Germans to recognize the independent state of Lithuania that the provisional government had proclaimed.

I left for Kaunas with Professor Padalskis to meet with the Prime Minister of the Provisional Government, Juozas Brazaitis-Ambrazevičius. We talked about what action was needed in Vilnius, which people we could trust and how we, the residents of Vilnius, could assist his Cabinet of Ministers. It was a promising discussion. We had high hopes that the Germans would permit Lithuania to remain independent, at least formally, and would recognize the provisional government.

Our next meeting with Professor Brazaitis took place several weeks later. It was far more disheartening. The Germans had declared all action by the provisional government illegal; it had lasted a mere six weeks. The discussion this time was about avoiding German repression. Our hopes that the new occupier would be better than the old one were rapidly dissipating. But we weren't yet at the point of organizing an underground resistance. We still believed that as soon as the war ended – it couldn't go on forever – we would again have the opportunity to claim our independence.

A *Gebietscommissar*, or Territorial Commissar, arrived to replace the Soviet commissar as the top official in Vilnius. He moved into quarters on Gedimino Prospect with an SS unit under his command for maintaining order. The commissar was one Hans Hingst, who did not get much involved in the work of our office. The Nazis permitted the municipality much more self-determination than the Soviets had. Apparently the raging war diverted their attention from such matters as city services. One thing I initially appreciated about them was that, at least, they spared us ideological indoctrination. Over time, however, they began demonstrating ever more openly that they were the masters in the city.

Colonel K. Dabulevičius was named the Burgomaster, or mayor, for the city; one of his assistants was Palevičius, a long-time resident of Vilnius, a former champion (representing Poland) of the European Motorcycle Races and a man of strong patriotic principles. The burgomaster had more interaction with the commissar and other German officials than anyone else, and the Germans were constantly issuing him all sorts of directives. His relationship with them was quite professional, if cool.

Well after the war, the Americans arrested Dabulevičius in Coburg, Germany. Someone had filed a complaint denouncing him as a collaborator. Knowing English, I was able to help gain his release. I testified that Dabulevičius had only handled city matters and had never collaborated or participated in the criminal activities of the Germans. He did not actually take part in the anti-Nazi resistance; however, he was in a position to know a great deal and he never informed on anyone.

Lėmanas, my direct superior, did not retreat with the Russians. Having done no harm to anyone, he was simply relieved of his duties as department head. I was promoted into his position and thus I became responsible for the work of all city services.

Initially our office routine altered little. The most noticeable change was that our Polish employees felt and acted closer to their Lithuanian colleagues than they had under the Soviets. The Poles recognized the German hostility toward them and believed that Germans had disdain for anyone and everyone other than themselves.

One event shook me to the bones during the early weeks under the new occupiers. The translator for the commissariat was a Lithuanian student from Klaipėda with whom I was somewhat acquainted. He spoke excellent German. One day I missed him – he was nowhere around. I went to the municipal administration office to find out where he was.

"They shot him." I heard the answer but could not believe my ears. "Why? What did he do?" No one knew much about the circumstances. The Germans had simply declared him a traitor, apprehended him and shot him.

I wondered whether he might have been a spy for the Soviets. It still seemed outrageous to execute a person so suddenly. Yesterday we had exchanged greetings; today he no longer existed. I realized that the Germans would shoot anyone that displeased them without the slightest ceremony. But, in another way, I was still trying to find reasons to justify their behavior. It's wartime, I told myself, and the boundary between life and death had become jagged.

But I could hardly keep using that excuse as, over time, their horrendous treatment of Jews became more and more evident. All Jewish Lithuanians who had not fled with the Russians were persecuted. During the very first days of the new occupation, the Germans issued an order that all Jews only appear in public wearing a visible Star of David. They were prohibited from walking on sidewalks – they had to walk in the gutter of the street.

There were several Jews in our department. One was a very diligent bus inspector. Several were employed at the municipal offices as skilled engineers, bookkeepers and other jobs. For the first few days, the Germans didn't catch on. It wasn't long, however, before an order was sent out that all Jews were to move into the Vilnius Ghetto and all Jewish employees at city offices were to be dismissed. The Nazis did provide an exception: with a special permit, a Jewish specialist could stay on the job. But it was necessary to prove that no other employee could take over his or her duties.

I requested permission to retain the Jewish employees at the workshop constructing bus bodies, explaining in a note to the *Gebietscommissariat* that I could not replace them. I was granted the permit. Our office had to take the responsibility for seeing that they did not run away – nor could they leave the workplace during the working day. At the end of their shift, they were to be led under guard back to the ghetto. I ignored these instructions and let them go to a nearby suburban area to shop. That way they were able to take food back to the ghetto. This state of affairs didn't last long. Our permit for retaining Jewish employees was revoked, and thereafter no more Jews worked for us. In all likelihood, these people suffered the same tragic fate that befell the great majority of Lithuania's Jews.

But we hardly fathomed the terrible tragedy that was to come. It was true, as we learned later, that the Jewish populations of villages and small townships were murdered en masse almost as soon as the Germans invaded Lithuania. Only many, many years later, after I was living in the United States, were the statistics about these horrifying events revealed. Apparently, historians have concluded that some 160,000 of the estimated 209,000 population of Jewish citizens (or residents) of Lithuania, including Vilnius, were executed following the Nazi invasion of our country. Although there is a dispute on the actual numbers by different scholars, the sheer volume of these tragedies shook me to the core of my soul. I have no idea what I would have done had I realized the extent of what was happening while I was still in Vilnius. Most of what we learned then was by rumors; aside from the underground press of our own resistance movement, the official news was heavily censored. The Nazis were no less adept at this than the Soviets had been.

The news about these slaughters did not reach Vilnius right away; it took some time before we learned about what was happening in the outlying areas. My first word of such events came from a member of our office staff several weeks after the start of the war. He told me he had heard that the Nazis had shot a hundred, perhaps a thousand Jews in the Paneriai Forest. Even children had been killed. My mind refused to believe this right away. "Even children, women, the elderly? It can't be possible ..." I was aghast and clung to the hope that it was a much exaggerated rumor. But the stories spread rapidly through the city. No healthy mind could comprehend the kind of viciousness we were hearing about. But finally we had to admit to ourselves that these stories were actually true.

One twilit evening in August 1941, Alexandra and I were walking down Gedimino Prospect toward the Cathedral. From far off we could see a long column of people coming toward us. As they came nearer, we saw that they were Jews. SS soldiers with automatic rifles were herding them towards Lukiškės Prison. We stopped dead as women, children and old people were marched past us. They walked with the quiet sort of gait of badly abused people. Their shoes scuffled over the cobblestones of Gedimino Prospect. A sense of utter helplessness swept over us, and we remained silent for a long time after the column passed. "They're being led to Lukiškės," one of us finally said. "They won't be shot there. They'll just be put in jail, that's all." We tried to hang onto this pathetic shred of hope. Alas, those people were shot. The next day I heard that sounds of gunfire had echoed from the prison the previous night. Any last doubts I still harbored about the truth of the tales I had been hearing vanished for good.

We spoke with Kęstutis Aglinskas, a young doctor friend. On the eve of the war, hiding out from the NKVD, he had bicycled to a village in Suvalkija. As soon as the Germans invaded, all the Jews in the area were rounded up, herded into the woods and shot. Entire families, even infants, fell under the bullets. Witnesses to these tragedies rarely came forth openly – at most they told one or another trusted friend or family member. Everyone was terrified of becoming victims themselves for speaking the truth. Aglinskas was the only one who actually told me he saw something. Others would say no more than, "I heard that someone said they saw..." Another friend whispered that near his home village a huge hole had been dug in the forest. Jews had been rounded up and marched out there; mercilessly, they had all been shot and all fell into the pit. One man had somehow escaped and crawled back to the village. Some people had whisked this injured man in the dead of night to an area several townships away to trusted friends who hid him. This story reminded me of my Aunt Grasilija's brother, Juozas, who had crawled out of a corpse-filled pit after facing a Bolshevik firing squad. We hated the Bolsheviks and the Communists for all their atrocities. Now we were faced with these hideous, unspeakable crimes from another enemy, one we had hoped would "save" us from Soviet enslavement.

Alexandra and I and all of our friends were horrified at the kind of barbarism we could never have imagined before. The new occupational government now repelled people but it also terrified them. We understood that no sort of morality or even the most elementary humanity held back the Nazis. They were entirely capable of any brutality. Our views about Germans changed radically over the first several weeks of the occupation. Anyone who had taken pride in having German acquaintances stopped talking about them very quickly.

My last meeting, at the end of 1941, with my beloved teacher, Mrs. Hofmanienė, deeply distressed me. She had written me that she would be visiting Kaunas and would like to meet me there. I drove over one evening, and we spent several hours at her hotel, talking about life. She was in a grimly pessimistic mood. She believed that Germany was doomed to lose the war, and that with its vicious policies – particularly the slaughters of Jews – Germany had brought down on itself a terrible fate. Although she was in no way involved and was powerless to change anything, as a German, Mrs. Hofmanienė felt a deep sense of personal guilt. She told me she had been considering suicide. Of course I tried to convince her to put such ideas out of her mind. "Look how much you've helped me over my life – and I'm just one person. You have to continue to work! Your students need you!" I tried to comfort her, but she only listened silently and sadly. When we said goodbye, she told me she never expected to see me again. She never did. When I returned to Lithuania many decades later, I tried to track Mrs. Hofmanienė down but I was unable to find a trace of her.

It is true that Jewish-Lithuanian relations had soured during the Soviet occupation. There were many Jews in Pasvalys, the town of my childhood, as there were in every prewar Lithuanian town. Back then I had not the vaguest notion of the phenomenon known as anti-Semitism. It never entered my mind that my Jewish friends might be inferior to my other friends; religious intolerance was not characteristic of my generation. I was never aware of animosity toward Jews as a group – until 1940. But from the start of the Soviet occupation, rumors were rife that many Jews were collaborating with the occupiers, and the result was a great deal of anger toward them. Nonetheless, I detected no specifically anti-Semitic mood at the start of the German occupation, at least not in my circle of friends and acquaintances. When talk reached our ears that Lithuanians had become stained with the blood of Jews in the Nazi-led murders, we were devastated and horrified.

Among my Jewish acquaintances was a young man I knew at military school in Panemunė. We had struck up a friendship. He had graduated with the rank of junior lieutenant in the Lithuanian army, and then our lives had taken their different roads. We hadn't seen each other for many years when, out of the blue, I spotted him one early morning in November 1941 and froze in my tracks. At daybreak a column of Jews was always marched to work from the ghetto. There, among the guards, was my old friend, wearing the uniform of a ghetto policeman and herding his own compatriots. The Germans had formed a ghetto administration and a police force out of Jews. Military officers received priority for these positions.

He caught sight of me and dropped his gaze to the ground. The column moved forward into the mist of an autumn dawn. I stared at him until they had disappeared from sight. I never heard another thing about him. It would be good to find out that he survived the Holocaust but, of course, I have very little hope that he could have. The entire ghetto administration of Vilnius was destroyed. Most died at Paneriai, some at Auschwitz or Treblinka. A rare exception or two managed, by some miracle, to survive to the war's end.

I also remember the chief of the ghetto. I would see him at the burgomaster's office; the features of his intelligent face are etched in my memory. He remained in charge of the Vilnius Ghetto to the day of its final destruction. He tried as best he could to find ways to ease the everyday lives of his people, trapped in such dire circumstances.

August 15, 1941

We were married today, during Žolinės, the day of our ancient tradition for blessing crops before the harvest, at Šv. Mikalojaus (St. Michael's), the oldest church in Vilnius. I borrowed a dress from my friend who had married a month earlier. I could no longer get the material to make one of my own.

Juozas and Alexandra on their wedding day, Aug. 15, 1941

The witnesses were Alė Rūta, the poet, and Vladas Kulbokas, one of Juozas' teachers. Professor Petras Katilius was best man. The guests were Victoria, Joseph Gruodis and Stasė, who had just escaped from the clutches of the NKVD.

From the church, we all went to the shrine of the Madonna at Aušros Vartai, the ancient city gates. Of course we couldn't have a big, noisy reception – our country is at war, and Juozas' mother died only a few months ago. We had our party at Victoria's apartment. It's been very hard to get good food lately, but Victoria managed to serve some delicious dishes. At nine o'clock, we now have Commandant's Hour, when no one is allowed out on the streets. We had to cover the windows with heavy drapes and party in near darkness.

Until today my last name was Kalvėnaitė. Today I am Kazickienė, the wife of Juozas Kazickas. I am proud and happy.

September 1941

We got our first apartment together! It's in our old neighborhood, Žvėrynas, on the same street Victoria lives – Treniotos Street.

Burdens of War

Before the war, the rise of the German economy under Hitler's leadership had strongly impressed Lithuanians. The 1936 Olympic Games in Berlin had helped solidify the image of Germany as a great power. We saw films of grandiose stadiums and the incredibly ostentatious parades in Nuremburg. We knew, on the one hand, that Hitler ruled Germany as a strict dictatorship but, on the other, that he seemed to have succeeded in mobilizing the entire nation to shore up its economy.

The fact that, in September 1939, Germany crushed the seemingly robust Polish army in barely two weeks elicited differing reactions in Lithuania. Germany had displayed the face of an aggressor, fomenting a World War, and that naturally was intimidating. But the show of power also aroused an apprehensive respect, colored not a little by Poland's role as a national adversary. Furthermore, our joy in regaining Vilnius overwhelmed the sense of catastrophe surrounding the war in Europe. Our euphoria was dampened when Germany tore the Klaipėda lands (also known as the Memel Territory) away from Lithuanian jurisdiction soon afterward. But, on the whole, Lithuanians did not consider Germany a foe after the Soviet occupation. Russia loomed in everyone's mind as the great enemy, and thus many Lithuanians greeted the Germans as liberators when they marched into the country in June 1941.

Initially the Germans appeared to be the opposite of the Russians. When the Soviet Army invaded Lithuania in 1940, the grocery stores in our country must have looked like a dream of luxury and abundance to its soldiers. They all but swept the products off the shelves, buying anything and everything indiscriminately. For a while, the shops had sufficient stocks on reserve in warehouses to operate reasonably well. Of course these shops could only impress someone who had previously experienced nothing but the privations of the Soviet Union. The great irony, of course, was that for all their condemnation and vilification of capitalism, the Russians chased madly after any and all the remnants of capitalism in the country they had newly occupied.

Their behavior evinced a peculiar sort of culture shock. Jokes abounded about their gaffes, as when the wives of some military officers showed up in theaters and restaurants wearing brand-new nightgowns they believed to be evening gowns. According to Lithuanian soldiers in the Soviet Army, these women wept with shame when they learned that they had actually worn bedroom apparel out in public. High-ranking officers showed off their position by wearing two watches at a time. Such ostentatious displays brought nothing from us but smiles of pity. As for the Soviet soldiers, they were simply thieves. Any apartments left empty for too long would be stripped of mirrors, door handles, even padlocks.

The Germans, on the other hand, behaved like arrivals from a wealthier, higher civilization. They had no need to shop in Lithuanian stores because they purchased their goods through their own internal supply system. Quickly, however, their arrogance and their contempt for every other nationality became just as offensive as the aggressive indigence of the Soviets.

That the war would take longer than most of us had expected and that a German victory would be no simple matter soon became clear. By the autumn of 1941, all sorts of indications had appeared. All the resources of the country were being mobilized for the needs of the German Army. First there were gasoline shortages in Vilnius. Then the Germans expropriated many of the automobiles belonging to the city (though I managed for a few months to keep my old but well-maintained Citroën). Our greatest headache by far, though, was managing the fuel supply for the public transportation system. We somehow kept the wheels turning but not always smoothly. Citizens had to wait longer and longer for a bus; walking became far more popular than it had been. But, despite all the difficulties, the system did keep operating until the German Army retreated and the Soviets reentered.

All day I was buried in city matters; in the evening I still rushed to lectures at Vilnius University. I was in my final term in economics when Germany invaded Lithuania. As the war expanded farther east and farther west, the length of time the university would continue operating became an open question. The Germans, furious at not having been able to draw more Lithuanian youths into the German Army, apprehended many professors and shut down the universities in Kaunas and Vilnius during the spring of 1943. By then I had already graduated. I had defended my dissertation, "The Collectivization of Lithuanian Agriculture," in June 1942 and was now a bona fide economist with a degree. Alexandra graduated at the same time. Despite the war, our student friends gathered for a modest celebration. As it turned out, we were the last class to graduate before the Nazis closed the universities. The students in lower classes did not get their diplomas until after the war in Germany. Some graduated much later – after they had emigrated from Germany to the United States.

During that final school year, conditions at the university were very trying. Winter was especially hard since the facilities were not heated at all. It was an odd picture with professors lecturing in their winter coats and students taking notes in their woolen gloves. Even so, the level of education never dropped; the professors never compromised their academic standards or lessened their demands on their students.

Work at the Municipal Services Department under wartime conditions was tremendously complicated. The one good aspect was that the German administration guaranteed our city services the most needed provisions from Germany and its other occupied countries. During the first winter of the war, we received a shipment of bituminous coal, which we distributed to the populace; therefore the winter of 1942 in Vilnius was not especially hard.

However, the situation kept worsening. It was especially difficult to get enough fuel for the gas utilities plant. I went to the burgomaster and even to the police for help. We switched from coal to peat. We needed huge quantities of peat which we had to bring in from the district of Varėna. We were never able to accumulate a surplus so we were constantly fretting over deliveries, which were made mostly by horse-drawn wagon since we had no gasoline to spare for trucks. Under these conditions, a complete stoppage at the gas plant was a constant threat; the pressure of the boilers frequently dropped to a dangerously low point. All of the larger apartment buildings in Vilnius had gas-generated centralized heating and, if the gas supply were to terminate, many people would freeze.

Then there was the dwindling supply of food to the city. Early on the shelves in Vilnius stores were adequately stocked. There were plenty of reserves, and the supply system from the villages continued to function fairly normally for a while. But the occupational government wasted no time in demanding food from the farmers for its army – a "tax payment" enforced by the Nazi-instituted civil administration. A number of farmers were shot for hiding products. And then, after a few months, the food-coupon system was put into place. People in the city could buy food only with coupons which, over time, purchased less and less. Even people with relatives in the villages found it hard to get butter and eggs or any other products. Lithuanian sausages and other delicacies that had been common before the war were now out of the question. The offerings at the cafeterias and restaurants grew ever more meager. Often you could get nothing but vegetable soup – a thin liquid with a few floating pieces of carrots and potatoes. I had the additional problem of being allergic to certain foods. Until I was fifteen, I was unable to drink milk because, if I did, I would immediately break out in a rash. Cafeteria food often caused me health problems early in the war. But a human being can adjust to any conditions. Over time, my organism stopped going on strike, even when the quality of the food I ate might have justified it.

But Lithuania did not suffer true starvation even during the war years. A minimum of the necessary staples covered by food coupons remained available for purchase at the stores in Vilnius. And relatives in rural areas made the lives of most Lithuanians easier. Alexandra's relatives came to our aid many a time; we would come back from a visit with bread, bacon and flour.

Once the coupons were introduced, though, purchasing food directly from villages was considered speculation and outlawed. The Germans set up road checks to inspect passing cars. A patrol officer once stopped me in my government car on my way back from a visit with Alexandra's relatives and ordered me to open my trunk. I did have food from the village packed there, but he didn't make an issue of it. I had shown him my work papers, and apparently that was enough to keep him from confiscating my treasures or even arresting me. The Germans were generally merciless in controlling speculation – more than one person was shot for it, probably as an example to dissuade others from pursuing this source of income. Life in Lithuania by now had become as perilous as it had been during the Soviet occupation. The most minor infraction of German laws could result in arrest or even execution. The major difference from the Soviet era was that the Nazi repressions were not class-based; greater affluence was no longer considered the offense it had been under the Soviets.

Toward the end of the war, when we wound up in Germany, we found, much to our surprise, that the supply system was operating smoothly there, even though the country was completely bombed out and war-torn. The Germans were better cared for with food than we Lithuanians had been up to the Nazi capitulation to the Allies.

Our Wee Great Miracle

Life became ever more difficult – but life went on. A great event blessed Alexandra and me: a daughter, whom we named Jurate, was born to us on February 18, 1943, at *Švento Jokūbo* 'St. Jacob's' Hospital. The inspiration for the name, a popular one in Lithuania, was "Jūratė and Kastytis," a classic ballad by Maironis based on a Lithuanian folktale.

It was a beautiful, sunny day. At work I was utterly unable to concentrate – all I could do was watch for my friend, Dr. Kęstutis Aglinskas, who worked at the hospital and had promised to dash over to my office as soon as Alexandra gave birth. In the afternoon it suddenly grew dark and began snowing hard. For a while I stood at the window, wondering what sort of world awaited my soon-to-arrive firstborn. I had no idea what the future held but I had faith that I would somehow manage to provide at least the bare necessities for our baby. I earned a respectable salary – that eased my worries to some extent. We lived in a nice, newly remodeled apartment. And I had inherited some property from my mother.

Finally Dr. Aglinskas came bustling in from the snowstorm. "Congratulations! You have a daughter," he announced. For weeks he had been assuring me that we were going to have a son but now he just laughed and said, "Her nose is like a little button."

An illness of some sort was then raging through the hospital, and it proved fatal to a number of mothers and infants. Alexandra got sick, but my physician friends saved us by procuring a very rare medication from the Germans: antibiotics. Ultimately this highly contagious disease closed down the hospital entirely. But Alexandra recovered in a few weeks.

Knowing how much she liked writing down her impressions, my gift to her on the occasion of our daughter's birth was a leather-bound diary. A year and a half later, she would use it to record the heart-rending details of our departure from our homeland and later of our wanderings in Germany.

February 20, 1943

Compared to others, we live quite well. Our apartment is really very nice. Still, I feared becoming pregnant during wartime. What will tomorrow bring? The future remains entirely unknown. But it happened all the same: late last spring I knew that I was going to have a baby. A great anxiety washed over me – though at the same time a strong self-confidence enveloped me. I have complete faith that, with help from Juozas, I'll be able to protect my little baby no matter what events shake the world.

With my pregnancy, Juozas became more attentive than ever. Winter arrived and, as if by design, an extremely cold one. The doctors told me that my baby would be born on Independence Day, February 16th. But she waited two more days.

That morning, I felt the first cramps of labor pains. Juozas held on to me as we walked to the hospital. Every few steps, I had to stop and take a deep breath. It was a cold, clear, beautiful morning.

Alexandra and Jurate at 7 months, 1943

We arrived at the hospital, and Juozas rushed off to work. I felt an overwhelming sense of loneliness. I was taken to a large room with several other women who were also waiting to give birth. There I was, with a table and a robe (there are no nightgowns anymore), as the pains were getting stronger. A single midwife takes care of the entire ward, walking from one woman to the next, offering words of encouragement, comforting each as best she can or, occasionally, delivering a scolding.

A snowstorm whipped up. Dusk filled the ward, which was gloomy enough as it was. The next thing I remember is hearing a baby's cry. The midwife was holding my squirming daughter in her arms, stretched out to show me. It was 3:30 in the afternoon. It looked like night.

The Anti-Nazi Underground

At the end of 1941, I became involved in a new resistance movement, this time against the Nazis. It didn't take many months for us to become convinced that the new regime was even more despicable than the Soviet regime had been. We revived the Lithuanian Activist Front. Its activities were conducted mostly by the same people who had earlier formed the anti-Soviet underground.

The Lithuanian Freedom Fighters Union was also part of the new underground. It had been established during the early part of the Soviet occupation in 1940. The two groups merged in April 1941 and together led the June 1941 uprising against the Soviets as the German Army was advancing toward Lithuania. We split the following August and thenceforth carried out our resistance activities independently. I knew a few members of the Freedom Fighters Union. They hewed to the ideology of the Nationalists League, which had been the majority party during the regime of President Smetona. We *Frontininkai* – members of the Front – were more oriented to Christian values. But the difference in our political outlooks didn't much influence our relationships. This time, however, our organizations did not combine, primarily because it was unsafe to form any kind of broad-based underground structure. Later on, in 1943, the VLIK [acronym for *Vyriausias Lietuvos išlaisvinimo komitetas* 'Supreme Committee for the Liberation of Lithuania'] organization, comprising various political parties, took over the job of coordinating the entire resistance movement.

My professors encouraged me to join the underground. In those days, professors tended to avoid personal interaction with their students. But since Alexandra was also an employee at the university, the usual distance didn't apply in her case; after our relationship became serious and especially after we married, my personal contacts with our professors increased. Of course the fact that I was a good student, as well as a Ramovė reserve officer, helped bridge the usual student-instructor formality. Notwithstanding their professorial status, when I was with them, I spoke and behaved freely as an equal.

I struck up an especially close friendship with Professor Pranas Padalskis, who was probably the first to urge me to join him in the anti-Nazi resistance. I also became very friendly with Professor Zenonas Ivinskis, a historian.

As we began deliberating over the nature of our response to the Nazi occupation, it was hard to imagine what we could really accomplish. But our patriotism was too strong to allow us merely to wait passively for the end of the war. Our hearts couldn't accept the situation into which Lithuania had fallen, so our minds refused to rest either. This restlessness is typical of young people and, in the autumn of 1941, I was twenty-three years old. My friends and I had grown up during the era of independence; we were passionate about maintaining the spirit of the Rebirth, the movement preceding reinstated independence in 1918 that had reawakened our sense of national self-identity and pride.

All those who joined the resistance knew that they were up against an overwhelming power. Germany appeared to be invincible. Actions against the Nazis were probably even more dangerous than they had been against the Soviets. We understood that we might very well have to sacrifice our lives. But we committed ourselves to the cause out of passion, not logic. The destruction of the Lithuanian Jews probably provided our strongest impetus. And our motives were not simply compassion or horror but also the instinct of self-preservation which seemed to whisper to us ceaselessly, "Today the Jews – tomorrow us." And, of course, we had already been hardened in the resistance to the Soviets.

Initially our activities were mainly ideological. We mimeographed newsletters and proclamations in an effort to disseminate the view that the German occupation was no better than the Soviet one. We had to plant the idea that Germany wasn't invincible. We were convinced that the nations enslaved by Germany could not simply wait for the Western Allies to win the war. We had to make moves on our own to undermine the rear flank of the Reich and weaken it internally.

Another question haunted us. What would happen if the Soviet Union won the war in the East? We believed that the British and the Americans would view the anti-Nazi resistance favorably; this would increase our chances of reclaiming statehood and preventing another Soviet invasion. We never thought the Allies would permit Stalin to occupy Lithuania once again.

During the winter of 1943, the tide turned against the Germans. They met with defeat at Stalingrad. From time to time, air alert sirens would go off, shattering our windows. Vilnius itself, however, was not bombed until the spring of 1944 when the front approached Lithuania.

In March 1943, a mere month after my daughter's birth, the universities of Vilnius and Kaunas were shut down. A number of the Lithuanian intelligentsia were arrested and imprisoned at the Stutthoff Concentration Camp in Germany. Among them were people I knew very well, including priests Stasys Yla and Alfonsas Lipniūnas, the chaplain of Vilnius University. Professor Padalskis, who lived under the threat of arrest as a former member of the provisional government, had to go into hiding. He stayed with us for a short time; afterward he left to live with the family of Jonas Vileišis, a prominent citizen who had been among the signatories of the 1918 Act of Independence. In time he managed to get to Austria. The Nazis were also searching for Professor Juozas Brazaitis, who was hiding out in Kaunas. I once tried to see him but I was only able to speak with his wife.

We went so far as to make contact with Soviet partisans operating in Byelorussia and the territory around Vilnius. We even worked jointly with them to some degree because, in the Nazis, we had a common enemy. The German military administration was ruling the rural Švenčionys district with an especially brutal hand. German units holding down the rear flank would shoot anyone who failed to execute a directive immediately. There were fairly large groups of Soviet partisans operating nearby and, in a few cases, we provided them with information about the German officials, so that they could plan a military action against them. They did exactly that.

When winter came, under the guise of bringing in their obligatory tribute of agricultural products by sled, the Soviet partisans shot all the German officials who arrived to take their pick. The German military did not succeed in punishing them, and the German officials who came in to replace the ones who had been shot were not as brutal as their predecessors. For once the Nazis hesitated, refraining from their usual reprisals against the people around Švenčionys.

Such actions were extremely dangerous, of course, particularly as the front moved closer to Lithuania. Another action by the Soviet partisans in the Varėna area ended in a frightening massacre, which one of our employees who worked in the peat moss fields told us about. He saw the village of Pirčiupiai burned down to the ground, and the entire population – several hundred people – murdered. He had been on his way into the village when he saw the Germans approaching and managed to hide. The Germans herded the villagers into a barn and set the barn afire. A child escaped somehow and ran outside; a German grabbed him and threw him back into the flames. The story made us sick.

Of course, there was no love lost between the Soviet partisans and the Lithuanians. Any long-lasting camaraderie was impossible because, although we were jointly against Nazis, the partisans fought for the Soviet Union, whereas we were for Lithuania. Our main reason for maintaining contact was to avoid circumstances that might result in clashes between them and other Lithuanians. We weren't always successful due to the confusion of the times. One example involved the military adjuncts, comprised of Lithuanian soldiers, for protecting railroad routes. They were being sent out of the country on duty by the Germans in command. Soviet partisans attacked them during their movements and, since they were indistinguishable from regular German units, more than one Lithuanian died at their hands.

Our most important goal was to make contact with the Americans and the British. In September 1943, the resistance underground prepared a review of the situation in Lithuania, beginning with the arrests of members of the intelligentsia who had participated in the anti-Nazi movement. We also gathered data on the deployment of German troops, not only in our own country but also in Byelorussia and a sizable part of Ukraine – information we received from the Lithuanian battalions spread out across the East. The leaders of the underground decided that this information was crucial and had to be transmitted to the Allies. They assigned me to travel to Berlin, where I was to pass the documents to a Lithuanian journalist living there, Julijonas Būtėnas; he, in turn, would transmit them to a friend of his, a Swedish journalist, who would be able to smuggle them out of Germany with relatively little risk.

Anyone who wanted to travel from Lithuania to Germany needed a permit from the occupation government. As head of the Vilnius Municipal Services Department, it was easy enough for me to dream up a pretext. It had become increasingly difficult to assure the fuel supply to the Vilnius Gas Plant. There was not enough fuel from peat coming in from Varėna. We had even begun using logs chopped from trees in the surrounding woods. Burgomaster Dabulevičius would provide me with an extra quota of whiskey to bribe the villagers who were providing timber for us, but the plant still operated under the threat of being shut down any day. Another headache was the constant necessity of supplying at least a minimum of diesel fuel to the city bus park.

I convinced the burgomaster that on a trip to Germany and Austria I could study the handling of raw materials and fuel shortages and learn what they were using to produce gas. Colonel Dabulevičius requested a travel permit for me from *Gebietscommissar* Hingst. The document I received contained an explanation in German of the purpose of the trip.

My colleagues in the Lithuanian Activist Front provided me with a map marking all the locales where, according to our inside information sources, German Army units were deployed as well as a review of the Lithuanian situation which was several pages long. I intermingled these documents with a lot of old newspapers; then I wrapped them all around a big slab of fatty bacon which I placed at the bottom of my suitcase.

The customs post for travelers to Germany was at Kybartai. A German guard opened my suitcase, pulled the bacon out from the bottom and unwrapped it. "*Speck* – bacon" was all he said before shoving it back in. The newspapers and the documents were all soaked in grease by then. I breathed more easily. If he had found the map, there is no question that the Germans would have interrogated and tortured me and then put me in front of a firing squad.

I arrived in Berlin in September 1943. Julijonas Būtėnas met me at the station and took me to a very fine hotel. Except for my early childhood in Russia, I had never been abroad before. Coming from Vilnius, which was actually rather provincial, I was stunned by the luxury and elegance of the hotel. Lovely drapes, thick and heavy, graced my windows. But at night it was necessary to draw them tight. Berlin was then being frequently bombed, and the slightest ray of light could not be allowed to escape. The danger of an air raid was announced on the first night of my stay. At the howl of the siren, all the hotel guests ran for the bomb shelter in the cellar, though fortunately there was no bombing.

I gave the documents to Julijonas the next day. Then we went to a restaurant on the Kurtfürstendamm for our midday meal. Food coupons were also required in Germany, but otherwise there was no comparison with Vilnius. There were far more dishes to choose from, and the food was of an incomparably finer quality. While I was thoroughly enjoying a luncheon of the sort I hadn't seen since the war started, I gave Julijonas a rundown of events in Lithuania, and he told me about life in Berlin.

After our meal, Julijonas took me to visit another local Lithuanian, Dr. Petras Karvelis, who lived in a beautiful, comfortable villa. He plied me with questions about Lithuania and mulled over the turn of events in the war. Although Germany was stalled in Stalingrad, it still appeared far from crippled. Karvelis guessed that the German Army was readying for a new attack but that nothing would happen on the eastern front before spring. We considered the possibility that the war might not end for a long time yet, even though the Allies had landed in southern Italy and their air raids were striking the cities of the Reich more forcefully with every passing day.

The official purpose of my trip was to learn how the utility companies in Germany were being managed under wartime conditions. I had no other time-consuming matters to attend to so I was able to walk around Berlin as freely as a tourist. Under Julijonas' guidance, I spent two very enjoyable days of sightseeing. We visited the Tiergarten Amusement Park. We saw the Brandenburg Gates and other majestic works of architecture that were not yet badly damaged. Julijonas informed me that he had passed my documents on to the Swedish journalist who had promised that they would reach England via the Swedish Embassy very soon.

After my two days in Berlin, I left for Austria. In Innsbruck I studied the workings of the municipal gas plant. The managers were quite hospitable, showing me around and explaining the steps they took when coal was in short supply, as it frequently was. In Vienna I met with Leonas Prapuolenis, who had managed to flee to Austria when he faced arrest in Lithuania and imprisonment in a concentration camp. Austria was relatively quiet. There were two other Lithuanians who had found haven here – my friends Pranas Padalskis and Petras Vilutis. By coming to Vienna, they had also evaded arrest.

These men welcomed me with all their hearts. They took me to the Vienna Opera. After that we went for coffee next door in the cafe at the renowned Sacher Hotel, famous in all of Europe for its excellent pastries. That evening we went to a nightclub. A corps de ballet of lithe young women kicked up their heels while delicately holding onto champagne glasses. I was surprised by the carefree lifestyle in Vienna; it was as though there was no war raging in the world outside.

After three days I returned to Lithuania. It was like coming home from a different planet. I met with Burgomaster Dabulevičius, who immediately informed me that my trip had raised suspicions. "Some police came to see me from the *Gebietscommissariat*, making a lot of inquiries about you – Who is that Kazickas? What's he doing in Innsbruck? Why is he visiting the gas plant?" Apparently, for all their friendliness, the managers at Innsbruck had not fully trusted the documents I presented and had immediately sent out an inquiry as to whether I truly represented the government in Vilnius. Dabulevičius explained who I was and the reasons for my trip – which, apart from this incident, the Germans took no further interest in.

We began laying the groundwork for an uprising. We organized fighting units, mostly Lithuanian army officers on reserve. As in the Soviet years, I was at the center of the political – but not the military – underground. We met approximately once a month and prepared briefs reviewing the political situation. Someone from the provinces would always come to discuss events there. I was also assigned the task of maintaining contact with armed resistance groups. Colonel Vitkus was in charge of the military underground in Vilnius. I regularly met with him to pass on decisions of the political center and to exchange information.

As I've already mentioned, Lithuanians by now made up a fairly low percentage of the population of Vilnius (due to the previous Polish occupation); as a consequence, our underground there was comparatively small. The main center of the anti-Nazi resistance was Kaunas. In Vilnius we took no direct military action against the occupation government. Some nights we heard sounds of gunfire, but most likely they came from clashes between Germans and Soviet partisans or the fighters of the Polish Armia Krajowa (with whom our relations were rather complicated owing to our rival claims on Vilnius).

The Lithuanian Activist Front concentrated on readiness for battle when the right moment presented itself – that is, when the German Army was already withdrawing. We also knew it would be vital to take up weapons should the Germans begin mass repressions. But, in the opinion of the political leadership, there was no point rushing headfirst into military action. First of all, as matters stood, it was impossible to do serious damage to the Germans; and second, any such attacks would cause a wave of harsh reprisals. It was more important to be ready for advancing events and to work at expanding the resistance base. The underground slowly accumulated weapons and stored them at reliable locations in the provinces. Once I managed to get several automatic rifles through Major Šimkus. I placed them in a box and handed them over to my wife's cousin, who disguised the box and drove it out to his village near the town of Rokiškis.

By the end of 1943, it was clear that Germany would lose the war. We knew that Germany was being bombed extensively and that the Allies, having been successful in Africa, had moved into southern Italy. News from the eastern front gave us cause for much deeper concern. After the Battle of Stalingrad, the Russians were on the attack. The Germans were retreating from Russia and Ukraine. For obvious reasons, we hated and feared the Russian army and placed our hopes on the likelihood that the British and American forces would be decisive in ending the war.

Just before Christmas 1943, I made another trip that was ostensibly on municipal business but was actually for the underground. I was traveling to Warsaw to make contact with the Polish resistance. This time the information I carried about the current situation in Lithuania didn't have to be wrapped around bacon, because travelers crossing the Polish border were not as strictly searched as those entering Reich territory. The first leg of the trip was from Vilnius to Varėna. Partisans were attacking trains quite often during this period, so our locomotive pushed an empty wagon in front to cushion the other cars in case of an explosion.

Warsaw looked terrible. The city was in ruins. Even those homes that were not completely destroyed had obviously not seen any repairs since the autumn of 1939. Practically no cars were on the streets; if one passed, there was inevitably a German behind the wheel. Horse-drawn sleighs appeared to be the major mode of public transportation.

The hotel room I found had no heat, which meant that there was no hot water either. An icy yellowish liquid was all that trickled out of the tap. I could barely force myself to splash a few drops on my face after dragging myself out of bed, numb from the cold as I unwrapped the layers of blankets I had pulled around myself. The occupation and the war were much more harshly felt in Warsaw than in Vilnius. Sullen German soldiers patrolled every corner of the city. Tension and fear were etched on every passerby's face. And yet I knew that despite the brutal rule of the Germans, the Polish resistance carried out frequent actions in Warsaw. Entire city blocks would be surrounded and hostages captured. I spent only a couple of days in the city and once I heard gunfire no more than a few blocks away. People on the street began diving into courtyards. Nothing like that ever happened in Vilnius.

The Polish resistance had received word of my arrival. I knew the pseudonym of the person I was supposed to meet. He dropped by my hotel room and informed me that Armia Krajowa representatives would meet with me the following evening at a certain apartment. I would probably have to spend the night at the meeting place, since curfew began at a very early hour.

I arrived at the address he had given me. The owner of the apartment, a woman of advanced years, met me at the door with her two adult daughters. The place was spacious, but only one room was heated somehow. That was where the four of us sat down. The women were most hospitable, offering me food and drink. My Polish was hopeless – I could barely form even the most rudimentary sentences when it came my turn to speak. I mixed in Russian, a language I knew a bit better. The women told me how horrible the Germans were and how Lithuanians and Poles had to resist them hand in hand. Apparently the Nazis had shot the old woman's husband.

After some time, two members of Armia Krajowa arrived. They introduced themselves as university professors but volunteered no more information than that. They did not tell me their names and only briefly and vaguely explained their relationship with the organization. Obviously they were wary of me. I might be a spy on a German mission. They had no way to be certain. Nor could I be certain about them – they could be provocateurs of some sort. We spoke German and, for the first time, I was sincerely sorry I hadn't studied Mrs. Hofmanienė's lessons more earnestly. But my Polish counterparts were no more adept at the language. When our German skills failed us, we communicated by gesture. Somehow we managed to understand one another. They were particularly interested in relations between Lithuanians and Poles in Vilnius.

I told them that, based on my own experience, relations were friendly enough under the circumstances. At the Municipal Services Department, nearly every driver was Polish, and they never got into arguments related to nationality with their Lithuanian co-workers. We had trusted Polish nationals in responsible positions, and it was a Pole in my department who had organized this meeting.

The supervisor of the garage for municipal vehicles had once been a colonel in the Polish army; he was orderly and aristocratic and always carried himself like a soldier, straight and tall. I never felt the least bit of animosity from him or any resentment that Lithuanians were now in charge. Actually he had some problems running our garage even though he had once headed the Fiat factory in Poland; ultimately he resigned. It was handled matter-of-factly, and he expressed no anger about leaving.

The review papers on the Lithuanian situation that I had brought were written in Polish. Naturally they contained no names or addresses since specifics were dangerous. We were primarily concerned about avoiding clashes with the Armia Krajowa units that were active in the territory around Vilnius. There had already been several shootouts between Lithuanians and Poles. We were making an offer to coordinate our underground actions with theirs. The Poles acknowledged that this was a very necessary initiative and promised to consider ways of maintaining contact with us. During the entire discussion, they never brought up the issue of Poland's claim on Vilnius.

The hour of curfew was almost upon us. The men urged me to spend the night at the apartment and left.

Upon my return to Vilnius, I reported on this discussion. The necessity of seeking contacts with Armia Krajowa units was becoming clear because the situations in both the West and the East were changing rapidly. The Germans were retreating on all fronts. We sensed that the fate of our country would be decided quite soon.

Doomed Hope: The Soviets Return

Throughout the war years, I tuned in to BBC, a practice that, naturally, the Germans strictly prohibited. Nevertheless, when I was home in the evenings, I would press my ear to a radio set at the quietest possible volume, concentrating very hard on hearing and understanding the news broadcasts from London. I can instantly recall the BBC catchphrase, which I heard hundreds of times. I still didn't know English well enough but I could glean the main ideas of the broadcasts. Other members of the resistance, far more fluent that I, would prepare reviews of war news and publish them in the underground press.

When we heard that the armies of the United States and Great Britain had landed in southern Italy in September 1943, we started waiting anxiously, convinced that the Western Allies would attack other European areas closer to thc Baltic. There were reports that England was concentrating troops and ships. We were also aware of the deluge of bombs being dropped on German cities – they were virtually being leveled. We would repeat the BBC announcements: "Hamburg is burning. Hamburg is burning!" Even the Germans were talking about how fiercely their country was being bombed. A new propaganda campaign bitterly accused the English and the Americans of destroying the cultural monuments of Europe.

These movements by the Western Allies strengthened our hope that their armies would liberate Lithuania. Naively we told ourselves that, from a military standpoint, it would be expedient for them to attack Germany in Norway, close to the Baltic Sea basin. We had heard nothing of any pact between the Western Allies and the Soviet Union and did not have the vaguest inkling that Stalin was in league with the West. We never expected that the Western Allies would refrain from military action in our region. Only later, as the war was ending, did it become obvious that the three major powers had agreed in advance which territories each would control.

Christmas arrived and then the New Year, 1944. The British and the Americans were still squeezing the Germans in Italy but slowly. They assembled their armies in the British Isles but still they did not begin any attacks in the direction of the Baltic Sea. As spring approached, we were growing very afraid we would never see the Allies arrive. We had heard that the Russians were attacking the Germans near Leningrad and pushing them out of Ukraine toward the Balkans and Byelorussia.

By June 1944, no illusions remained. The Western Allies landed in France; the Russians were returning to Lithuania. They were literally chasing the Germans out of Byelorussia and moving closer and closer to Vilnius each day. Multitudes of Soviet partisans who had forced their way out of Byelorussia were now active in the woods around Vilnius and through all of eastern Lithuania.

But hope dies last. Just as in 1940, in 1944 we still wanted to believe that the Russians, pressured by the West, would be forced somehow to permit at least a puppet state in Lithuania and that, in the long run, they might have to withdraw completely. But a gloomy mood hung in the air all the same. We had no idea what to expect from a returning Soviet regime and we very much feared that a new occupation could last a long, long time.

I was assigned responsibility for the evacuation of the employees of Municipal Services. In June, with the Russians very close, an order was issued that any citizen with relatives or friends in outlying villages was to leave Vilnius. I decided to send my family out of the city. Alexandra and Jurate, who was just over a year old, went to stay with my Uncle Feliksas in the village of Žalioji, in the Vilkaviškis district, very close to eastern Germany. I intended to join them as soon as the department was evacuated. At that point, I already suspected that we would probably have to keep going out of Vilkaviškis and on to Germany. The thought was extremely painful. The first time I saw Lithuania, for so long the object of my parents' and grandparents' dreams, I was four years old. Now I was twenty-six and I was once again leaving the homeland of my ancestors. And I didn't have the vaguest idea how long I would have to stay away.

Christmas 1943

All my days and nights in Vilnius, I spend with our tiny Jurate.

There's been a shortage here of food for infants. I manage to get milk one way or another but then I get it home and start pouring it and – look, it's already curdled. It's been hard enough to get clothes for her, harder still to find what I need to keep her clean and tidy.

Winter went by, then spring and then the hot summer of 1943. I was so wrapped up in my day-to-day concerns that I didn't even notice the falling leaves. Then it was snowing. And now Christmas has come again.

This morning I cleaned our apartment as best I could and set our holiday table, although it certainly wasn't groaning under the spread the way it used to be. We were playing with our little girl when she gave us a real Christmas surprise. We weren't holding on to her, and suddenly she took a step all by herself, then another. She walked several meters in al, from where I was standing over to Juozas and fell into his outstretched arms.

Juozas gave me this new diary as a present.

And this event is indeed worth an entry. December 25th: Jurate, at ten months and one week, took her first steps.

February 18, 1944

We celebrated Jurate's first birthday quietly. She's now running all over the apartment, with a spring in every step.

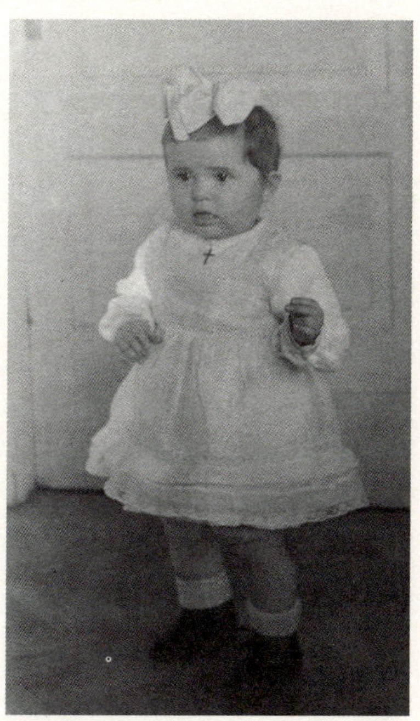

Jurate on her first birthday, 1944

Spring 1944

The war is approaching Lithuania like a roll of thunder. The Germans are still boasting they'll celebrate the final victory, but we know that things are getting worse for them. A big map hangs in a display window on Gedimino Prospect with tiny flags marking the front. The Germans have cleverly marked it to look as though they were merely straightening out the front line – not that they were being pushed back. A little later the line would slink back by a bit, so that even their understated map, if you observed it over a longer period, reflected the fact that they were retreating westward. The Germans, meanwhile, vent their rage at the Americans who are taking a greater and greater role in the war against them. Caricatures of U.S. government officials as Jews with big noses, droopy stomachs and cigars clamped between their teeth hang in the window.

These efforts by the Germans to show they're still in control are looking more and more pitiful. The news from London is that they're being forced back on all fronts now. Their approaching defeat, however, is more obvious from the columns of soldiers moving through Vilnius. A couple of years ago, the Germans rolled east with their chests puffed out in their shiny uniforms, eating chocolates and offering candy to children and pretty young ladies. Now we're seeing them as they return from the front: shabby, with their arms and legs wrapped in thick bandages, probably frozen. Many have no arms or legs at all.

We hate the Germans but we can't muster up any joy over the Russian victories either. All I feel is the sense of an absolute unknown. What will happen to us? If the Germans win this war, a sad fate awaits us. But if the Russians return, it will be impossible for us to stay in Lithuania. We are keenly aware that anyone who has worked in a government job under the German occupation will be arrested and exiled or possibly shot. We already know that no mercy will be shown to families as well.

Spring has arrived. With every passing day I feel more anxious. With each day we see more caravans of ambulances carrying the wounded from the east. Every evening the broadcasts from London report new German defeats. We've been seeing more Russian planes in the sky over Vilnius. The railway station and other buildings in the city have been bombed. We know that the Russian army is advancing through Byelorussian territory in the direction of Lithuania.

June 1944

One day early this month, Juozas told me, "Alytė, you and Jurate are going to have to leave Vilnius. It's become too dangerous for you to stay here any longer." He asked me to start getting ready for a trip to the village of Žalioji, in Suvalkija, to stay with his Uncle Feliksas.

I told him, "I'm not going anywhere without you." But he kept after me the next day and the next, telling me again and again that we can no longer delay. He promised to follow us as soon as the burgomaster releases him from his job. "Please believe me. In a few days I'll join you in the village. It will be a lot easier for me to get out of Vilnius, even if it's at the very last minute, if I'm alone." He wouldn't let up.

I packed the things we needed most. There isn't much really – just some bedding and a few clothes. Juozas arranged for a small truck to take us. Some other city employees and their families traveled with us.

I held my most precious treasure, Jurate, in my arms.

As I walked out of our apartment in Žvėrynas, I cast a last look over the rooms which seemed so sad and empty now. I had a feeling that I would never again return. As I closed the door, I felt my heart clench. This was our first home together, the beginning of our married life. Three hard years of war have

In Vilnius, 1944

passed but they've also been my years of joy – the joy of being with Juozas and, in time, with my daughter.

By that evening we were in Suvalkija. We spent the night in a farmer's barn, sleeping on hay. The next day we arrived at Žalioji. Uncle Feliksas and his family greeted us warmly. Victoria and her children are also here and happy to see us. She wasted no time in telling me how worried she is about her husband who's serving in one of the combat units that General Povilas Plechavičius has consolidated to try to reestablish our independence. Naturally her concerns went straight to my heart and, right away, I began worrying about Juozas. What's happening in Vilnius? How will he get out? When on earth will I see him again?

Evacuation

As the Russians approached Vilnius, I was seriously considering leaving for the West on my own, now that my wife and child were safe with my uncle in the village. It was much too dangerous for me to remain in Lithuania. Since I had held a managerial position in the municipal government under the Germans, I would inevitably be arrested. For some reason, I thought the Russians would leave my family alone. I expected the war to end soon and then I could return and rejoin them. As soon as peace settled over Europe, the West would exert pressure and Lithuania would regain its independence, at least formally; repressions would end.

The Sts. Peter and Paul Day of Indulgence in June had been an important Lithuanian religious holiday before the war. On that day I sent Alexandra and Jurate to Žalioji while I remained in our nearly empty apartment. All the city employees were ready to evacuate at any moment. Russian reconnaissance planes were flying over the city much more frequently. Finally one night when I was at the municipal building with Burgomaster Dabulevičius, the sound of cannons came rolling in from afar. We immediately understood that the front was no more than a few dozen kilometers away.

We decided to evacuate the remaining city employees without further delay. At sunrise an announcement from the burgomaster went out to the residents of Vilnius informing them that, due to possible military action, they would be safer out of the city for the time being.

Then panic ensued. Crowds of people took to the streets in confusion. The Lithuanian city employees gathered at Cathedral Square to talk about what to do; after all, they could hardly travel on foot to their relatives in rural Lithuania. The Polish employees were also anxious but they had nowhere else to go – their families were mostly in Vilnius. There was little we could do to help. We had no means of organizing a mass evacuation. The Germans had already mobilized most of the city's transport vehicles – not only the buses, trucks and cars but also the motorcycles and even the horses and wagons and carts.

Columns of soldiers were still marching through Vilnius. People would try to plead their way onto a passenger train; a few probably managed to do just that. Others, getting hold of a horse from God knows where, took off in wagons. Others grabbed bicycles and still others left on foot. The roads out of the city were mobbed.

July 6th was a warm and sunny day. The German Army swarmed through Vilnius. These soldiers were entirely different from the ones who had marched through on the way east in June 1941. They were exhausted and miserable. Dust covered their faces and they wore torn, dirty uniforms. Trucks drove by filled to capacity with soldiers. Horse-drawn wagons rolled alongside, piled high with furniture from military command offices. I took a car with Lenkaitis, the Director of the Vilnius Department Store, who had managed to hold onto one somehow. I drove. First we stopped at the hospital to see Lenkaitis' wife who was a patient there. We picked up Juzė Augaitytė, a well-known singer who was very ill, and another woman. By evening the four of us were on our way to Kaunas, driving down a road jammed with military vehicles and civilians fleeing the city. I took the women to their homes and then, as agreed, gave the car back to Lenkaitis.

In Kaunas I joined my brother-in-law, Joseph Gruodis, who had been serving in the officer corps of General Plechavičius; he too had made his way out of Vilnius. Joseph informed me that the Germans had managed to slow down the Russian attack, and Vilnius was still in their hands. I spent the night with him at his brother's house in Kaunas.

A day later I managed to get a seat on a train heading for Karaliaučius (the Lithuanian name for Königsberg, now Kaliningrad). I got off at the Vilkaviškis stop. From there it was easy to get to Žalioji.

First week of July 1944

Day after day I waited for Juozas to arrive from Vilnius. My eyes constantly scanned the road from the fields to the farmhouse. At last one day I spotted him coming down the road, carrying a small suitcase. He was covered in dust and looked exhausted. I ran toward him and fell into his arms; for an instant I forgot there was a war going on.

Now that Juozas is here with us at his uncle's farm, it's easier to forget the way things really are. There are no German soldiers in the village; there's no inkling of the war that is raging all over the rest of the world. We have plenty of food. The children play happily in the orchard. Our sprightly little Jurate is running around and keeping up with the others. It's as though we were simply spending a summer out on the farm.

Several days later

However, our idyllic village life is no more than a fleeting fantasy. Broadcasts from London keep delivering upsetting news. Planes fly over Lithuania at night, dropping out saboteurs. Rumors fill the village; somebody has noticed a suspicious type hiding out in the rye fields.

Now we hear that the Russians have overtaken Vilnius and are already advancing in the direction of Kaunas. All we can talk about is: What should we do next? Should we flee to East Prussia, or should we stay here in Žalioji and wait to see what happens? The Germans claim they're regrouping in Lithuania for a fierce counterattack that will knock the Russians back east. We know this is just propaganda. On the other hand, everyone in Žalioji has been saying that the Germans are going to give their all here in Lithuania to stop the Soviet Army at the Nemunas River. The river is their final line of defense – any farther back and they'll be in their own territory of East Prussia. Which is true. We have news that the front has stopped moving. The Russians seem not to have gotten any closer to Kaunas. We've also heard that secret meetings have been held between the Germans and representatives of the Western Allies. We keep clinging to the hope that Hitler will capitulate, a truce will be reached and the Russians will fail to overtake Lithuania before the war ends.

Juozas says that such hopes are just so much rubbish. He believes the Russians will move into Suvalkija as well. He thinks the women should stay in Žalioji with the children while the men head into East Prussia for a while. He says we won't be separated for long because the West will never allow the Russians to rule Lithuania. In his opinion, the war will end and the men will be able to come home from Germany, as soon as the situation stabilizes and a democratic order is reestablished in Europe.

I wouldn't hear a word about such a plan. "I'm not letting you go anywhere alone," I told Juozas flatly. "If we have to run, then all three of us run together. If we stay, then the three of us stay here together." I turned a deaf ear when he tried to argue that refugees might have to suffer unbearable conditions that our little daughter is too young to withstand.

A week later

The days go by tensely. It's been a week since our argument. The news has only gotten worse. The Russians are attacking again while the Germans retreat. The other night we heard an echo of exploding artillery. The sound was weak but it was unmistakable. That means the front is very close to us. We stood outside and saw flashes of light in the night sky.

Juozas said, "Well, Alytė*, there's nothing else we can do. We have to get ready for a journey. We'll all leave together for East Prussia." His voice was very sad.*

When the sun rose, we could no longer hear the cannons. Juozas is taking his time, walking around wordlessly, deep in thought.

July 16, 1944

We're getting ready for our trip. Uncle Feliksas and Aunt Elenora have decided to go to East Prussia with us. They're about fifty, rather old for such a journey. We can all feel the pain in their hearts. They live very comfortably here. Uncle Feliksas runs an exemplary thirty-two hectare farm. He and Elenora have built themselves a beautiful new house. Now they have to abandon the things they toiled so hard for. We keep telling ourselves that the war will end soon and we'll be able to return to Lithuania in no time at all.

Aunt Elenora put her silverware and her porcelain dishes into a box – few farmers have such things – to bury out in the orchard. Two Russian prisoners work on the farm, and she was afraid they might see where she was hiding it. Not so long ago, these prisoners were thrilled to have wound up on a good farm where they could eat their fill. Now that the Russian army is getting closer to Suvalkija, they've started acting much bolder. They're keeping their eyes open, watching everything that goes on at the farm. But we managed to find a time when they were off in the fields and buried the box in the ground.

Uncle Feliksas slaughtered a pig and a calf. The men salted down the meat and put it up in metal containers with tightly sealed covers. The women pressed cheeses, churned butter and made noodles. We packed quite a lot of food. Juozas and I decided to take only our clothing with us. Our belongings fit neatly into two suitcases.

Uncle Feliksas picked his largest wagons and his finest horses. He brought his best milk cow in from the fields. The cow will be very important for feeding the young children on the trip. Jurate is just a year and a half old. Victoria's son, Gediminas, and Feliksiukas, Uncle Feliksas' and Aunt Elenora's adopted son, are barely two. We have no idea how many days we'll be riding in a rattling wagon over the roads into East Prussia. Without milk it will be very hard on the children.

July 18, 1944

The day of our departure has arrived. Uncle Feliksas and Aunt Elenora took a last walk around their property, wiping the tears from their eyes. We have three wagons for our caravan of refugees – twenty-one of us in all. Professor Antanas Vasiliauskas and his wife and their four children are leaving with us in their own wagon. Then there's the three of us, Uncle Feliksas, Aunt Elenora and little Feliksiukas, Victoria with her three sons and her sister-in-law with her four daughters. The sister-in-law's husband, a colonel in the Lithuanian army, has been imprisoned by the Germans at Stutthoff Concentration Camp. Meanwhile we still have no idea what has happened to Joseph Gruodis back in Kaunas.

[He joined us quite a while afterward when we were living in Germany.]

The wagons clattered slowly toward the closest border crossing at Kudirkos Naumiestis. We had to move slowly because of the cow, which plodded along behind our wagon train; she just couldn't go any faster. We also had to stop from time to time, so the cow could graze on the grass growing alongside the road. Naturally Uncle Feliksas also packed a lot of hay in the wagon for the cow and the horses.

July 19, 1944

It's a good thing we had the hay. Our first night on the road, we had to sleep out in the fields and used the hay as our bedding.

The closer we got to Kudirkos Naumiestis, the more wagons we saw along the road. The long line of wagons rolled slowly as we approached the German border. Finally our turn at the control post came. We showed our documents, the ones Juozas had arranged with the Gebietscommissariat *while he was still in Vilnius.*

The Germans didn't bother us with too many questions but they ordered us to leave the cow behind. "We cannot permit the cow to cross into Germany," they barked at us, ignoring all our arguments. They filled out a very proper-looking document stating that the cow was confiscated at the border. When the war ends and we return to Lithuania, they assured us, we'll be compensated for it.

PART III

Homeland Lost: Refugees in War-torn Europe

As I gazed fondly over the slowly distancing fields of Lithuania, little did I know that this was the last vision I would have of my homeland for the next thirty-five years.

Evening was approaching. We drove about 10 kilometers from the border and stopped for the night at the home of a kind-hearted farmer where several families who had fled Lithuania were already staying. The man offered us food and brewed tea but he had no place for us to sleep, so we slept outside. Some of us bedded down in the wagons while others lay down on hay underneath.

I remember that the night was warm and clear; stars twinkled at us from the sky. Peace and silence enveloped us. The raging war seemed so far away as if it did not exist at all. Such an illusion was short-lived. Somewhere in the east, flashes of light sent a quivering glow to the darkness. As we listened intently, a faint sound of cannon fire drifted into our ears. The war front was crossing Lithuania.

Alexandra and I lay on the ground with our arms wrapped around each other. We could not sleep. We just stared at the stars high in the sky, wondering what would become of us.

The next morning we got back in our wagons though we were not sure exactly where we were going. Only our direction was clear – we were westward bound heading for East Prussia, the land often considered Lithuania Minor because so many of our fellow nationals lived in the territory. But alas, we ourselves did not know a single soul in Prussia. Only Gruzinskienė, the wife of Victoria's brother-in-law, had some acquaintances who had been living in the town of Wehlau, about 50 kilometers from Insterburg, for quite some time. These folks had given her the address of a Doctor Danilevičius in the town of Breslau. So our plan was to leave the horses and get onto some train going to Breslau (now known as Wroclaw, Poland) in the Silesia area at the opposite end of the Germany of those times. We had no clue if we could expect any sort of support there but we did not have any better ideas of where to go.

Our wagons rolled on a wide, smooth asphalt road. We were in awe of the large, well-kept German farms that we passed. There was electricity everywhere, a convenience that very few Lithuanian villagers enjoyed.

The other Lithuanian refugees who had crossed the border with us went off in other directions and most reached Pilkalnis. When we arrived at Gumbinnen, we learned that they had been put on a train to a refugee camp. In the meantime, we found ourselves traveling alone on a nearly empty road.

We had several bicycles with us. The older children would take turns riding on the bikes ahead of the wagons. By the time we would catch up with them, they would have had ample time to pick some peas for us from alongside the roadway.

Our little caravan caught the attention of the Germans. We looked like the settlers on the Western prairies that you see in American movies, rolling along in our wagons (one was even covered) with more than a dozen chattering children. The police stopped us several times but after they checked our documents, they let us travel on. We were making very good time. Occasionally we'd stop by some farmstead, eat, rest and feed our horses. The Germans were friendly. They gave us something to eat and drink, boiled water for us so we could make tea and offered the children milk and porridge.

The second day of our trip, we passed Schlossberg (Pillkallen before 1938) and Gumbinnen. About 7 kilometers from Insterburg, we stopped to spend the night on the grounds of a manor estate. Again we slept under an open sky.

In no time at all, on July 20th, we reached Insterburg. When we got into town, people surrounded the wagon of Professor Antanas Vasiliauskas.

No one in this town had seen any refugees from Lithuania yet. People asked him why we were running away from our own country. Had the front reached East Prussia by now? The professor, who spoke German, barely had time to tell them anything before a policeman showed up and took him away to the police station. There they checked his documents, asked a few questions and, fortunately, released him quite quickly. We were able to continue on our journey.

Evening came. We were talking among ourselves quietly about where we should spend the night. Suddenly a car passed our wagon train and turned sideways in front of us, blocking the road. An SS Legion Major jumped out and demanded to see our documents. I gave him our passports and travel permit for Germany. My language skills were too weak to tell him much, but Vasiliauskas took over and provided a clear explanation – we are Lithuanians; we have fled to Germany from the Russian Army that has invaded our country.

However, the SS Major told us that we could not go any farther. It seems that the road on which we were traveling was designated exclusively for military vehicles. He ordered us to turn back at once and return to the nearest town. There we would have to register and only then could we continue our journey by a different road. He wrote down our names, politely bid us goodbye and drove away. We did not dare disobey; we turned our wagon train around and proceeded back.

After we'd gone a couple of kilometers, Professor Vasiliauskas' wagon broke down. As we wondered what to do next, along came a gendarme. Once again, our documents were checked. "You are forbidden to drive any further!" the officer shouted. "You must immediately follow me to Insterburg and spend the night there."

We were reluctant to obey his orders. We knew we wouldn't get into town until late at night, and by that time there would be no food or an available place to sleep. We pleaded with him to let us spend the night at some farmstead so the children could get milk for their supper, and we could feed and water the horses. But the gendarme just kept yelling at us and refused to discuss the matter. With all the German that I could muster, I asked him, "Why are you treating us this way?" After all, our documentation was in order, and the SS officer who had checked us a short time ago had not ordered us back to Insterburg.

He shouted at us even more angrily. "I will arrest all of you right now if you argue with me any longer!" He motioned to us with his arm to ride behind him. There was nothing else that we could do but follow.

Apparently the gendarme realized it was too late after all to drive all the way to Insterburg. Not far down the road, he turned off to a small manor estate. He ordered us to remain there for the night and said he would return in the morning, when we would have to go to Insterburg with him. As soon as he disappeared from sight, we breathed a bit easier. The family there acted entirely differently with us. The housewife made us some coffee and offered us a supper of potatoes and milk.

Talking to our hosts, we discovered that a most important and ominous event had taken place that same day in Germany – an attempt had been made on Hitler's life! Therefore all roads were blocked and all documents checked, and all persons arousing any suspicions were arrested.

The farmer and his wife were worried. They began asking us the same questions we had heard before: "What has happened? Why are you running away from Lithuania? Are the Russians really that close to the Prussian border?"

We told them that the Russians were forcing their way into Suvalkija. The war front had already shifted and was indeed very close to the border. This news made the Germans very nervous. "Are the Russians so terrible that you have to run away from your homes, leaving everything behind?" they asked. "What kind of trouble would you have faced if you had stayed at home?"

We told them, "You could be shot for the least little mistake. At best, they could pack you into a cattle wagon and ship you out by rail to Siberia. Russians will rob and rape everywhere they pass."

The Germans became completely morose listening to our stories. The wife was especially fearful about what might happen to her 18 year-old daughter should the Russian army break through the East Prussian border. We advised them that it would be better for them not to stay; their entire family, not only their daughter, should head out somewhere into the depths of Germany. Sadness overwhelmed the Germans. They told us they would probably soon experience the same fate as ours; they too would become refugees.

The gendarme who had detained us showed up the next morning exactly as he had promised with an older German. He explained that this man would be escorting us. We would travel even farther than Insterburg to Gumbinnen Town. There we had to present ourselves to the local police. Apparently the gendarme had received such a written directive from the SS major who had stopped us on the road.

The professor and I decided we needed to get to Gumbinnen ahead of our families. We hoped to reach some agreement with the German governmental officials to permit us to travel further into Germany.

The overbearing gendarme left us with our elderly escort. We had a much easier time talking to this man. First we treated him to our home brew whiskey from Suvalkija and our smoked Lithuanian bacon. This German just smacked his lips and praised our food and drink. The next thing we knew, he became weepy. He said our fate was terribly hard, because we had to leave our homes and travel like a group of gypsies across Germany. He sighed deeply, saying that the same fate probably awaited his family. Naturally, after such a breakfast of whiskey and heartfelt feelings, it was much easier to get his permission for the professor and me to leave ahead of our families.

Alas, our plan to get a permit for longer travel fell apart right away. As soon as we got to Gumbinnen, we realized that the situation was a good deal more serious than we had expected. The German police were astounded when we showed up. They couldn't believe that we had managed to travel this far. They had no interest in discussing any permit to let us proceed farther. We were told that apparently all other Lithuanians who had crossed the border had been gathered up and put on a train for a refugee camp. According to these policemen, we were the only ones who had somehow fallen through the cracks of this planned German order. What should be done with us? Here we were, wandering over German roads in a disorderly fashion whereas, throughout the Reich, the strictest orders had been implemented after the attempt on Hitler's life. We were told to find our families, escort them to a manor near Gumbinnen and present ourselves post haste at the local commandant's office.

We met up with our folks, still rolling down the road in their wagons towards Gumbinnen. When we found the designated manor, we were allowed to stay in a hay-filled barn. We quickly unloaded some of our things and went to see the military commander. However, our talk with him was very discouraging.

"You men will be sent near the front to dig trenches. The women and children will be taken to the war refugee camp at Szczecin," announced the commander in an intimidating voice. "Don't you dare argue with me."

We showed him our documents and the permits, all in order with the appropriate stamps that allowed us to travel in Germany. "We have relatives in Breslau; they will care for us," we explained. But the German did not seem to hear a word we were saying. However he did not order us to leave immediately. We were simply told to return to the office again the next day.

Feverishly my mind searched for a plan – what should I do next? I sensed that this commander held our fate in his hands. If we can't persuade him to back down from his decision, our families would be separated. The mere thought of how our women and children would live alone, not knowing a word of German, was very distressing. And what would happen to us men? God only knows where we might be sent in the war zone. We could be forcibly mobilized into German military service; we could be killed. We had to get out of this situation. There just had to be a way!

One idea came to mind. I was aware that the German officials were weary from the hardships of the war; possibly a bribe could break through their usual resistance. I wondered what would be the best thing to offer that commander and how I should go about doing it. Then I thought of my earlier tactic – the lure of homebrew and bacon – which had met with such success.

As days passed and we were not ordered to the front, we tried to engage the commander in conversation about our fate as war refugees and all the hardships we endured. On the third day, he agreed to come and have supper with us at the manor where we were staying so he could see for himself just how many of us, including children, were traveling. That proved to be our victory.

The women fried up some bacon bits and made an omelet. We men pulled out a couple of bottles of our best whiskey. After a few drinks, the commander softened. He began telling us that he understood how hard it was for us. After downing a few more shots and enjoying the hearty meal, he said that he would allow us to travel to Breslau to our relatives. "Naturally, you will not be allowed to travel with harnessed horses. I am going to issue a permit for you to go by train to Königsberg [Kaliningrad today]. From there you can get to Breslau easily," he promised us. And what a great promise that was! We thanked the commander and sent him home with a basket filled with sausages, bacon and whiskey.

We were all bursting with happiness. We would be able to travel onward and even go by train. That meant we would get to our destination faster and be much more comfortable in the process. Only Uncle Feliksas felt sad about losing his horses and wagons. Even the manor owner was pleased; he jumped at the chance to safeguard our property until we would return. The commander wrote us an official promissory note that once the war ended, compensation for the horses would be honored.

"We do not know the ways of our Lord. Who knows? Maybe someday they will pay us," sighed Uncle Feliksas. He carefully attached this note to the same sort of document promising compensation for his cow that had been left behind at the East Prussian border.

Alexandra packed all of our family belongings into two suitcases, one for our clothing and the other for the food from our uncle's farm. The next day, on July 26th, we boarded the train for Königsberg.

When we arrived there, we never left the station to go into town. We were afraid that some gendarme might accost us. We wanted no more interruptions in our journey. I was able to get tickets for a train that was leaving for Breslau that same evening, so we did not have to wait at the station very long. There were so many of us that we took up an entire second-class wagon. Of course it was not all that comfortable. Only the children could lie down to sleep. We adults sat pressed to one another all night long. We'd snooze a minute here and a minute there, nodding off until our heads bumped into a neighbor. Actually I was not particularly sleepy. Thoughts about what we would have to do once we reached Breslau filled my head. Where would we stay after we got there?

Thursday, July 27, 1944

We got out at the Breslau Station at 8:00 a.m. As soon as we left the train, we spotted an NSF Point [run by the Nationalsozialistische Frauenschaft *'National Socialist Women's Organization for the care of war refugees in Germany].*

Women working at the Point began helping us. They explained to us how we could reach the place where Dr. Danilevičius, the acquaintance of Gruzinskienė, lived. They directed us back to the station, where we were able to wash up a bit after our exhausting 24-hour trip from Gumbinnen to Breslau.

Traveling by bus towards the home of Dr. Danilevičius, we were surprised to see that Breslau had not been badly bombed. The streets and square are well kept and repaired. All the home facades appeared in good order. This city must not have been strategically important to the English and American Air Forces. And the Russians probably lacked the power to launch an air attack over Silesia since it was quite far from their front.

Dr. Danilevičius took our entire group under his care. He has been so good-natured, offering us all his help. There isn't enough space for all of us, not even to stretch out on the floor, but at least we have a roof over our heads. We realize that we can stay here no more than a day or two. Being so tightly squeezed together, it would be hard to stay any longer. Besides we certainly do not want to try the patience of our host any more than necessary.

Another problem has come up for us – we have to get a permit to live in Breslau.

We learned that next Sunday, all the Lithuanians living in Breslau would be gathering for 11:00 mass at the local church.

Sunday, July 30, 1944

Apparently there is quite a large group of our country folk here in the same situation as us. When we went to mass, we met some old friends and made some new acquaintances. We all felt as though we were close relatives – all of us are left without a country. Without our own home and hearth, we are like orphans; we have only one another to lean on. Lithuanians are generously sharing any support they can muster. Some have managed to establish themselves decently since they've been in Breslau long enough by now. Physicians are especially privileged. They immediately got jobs at local hospitals along with apartments and food coupons.

Lithuanians that are well situated offer to help others, especially the recently arrived war refugees. They have taken in people to stay in their homes and have helped them find work.

Unfortunately our group was too large to get a place to stay for any length of time. We decided that we would have to turn for help to the NSF. This organization has dormitory type rooms, established especially for war refugees.

The NSF took us in. We women and children have been housed in a building in Gartenstrasse. The men went to a nearby building where a common cafeteria is located. We are all amazed that the Germans can uphold this degree of order in their lives. After all, the Western Allies and the Russians are squeezing Germany between two war fronts. Bombing of the entire country has been non-stop, day and night. The feeling that Germany is going to lose the war soon hangs in the air everywhere. Nevertheless, the facilities provided for the refugees are neat and clean. We seem to have all the basics for our household needs.

What a blessing it is to be able to bathe our children and ourselves after the many days of traveling! The best thing is that, compared to what we've had to eat lately, we were treated to a really good meal.

Monday, July 31

It is too bad that we cannot enjoy this comfort for long. We found out that we can only stay in these dormitories for a few days. This, as it turns out, is only a distribution center for the different refugee camps. Everyone has to move out. We have two choices – to be sent to another refugee camp or find a job and apartment in Breslau by our own wits.

Locating an adequate apartment is clearly a problem. If it was only our family of three, we probably could find a roof over our heads one way or another. But we are not alone. Victoria and Gruzinskienė and all their children are with us along with Uncle Feliksas and Aunt Elenora. Meanwhile Professor Vasiliauskas has left with his family for Dresden, where he knows some people.

We don't know what to do. At first Juozas thought we should go on to Vienna. Since it's a huge city, we might have an easier time finding a place to live. Besides Juozas has already been there once before. Now he has changed his mind about Vienna. He says there are too many of us in our group. Food is likely to be a greater problem in a big city. I think Juozas is just too exhausted to come to a firm decision. After all, he's been looking for work and a place to live non-stop since we got here.

While we were discussing our options, some unexpected news came in. It seems that the authorities are planning to take us somewhere else. New refugees have been coming in every day, and there is no more room here.

All of us women are relieved. We would be happy not to have to worry every day about a home and food. The German government is sure to provide us with at least minimal living conditions. Juozas, however, is not optimistic. He says we don't know where we will be taken or what sort of life we will face. What if we end up in some place that is being heavily bombed? Now he is wondering – would we be better off forgetting about NSF care? He has decided to try to find work on his own in Breslau.

A couple more days have gone by without any luck. Not a single matter has been resolved. All of us adults sat down together and made a decision. The women and children will go wherever NSF takes us. Juozas and Uncle Feliksas are going to stay in Breslau and try to find any kind of job. They will keep looking for a cheap apartment to rent. Then we can come back and join them in Breslau. We agreed to one more thing. If we should happen to end up at some refugee camp where conditions are extremely hard, Juozas promised to come and rescue us without delay.

We have to leave tomorrow. Juozas and I spent our evening walking around town. A strange feeling came over us. There is a war going on. Germany is being bombed constantly. We are about to be separated – Jurate and I are going off to heaven knows where, while Juozas is going to stay here in Breslau. We have no idea when we will see each other again. Despite everything, here we are, walking around like carefree tourists sightseeing in the beautiful Old Town of Breslau. Cafes bustle everywhere. We stopped in one place. Music was playing; the room was filled with people and laughter. A pleasant aroma of good coffee filled the air. It is hard to believe that we are in a country which has been at war for so long and is about to lose the war. Breslau is an illusion of peace and calm on this day of July 31, 1944.

August, 1944 in Kliosterle, Czechoslovakia

On the morning of August 1st, we said goodbye to Juozas and Uncle Feliksas. Then we took the bus to the Breslau Train Station. Our train headed towards Czechoslovakia. We got off at Tropau Town. The NSF representatives were already waiting for us. They registered all new arrivals and gave us certificates for our food coupons. They told us not to go anywhere far because we were to be taken on to Hohenstatt. However, we did have time for a walk.

There was a large and pleasant looking park near the station. We decided that we would not find a better place for a rest with the children. At a corner of this park were some cages with exotic birds. Seeing all these birds, the children shouted in glee. I was tired from our trip and the walk in the park, so I sat down on one of the benches. Four elderly women were already sitting there. One of them started to protest right away. She complained loudly that there wasn't enough room for more than four on the bench, although I could see five sitting easily on the other benches. Of course I moved. One old woman, frowning angrily, was mumbling something, expressing her displeasure, all the while staring at me. She must have realized that we were refugees from somewhere because we were so very tired and poorly dressed. This really hurt me. I felt so lonely – without my birthplace, with no home and now without my husband either. I wanted to cry but I knew I couldn't. Holding Jurate's little hand pressed tightly in mine, I held back my tears, knowing I had to be strong.

We went back to the station where we were told that our trip would be delayed until tomorrow. Members of Hitlerjugend, *the Nazi youth organization, were in charge of looking after our baggage. We were taken to some gymnasium to spend the night. I wanted to take Jurate's bedding, but a German from the NSF told me that everything was already arranged, and we didn't need to take anything with us.*

As things turned out, I was sorry that I listened to him. There were only some worn and dirty mats tossed all over the gym floor. We were not given any sheets, pillows or blankets. But there was no other choice at this point. I couldn't very well sit up all night with a toddler in my arms. I laid my dress down for Jurate to sleep on and used my raincoat as a blanket.

But I couldn't sleep. My little girl tossed and turned all night and kept kicking her cover off. I was afraid that she might catch cold so I kept watch to be sure she was covered. At midnight there was much clamor and noise. A large group of people who looked like gypsies was brought into the gym. I had no idea what country they came from. Their behavior, though, was most uncivilized. They didn't care at all that other people were already sleeping. They talked loudly, bickering about something. I couldn't help but think of my cozy, lovely home in Vilnius. I pulled the raincoat over my head and quietly cried most of that night.

We all got up as early as possible in the morning and returned to the train station. It was scary being together with that crowd of aggressive people who had been brought in at midnight from God-knows-where. Even though I had tried to keep Jurate warm, she caught a cold anyway. Then she was struck with another malady – a bout of diarrhea, probably from all the irregular meals and bad food. I am so concerned about my daughter. She is just a little girl with a small build. Over the past two weeks of our trip, she has lost quite a lot of weight. She is nothing but skin and bones.

Another group of war refugees joined our group. Finally, about ninety of us in total were put on a train at about 1:00 p.m.

The train chugged onwards over narrow mountain passages and through tunnels. It ran across sun-drenched valleys, surrounded by mountains carved with caves and overgrown with forests. We passed streams with gushing torrents of water along the way. The views were so beautiful we couldn't take our eyes away from the windows. It was fascinating for all of us who had come from the relatively flat lands of Lithuania. We stared at the mountaintops engulfed in a mist. When our train moved up a slope, we were in awe of the pretty villages and neatly laid out towns below us.

Our train stopped in Hohenstatt. We were told to disembark and get on a bus to Heilendorff, which was about 4 kilometers from the railroad station. This charming little town seemed entirely untouched by the war.

We were housed at a spacious school. Three groups formed by nationality – Germans, Lithuanians and Ukrainians. Although twenty people had to sleep in each room, living conditions were relatively tolerable here. Each person was provided with a separate bed, a clean, new mattress, a sheet and a blanket. We settled in. Then we were invited to come for supper, which was a pleasant surprise – a tasty porridge of rice and meat.

Ten days flew by. We didn't do anything except walk around in Heilendorff. The only language heard on the streets was Czech.

The German war refugees were taken away in small groups to different locales. We Lithuanians were left to share the school facilities with Ukrainians. Interestingly, the food became noticeably worse. But it is the unknown that depresses us the most. What will become of us?

The Germans did not speak to us at all; they did not explain anything. We talked amongst ourselves. What should we do? Should we let Juozas know about our uncertain situation in some way? Victoria and my auntie said that he is so shrewd and smart he will be able to find common ground with the Germans and help us out of this situation.

Then a near-miracle happened. The door to our room opened and Juozas walked in! He found a job in Breslau! Unfortunately we could not leave with him right away. He said he needed some more time to get used to the new situation and find us a place to live. Besides we certainly couldn't leave Victoria all alone with the children. We decided there was nothing else we could do. He will work in Breslau, while the rest of us will remain under the care of the NSF.

Juozas wasted no time taking care of our difficulties. The next day he went to Hohenstatt and convinced the NSF people to move our group to Kliosterle Village where our living conditions were much improved.

Since I have a child, I was provided with my own separate room. However I prefer staying with Victoria and her three children in the large room they had been given. We are rather tightly packed in, but there is enough space for all of us. It's more fun being together and it's easier getting our household chores done. All we really have to do is watch the children and cook. At first we had no stove, so it was somewhat difficult, going around the village to ask people if we could use their kitchens. Not long afterwards, though, we did get a little stove.

Life seems to have taken a turn for the better. We get our supplies with coupons. The Germans also provided an extra allocation of food for our four children, two of whom are babies. We also still have some left over food, which Victoria had brought on the trip.

The Allies have not been bombing this town.

The days are warm. We can enjoy the beauty of the mountains and the peace of village life.

Of course the sense of peace is very relative. We have to forget about the raging war first, and that rarely happens. We are always talking, wondering what is happening in Lithuania. Where are our relatives; where are our good friends? Victoria starts sighing mournfully, especially at night, nervously talking about her husband. Is he still alive? We have not had a word of news about him.

The days pass monotonously; we have the same routine every day. The villagers are nearly all Czech and they are very friendly to us. We sense that they do not much care for the Germans. Most of the Germans here are locals; they hold all sorts of supervisory jobs.

September, 1944

Saturday is the day that I live for. Juozas comes in during the evening from Breslau. As soon as we hear the whistle from the train that is still far off in the mountains, Jurate starts jumping up and down, shouting, "Here, here, te-te." Together, we go to meet him at the station.

Jurate has been pronouncing whole words and even pulling together some sentences. Nonetheless all of our wanderings over Germany did have an effect on our child. She is very nervous and excitable. She wants me to pick her up all the time. Victoria's youngest, Gediminas, whom we call Gedutis, always walks peacefully behind his mother when we come back from the store. And he is only a half a year older than Jurate. In the meantime, she demands that I pick her up. How can I possibly carry her when my hands are full of packages? Once I actually had to leave Jurate lying in the street. She fell down and refused to get up, no matter how much I pleaded with her. All she did was scream. I had no way to carry her and my parcels. There was no other choice. I had to rush home, toss my things down and hurry back to get her.

For the weekends, Juozas and I rent a little room from some people who live not far from my place. Their house is on the slope of a mountain. We have an outstanding view from our window. But the weekend whizzes by so fast, and early Monday morning arrives too soon, colored in sadness for me. Juozas has to go back to Breslau.

This living apart is starting to annoy me. Besides, whenever he leaves me, I am constantly worried about him. Anything can happen during a war. The idea of losing him puts me into an absolute panic. After the last visit, I pleaded with him to take Jurate and me to live with him in Breslau. On the other hand, I don't really want to leave Victoria alone with her children. We still can't invite them to come with us. Juozas says that he is simply not able to support all of us in the city.

One fine autumn day, our problem got resolved all on its own. Out of the blue, Jozeph Gruodis showed up in our village! Victoria's husband got out of Lithuania successfully and made his way to Germany. Somehow he found out that his family was here. Oh, tears of joy flowed in streams. Victoria wants nothing more but to be with her husband. I am just as happy as she is.

I can hardly wait for the weekend. I have already packed our bags. Juozas is coming to take us to Breslau with him.

After Alexandra and my relatives left for Heilendorff (Kliosterle), I was able to find work quite quickly in Breslau. The German government provided support for the women and young children since they were not obliged to work. The men, however, had to indicate their profession at the time of registration. They were then offered jobs for which they were qualified or they had to find work on their own somewhere.

I registered as an economist. On the questionnaire I included the title of my dissertation, "Forced Sovietization of Lithuanian Agriculture." My expertise seemed to interest the Germans. I received an offer to work at the East European Research Institute of Breslau University.

This was a small academic office which continued to do research on countries occupied by Germany even as late as the latter half of 1944. My assignment was to write a study on Soviet economic policies in Lithuania. I needed to describe the methods of Sovietization employed in our country and the ensuing damages to the economy of Lithuania. It's difficult to surmise what sort of practical benefit such a study had for Germans, particularly since they were already being forced out of most Lithuanian territories. The facts which I presented were not of much value for propaganda purposes either. Apparently it was scholarship for the sake of scholarship.

However I was incredibly happy to have gotten such a job. The institute started paying me a salary. It may not have been much but it was sufficient to live on and rent an apartment. Even better, I received my salary in actual Reich marks rather than the so-called Ost marks, the currency circulating in German occupied countries.

Ost marks were freely converted to regular marks in Germany earlier. I had enjoyed a comparatively high salary working for the Vilnius Municipality. Thus I had saved a thousand or so Ost marks. But as soon as we got to Breslau, I heard over the radio that conversion of this currency was not permitted. We panicked! As soon as we heard this distressing news, we rushed to change our money. Unfortunately we were too late and got nothing.

Instantly another plan came to mind of how we might save at least a hundred or so marks. We raced over to the railroad station. It was still possible to pay for train tickets with Ost marks. Thus we started buying the cheapest tickets available to some station close to Breslau. Luck was on our side. The cashier would accept our Ost marks and give us change in valid official marks. By going from one cashier window to another, we managed to change most of the money we had. Naturally we incurred losses but at least we had some workable cash in our pockets.

All the while in Germany, we were impressed by the clear efficiency of the iron-handed German order. Germans were retreating from territories that had been under their control, as though they were shedding their skins, while the Allies beat on them. The ruins of their cities made it obvious that the end of the Reich was near. Nonetheless, the usual pandemonium that went hand-in-hand with a military defeat was not felt in Germany. Even though it seemed that every last bridge, every train station, warehouse and factory had been bombed and it was almost impossible to walk the city streets due to the rubble of destruction, the order of Germany never fell apart. A system of supply continued. No one died from starvation, not even a single war refugee.

We received our food coupons regularly and we were always able to acquire the products indicated on the coupons. The weekly coupon contained a notation about the allocation of food. If it read, for example, a kilogram of bread, two eggs and 200 grams of meat, then it was possible to buy all of those items. Obviously we were never able to eat our fill but we certainly did not starve. This was a particular blessing during the early months after leaving Lithuania. But the ration became somewhat leaner over time, and we were rather deprived by the time the United States Army arrived.

I also managed to win some extra benefits for war refugees. Coupons for refugees included provisions of winter clothing, textile materials and bedding available for purchase. I used ours to buy a good coat for Alexandra. We also dressed up Jurate in warm clothes – shoes, a coat and a thick jacket. Alexandra was thrilled, telling me happily, "Well, we will surely have enough clothes to last us until the end of this war."

As for housing, at first I rented a room from an owner of a sewing shop. These quarters were tight but sufficient for one person. But I was unhappy being away from Alexandra and Jurate. I wanted them with me as soon as possible.

Visiting my family on the weekends at that little town in Czechoslovakia was a complicated affair. I had to travel by train for a couple of hours, sometimes longer. Besides that, I had to get a new permit to leave Breslau each time I went to visit my family.

Finally Alexandra and Jurate were able to join me. I rented a fairly large room with kitchen rights from a German colonel. The wife lived in the house with her two daughters while her husband was off fighting the war in Russia. Alexandra got along well with her.

Our landlady was a great cook. She always managed to make a delicious meal from the most ordinary food. Once in a while she would invite us for a meal. Then she would question me about military conditions and the Russian threat. I could never speak entirely freely with her – after all, she was the wife of a colonel in the German Army. There was a clear sense, however, that she no longer had any remaining illusions about the fate of Germany. Sighing deeply, she would speak of her husband in battle at the front. She complained about the future before her eyes. All we could do was to agree with her and console her.

At the East European Research Institute, I became friendly with its president, Professor Seraphim. He was always interested in the progress of my work. He'd invite me into his office for a talk which did not avoid the topic of war. I quickly surmised that the professor had no sympathies for the Nazi regime and I could discuss politics with him quite openly. He invited Alexandra and me to visit his home at Christmas. This was a good sign. Germans were generally never quick to accept guests, and here we were, Lithuanian war refugees! We were truly honored.

Ten years later, when I was living in the United States, I was in business supplying coal to the German steel industry. On one occasion, the Dortmund Steel Mill President, Dr. Ellshoff, visited me in New York. As I was telling him about my life in Germany at the end of the war, I happened to mention Dr. Seraphim. "Professor Seraphim?" Dr. Ellshoff was terribly surprised. "Why, I was his student!"

"I haven't heard a word about the professor since the day in February of 1945, when we left Breslau. Could he have wound up in the Russian Zone? Is he still alive? Do you have any clue about his fate?" I asked Ellshoff.

"*Ein moment,*" Ellshoff told me and picked up the phone to call Germany. It was hard to believe that we could learn anything but we did not have to wait long for an answer. One of his assistants found Professor Seraphim's telephone number. Dr. Ellshoff immediately dialed it. "Is this Professor Seraphim?" he inquired over the phone. I heard Ellshoff mention my name and then he handed me the phone.

"Kazickas?!" I heard the familiar voice of my former boss, who was stunned to be talking to me again. I learned that he had successfully escaped from Breslau and settled in Frankfurt on the Main. He asked me all sorts of questions about how life had unfolded for Alexandra and me. Ten years had gone by, but finally I was able to thank him for the help he had given us. Unfortunately an opportunity to visit Professor Seraphim in person never did materialize.

I remember well the other professors who worked at the Institute. They came from Croatia, Bulgaria, Rumania and Poland. The Rumanians and Croatians were from aristocratic families, the upper class of their countries. However there were no nationalistic rivalries or snobbery among us. We interacted as friends. We always discussed war events in our own countries and freely exchanged opinions about the future of Eastern Europe after the war.

Autumn passed. Breslau was not bombed at all because of its remote strategic position. Apparently the Russians did not have enough long-range fighting planes and never bombed very far from the front line area. Breslau was at the edge of eastern Germany near Czechoslovakia and Poland. It had no key military industry. The town was also of no special importance to the Western Allies. Nonetheless, air raid sirens went off here as well. At autumn's end, alarms would sound more frequently even though air strikes, which were devastating most of Germany, were still not being aimed at Breslau.

The alarms made Alexandra nervous. The sirens usually went off after noon, as if on purpose, just as soon as Jurate fell asleep. Alexandra would have to wake her up and run down into the cellar. First of all, everybody was required to go into shelters. Then, there was no way for anyone to know whether or not bombs would actually begin falling all over town. Alexandra finally got sick and tired of running back and forth into the basement. It got to the point where she would simply stay in our room, ignoring the sounds of the alarms.

Christmas of 1944 was approaching. Lithuanians living in Breslau made up a fair-sized community as new refugees from Lithuania kept coming in. We got into an especially good relationship with Dr. Vytautas Slavinskas, who worked for the town hospital, and his wife, Maria. He helped our family a great deal. I was the first to catch a bad cold. Later Jurate came down with a severe ear infection. Even the most basic of medications were hard to come by under wartime conditions. A person's life often depended on the help of a private physician. We were aware of this and appreciated the efforts of Dr. Slavinskas on our behalf. Along with the Slavinskas family, we gathered around our special Lithuanian *Kūčios* table with straw under the table cloth, a Christmas Eve tradition. With heads bowed, we prayed to God to keep us safe during the upcoming year.

The whirlwind of war nonetheless did finally reach Breslau. In January 1945, while listening on the sly to BBC on the radio, we heard that the Russians had launched a major attack on Poland, and the line of the front was edging towards Breslau. This news raised the anxiety level for everyone. One day early in February, Professor Seraphim called me into his office and said, "Apparently the Russians are going to overtake Breslau very soon. I would advise you and your family to travel somewhere further west." It didn't take long to realize that his advice had been very timely. By mid-February, the Russians had surrounded Breslau and the city became a battle zone for nearly three months.

Professor Seraphim displayed an incredibly generous spirit. He filed the necessary paperwork to send me on an official trip to Würzburg on behalf of the institute and made sure that I received a permit to travel with my family. It was my own choice to go to Würzburg since my sister Victoria and Uncle Feliksas had settled in a village not far from this area. I had received a letter from them (German mail service was still operating normally) so I knew where they lived. I believed that by pulling together we could survive to the war's end, and I intended to find them. Most importantly – we had to avoid falling into the clutches of the Russians.

Our plan was to leave Breslau during the latter part of February. I did not want to rush matters because Jurate was still sick from an ear infection. But on the night of February 12th, the air raid sirens went off. This time it was not a false alarm. Explosions somewhere at the outskirts of Breslau shook all the windows. After we came up from the cellar, I told Alexandra that we absolutely had to leave without any further delay.

Again our worldly goods fit into our two small suitcases. All our clothes went into one and food into the other. Most of our food was still what we had brought from Lithuania; the rest was our leftover stocks of bacon and ham, which we had saved by rationing them sparingly. Later that night, we bade farewell to our highly distraught landlady. She jumped up to ask us, "Why are you leaving so suddenly?" She asked for our advice – what should she do? I suggested that she not remain in Breslau so that she would not find herself in a zone occupied by Russians.

It was a cold, snowy night. We had no choice but to walk to the train station which was quite far away. The sirens were howling again, and we could hear the roar of airplanes. We ran as fast as we could. I lugged the suitcases, while Alexandra carried our sick daughter wrapped in my fur coat. I was wearing my other fur coat which I had saved for an emergency. Such a coat could easily be sold in winter and traded for food. Loaded down this way, we couldn't really move easily but finally we made it to the railroad station.

The vision at the station is etched forever in my mind. Masses of people, moving as if in a wave, were crammed into a huge hall. Most were women with children surrounded by suitcases and bags. A few elderly men huddled in the crowd. The building was so crowded that it was virtually impossible to get inside.

It was now obvious to everyone that the Soviet Army had broken through the German front and was advancing towards Breslau. The sharp sounds of artillery filled the night sky. Panic ensued. Thousands of people had jammed the railroad station, hoping to squeeze into any one of the departing trains.

It was nearly midnight. We realized that we didn't have a prayer of getting into the building, so our sick little girl might warm up a bit. Even though she was completely wrapped in furs, we were still afraid that she would get chilled. We stomped in place from one foot to the other at the edge of the crowd. People continued to pour in from town. Slowly we inched closer to the station. We found ourselves pressed into the gradually increasing throng of bodies. We were so afraid of losing each other – that would have been a terrible calamity. How could anyone find anybody in this madhouse? There was no way to shout out a name. The loudest scream would drown in the clamor and tumult of this mass of desperate humanity.

Suddenly the screech of air raid sirens cut through the noise of the crowd. Police and SS troopers started herding people out of the station into shelters. The crowd, however, was beyond control. Everyone was shoving; children were shrieking, women were crying and there was cursing of the war and Hitler. One way or another, some of these people ran for the bomb shelters. Nobody really wanted to leave his or her established place in the station, but the idea that the railroad station could become the first target of a bomb was even more frightening. I took advantage of the flow of people moving out through the door to elbow my way inside. I grabbed hold of Alexandra's arm and pulled her and Jurate inside with me.

Fortunately the station was not bombed. The bombers flew somewhere else. We heard an echo of a hollow rumble from afar. The crush inside the station hall became stronger. Everyone was craning their necks to see the schedule of departing trains on the hanging signboard. The closest large city to the west was Dresden. The train headed there should pass through Breslau, but I could see that we would be unable to push our way up to the platform where it was to stop. People stood shoulder to shoulder in the underground tunnel leading to the platform for the Dresden bound trains.

It was clear to me that we would never succeed in getting on the train, even if several were to arrive at once. I glanced over at Alexandra; I could see hopelessness in her eyes. She stood in silence. Even our little girl, who cried so very often, was silent. All of a sudden, something broke inside Alexandra. She shouted at me, "Why on earth are we standing here, frozen to this spot? We are going to die here! Do something! Hurry up and think of something to save us!"

Faced with a critical moment such as this one, people often have a brainstorm. An idea shot through my mind. I looked around and saw that everyone was pushing towards the westward platform. Over where the trains were heading east, there was not a single soul. The idea I had was a simple one. We would go down the eastward tunnel and get out at any empty platform. From there we would follow the tracks in the opposite direction from the station and work our way over to the spot where the Dresden train was to stop.

However, walking on the train tracks was strictly prohibited, even during peacetime. Control was more strict during wartime due to the threat of diversionary actions that appeared everywhere. Should the police or SS Security officers see us, we would undoubtedly be arrested. They might even fire off some rounds from their rifles. Nonetheless, I still thought my strategy was worth the risk. Besides, there was no other way out of this mess.

My plan worked. We got out of the tunnel at the Warsaw platform. We saw that we had gotten around the crowd from the opposite side. The crushing mass of people was about five or six platforms away from us. I jumped down on the tracks and took Jurate in my arms. Alexandra followed me, dragging our suitcases behind her. Our highly risky march proceeded onward. We climbed up the platforms and back down on the tracks as we slowly worked our way towards the Dresden platform.

At last we reached our goal, unnoticed by the police. The problem was that there were so many people there we couldn't climb up. Not a single spot remained where we could lift a foot and pull ourselves up. By now several German women spotted us. They were shocked to see us suddenly appear on the tracks and stared angrily at us. However they were more concerned about holding their places in the crowd or pushing to a better location to get on the train than worrying about our "misdeeds."

Somehow I worked my way up to the platform and swung my shoulders from side to side to gain some space. I took Jurate, pulled up our suitcases and offered my arm to help Alexandra climb up the side. And so we found ourselves in the middle of the crowd of people, standing at the very front. The train should stop right alongside us. Of course we still had no way of knowing where the door of the train car would swing open or if and when a train might come at all.

Patiently we stood in the crowd, pleased that our plan had worked out so well. The air raid again sounded danger. The police were trying to herd people off the platform. They yelled over the loudspeakers that no train would be coming "You are risking your lives! There's no sense remaining at the railroad station!" But not a single person moved.

We simply did not want to believe that all our efforts to get to the front of the crowd were in vain. I decided to take a look at a train schedule hanging on a nearby board. I left Alexandra alone with Jurate in her arms to watch our suitcases. Then I elbowed my way through the crowd.

Just as I managed to push ahead, the crowd moved in a huge wave. Suddenly, a shrill whistle announced the arrival of a train. SS storm troopers armed with automatic rifles jumped out at the edge of the platform, trying to push people away from the cars of the train as it pulled into the station.

February 13, 1945

Flashing past my eyes were the wagons of a military hospital train. Suddenly it slowed down. People were shoving me; I was in danger of falling onto the tracks. SS troopers were trying to stem the surging crowd, threatening and forcibly pushing people away from the train. By now nothing was going to stop this crowd. Panic washed over me; I looked around, trying to spot Juozas. I couldn't see him anywhere in the mass of people, shouting and streaming towards the train. It came to a full stop and the door of one car opened not far from me. I could see that the car was filled with soldiers, most of them injured, their heads and arms wrapped in bandages. Several soldiers were looking out a window at the crowd right in front of me. Unexpectedly one of them called out to me, "Give me the girl. Climb in the window here, over to us!"

I have no idea why I listened to him, but that instinctive reaction probably saved our lives. Mechanically I lifted Jurate up to him. The soldier pulled my little girl into their car; she was now completely quiet. For a moment, I was paralyzed by fear – what would happen if the train starts to move?

But I froze for no longer than a blink of an eye. I saw the outstretched arms of another soldier. I grabbed hold of him with one hand and the ledge of the window with my other hand. I swung myself over the ledge. Several other soldiers grabbed me and in a flash pulled me in. I immediately took Jurate into my arms.

At that point, I came back to my senses. I was alone in that train with my little daughter. Juozas was still out there somewhere on the platform. Our suitcases had been left behind. I stuck my head out the window and started screaming hysterically, "Juozas, my Juozas! Juozukas!"

The soldiers rushed to calm me down. I kept hearing them repeat the word – "police, police!" I caught hold of myself. They were shushing me, explaining that I might be noticed by the police. Then it would be bad for me and for them. After all I had no right to be on this troop train.

*I noticed Juozas in the crowd. He is so tall that his head stood out above the others. I waved my arms at him from inside the wagon. When he spotted me, he started shoving his way towards the train, looking at me and smiling. With tears in my eyes, I motioned with my hands to the soldiers. With as many words as I could muster in German, I pleaded with them to help Juozas climb in. "*Meine man, meine man,*" I cried. "My husband, my husband."*

But then some policemen appeared by the window. They were trying to push back the people who were surging for the door of the train. The locomotive whistle shrilled. The wheels clanged on the tracks, and the train jerked as it started rolling slowly forward.

It was very dark in the wagon. That was to guard against being visible to the air forces of either the Russians or the Western Allies. The wagon was packed with soldiers, many of them badly hurt. I was surprised at first to notice that even the injured seemed to be happy as though they were completely healed and heading for a vacation. It did make sense though. They were on their way home, away from the eastern front which promised nothing but death.

*The men led me over to a corner in the hallway of the wagon. One soldier started talking to Jurate, trying to play with her. I looked over at my baby. She was all scrunched up and frightened. Tears filled her eyes, but she did not make a single sound. I put my hand against her forehead; she was burning with fever. I was afraid to say a word, because the soldiers would instantly understand that we were "*auslanders *[foreigners]". Who knows how they might react? So many Germans had been left behind at the Breslau Station, and here they were, rescuing some foreign woman.*

Suddenly there was a noise in the wagon. Someone turned on a flashlight. Gendarmes were pushing their way through the darkness, looking for any civilians who might have gotten on the train. The soldiers immediately threw their overcoats over Jurate and me and lay down next to us, pretending to be asleep. It was unbelievable. Jurate was completely covered up and pressed against my chest. But she didn't make a single move or a single sound as the gendarmes searched the wagon.

After they had passed without noticing us, I broke down and started to cry. Of course I wept as silently as I could because I didn't want the soldiers to hear me. All these thoughts were racing through my mind. Where am I going all by myself? What am I going to do without my husband? How am I going to get by without a single thing with me, without a single coin in my pocket?

All of a sudden, the train started slowing down and stopped in a forest. I could hear the thunder of a far-off explosion. Bombs were falling somewhere. Under such circumstances, trains will stop in a forest to be less noticeable to the planes overhead. Thus they are almost invisible from the air at night. After about a half hour, the train began moving again. Stopping and starting, our train rolled west at an incredibly slow pace.

Jurate had stayed silent all this time. However, when we stopped at one station, she uttered her first words: "Siu, siu." She had to go to the bathroom. With my life in chaos, now I had to deal with this! The simplest act of placing a child on a potty suddenly became a huge problem here. It was entirely unrealistic to find a toilet somewhere on the train. We were in total darkness in the car and surrounded by snoozing soldiers. Climbing out of the train was also not an option, because we might not get back on. I couldn't think of anything better to do. I asked a person standing outside the window to take Jurate and hold her while she relieved herself in the bushes. Some kind-hearted German caught on to the situation quickly and did just that. Naturally all this was extremely stressful for a child, not quite two years old. Here she was being lifted out of the train and given to some stranger, while her mother stayed in the car. On top of all that, it was cold outside – around 10° C below zero [15 F]. Trembling I watched my little girl – feverish, her little bottom bare – endure this entire process. But she never uttered a single cry.

When Jurate was in my arms again, I huddled back in our corner and started to snooze. But I did not fall into a deep sleep. My head kept snapping back to reality. I kept checking to see if Jurate was still breathing. She had never been so silent for so long, and I was afraid for her. Her stillness kept waking me.

Dawn finally broke. I began to make out the faces of the soldiers. They looked tired though pleased at their good fortune, having escaped the hell of the front. I saw several more civilians in the wagon. I wondered how they had gotten in. Did they board the train in Breslau, as I had done, or at some other station where the train had stopped? A tiny ember of hope glowed within me. Maybe my dearest Juozas had managed to push his way onto this train. I prayed to God for such a miracle.

I was still praying when suddenly I noticed my husband through the open door, carefully picking his way forward. It really was a miracle! I shouted out in disbelief and happiness as we embraced.

But once again, fear took hold. I was incredibly worried about Jurate who was squirming and moaning. Her forehead was on fire. I knew she needed medical attention as quickly as possible. The soldiers told us that the train would stop soon in Dresden. I relaxed a bit. I assumed there would be an NSF Point at the railroad station. There we could find a doctor to give our daughter the right medicine.

At long last, we rolled into Dresden. Its huge, decorative railroad station was filled with soldiers and tired civilians, pushing each another in the crowded hall. Possibly some of these people were refugees, just like us. We said goodbye and thank you to the soldiers who had saved us.

[I have often wondered about the fate of those good soldiers. I wondered if they might have fallen in battle on the front or if they had been bombed. With all my heart, I hoped that they survived the horrible final months of the war. I would have liked to see them again, but that was not to be. In all the turmoil, I never even asked them their names nor where they had come from. However I will always remember their young, war weary faces.]

Germany in Agony

The first thing we did at the Dresden Station was find the NSF Point. There a whole crowd of people was waiting to see a doctor. Women, children and old people, all were war refugees. We waited in line for several hours. The doctor, a young and gracious woman from Yugoslavia, examined Jurate and told us that she had caught a bad cold. Although pneumonia had not yet developed, she was at risk for it. Under normal conditions, the child should immediately be put to bed. However, the doctor advised us to move on, especially since we did not know anyone in Dresden. "The Americans and English are bombing the city. It is absolute chaos here. Try to find a way out of here as quickly as possible. The girl will endure the trip somehow," the doctor said and gave us some medicine.

We then returned to the platform for trains running in a westward direction. The situation here was no better than it had been in Breslau. The only difference was that in the Dresden Station, trains ran more frequently. Most of the people were flailing about, going from one overcrowded train to the next, trying to squeeze inside any car without caring where the train was heading, just so long as they were on board. Everybody was desperately trying to get out of Dresden. Then an announcement came over the loudspeaker that men were not allowed to get on any train. Only women and children were permitted to leave.

A long train came into view. It was already getting dark, and the platform was poorly lit. Policemen were walking around, using their flashlights to check the surroundings. I had no idea where that train was going and I did not make any effort to find out. All that mattered was that it was traveling westward. There was a tremendous crush at the doors as people shoved each other to get on. The train was moving very slowly when an open door appeared. I took advantage of the moment and lifted Alexandra on. I handed our child to her and then, threw in the suitcases. But I did not have time to jump on the car myself. So I ran alongside the train – the adjoining car was the last one – and grabbed hold of the door railing. There I was – balancing on one stair and hanging on to the door handle. I knew that men were not allowed on the train, as the announcement had made clear. However, the police either did not see me or possibly did not want to bother about the situation. The door clanged shut. There was no way for me to open it from the outside, so I rode along, clinging on for dear life.

The city faded away in the darkness. Then luckily the train started to brake. I figured that an air raid alarm must have signaled danger. I jumped off and ran for the car in front. There, still standing by the doors, were Alexandra and a frightened Jurate. As though she had been waiting for me, Alexandra opened the door immediately. I embraced her. "Everything is fine now. We are together," I said, trying to calm her because her entire body was still trembling with fear.

The train again rolled forward for a while and then stopped. It was another air raid warning, but we couldn't hear any bombs exploding. I told Alexandra, "Come on, let's try to find a spot in the wagon. We can't stand here in the doorway the whole time."

The train was filled beyond capacity. But in the very last car there was room for us, as long as everyone pressed in closer together. All the people sitting there looked up at us. We exchanged greetings with two young soldiers and a couple of women, one of whom was dressed quite elegantly. But two men in SS officer uniforms did not so much as nod. The atmosphere was tense. Still, all the passengers huddled together more tightly and made room for us on the edge of the seat.

We sat without uttering a word. We sensed that we'd best not speak Lithuanian. The others did not talk either. Suddenly, Jurate mumbled something, and Alexandra automatically answered her in Lithuanian. She spoke quietly, pressing the child against her bosom. The SS men leaped up as if they'd been stung. "*Polen raus! Polen raus!*" the Nazis shrieked, rolling their eyes and flailing their hands, that the Poles should get out.

I felt a flash of fear. But then a sense of strength and calm came over me. I looked them straight in their eyes and said in German, "We are not

Poles. We are Lithuanians. We have left our country to get away from the Soviets who have occupied our land. We have a permit to live in Germany from the German government."

The SS-ers calmed down just as suddenly as they had gotten riled. They said nothing to me in reply but sat back down in their places. Apparently Lithuanians did not antagonize them like the Poles did. They did not even ask to see our documents.

The silence, however, got more and more uncomfortable. Only Jurate, who seemed very frightened, whimpered in a weak voice. I could see that the soldiers and the women were ill at ease. They sat with their eyes downcast or just stared into the blind darkness through the windows. The elegantly dressed lady pulled an apple from her basket and offered it to Jurate who did not respond; she only snuggled closer to her mother's chest. Without much ado, Alexandra thanked the woman for the apple and took it. She had a bite herself and tried to persuade Jurate to take a piece.

About another twenty minutes went by and the train stopped again. This time it remained standing nearly the entire night. The German anti-aircraft missiles flashed in the sky over Dresden, which was a few miles away. Bomb explosions reverberated in the night air. It was February 13, 1945. The massive bombing of Dresden had begun.

Our train had stopped in a forest. A glow from the burning fires spread across the sky, and it became peculiarly light. The rumbles of the explosions intensified into a seemingly never-ending roll of thunder. We sat in the darkened wagon in stunned silence staring at the flashing sky. Minutes turned into hours. The ground under us shook.

(Several years later, after we had already settled in the United States, we met the Varnas and Giedrikas families. They had been in Dresden on that night of February 13th and survived. They told us how furiously and ceaselessly the bombs fell. It had made the air so hot that even the asphalt of the streets had started burning. Thousands of people smothered and died inside the bomb shelters. "Only by some miracle did we live through that hell," both families agreed, remembering that horrendous night. The unbearable heat had scorched their faces and they had been on the verge of losing consciousness.

"I felt as if we would all die," recalled Mrs. Varnas. "I opened my eyes a crack and unexpectedly, I saw the rays from flashlights flickering in the darkness of the hideaway shelter. Rescuers had forced their way in from the outside, searching for any survivors. They dragged us out into the street over piles of corpses. The bombing of Dresden had ended, but the demolished city was still in flames. Ruined buildings were crumbling into ashes. Melted asphalt flowed down the streets like lava. Survivors stumbled in the rubble and smoke, crazed, not knowing where to go.")

Meanwhile, during this horrific battle, we had been sitting speechlessly in the dark car, listening to the bombing of Dresden for several hours. Our train moved again only at daybreak. We pulled up to an unknown railroad station. The walls of the building were all that were left standing. It had no roof and no windows; it looked like a strange skeleton looming up from the ground. It was snowing hard. People were huddled together, hiding in a shed of nailed-up boards.

We stayed on that train making frequent stops for two full days. It became clear that we were heading for Coburg so we did not have to transfer once. We got off in the darkness at the Froenlach Station, not far from Coburg. The town itself was nowhere to be seen. There were no buildings, nothing but a flat field. We knew that there had to be a little town somewhere not far from here, where Victoria's and Uncle Feliksas' families had settled several months ago.

The snow was up to our knees, as we waded through the drifts. I dragged our two suitcases, while Alexandra carried Jurate. We had no idea if we were going the right way. There was not a soul in sight to ask for directions. After we had walked a while, we noticed a young boy sledding down a hill. We asked him how we could get to the address of our relatives. It turned out that we would have to walk another several kilometers. I immediately tried to convince this young lad to be our guide and let us use his sled to haul our suitcases. The boy looked at me distrustfully. I pulled a few marks out of my wallet and offered him compensation. The money tempted him. And he spoke, "*Gut.*"

We piled our belongings on the sled and placed Jurate on top. The boy led us. Our steps were swifter now, and soon we got to the house where Victoria lived.

With Victoria and her two sons in Germany, 1945

February 16, 1945

We were so relieved to see our relatives again that we just fell into their arms. We had been traveling for almost a week. We had not washed nor had a chance to change our clothes; we had had little to eat and very little sleep. Despite all these hardships, we are incredibly happy to have escaped all the bombings and be together again with the people we love.

Victoria and Joseph Gruodis have settled their family in a spacious, well-heated room. Their stove was lit and the day's meal gave off a delicious aroma. We pounced on the pot of soup without even bothering to wash first. Uncle Feliksas, who lived nearby, also came by soon after. We all ate and talked. We told them about our lives in Breslau, how we traveled to Dresden and finally reached them in Bavaria. Our relatives did not hold back their stories either. They are very happy to be here in a little town where it is peaceful, at least for the time being. They have been able to live reasonably normal lives.

Today Juozas went to the town burgomaster to register. The office allocated a place of residence for us. It turned out to be a small, poorly heated room but, most importantly, we are able to use the common kitchen in the building. This is where we intend to spend most of our day, sitting and getting warm by the stove. I feel blessed in a strange way – we are far from the front, and the sounds of bombings are no more threatening than the quiet crackling of logs in the fire.

February 17, 1945

Our landlady is a Nazi who believes fanatically in Hitler. Her husband and son both fought on the eastern front. To us it was obvious that the surrender of Germany was now inevitable, and that day is not far away. However, she boasted constantly that Germany would prove victorious at the last minute. We don't argue with her or get involved in any political discussions. We just listen to her politely. I can see she doesn't like us very much. Maybe we don't seem loyal enough to Germany for her. Maybe she just doesn't like us, because we're not German. I think, however, that she will get to like us more in time. I have already seen her offering Jurate a piece of bread spread with marmalade.

We have met some of the other residents of this town. Some acted very cold towards us and did not want to engage in conversation. Others were friendly. They expressed some compassion for the plight of war refugees. We have developed a warm relationship with the owner of the local bakery. She told us that her husband had been taken prisoner-of-war by the Americans and brought to the United States. He writes letters to her from there. She is delighted that he is now safer and less hungry in America than he would be in Germany. She says she wants to help us care for Jurate. Right away she gave her a sweet roll. I am quite sure that she cut us a slightly bigger hunk of bread than the ration noted on our food coupon.

February 18, 1945

Today we celebrated Jurate's birthday; she is 2 years old. Probably the best present for her is that we have arrived in this little town and are safe. Viktutė, as I call my dear Victoria, made a dress for Jurate using the material from her christening gown. Our friend from the bakery brought over a doll as a gift and a small cake. Even our landlady came and brought apples. It turned out to be a true party and a feast in comparison to what we have had. The children and the adults all had fun.

March, 1945

Formally Juozas is still employed by the East European Research Institute of Breslau University, writing an academic report on the economic damages done to Lithuania by the Soviet occupation. Therefore he is relieved of the legal obligation to work at some company or on a farm. Our lives are peaceful, and we are happy. We are not hungry or cold. There is a forest nearby; we go there to bring back logs. Chopping down trees is prohibited, but we quickly noticed that the locals don't pay attention to this edict. So we dare to do the same. We go out to find some dried up tree, look around to make sure nobody is watching, cut it down and chop it into pieces. Then we haul our load home. This way we are helping our landlady by providing her with much needed firewood.

Nevertheless we fully understand that our quiet lives are no more than an illusion. Without a radio, we have no idea of what is going on in the world or the situation on the war front; this adds to our anxiety. There is no sense in asking our landlady about such concerns, because all she does is praise Hitler. She insists that the Germans are not in any trouble; they are simply straightening out the front lines now and getting ready for a huge counter attack. Her comments seem pitifully comic to us. Every day we see hundreds, and sometimes thousands, of allied bomber planes flying overhead to bomb German cities. Occasionally we see soldiers returning from the front. We have heard them say that the German Army is constantly retreating from one city after another.

April, 1945

Spring has arrived at long last. The Nazis in our town are getting extremely nervous. Only our landlady continuously insists on praising Hitler to the skies.

Palm Sunday we went to church. We found out that there is a Catholic Church about 10 kilometers outside of our town. We decided to ride our bicycles to attend mass there. Since we only have three bicycles, not all of us could go. Victoria, her husband and I went together. Juozas stayed home with the children.

It is dangerous to ride around on the roadways even here. The airplanes of the Allies often circle our area. We have heard stories that fighter planes have been known to shoot at civilians on the road or out in the fields. Witnesses have heard the blasts of machine guns. There has been talk that many people have been killed like this. It surprises us to hear that pilots from Western countries, which we thought to be highly cultured, would shoot at unarmed citizens. But these things are really happening. Sometimes airmen fire shots at a person who is running away, as though this were a game or a hunt for an animal.

The three of us rode mostly by way of forest paths and arrived at our destination safely. Vierzehn Heiligen *'Fourteen Saints' Church stood atop a hill, so we saw its splendid towers from a distance. It has been a long time since any of us has attended mass. It was thrilling to listen to the priest's sermon, even though we did not really understand much of what he was saying. We all went to confession so we could properly receive Holy Communion. I confessed to the priest half in German and half in Lithuanian. He most likely understood less of our confessions than we understood of his sermon, but I'm sure he forgave our sins anyway.*

After church we rolled downhill on our bikes, feeling sheer happiness. All of a sudden, we heard the sounds of airplanes and then we saw some low-flying planes not far away. Along the road were some scrub bushes, so we tossed our bicycles to the side and dove to hide under them. The planes flew by. We got back on our bicycles and pedaled as fast as we could to get out of town. The forest was in sight. In a little bit, we could hide in the shadows of the trees. Again we heard the roar of approaching planes. My brother-in-law, Joseph, shouted at us to hurry with all our might into the forest. There was not a bush or a ditch along the road at this point.

I don't think I have ever pedaled so fast in all my life! Meanwhile, the seat of my bicycle had slipped to the side. Standing up I pushed those pedals like crazy, but the roar of a plane was right behind me. It seemed as though it would swoop down on me at any second. Time stopped – a second seemed like an eternity. I dove into the forest and fell under the first trees I saw. The plane whizzed past just above the treetops. A second one followed. We lay there on the mossy ground, crying and laughing at the same time.

[My brother-in-law teased me for many years about this day. He would laugh, remembering how I had broken all world speed records, racing on my bicycle with the seat dangling over the side.]

Juozas met us at the doorway when we got home. He was very distressed. Apparently several fighter planes had attacked our town. He had to run and hide in the cellar with the children. He was concerned about us because he noticed that the planes flew off in the direction where we had gone for church. Those must have been the same planes that we encountered on our way home.

The next Sunday was Easter. We wanted to go to church again despite our last experience. Because we decided to take the children with us, we went by train and got to church without incident. Unfortunately the return did not go as well. Fighter planes attacked our train. We managed to jump out of our car just in time and fell into a ditch under some trees at the edge of the forest. I was terrified as it was but even more terrified for the children. But they seemed much less frightened than we were – they were still too little to understand the notion of danger. They simply watched with big round eyes at the cascade of bullets hitting the train. The windows of the cars were shattered, but the planes flew off without killing anyone or doing any serious damage.

Spring has arrived and the days are getting warmer. The war continues. The local Germans whisper in fear that everything will soon come to an end. Clearly the "end" means that Germany will be forced to capitulate. From time to time, we are able to listen to the radio but all we hear are hysterical speeches by Hitler.

In the meantime, we see many deserters in town. Some injured soldiers, having been sent home for a holiday, did not want to return to the front. Others, taking advantage of the opportunity, simply ran away from their army divisions. Their families hide them, terrified of revealing the situation even to their closest neighbors. There are still many fanatical Nazis around like our landlady despite the fact that the war is ending so badly. Gendarmes or SS legionnaires have the right to hang any deserter they catch right in the town square without any sort of court trial. We once saw four young men hanging from ropes in the town square at Coburg. They had signs on their chests that read – "Deserters. German traitors."

One day this month, we heard talk that the western front is approaching our town. The so-called Folksturm, *which means storm troopers of the people, an army composed of mostly old folks and teenagers that is not the regular army, is taking over all governing functions from the civil administration. The only supporters of this group are the young members of* Hitlerjugend, *the Nazi youth organization, which has also joined the* Folksturm. *It is pitiful to see 16-year old boys, the milk barely dried on their chins, carrying guns and automatic rifles, heady from Nazi propaganda. These kids are marching up and down the streets of town, determined to stop the United States Army which is forcing its way into Germany ever more aggressively.*

A rumor has swept through town that the German Army is liquidating its warehouses and distributing all leftover goods to the people for free. Presumably this is being done so that goods do not fall into the hands of the enemy. This sort of information means one thing to me. The soldiers are no longer bothering to pretend that they can stop the American army. This whole affair struck me as being especially hilarious, when I saw the pathetic things that were being distributed to the public. Do the Germans really believe that the rags being passed out could possibly interest the army of the Western Allies? Of course we poor refugees were happy to get anything for free. We went by bicycle to Coburg to pick up anything which might be useful in the future though we have no idea what the future will hold for us. We stood in a long line and ultimately got some sheets. I decided that I can use these to make some clothing for us.

On our way home, we heard a thunderous noise that continued to get louder. Then the ground started shaking as well. We tossed our bicycles to the side and threw ourselves into the ditches along the road. Never before had I seen such a mass of planes flying at once. We tried to count them while we lay on the ground. There were at least 1,000 bombers. Circling this squadron were groups of fighter planes which flew faster than the bombers. All these planes nearly blocked the sunlight; their shadows drifted out across the fields. They flew high and did not shoot up or bomb this area. The German anti-aircraft defenses were silent. By this time, the Allies are able to bomb German cities uninterrupted day and night.

We got home. A strange silence hung over our town. There were no army or SS troopers in sight. The Folksturm *troops had disappeared. Planes again roared overhead. This time they were flying low. We all got nervous, fearing that the pilots might attack our town. We looked again. Snowflakes seemed to be falling from the sky – only they were pieces of white paper. Several fell into our yard as well. Printed on the papers was a message: "Germany has lost the war. Armies of the Eastern and Western Allies are united. Berlin will be taken soon. Hitler has fled; he is in hiding. The* Folksturm *advises all to lay down their weapons. Resistance will no longer serve any purpose."*

All residents are instructed to raise white flags. This sign of surrender will indicate to the Allied Army that only peaceful civilians remain in that house. The planes were still circling above when we saw white sheets flapping from the windows. But as soon as the planes flew off, all the sheets disappeared from view. People are still afraid of displaying such sentiments because Nazis and SS-ers are still around.

*Of course we did not dare hang white sheets from our windows. Our landlady would not have allowed that. She was completely hysterical. Over and over she shouted, "*Sieg Heil!*" She cursed the Allies and spared no angry words about us, the war refugees.*

The stress of waiting to find out what was going to happen next lasted for three days. The Americans overtook Coburg. The last of the retreating German Army ran around the fields and through our town. We have to remain alert and careful. A couple of SS-ers shot at some people who had accidentally gotten in their way.

April 20, 1945

The other day we could hear American artillery firing very near our town. The whistling bombs began to explode all around us. We huddled in the cellar, praying to God that no bomb would hit our home. There would be silence for a while; then the shooting would start up again. At long last, we no longer heard bombs exploding. Juozas said he was going up to look around and see what was happening in town. Suddenly we heard a roar of motor vehicles. I shouted at him to be careful – the SS might still be riding around. "No, these are tanks rolling by and they're not German. They're American tanks," Juozas replied in a happy voice.

It was true. I went outside with Juozas and looked down the street. Tanks were rolling past our house, and it was instantly obvious that the Americans had arrived. A heavy-set black man was standing halfway above the opening in a tank, glancing from side to side, smiling and gnawing on some chocolate. A sensation of ease and joy washed over me. Juozas and I had the same idea at the same time – we both started waving at the Americans, greeting them. We don't have to worry about the Germans, standing on the street with their gloomy faces anymore. The reign of the Nazis has finally ended. Ironically, today is Hitler's birthday. He is celebrating from a hideout in a bunker somewhere in Berlin.

The tanks stopped in town. Some very cheerful Americans climbed out. Laughing and waving their arms at the Germans, who were staring at them, they passed out candy to the children. Slowly the tension in people's faces seemed to melt away. The Americans have started bartering with the Germans. They offer canned goods and cigarettes in exchange for fresh eggs or a glass of milk. We just watch all this in amazement. We have already witnessed one occupation follow another in Lithuania – the Russians and then the Germans – but this invasion of Germany is completely unlike anything we have ever seen.

May 1, 1945

The Americans have taken over, but life in our little town doesn't seem to have changed much. True, the Folksturm *kids are no longer running around all over town and the Germans, who never before bothered to say hello to us, are acting friendly all of a sudden. But none of our household concerns has changed. We still receive the same food quotas according to the same old coupons issued by the German government.*

Still, there is one big change. It just hit us at once. All of us, all of a sudden, feel much braver. I still cannot envision what the future holds in store for us. But, now, we have developed a sense of pride that is different from what we have felt ever since we have been on the run.

Juozas taught me to say one sentence in English: "I am not a German. I am Lithuanian." He said it is important for me to say this whenever any American stops me and wants to see my documents.

May 8, 1945

News is spreading fast all over town. The war has ended! Germany has surrendered.

The military command of the United States has already issued an order that all residents are obligated to turn in all of their weapons. Foreigners must register at the headquarters office. We heard from others that all prisoners-of-war, refugees and persons forcibly brought into Germany are going to be sent back to their own, now liberated countries. The organizational work to accomplish this is already underway. This is very bad news for us. Where on earth are we supposed to be sent? To what country can we possibly return? Our homeland is again Soviet occupied. Our family is bound to be under a much greater threat from the Soviets than from any Germans here.

We don't exactly know how to explain this to the Americans since Russia is still their ally. We decided on a version of our story. We are not going to tell them that we ended up in Germany running from the approaching Red Army. Instead, the story is going to be that the Germans forced us to leave our homes along with their withdrawing army, and that's how we got to Germany. Then we thought this over again. There is still a problem with our story. If Germans had forced us to leave, then what is stopping us now from wanting to hurry back home?

June 3, 1945

The military administration of the United States started gathering up war refugees who are scattered throughout different villages all over the country at the end of May. Refugees are then taken to camps especially designated for them. We've been directed to go to Würzburg.

We said goodbye to our landlady on June 1st. The German surrender seems to have completely crushed her. Our neighbors saw us off, wishing us well and waving their farewells. We loaded our meager belongings on a wagon and piled in. Again we left on another trip into the unknown.

The wagons carried us to the railroad station. From there we got on a train heading for Coburg, where we spent the entire day. Walking around, we could not believe our eyes how badly this very old town had been demolished during the final weeks of the war.

Today we arrived in Würzburg. Our first impression, when we saw where we would have to live, was complete shock. These huge buildings, formerly German military barracks, are close to ruin. Several thousand people of different nationalities – war prisoners, refugees and forced labor recruits – were shoving their way inside. People were shouting, singing and embracing each other. Some danced in the courtyards of the barracks.

The worst horror is that, apparently, a large number of Russians, former prisoners-of-war, are being housed at this camp. They are celebrating the victory against Germany and their own liberation. Stunned we stood watching them racing around, fueled by vodka, waving little red flags with crude portraits of Lenin and Stalin. We've been running away from those people all this time, but now they have caught up with us, here in Bavaria.

June 5, 1945

Our first night at the camp, four of us Lithuanian families lay down to sleep in one large facility. However, I kept hearing different sounds in the room – people tossing and turning, sighing, whispering to each other. It seems that nobody could sleep. All night the singing of Katyusha *[a popular Russian song] and the squeals of a harmonica outside kept us awake.*

What weighed us all down and distressed us the most was the unknown – what will become of us tomorrow? Another concern adds to our duress. We were brought to a camp that is full of Russian prisoners. Does this mean that the Americans consider us Soviet citizens? Moscow is arguing that this is the case. What do we do if the American government decides to turn us over to their Russian ally? Should we run again? And where on earth can we go now?

Obviously this is the camp where we must stay for some time. First we have to locate a stable residence for our family. From what I can see, these people in the barracks have organized themselves by nationality. In one group, there appears to be a hundred people; at the largest barracks, a group can certainly number many more. All members of a single nationality have gathered their beds in one area; families hang sheets to separate themselves from neighboring families. New arrivals quickly claim any spare cot but always in the area of the floor taken by members of their own nationality. But there are not many of us Lithuanians.

After our sleepless night in the camp at Würzburg, Uncle Feliksas and my brother-in-law, Joseph, went out in the morning to look over this town, which consists mainly of soldiers' quarters. When they came back, they said they had seen a garage that could house us. We all went to have a look at it. This garage is badly damaged. It has no windows, but there is a roof which is in good shape. Inside it is a horrid mess, filled with piles of brick and tile shards, garbage and human waste.

"The most important thing is the roof, and it's a good one. We can patch up the holes and shovel out the trash. You'll see, we'll be able to live in it," the men explained to the rest of us. The men are right. There is enough room in the garage for all three of our families. But there sure is a lot of work before our eyes.

June 8, 1945

It only took us a couple of days to fix up the garage. The others at the barracks are jealous. We are the only ones who have our own separate little house. A few people asked us to let them join in, insisting that there is room for one more family. It makes me laugh. Nobody asked to come in with us before we got the place cleaned and patched up. A couple of days ago, these people didn't even cast an eye in this direction.

late June, 1945

We are like prisoners at this camp. A guard stands at the entrance gate; no one is allowed to leave the army town without a permit. The official explanation is that we must be protected from German vengeance. Actually this is also to protect Germans from various criminal types. There seems to be plenty of them at the camp – thefts and robberies are common.

Soon after our arrival, Joseph Gruodis' bicycle disappeared – the same bicycle he had with him for all his wanderings in Germany. That really pains his heart.

Besides thieves, there are Russians, former prisoners, who hold a smoldering hatred for the Germans. Americans are well aware of this, and that's why they don't let us out into town. That is what our lives are like within the confines of this camp. However, we have gotten used to it.

Food, though basic, is not a problem. Everyone eats together out in the courtyards, where huge kettles are set up for cooking. The fare is simple. Usually we get a thin soup which seems to be pea soup most of the time. [Since those times, I haven't been able to look at a bowl of pea soup.] Nevertheless we certainly are not starving. The children are provided an extra helping with their meals.

In a way our lives might seem almost carefree. Children play in the yard in small groups. We women handle the usual household chores like laundry. Our men walk around the camp. They have been meeting more and more Lithuanian acquaintances.

end July, 1945

The number of Lithuanians at Würzburg Camp has gotten larger quite quickly. We are a full colony of our own now and busy with all sorts of activities. A Lithuanian school has been organized for our children. We found a spot to put up a small shrine for our prayers. A choir and a dance group performed their first show after a mere month of rehearsing. I don't see any of the other national groups organizing anything like this. A lot of them look at us and shake their heads in wonder.

There are fewer Russians in the camp by now. Ukrainians, though, are having a terrible time. They are being forced into trucks and driven out into the occupational zone of the Soviet Union. This is causing so much suffering – Ukrainians are hiding anywhere that they can find. Some have jumped out of windows, as authorities chased after them. These people would rather die than be handed over into the claws of the Russians. We have heard of many Ukrainian suicides. But the deportation policy continues as usual.

The fear that we might be deported to the Soviet Union has lessened. Americans do not bother us Lithuanians. We simply go about our daily routine at the camp. It has to be the international status of Lithuania that is saving us.

[Despite the intense efforts of Soviet propaganda, the United States did not recognize the lawfulness of the occupation of Lithuania. Since we have lived

in the United States, we always leapt in fiery defense at the slightest provocation of the status of Lithuania as an occupied country. We know from our own experience the importance of diplomatic formalities.]

A few of our fellow Lithuanians are searching for blood relatives in North America. All I think about is how much I want to go back to Lithuania. Many refugees, I believe, are also ready to return home. But two concerns are always on our minds – when will the Soviet occupation end? When can we go home?

The days are passing by quickly, but the future is just as clouded as it has ever been. There is nothing else to do but worry about how to make our lives as comfortable as possible here in Germany.

Juozas started a job working for the Americans. The administrators in charge of our camp have had a difficult time interacting with us DPs (officially Displaced Persons that Lithuanians always call "dipukai"*.) We are the people who have lost our homes and most of us do not know a word of English. Americans, meanwhile, rarely know any other language except their own. They are pleased to have found Juozas. He can speak a little German and Russian and already manages quite well with English.*

After several weeks of living at Würzburg Camp, I happened to answer an American official in English. He, like all other Americans, communicated with me and the rest of us mostly in sign language. The man was taken aback by my reply. He asked me, "Where did you learn English?" I told him that I had studied English in school in Lithuania. Right away he invited me to see the commander in charge of the camp who asked me a few questions and then offered me the job of translating for them.

My first days at work were incredibly difficult. I had to translate English, not only into Lithuanian but also into German, Russian and even Polish. My school-level English differed greatly from the colloquial English spoken by the Americans. At that time my German was weaker than my English, and I barely knew Russian and Polish. I would come home completely drained and exhausted.

The worst thing was that I had to translate mostly for the commander, a major in the United States Army who was from Texas and had such a heavy accent that I often could not understand a word he was saying. I could not bring myself to admit this to him as I surely didn't want to lose my job. I did not know what to do.

The major delivered all sorts of speeches that I had to translate to the people settling into the camp. I could barely comprehend some of his sentences but I had to pretend that I knew what he was saying. In reality two independent speeches would be delivered in such cases – his in English and mine in German or Russian. One talk, I'm sure, was not like the other. Luckily the Americans did not understand my translations. I must have had a reasonably good sense of what the major said because somehow I never got into trouble. In a while I got to the point where I understood him better. The level of my English skills improved greatly in a matter of a few months while working for the Americans.

Once a very funny thing happened. A fellow DP came in to see the commander. In a terrible English accent, he tried to explain that I was doing a very poor job of translating; obviously he was after my job. The major was rifling through his papers and not listening very intently. When the man paused in his tirade, the commander turned to me and said, "Joe, why aren't you translating what he is saying?"

Naturally the man understood what the commander had said and he looked as though someone had slapped him in the face. "He says that he wants to translate for you," I said.

"Tell him that we don't need him; we already have a translator," answered the major without raising his eyes from his papers. That poor man's face turned completely red and he left the office. Never again did he try to push me out of my position.

Once I started working at the camp command headquarters, our lives changed dramatically. I did not get any salary, but my family was allowed to move out of the camp into a house where the American employees for the camp and UNRRA were housed. (The United Nations Relief and Rehabilitation Administration was the major organization aiding war refugees at the time.) I was provided a separate apartment which had spacious rooms with all the conveniences.

The best privilege was that we could eat in the American cafeteria. We felt as though we had landed on a different planet; the contrast to the poor food at the camp was huge. We got to taste the soft, white bread that Americans ate. There had never been any such bread in prewar Lithuania, and maybe that is why we thought that it tasted so delicious. Alexandra developed a special fondness for peanut butter. Because of its brown color, Alexandra thought that it was mustard at first. (Later, when we lived in the United States permanently, this was our family joke – we made "mustard" sandwiches.) Another new delicacy for us was orange marmalade. For dinner we devoured American chicken which seemed to melt in our mouths. Our favorite snacks were dried fruits, which we gulped by the handfuls.

In a way it was disturbing to be enjoying all this delicious food while the others got such meager fare. It especially distressed Alexandra that Victoria's poor children could not get such food at the refugee camp. The head cook at the American cafeteria was a Lithuanian woman from the United States. She took us under her wing and gave us some extra provisions whenever she could. Alexandra would spread slices of white bread with a thick layer of peanut butter and orange marmalade and secretly take them for our relatives to enjoy.

No one who did not actually live at the camp could enter there without a permit. But this did not discourage Alexandra. She discovered a hole in the wire fence and would squeeze through the opening into the camp. It did not bother her that she risked having security detain her every time she did this. Had she been discovered smuggling food from the American cafeteria into the camp, most likely I would have lost my job. But Alexandra was so joyful after these secret trips that I overlooked any potential danger. She would glow with delight, telling me how Victoria and her children had smacked their lips eating the sandwiches. These were named "*buterbrodai à la* Alexandra" (*buterbrodai* was the Lithuanian adaptation of the German words for butter and bread to mean sandwich). I knew from the example set by my parents that shared happiness is the only true happiness. Peanut butter and jelly sandwiches were a pleasure for all, weary from the horrors and hardships of the war.

But this unaccustomed food, no matter how good it tasted, turned out to be a hazard. Since early in my childhood, I was very sensitive to food. All of a sudden, I was eating so many new products, and that must have caused some sort of allergic reaction. For three months, I was hardly able to eat a thing. I was well over six feet tall, but my weight dropped to about 120 pounds.

Several lower-rank American officers also worked with the major at the command headquarters of the gigantic Würzburg Camp. They had a lot of work to do dealing with all the newly arrived Displaced Persons who were grouped by nationality. Some people had to be transferred to different camps; others were deported to their native lands. Deportees primarily comprised Russians, Ukrainians and others from countries under the Soviet Union.

Russians living at the camp were definitely not all the same; some did not want to return to the Soviet Union. The situation was especially dangerous for the so-called White Russians who had fled Russia right after the revolution and settled in Poland, Hungary and Czechoslovakia until the Second World War. When the Soviet Army advanced towards these countries, the White Russians ran to Germany. Death was a near certainty for them if they should again fall into the hands of the Stalin regime. Nonetheless, Americans intended to give them over to the Soviets. United States officers had no idea that prison camps awaited these people back in their country of origin. In general most Americans did not understand the true nature of the Soviet regime. They simply considered Russia to be their ally in the war against Germany.

We Lithuanians often had to answer one especially naive question – "Why don't you want to go back to your home country?" I remember a time in Nürtingen where I had a discussion with a young American officer who had just graduated from Princeton University. He sincerely tried to convince me that Lithuanians should go back to Lithuania to rebuild the country and that the Bolsheviks were truly not as horrible as I believed.

Once a report came in that a long procession of trucks was arriving to carry some 1,000 refugees from the camp. Earmarked for deportation to the Soviet Zone were several hundred Russians and all the White Russians at the camp. All of them were intelligent people from the aristocratic class – counts and dukes who still used their appropriate titles. Some knew German, so I was able to talk with them. I especially remember the unofficial leader of their group, a tall, lean man with slightly graying hair and a noble face.

I tried my best to explain to the American commander that these Russians, despite the fact that they had been born in Russia, could not be lumped into one group with all the others from the Soviet Union. These people were absolutely not Soviet citizens. I thought I was explaining all this most thoroughly when one young lieutenant merely shrugged his shoulders and asked, "But are they Russians?" A Russian was a Russian to the Americans and should be returned to Stalin.

I realized that it was impossible to convince a single person; all of them simply adhered to the policy of the United States. Therefore I went to see the leader of the group and told him about the danger that threatened. "You must leave tonight. Otherwise you will be taken to Stalin's camps tomorrow," I warned them.

The facilities were always under guard. However the guards were refugees themselves and they were not always attentive to their duties. That night all the White Russians of our camp slipped away.

The following day, the Americans began seating people into the trucks, checking them off their lists as they got in. The officials soon realized that some people were missing. However, nobody rushed to go out and search for them. War refugees, at that time, were counted by the millions. The Americans did not trouble themselves over a few dozen refugees.

By this time, a great many Lithuanians were living at the Würzburg Displaced Persons Camp along with a smaller group of Latvians. One day the camp commander told me that the Baltic people were earmarked for a move to other locations. Because they could not be turned over to Russians against their will, only those who so desired would be returned to the country of their birth.

In the meantime, the boundaries of the occupational zones were shifting, and Würzburg was probably going to be put under the jurisdiction of the Soviet Union. As it turned out, this did not happen. Nonetheless the boundary of the Russian Occupation Zone did pass very near Würzburg. I was not comfortable with this situation. When the American administration provided people from the Baltics a choice for their destination out of Würzburg, I decided we should travel to Nürtingen where a large colony of Lithuanians had settled.

November, 1945

We have spent nearly half a year at Würzburg without any great worries. The Displaced Persons Camp has gotten smaller, as some left for their homelands on their own free will and others were forcibly deported. Still others left for different

German towns and cities. The moment Juozas learned that Würzburg might transfer into Russian hands, he no longer wanted to remain here. Even though our living conditions are very good compared to the usual postwar situation, there is no future for us at Würzburg. Our days are routine and monotonous. I can sense that Juozas is anxious to get actively involved in more endeavors and make contacts with other Lithuanians.

Juozas started investigating how he might enter some German university to study. He got the idea to move to Nürtingen which is alongside the French Occupational Zone. We heard that many of our acquaintances have settled there, and Lithuanian organizations are being formed. Moreover the famed, old Tübingen University is not far from the city and located within the French Zone. Juozas spent some time devising a plan whereby he could study at the university. In the meantime, we could live in Nürtingen where we could participate in the activities of the Lithuanian colony.

I liked his idea as well. Juozas put in a request with the commander to relieve him of his translating duties, and his resignation was approved. The UNRRA branch administrators thanked Juozas for his work and presented him with a fancy leather briefcase as a gift of appreciation.

When the day of our departure was near, the Lithuanians of Würzburg Camp organized a going away party to bid our final farewells. It is sad to part with our relatives and friends; we can feel that everyone is sincerely sorry to see us leave. The entire colony presented us with a lovely picture. Then the community treated us with a concert. Afterwards we all gathered in a room where speeches to honor Juozas were delivered, highlighting his contributions to the Lithuanian colony at Würzburg.

Early the next morning, we loaded our belongings into a car provided by the UNRRA and off we went to Nürtingen. From there it is about 28 kilometers to Tübingen. Stuttgart is also nearby. Electric trains run frequently between cities. So this is really an advantageous location.

At Nürtingen we learned that Lithuanians live in private apartments, not in a camp like Würzburg. The first thing we did once we arrived there was to visit the Aglinskas family, who has been here for some time. Juozas went to the landlady of their apartment, and immediately she agreed to accept our family as well. We were provided with our own little room. Then we went to the UNRRA and registered our residency. That organization has the responsibility for supplying our food.

Jurate (top row, third from left) with her classmates in Nürtingen, 1945

Picnic in Nürtingen with Juozas' sister, Victoria, and her two children, 1945

We stayed in the room provided by the Aglinskas landlady for a very short time because the UNRRA decided to relocate all Germans to a nearby block and move displaced persons into their residences. Along with Dr. Aglinskas and his family, we have settled into a nice house. They moved to the second floor, and we took the first floor. We have three whole rooms to ourselves!

Juozas made contacts with Americans in no time at all and he occasionally translates for UNRRA officials. The Americans at Nürtingen invite Juozas when they need to resolve matters at the Lithuanian colony.

There are many Lithuanians in our colony here at Nürtingen. Despite the obvious German resentment, Lithuanians are comparatively well established. They took over the excellently installed homes of former Nazis. Life in our community is quite lively. A Lithuanian school has even been organized that Jurate and Victoria's son, Gediminas, have started attending.

[Many years later, Juozas had the opportunity to speak with Dwight Eisenhower after his term as President of the United States. Eisenhower expressed high praise for Lithuanians during that talk. While Commander of the United States Occupation Army in Germany during the postwar years, he said he visited war refugee camps. Eisenhower remembered that Lithuanians had amazed him. We were ahead of other national groups in terms of our living arrangements and public and cultural activities. Only Lithuanians had managed to establish schools, publish newspapers and books and form theater troupes, orchestras and even a ballet studio. Lithuanians even maintained their own police force to protect the refugees from the frequent thefts and attacks in the camps.]

December, 1945

Juozas started his studies at Tübingen University which will lead to a master's degree in economics. He is attending lectures daily. He didn't have to take the entrance exam since his diploma from Vilnius University was sufficient for acceptance. But he is having a hard time with his studies, because classes are held in German, and his language skills are not that strong. Most of the students are, of course, Germans; many of them came to the university directly from the front. Juozas tells me that they are very hostile towards people from the victorious West and all other nationalities.

During one lecture, a professor dared to criticize the Nazis and Hitler, stating that Germany, which had given in to the influence of their demagogy, met with a terrible national catastrophe. The entire auditorium of students started stomping their feet and whistling to stop the lecture.

Juozas is definitely not lonely at Tübingen University. A whole group of Lithuanian refugees is studying there. A large community of our countrymen has also settled in the French Occupation Zone, very near to another Lithuanian colony in Reutlingen. At Pfullingen, which is also close to Tübingen, VLIK [acronym for 'Supreme Committee for the Liberation of Lithuania'] set up an office for its operations. Monsignor Mykolas Kuprevičius has been heading the organization. Juozas Brazaitis, the former Prime Minister of the Provisional Government, and Steponas Kairys, the first VLIK Chairman, live in Reutlingen along with many more activists of the Lithuanian community. Members of the Lithuanian Activist Front are also around, and Juozas is in contact with them already.

I enjoy going to Tübingen with Juozas from time to time. We meet up with some of our old-time friends and acquaintances from Vilnius and Kaunas – Professors Zenonas Ivinskis [a distinguished historian who authored numerous works on Lithuania during the Middle Ages], Antanas Maceina *[one of the best-known interwar Lithuanian philosophers in Catholic existentialism], Antanas Salys [a famed linguist who specialized in Baltic cultures and comparative research in languages], Juozas Girnius [a publicist and philosopher], Jonas Grinius [a literary scholar and dramaturgist] and Adolfas Damušis [one of the organizers of the anti-Soviet, June 1941 Uprising, then declared a Minister of the Interim Government of Lithuania, later a participant in the anti-Nazi movement and one of the organizers of VLIK, the 'Supreme Committee for the Liberation of Lithuania' who returned to live in independent Lithuania after 1990]. We've made new friends there as well. Juozas has formed a tight friendship with another student at the university, Kęstutis Valiūnas.*

Christmas 1945

Our first postwar Christmas has arrived. Our future remains as uncertain as ever. All the Lithuanians of Nürtingen sat around a common table at the UNRRA cafeteria on Christmas Eve night to celebrate our Kūčios. *This was not a happy night. The only thing that everyone talked about was – when are we going to be able to return to our homeland? I'm beginning to think that it's no longer very realistic. But I try to be positive. I believe that it is essential to try to find happiness in life, no matter in what situation people might find themselves.*

As soon as we got home after our supper, we put Jurate to bed and decorated our Christmas tree. The joy of our child, when she saw the tree upon awakening – the first Christmas tree that she has ever had – made this day a special one for us too. Hope for a brighter future seemed to light up in our hearts.

February 18, 1946

Today Jurate is three years old. Now she understands that we are celebrating her birthday. I baked a cake for her, and we lit three candles on top of it. Jurate's godfather, Vladas Kulbokas, and his wife came over and brought her a doll. The Aglinskas family also came with their son, Audrius, who is only a few months older than Jurate.

It is so wonderful to observe our child and watch her develop into a personality with her own ideas and desires. She doesn't like to play alone; she keeps running after Audrius. Eventually he starts whining because Jurate is bothering him. Then I run over to make peace between them. Jurate is very frisky. She no longer sleeps during the day; she wakes up early and goes to bed late. I always worry that she doesn't eat enough. She has gotten taller and thinner; she looks peaked to me. I wish spring would come soon, so she can play out in the yard. That would make my days happier as well.

By the house provided for us in Nürtingen, 1946

Spring, 1946

Springtime brought us some good news – the Gruodis family left Würzburg at the end of March and came to live in Nürtingen. Now I don't have to be alone all day at home when Juozas leaves for Tübingen in the morning.

I have a feeling that Juozas is not getting much from his studies at the university. It takes a lot of time for him to travel back and forth every day. He eats nothing but sandwiches all day. He comes home later in the evening. But right now he is just happy to have something definite to do since finding a job is nearly impossible these days.

3-year old Jurate, Nürtingen, 1946

Time seems to pass more quickly for us women. We have the children to look after, our homes to clean and laundry and sewing to do. Some men have started teaching or gotten involved in politics or cultural endeavors. Some have taken up speculating. But most of the men can't think of anything specific to occupy their time so they spend their days and nights just hanging around, playing cards, drinking and looking for casual romances.

The administration of the United States seems to have realized that the current lives of war refugees, which are without the slightest hope for the future, cannot continue forever. This problem must get resolved. Forcible deportation to Eastern and Central European countries, now occupied by the Soviets, is no longer a threat. The relations between the Western Allies and the Soviet Union have clearly started to sour. In the meantime, Germany is demolished and impoverished. So many German cities are in total ruin. It looks like it will take the country many decades to get back on its feet.

It is obvious that millions of war refugees cannot be accommodated here indefinitely. To add to the problem, the German outlook towards refugees has grown more hostile. Germans have to live in near-hunger themselves and, when they see the idlers and the drunkards, they can't hide their disgust with the "freeloading" refugees. Any Germans who have displaced persons renting rooms from them are making every effort to evict them from their homes.

late Spring 1946

We are living in a separate house which had been confiscated from a Nazi. We thought that we were under no threat of eviction. One evening, however, I returned from town to find a very agitated Aglinskas family at home. It was hard to believe what they told me. Several Germans with an American army officer in the lead were here, demanding that we all move out immediately! I stood frozen to the spot; I had no idea what to do. The American started ordering us to take our things outside.

Luckily Juozas came back from Tübingen in the nick of time. In English he immediately demanded that the American officer show his identification and a written order for evicting us from the residence which the United States administration had designated for us. The man was at a loss for words. He quickly disappeared from our home along with the Germans without showing us any documents.

Today Juozas told me that the American who had tried to move us out was only a lieutenant. When Juozas went to speak with the higher-ranking American officials, apparently they were very surprised to hear what happened. They were not aware of any order to evict us. It seems that the lieutenant had done this entirely on his own accord. It seems that he has a German lover, and she convinced him that he should kick us out and turn over the house to her family. He assumed that his American epaulets were enough to intimidate a war refugee. Completely self-assured, he swaggered over to us, fully expecting that we would instantly obey him and never complain!

Departures – To Return or Not To Return?

The first year after the war flew by in lightning speed. The second one, since we had left our homeland, was half-gone. Lithuanians still waited for a miracle. Most everyone expected that the Western countries would start a war with the Soviet Union and liberate all the enslaved nations. I, however, had stopped believing in miracles even as relations between the United States and England with Russia had become much more strained. In truth, a new war was developing. Only this time, it was a Cold War and it would last five decades.

While I was translating for the Americans, I had the opportunity to read *The Herald Tribune, The Financial Times,* and the *Stars and Stripes,* the

United States Army newspaper. Summarizing the information from these newspapers, I wrote reviews and commentaries on international events and published them in *Žiburiai 'Lights'* (one of the first of many Lithuanian newspapers published in Germany in DP camps). I also gave lectures to the Lithuanian colonies at Nürtingen and Tübingen on world events. I spoke my own opinion openly; I did not avoid voicing my skepticism regarding the resolve of the West to use military force for liberating the occupied countries of Eastern and Central Europe. It was entirely clear to me that multilateral treaties had laid the foundation for the existing situation. The world had already been divided up into spheres of influence. A long and exhausting confrontation had begun but it was one which avoided any direct military clash with the Soviet Union. This confrontation was on ideological, political and economic grounds.

Much to my surprise, General Povilas Plechavičius stood up during one of my lectures. "You, young man, do not have the slightest understanding about politics or military strategy. You are simply misleading people!" he said with anger. The General then proceeded to outline his own viewpoint on the matter which was contrary to mine. He said that tremendous allied forces were concentrating near the Eastern borders, developing modern munitions facilities and delivering strict warnings to Stalin. The West was forced to act this way to protect its geopolitical interests; the logic of world occurrences demanded no less. He argued that a war should erupt any day now. "We will all be able to return to Lithuania by the end of this year," the General predicted.

The audience broke out in applause. I had to stand by silently. It was entirely understandable to me that all those gathered to hear the talk longed desperately to believe in the words of General Plechavičius. Deep in my heart, I also wanted him to be right. But I felt our general was naïve in his thinking, and that my views were probably closer to the truth.

People were very distressed about what the future held in store for them. Psychologically they were inclined to cling to any rumor about some sort of Western ultimatum to Stalin and the liberation of East European countries which, they believed, was due to begin any day.

The news coming from Lithuania also solidified such hope. Our partisans were engaged in a harsh war against the Soviets. (After the defeat of Germany, when Lithuania fell under Soviet jurisdiction, some

10,000 Lithuanian men retreated to the forests to fight the Soviet regime in what has been termed the Partisan Movement.) Accurate reporting was sorely lacking. Information consisted primarily of various rumors, which spread like wildfire. Once Jonas Deksnys, a journalist and an initiator of the Lithuanian Freedom Fighters Union (a strong anti-Nazi underground organization), forced his way out of Lithuania into the West, we received more reliable news about the Partisan Movement. We heard that British Intelligence was particularly interested in the events in our homeland. But, obviously, Great Britain did not share any of its information with us.

I had many discussions with my friend, Julijonas Būtėnas, about all this. One question never gave him any rest – what should be done now? What could one man do to help his homeland?

Julijonas Būtėnas – an Unforgettable Friend

The story about this noble and grand man must be told. I cannot forget his place in my life as I pen my memoirs. Even now there are people still alive who knew him and appreciated his friendship and for whom his tragic death remains a painful remembrance. Before my eyes, I can still see a young man, more than six-feet tall with a strong build and masculine facial features. He will always be young in everyone's memory because he was only 36 years of age when he died.

Julijonas attracted all who knew him with his charisma. There was one important secret to his charm. He had a rare gift from God: whenever he interacted with anyone, he would focus his entire attention on that person. It was as though his own personality had no importance. If you happened to ask him about his current endeavors, he would simply change the topic of conversation. He was never interested in any compliments about his own many accomplishments. With a gracious flair, he would turn the conversation around to draw others into talking about their own ideas and projects. This was far more than the good manners of a well-bred man – he was sincerely interested in others. He never failed to observe the work and activities of his friends.

I got my share of spiritual support when I'd run into Julijonas during my student days in Kaunas and later in Vilnius. "You know, Juozas," he would tell me, "I read your last work. Your thinking is right on point..." And off he'd go, discussing my ideas. Excitement and joy sprang naturally from within him as he would compliment some article of mine. Naturally it gratified me to hear that and inspired me to take on yet another project.

Julijonas graduated from Kaunas Military School a year after I did although he was about three years older than I. I met him by chance at Vytautas Magnus University in Kaunas. Afterwards we continued getting together from time to time to discuss different topics.

He was the political analyst for *XX Amžius '20th Century'* newspaper and was widely known for his many talents. Julijonas was an excellent linguist. He was fluent in English, even though, between the World Wars, German was the main foreign language studied in Lithuania. Not only did he speak English but he also had a flair for the written word. In addition to German, he had a decent command of French, Russian, Spanish, Latvian and Swedish. He had learned most of these languages entirely independently from books without attending any courses. He read various newspapers, listened to foreign radio stations and used the information he gathered in the articles he wrote for the press.

After I left for Vilnius University, I did not see Julijonas for a few years. It wasn't until the Soviet occupation that we again struck up a relationship. Some of my underground activities led me to Kaunas to meet with members of the Lithuanian Activist Front. During one of these trips, I had occasion to see Julijonas and speak with him about the developing situation.

I remember how much he worried about the looming threat that I could be arrested in Vilnius because Lithuanians were the ethnic minority in the city. From the first days of occupation, Julijonas clearly saw that a catastrophe had befallen our country. Independence was completely lost, and the Soviets did not intend to allow it ever. At that time many people still clung to the illusion that Stalin was only seeking military and political domination to prevent Germany from getting a foothold in this region. Many refused to believe that Stalin intended to destroy our statehood.

Shortly after our talk, Dr. Ignas Skrupskelis, the editor of *20th Century* newspaper, was arrested. Julijonas was also in danger of being arrested, but we heard that he had managed to flee to Germany. That was no simple matter. Russia had already isolated Lithuania from the rest of the world. At all the borders, the fields were plowed and Russian soldiers, patrolling with dogs, would shoot anyone attempting to get into Germany.

Julijonas Būtėnas wasted no time in returning to Lithuania as soon as Germany attacked the Soviet Union and occupied our land. Once again he proceeded to publish articles in newspapers, primarily *Į Laisvę 'Towards Freedom'* and *Ateitis 'The Future'*.

In 1942 he left for Berlin and sent correspondences to the Lithuanian press. Professor Pranas Padalis and other activists from the political headquarters of the Activist Front said that Julijonas was their representative in Berlin. There he made contacts with journalists from neutral countries and organized a channel for sending news from Lithuania to the West. Informational reviews that our underground prepared about the situation in Eastern Europe and the dislocation of the German Army in this region (similar to the one which I delivered to Berlin in September of 1943) were sent to the Western Allies via this channel. The two days which I spent in Berlin with Julijonas provided the opportunity for us to get to know each other better and become fast friends. As he showed me around Berlin, we discussed the future of our country. The occupational regime was becoming increasingly more brutal in Lithuania at that time. Julijonas had also heard that Nazis treated Lithuanians not much better than the Poles whom they totally disparaged. He was also aware that the Nazis considered Lithuanians to be inferior to the Latvians and Estonians, since their countries had historically been more influenced by German culture.

After my Berlin trip, I again lost contract with Julijonas for a time. I heard that he returned to Lithuania that same year of 1943 and took on aide-de-camp duties for the rudiments of a Lithuanian Army which General Povilas Plechavičius was attempting to form anew. After Russia had taken over a large part of the territory of Lithuania, its military units were sent into Latvia. Here German divisions surrounded them along with enemy forces. The German military command, infuriated by General Plechavičius' actions, ordered that all Lithuanian soldiers be disarmed and the officers of our Army imprisoned at Salaspil Concentration Camp outside of Riga. Actually this saved the men from sure death. Once the Russians launched their attack, the arrested Lithuanian officers were evacuated to Germany by boat. In the meantime, German units in Latvia were surrounded and completely destroyed. The Soviets took all German survivors as prisoners of war.

Julijonas escaped from the prison camp in Germany and witnessed the arrival of the Allied Army.

We met again in early 1946 when I began studying at Tübingen University. Julijonas lived nearby in Reutlingen at the time. He had started to work for the VLIK informational service. The moment we saw each other, we embraced, remembering our days in Berlin when I had brought underground information earmarked for the West. Henceforth we maintained frequent and close contacts. Both of us were writing articles for *Žiburiai 'Lights'* Newspaper. I wrote reviews of the American press, whereas he wrote political articles.

I lost touch with Julijonas and soon afterwards I left for the United States. Four years later, I met with Adolfas Damušis, who had just emigrated from Germany. He told me about the last deeds of Julijonas Būtėnas. Julijonas decided to fly back to Lithuania from Germany. He parachuted from a plane over its territory and actively joined the Partisan Movement, which was badly undermined by that time.

This news stunned me. I may have been the only one who knew the kind of insane resolve that was required to undertake such a drastic action. Once Julijonas and I went into the Alps for a mountain excursion, where he confided in me that he had a mortal fear of heights. I could only imagine the strength and will power it took for Julijonas to train for parachute jumping, much less actually to do it. What stress Julijonas must have experienced, leaping from a plane down into the forests of Lithuania! The love for his homeland overcame his fear.

He must have innately known that this was a leap to his death. NKVD henchmen surrounded Julijonas a month later in the Kazlų Rūda forests, where he was killed in April of 1951.

Fateful Decisions

I was already making plans to leave for the United States while traveling in the mountains with Julijonas. It was entirely clear to me that Lithuania would not be liberated any time soon, notwithstanding the popular opinion of the Lithuanian colony. I realized that I would have to make a new life for my family and myself in a foreign land. There was no reason to remain in a demolished Germany. By that time, other Lithuanians were also thinking that their only choice was to emigrate somewhere. Some options were Canada, Brazil or Argentina, where there were colonies of Lithuanians who had settled there during earlier periods. I considered the United States to be the most suitable place for us. I knew that the wealthiest country in the world would hold the most opportunities for a normal life. Kęstutis Valiūnas, my friend at Tübingen University, thought the same. He was already encouraging me to leave for the United States and even go into business with him there.

Western countries were already planning to relocate millions of war refugees from the Soviet occupied countries of Eastern and Central Europe for more stable lives. By the fall of 1946, the UNRRA began moving people from Germany on a predetermined quota basis. The United States agreed to accommodate the greatest number of displaced persons. Canada allocated another large quota, and Australia, New Zealand, Columbia and even South Africa provided for certain numbers of immigrants.

Nevertheless, that was only the start of the wave of emigration from Germany. The only people able to leave at the outset were those with relatives at destination countries who would agree to guarantee care for them. Therefore Jews were granted most of the initial emigration visas because the Jewish community in the United States was the most numerous and retained the strongest organizations. In addition the world showed Jews the greatest empathy as the national group which had suffered the most from the Nazis. A few Lithuanians who had close family ties in the United States also left during 1946.

By this time I could speak English comparatively well. At the American Consulate at Stuttgart, I found out that visas were provided without limitations for persons who were going to the United States to study. I

In Germany, just before leaving for the United States, 1946

decided that I should try to get accepted at some university in the United States. Another idea crossed my mind. I would ask for a scholarship from any institution of higher education that was willing to take me. I discussed my thoughts with Hugh Toomey, a representative for the National Catholic Aid Organization in Stuttgart.

"What a great idea!" he told me. "If you happen to get a positive response from any university, I will make sure that our organization pays your travel expenses. Then you would be able to leave with your entire family," he promised.

Up to that time, I knew nothing about colleges in the United States; I had not even heard of any of their names. Reading the newspapers, I noticed that Harvard and Yale were often mentioned but I had no idea what made them special.

When I asked Toomey where I should apply, he recommended that I write letters to universities on Long Island, in Pittsburg, Pennsylvania and a few other places. However, I was not sure that I should follow his advice. Looking through an old World Almanac, I found listings of several thousand universities and colleges in the United States along with information about student enrollment and professorships as well as the size of their endowments. I made note of which universities were the richest and had the highest budgets at their disposal.

I met with Toomey again and told him that I intended to send applications to the ten richest universities, starting with Harvard and Yale. "They control the most money, so it seems to me that they will be the most likely to provide me with a scholarship," I explained my reasoning to Toomey.

"Oh, no," he frowned. "This is not a good idea. These universities are definitely not for you. All of them are Ivy League," he explained.

"What does that mean – Ivy League?" I asked him.

"Those are the most prestigious universities. They are very selective. Only the children of the most prominent and affluent families are able to study there. You will be much better off applying to smaller schools in places like Detroit or Tennessee," Hugh tried to convince me. He himself had graduated from Springfield College in Massachusetts and could not imagine that Harvard or Yale would accept someone like me, a poor war refugee who was still dreaming about gaining entry into the United States. Such universities were inaccessible even to him, a citizen of the United States.

Toomey had grown up in a family of modest means. His father worked as a shoe salesman in a store. I had a chance to visit his family much later when I was living in the United States and found them to be warm and delightful people. It turned out that after I went into business, I was able to hire Toomey, who had been so helpful to me in Germany. (This old friend of mine has since died, but his son, whom I have known from birth, still visits us from time to time.)

Although I knew nothing about America at that time, my intuition told me that I should not follow my friend's advice even though I'm sure it was well-meant. Without saying anything more to him, I concluded that the most affluent schools would be more generous in providing financial aid for my studies. Besides I was already following a principle that I adhered to all my life – always reach for the highest goal. A lesser pursuit often takes as much time and effort as the grander one.

I discussed my thoughts with Julijonas Būtėnas. He did not intend to leave Europe because he was so involved in his activities with the VLIK organization. Nonetheless he backed my idea. "Why not try? After all, you have nothing to lose." He promised to help me write my entrance applications.

Julijonas filled out my forms and wrote the letters to the universities in the United States. To those he attached notarized copies of my diploma from Vilnius University, a listing of my final exam grades (I had passed all my classes except two with the highest ranking of 5) and my photographs. I sent out my applications to the top ten schools.

I was beside myself waiting for replies from America. I prayed to God that at least one of those universities would accept me and give me a scholarship. The first reply arrived at long last. My hand trembled as I opened the letter. I was accepted! I wanted to dance with joy. Then a second and a third letter came in. Unbelievably all ten universities had accepted me.

I was dazed by all this unexpected good fortune. All the time I kept wondering, which university should I accept – Harvard or Yale?

Yale informed me that it was able to provide me with a doctoral study program at no cost and a grant of $500. Harvard also offered me a scholarship but said it would resolve the matter of further financial assistance only after I had arrived in the States. Well, being a Lithuanian, I came to the conclusion that a sparrow in the hand is worth more than the eagle in the air. I selected Yale University.

With the letter from Yale in hand, I went to the United States Consulate in Stuttgart to apply for a visa to the United States. The Vice Consul was astonished as he read my letter. "Do you realize, young man, that you have been accepted by one of the finest universities in the United States? A great many Americans would love to change places with you right now."

This tremendous success marked the fate of the rest of my life. A prestigious university offered even more than an excellent education. I understood that social status was also important in the United States. And I knew that forming advantageous acquaintanceships could lead to many opportunities.

I've often wondered why I was one of the few Lithuanian war refugees who was so lucky to meet with such early success. Apparently I was the first with the idea to seek out the best universities in the United States.

It was only 1946, and many still clung to the hope of returning to their homelands. All in all, no one really knew about such possibilities; therefore no one thought of knocking at the hospitable doors of an American university. A war refugee from Eastern Europe was a novelty and deemed worthy of charity. I am a living example of an old American truism – it's important to be in the right place at the right time.

The letter of acceptance from Yale arrived in November of 1946. The diploma which I held from Vilnius University did not grant a formal master's degree in economics but did permit me to pursue a doctorate, skipping over the work for a master's. My studies were to begin in September of 1947, for a duration of four years.

All we needed now were our visas and we could pack our bags. The United States had a quota policy, permitting certain numbers of people from different countries to immigrate on a yearly basis. But these rules presented no problems for me. The Vice Consul explained that my student visa would be in my hands soon.

We spent Christmas with our friends in Nürtingen. A sense of adventure pervaded the mood of the holiday. We would be the first in our social circle to immigrate to the United States. Not a single person had a word to say against our decision. Julijonas Būtėnas, Professors Antanas Maceina, Zenonas Ivinskis and all our other friends were all sincerely delighted that I had managed to be accepted by Yale. They wished us luck and bid their fondest farewells.

There was only one note of sadness. We would soon be traveling out of Europe for thousands of miles from our homeland and we would be far away from our relatives and friends in Germany. I consoled myself with the thought that, if Lithuania should again be independent, I could always return home. A Yale education could prove very useful in rebuilding our country in the future. Nevertheless, anxiety about the unknown weighed upon me.

The letter from the U.S. Consulate with our visas arrived right after Christmas. It informed us that we should go to a distribution camp in Stuttgart. We will reside there until our turn comes for passage on a ship, carrying war refugees to the United States.

Fare Thee Well, Europe

January 28, 1947

We had to wait nearly a month for our ship. Just now we learned that we have to go to Bremen and from there we will sail for America. The saddest part was having to say goodbye to Victoria and her family. I will miss them terribly.

We had to go through customs control before getting on the bus to take us to Bremen. American officials rifled through our baggage, checking for any illegal items which we might be trying to take into America. They were even suspicious of Lithuanian books and notes. I was afraid that they might take this diary that Juozas gave me on the occasion of Jurate's birth in which I have written my experiences and most secret thoughts. I hated to think that some stranger might start reading my diary. I handed it over to Victoria, telling her, "Hold on to this until you get to America yourself or just burn it." Just then I noticed that the official who had been examining our bags moved a bit farther away. He was talking to somebody with his back towards us. Victoria quickly sneaked the diary back into my hands. We have saved my memories!

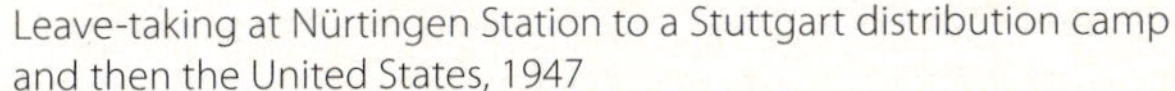

Leave-taking at Nürtingen Station to a Stuttgart distribution camp and then the United States, 1947

January 31, 1947

It's awfully cold in Bremen. Jurate and I both caught such bad colds that we had to miss the first boat assigned to us. Luckily it was not a big problem. We're both back on our feet, and our new ship leaves in just two days.

February 2, 1947

Today we will be leaving for the United States from the Port of Bremerhaven. Our ship is named the Ernie Pyle in honor of an American journalist who had been killed in the war. To us it seems like a high-class ocean liner but actually it's a basic military transport carrier. In comparison to other carriers, this is a small one. Before it was used to haul troops from America to Europe. Now several thousand civilians are traveling on this ship to the New World. The majority of the passengers are Jewish. They were first on the list for emigration to the United States because they had suffered the most from the Nazi regime. Few Lithuanians are immigrating to the United States right now. There are only about twenty Lithuanians on board with us.

I am filled with mixed feelings. I am very happy that the period in our lives of just waiting and having no clear objectives has finally come to a close. Though America is very far away, beyond this ocean that is endlessly rising and falling in waves, my heart pounds in anxious anticipation. I believe we're sailing to a land of freedom and endless opportunities.

Aboard the SS Ernie Pyle, Feb., 1947

We are on our way with a scholarship from Yale University for Juozas to study for his doctorate degree. His studies are not due to begin until the fall. In the meantime, the wind is whistling through our pockets – we don't have a single dollar. We also don't know anyone who might help us in America. But I feel confident about my husband. I am sure that, as always, he will think of a way for us to get settled and survive the half-year before he starts getting his scholarship payments.

Another feeling weighs heavily on me – a sense of loss. Visions of Lithuania and pleasant memories of my life there appear in my mind. I fully realize that we have to leave Germany, now in ruins from the war. Nevertheless, tears rolled from my eyes as I watched Europe's shoreline slowly disappearing in the distance. Will I ever see these lands again? The stretch of water between our ship and the Port of Bremerhaven became ever wider until the knot in my chest burst, and I started weeping.

"Alytė, my dear," Juozas consoled me in a calm voice. "I swear to you that we will come back to Europe one day and visit all of its most beautiful places."

I don't really believe him, but he did such a good job of comforting me that I calmed down and started feeling better.

February 4, 1947

The first two days at sea have been fun.

The way the boat is set up, the women and children are separated from the men. However, we got the better deck and the more comfortable cabins. The one problem is my bed which is right under the ceiling. The upper bunk sways and at night I'm afraid that Jurate and I might fall out while we sleep. I found a way to snooze, holding tightly on to my little girl with all my muscles taut. Naturally I haven't gotten much rest this way.

The food on the ship is delicious. Children and women eat in their own cafeteria, away from the men. White tablecloths cover all the tables and very polite waiters serve us. The conditions for the men are much less pleasant. They ended up on the lower deck in one facility that Juozas says is hot and stuffy. The men have to eat in a self-service cafeteria and stand in long lines with their utensils in hand to wait for their turn.

Juozas and I only see each other on the common deck. Still, I'm glad there is this separation of the men from the women. Otherwise we would have to push our way with our children past the men all the time. Besides there are some noisy types among them who do nothing but play cards and drink all night long.

February 12, 1947

The third day at sea, the waves became especially powerful as we sailed past the English Channel. The ship swayed monotonously up and down the waves. I had a terrible bout of seasickness. A lot of other women also became sick. Fewer and fewer come to the cafeteria; more are lying around in the corners of the deck or along the sides of the ship. My situation has been difficult, because I am the only one with a small child on my hands. I was so nauseous that I felt too weak to look after our daughter properly. Juozas, in the meantime, can't help me in the women's quarters.

Our four year old Jurate definitely did not succumb to the rocking waves. She has not been the least bit seasick; she runs around the deck, shouting in glee. She actually likes the rocking of the boat and tries to sway to the rhythm of the rolling waves. Just watching her makes me even more nauseous. At breakfast, lunch and dinnertime, a gong sounds, inviting us to eat at the cafeteria. I can not bear to look at food. My daughter, however, pulls on my sleeve, urging me on, "Mama, let's go eat." Even the smell of food bothers me. I have to ask some other woman to take Jurate for her meals.

This seasickness has lasted for days. I only feel better on the open deck where the gusts of fresh wind refresh me. We have sailed across a zone of strong storms. The waves were gigantic. The ship would struggle upwards and then it would crash down as though aiming for a bottomless ocean. I still go up on deck though because I can not bear being sick in my cabin. I stand there, hanging on to a pole, getting sprayed by the waves.

Once some sailors came over and tried to force me to go down below, telling me that being out in the open is extremely dangerous. Every wave that hits floods the deck. I begged them to let me stay and breathe the fresh air for a bit longer. Juozas finally convinced me to go back down to the cabin.

Another time we were all on the common deck, when the boat tipped suddenly to the side. Jurate rolled across the deck like a little ball. Juozas told me later that before he had a chance to shout, I leaped like a tigress after my daughter. I managed to grab hold of her before she disappeared but I took a bad fall and hurt my leg. It was bleeding from several scrapes. We were brought to the ship's nurse, a very kind-hearted woman who took good care of Jurate and me. She brought me some medicine, but I could not keep it down. She kept telling me that it is essential to drink tea and chew on a cracker. That seems to help a little bit.

Nevertheless, I've only stopped being sick now that we are half way across the ocean.

On the way to the United States – Jurate dances with a young Lithuanian onboard, 1947

The ocean journey did not affect me as it did Alexandra. Only when the ship sailed into the storm zone did I get sick. True, it was hard to sleep. I got the worst cot on the ship – at the front of the prow. When a storm hit us, the boat would smash into a wave and shoot upwards; my cot would flatten me against the wall. Then the ship would dive down. I would hit the ceiling and fall like a rock back onto my cot. There were some strong bouts of stormy waves where I would get tossed up and down like this all night long. Little by little, I got used to the conditions of my surroundings. I was mostly worried about Alexandra who was suffering terribly from seasickness. (To this day, it is hard to persuade her to climb on any boat.)

Lying in my bed on the stuffy deck, unable to sleep, I would fret about how I would get money for us to establish our lives in the United States. I did not have a single dollar in my pocket. The National Catholic Aid Organization had bought our tickets to the United States – the price of the trip for a family of three back then was $660. However, the money was a loan – I had to sign a promissory note to repay the sum within a year. Back then $660 seemed like a huge amount to me. Tossing and turning, I kept wondering how much money I would have to earn each month for us to survive and still have enough left to pay back this huge loan. When I was signing that note, I told the Catholic Aid representative that their organization was not being realistic to assume that an immigrant, just entering the United States, would be able to save over a half thousand dollars in a year. The man did offer me some comfort though. He said, "If you can't manage to pay us back in time, it's not all that big a deal. We will simply wait longer for your payment."

Actually many never did repay this loan which was a moral obligation to compensate for the assistance received. This money had to circulate, so that it could be allocated to help more new refugees. I had been accustomed to living debt-free in Lithuania so when I signed a payment contract, this weighed heavily on my mind.

I noticed that the Jewish refugees sailing on the Ernie Pyle looked better equipped to start a new life in the United States than the rest of us. It was obvious that their organizations had provided them with solid support. In the evenings, they would walk around wearing comfortable slippers and wrapped in silk robes. When they went to bed, they wore colorful pajamas. In the meantime, the other refugees seemed to have no more than one change of underwear.

The Jewish refugees also had dollars. Many spent day after day playing cards for money. Sometimes, when I had nothing to do, I would watch their games.

One day a storm started to rock our ship. One member after another of the card playing group got seasick and fell out of the game. The more stalwart players simply rearranged their teams and continued dealing cards. When there were only three players left on one team, I was asked if I knew how to play bridge. I told them I knew the game but had no money. "That's OK. We'll cover for you. Just be our partner so we can at least play." I was happy to join them under those conditions. Amazingly I actually won ten dollars! So, when I finally stepped out on the shores of America, I was not entirely penniless thanks to a lucky game of bridge.

We made friends with several Lithuanians who were also on board with us. Our Independence Day arrived on February 16th as the ship was nearing the American continent. We Lithuanians decided to hold a commemoration. The ship captain attended our gathering, and a Catholic priest celebrated mass. Speeches were delivered about how our nation would have sufficient determination to rebuild its statehood. Some women recited patriotic poetry, and we all sang the Lithuanian National Anthem. After the formal part of the meeting, as is traditional, we all sat down for a festive dinner. The array of food was decent, and even some alcoholic drinks had been arranged for the event. (After living in the United States for a time, I was convinced that our February 16th holiday was a symbol of unity for the émigré Lithuanian community. Since that commemoration of Independence Day on the ship in 1947, we have never missed a year to celebrate this day. We always get together with other Lithuanians on February 16th, no matter where we find ourselves in the world.)

February 17, 1947

This morning an announcement came that our journey, which had lasted over two weeks, was at an end. Late tonight the boat will reach the shore of the United States. Tonight we will still sleep on board. The Captain's assistant urged us over a loudspeaker to look over our baggage and make sure that we were not bringing a bunch of useless rags with us. "There is as much as you want of everything in America. You will buy new clothes, much better ones than what you have now. This is your best chance to throw away all your junk. Toss it out into the sea," he instructed us.

We looked over the wealth of our belongings. Juozas says that we should discard nearly everything. But I am worried. Where will we get the money to buy new clothes? Still, I did agree to toss a few things into the ocean waters. I realized that in the United States, we would never wear the pants and skirts which I had once sewn from old sheets. But I want to keep my winter boots which Juozas gave me right after Jurate's birth. I have taken good care of them and after four years, they are still not worn.

[When I started walking around wearing those boots in the United States, I was immediately identified as an immigrant since they had long since gone out of style. No one had been seen on the streets with boots like mine for several years. Then several decades passed. Much to my surprise, what did I see? The fashionable young people on the streets of New York City were wearing boots just like my old winter ones. Fashion had simply come full circle.]

At midnight our ship stopped suddenly. I ran out of my cabin to see what happened. I climbed out on deck and shrieked in surprise. Multitudes of lights twinkled across the entire shoreline – New York was in sight!

Juozas also showed up on the deck. We put our arms around each other and looked out at the dazzling lights of America. I told Juozas, "We will never have to run from here. Maybe now, at long last, we can start a normal life and create a better future for ourselves."

We were told that we would have to wait until morning to pass immigration control. I can't sleep tonight. I can hardly wait until morning. Tomorrow is the start of our new lives.

February 18, 1947

At daybreak I went out on deck. There was already a huge crowd craning their necks to see the skyline of New York which was looming ahead about a kilometer away. The skyscrapers I had seen only in movie magazines are taller than I could have ever imagined. All the people were crowded over on the side of the boat that looked out on the city. The captain started to plead over the loudspeaker for people to pull back for fear that the ship could tip over. However, no one paid any attention to him. People balanced on tiptoe to look over the heads of others. New York in all its splendor lay before our eyes.

The ship anchored, and the immigration officials came on board. They asked all of us to stand in one orderly line, but that was asking for too much! The strongest pushed and shoved their way forward to get as close as possible to the exit. This was especially hard on the children because nobody paid any attention to them. Everyone was so crushed together, it was hard for the little ones to breathe. Even those babies held in their parents' arms had a difficult time. Children were crying everywhere.

In all that chaos, somebody pushed against us, tearing the head off Jurate's rag doll. Oh, the cries and screams which filled the air! My little girl was sobbing bitterly, but I had no way to calm her down in this mass of people. Suddenly I remembered – today is Jurate's birthday! February 18, 1947 – the day that we have arrived in America.

I pressed Jurate tightly against my chest, trying to soothe her. I told her that we will soon buy her another doll, a much prettier and much bigger doll. I said, "Throw this one away. It has no head. It's not nice enough for America." My little girl calmed down a bit but she did not want to throw away her headless toy. This doll is a big part of her life. She has been going to bed and waking up with it for months, even though it was no more than a wad of rags. It took quite some doing to convince her, but she finally gave in. She raised her little hands as high as she could and threw her doll over the railing. The doll splashed into the water. Again tears were rolling down the cheeks of my child. I felt sad myself, watching her headless rag doll floating on the waves in the murky waters of the New York harbor.

The line which kept changing and regrouping moved forward at a very slow pace. We suffered patiently. Finally, an immigration official reached us. He asked some questions, and Juozas answered him in English. He stamped a seal in our Lithuanian passports with our United States visas for an unlimited length of time. At the end he bid us a farewell wish, "Okay. Good luck to you."

Then – my feet alighted on American land.

Lithuanians en route to the United States, February, 1947 –
Juozas and Alexandra are first to the left and Jurate, about center

PART IV

Blessings of the New World

Settling in the United States

Masses of people greeted us upon landing. Most passengers fell into the arms of their relatives right on the gangway as they disembarked. In the meantime, Alexandra, Jurate and I, carrying our two little suitcases, stopped, wondering where we should go next. Right then we noticed a man and woman with a sign in their hands written in Lithuanian – "Welcome arriving Lithuanians!" Mr. Simutis from the consulate office of Lithuania in New York and Mrs. Valatkienė, representing the Lithuanian Women's Club of the United States, had come to meet us. The UNRRA had informed them that a small group of Lithuanians was sailing in, and they had come to the harbor. We were deeply touched by such attention since we had no idea where to go or what to do. Right away they started advising us about matters that we had to handle first, including the best way to find an apartment. These people graciously helped us even later while we were still learning about life in the United States. (Anicetas Simutis went on to serve as a Lithuanian diplomat in the United States from 1951. After independence he was the first Ambassador to the United Nations [1991-1994] and later a special advisor to the Permanent Mission of the Republic of Lithuania to the United Nations.)

Simutis told me that a well-known Lithuanian journalist, Juozas Laučka, had been asking about me. For a time he had been the editor of *Darbininkas 'Worker'* newspaper, published in Brooklyn, and was now working with the *Voice of America* radio broadcast. The most pleasant surprise, however, was learning that my old friend, Professor Padalskis (who had shortened his name to Padalis), had also recently arrived in New York. As we were chatting with Mr. Simutis and Mrs. Valatkienė, we learned that representatives of the National Catholic Aid Organization had also come out to meet us. They gave us a few dollars and an address where we could find a place to live for our first days in New York. Apparently we were the only Lithuanians who needed help. All the others on the boat had been met on the landing by their relatives.

Consul Simutis escorted us to a taxi, and we left for the Catholic Aid Shelter on our own. On the way, as we stared at the snow-covered streets, the taxi driver asked us where we were from. I told him we were war refugees from Lithuania. He had never heard of such a country. Besides that, he was amazed to find out that we did not have a single relative in the United States and had no idea where we would be living or how we would earn a living. He shook his head and said over and over, "What a guy, what a guy!"

The shelter was located in some vacated apartments of a large multi-unit building. The sorry-looking apartment was in disrepair; the doors stuck and the window shutters had huge cracks through which the wind whistled. We told ourselves that it was just a temporary stop, an odd sort of transition until we could find a better home. The future was still a mystery, but we were just thrilled to be in a free country and one that was not in ruins.

The next day Padalis came over. We were so happy to see him. After embracing each other, we sat down for a long talk. Afterwards he invited us to join him for supper with Mr. Laučka.

On our first day in New York, we didn't step a foot outside of our shelter. It wasn't until our second day that we finally decided to have a look around town. We hadn't really seen all that much through the taxi window, but the sheer size of New York and its massive buildings already had us in awe. The restaurant where we went for supper also surprised us. It was in a huge hotel and its dining halls could serve several hundred people at once. We had never seen such a grand restaurant before anywhere. I immediately sensed that everything in this country was on an entirely different scale.

Since my studies at Yale were not due to start for another six months, I had to find something to do and a place to live. I discussed my situation with Professor Padalis and Juozas Laučka, the journalist who had tracked us down at the shelter. Laučka said he would recommend us to a certain Jurgis – or George – Diržys, a Lithuanian émigré from an earlier era. He was the owner of a fairly large sewing plant and had a home in Queens.

A few days later, we went to live with the Diržys family. They provided us with one small room and refused to take any rent for it. That should have been a blessing, but living there was not easy. Psychological tension constantly hovered in the house. Mr. Diržys had a girlfriend and did not always return home to sleep with his wife. Mrs. Diržys knew the reason for her husband's disappearances, and that spoiled her disposition greatly.

Mrs. Diržys also had a superior attitude about being a "real" American. Since she had been living in America for many years, she felt quite a cut above all other immigrants even though she still spoke English with a terrible accent. She didn't have much of an English vocabulary either because she spent nearly all her time with other Lithuanians. But she would throw in an English word after nearly every Lithuanian one. Naturally I would have to sit there and listen respectfully. It was unthinkable to let her know that I knew English better than she did, even though I had just arrived in the States.

Overall, a certain tension developed in the long run between the older generation of Lithuanian immigrants and us, the immigrants from the war. But it was our own country folk who helped us to get settled here. Most of us, just off the boat, stayed with them at least in the beginning. They were often the ones to provide us with our first jobs. We were grateful to them for all that. Nevertheless, the older émigrés looked down on the newly arrived Lithuanians. There were very few truly affluent people among them but, in spite of that, they considered us to be "greenhorns" – essentially beggars – who had moved to the United States by virtue of their favors. Nearly everyone, including me, sensed this hostility during the early years of our life in the new country.

Such an attitude deeply hurt the Lithuanians coming in from Germany, many of whom were well-educated people who had held intellectual positions back in the home country. Here in the States, some were forced to take blue-collar laborer jobs. (The younger postwar immigrants, however, who had learned English, were able after a while to work as physicians, engineers and even lawyers.) Thus the unavoidable loss of social status alone was enough to cause psychological problems for many people. Sensing contempt from certain members of the older generation of émigrés, the new arrivals began to interact mostly with one another. They began forming separate Lithuanian organizations and their own cultural collectives in music, drama and art. (I hate to say it, but a similar tension sometimes exists between today's arriving immigrant Lithuanians and us, now the older generation of émigrés.)

Initially Alexandra's and my life revolved entirely around the Lithuanian-American community. The first Sunday after our arrival, our Independence Day was celebrated in Great Neck, Long Island. When Monsignor Juozas Balkūnas of the Lithuanian parish in Queens found out that I had arrived in New York, he immediately invited me to make a speech about the current situation in Lithuania and the lives of war refugees.

I told the audience about the 1940-1941 Soviet terror and declared that, in my opinion, much more difficult times were ahead even after the war. Also I was entirely candid and predicted that Lithuania could be occupied for a long time. The audience had been attentive throughout my talk and, when I was through, they gave me a friendly round of applause. Afterwards Monsignor Balkūnas came on stage and angrily began lambasting Communists, calling them bloodthirsty killers. I noticed that this greatly annoyed some in the audience. Hoots of protest, whistles and sounds of foot stomping filled the hall. I had no idea that there were so many leftist thinkers among the older generation of Lithuanian immigrants. I learned that some actually belonged to the Communist Party of the United States and openly sympathized with the Soviet Union.

This realization confounded me. Up until then, I had thought that the older Lithuanian-Americans felt nothing but hatred for Communists, just as we did. While Monsignor Balkūnas was driving me home after the commemoration, I asked him how there could be so many Lithuanian communist supporters in America. "Don't be surprised. This whole country is crawling with Reds!" he said. "Among Lithuanians, if you take a hard look, every other one is a Bimba follower."

I had never heard of Bimba. Monsignor Balkūnas told me that Antanas Bimba was the leader of the Lithuanian Communists. An early immigrant to the United States, he participated in the formation of the Lithuanian Communist League of America, which had joined the Communist Party of America in 1919. His supporters were apparently publishing newspapers and making every effort to justify the actions of the Soviet Union, including the occupation of Lithuania by Stalin. One thing was clear, though. Even the "Reds" had come out to celebrate our Independence Day on February 16th.

That was my first meeting with the Lithuanian-American community. For a long time, I was always invited to deliver speeches, which I enjoyed doing. Because I never had stage fright, I was able to speak easily, even without a prepared text. From 1947 to 1949, I attended many holidays, commemorations and celebrations of Lithuanian settlements along the East Coast, scattered from Florida to Maine. Everywhere I openly declared my opposition to communist ideology. However, I tried to express my arguments, not by cursing Communists, but by presenting facts and evidence. This way I was usually able to avoid protests even from the supporters of Bimba. Naturally Catholic audiences, being vehemently opposed to atheistic communism, reacted to my speeches much more favorably. They were very curious about war-time events in Lithuania and our subsequent lives in the refugee camps.

Additionally it was the older, Catholic generation of immigrants who quickly joined us, the new arrivals, in activities involving the defense of Lithuanian statehood. These people did not shy away from the new wave of immigration. They did not mind that the newcomers became, over time, entrenched in the same organizations which they had initially established or that we were forming new organizations like the *Amerikos Lietuvių Bendruomenė* (ALB) 'American Lithuanian Community' and *Pasaulio Lietuvių Bendruomenė* (PLB) 'Lithuanian World Community'.

The new immigrants also took over the press and made strong contributions to Lithuanian media overall. Some of our country folk, born in the United States and quite Americanized, experienced a new surge of patriotism. They began getting involved in Lithuanian politics and often provided financial support. As fully-fledged citizens of the United

States, they pressured members of Congress to pay greater attention to the situation in Lithuania.

I had several opportunities to speak to bona fide American audiences. Invitations for such lectures often included offers of payment, which were most appreciated. Probably the greatest ovation after a speech that I ever received in my entire life was during an event sponsored by the Knights of Columbus in New Haven.

Many participants in the activities of this organization were Americans, descended from Italy and other European countries and included an occasional Lithuanian. The members invited me to join in their traditional annual morning mass and afterwards deliver a speech during the ceremonial breakfast. This was one lecture for which I seriously prepared, especially since I had to speak in English. My speech on the danger of communism in Europe was based on my experiences in Lithuania with ample use of metaphors and journalistic rhetoric. When I was finished, the entire audience stood up and applauded at length. I was astonished by the response and incredibly happy that I was so well received by true Americans in the United States.

It wasn't long after we had moved in that Mr. Diržys offered Alexandra a job at his sewing plant. My wife had to learn the craft of sewing on buttons en masse. The pay was miserably low at first because she was not paid by the hour but rather by how many buttons she could successfully sew. Alexandra, who had never in her life worked at such a job, had a very hard time keeping up with the other women who were mainly Italian and experienced.

Alexandra was exhausted but delighted when she got her first pay check – $20! That may have been a miserly salary in New York, even back in those days, but it made us feel rich after having come from poverty-ridden Germany. It goes without saying that the money quickly disappeared.

As the days went on, Alexandra slowly gained the skill to sew on those buttons nearly as fast as her co-workers. She learned from them to arrange her needles and threads at home before going to work, so her earnings rose considerably. The downside was that she had to spend her entire day at the sewing plant away from Jurate. Fortunately Mrs. Diržys, who did not have children of her own, took good care of our daughter, showering her with toys and clothes.

Jurate with Mr. Diržys, May, 1947

I landed a job very soon as well. Juozas Laučka, who was also a member of the board of directors for a Lithuanian Roman Catholic insurance company headquartered in Wilkes-Barre, Pennsylvania, suggested I consider working as an insurance agent. "You sure do talk well. It seems like you can start up a conversation with anyone. Try out this job. You could be good at it," he encouraged me.

The General Director of the company, a third-generation Lithuanian-American, came to visit me in New York. After a brief interview, he offered me a position in the Wilkes-Barre office that he managed.

Though I did not want to be away from my family, I really had no other choice. I left Alexandra in New York at her sewing job and went to Pennsylvania to pursue some good fortune for us. It took more than four hours to travel by bus between our two residences. It was impossible to live in New York and commute to work, so I only saw Alexandra and Jurate on the weekends.

In Wilkes-Barre I rented a room in an attic from an older Lithuanian immigrant, a printer. I wasted no time in getting to work. My job involved finding new clients for the company from the Lithuanian community. I was paid a commission which was a percentage of the total sum of the insurance payments. The most important aspect of this business was the ability to convince someone that an insurance policy was truly beneficial for the family.

This insurance company was small-scale for America. Nonetheless it carried policies for several thousand Lithuanians in the area. The company only handled Lithuanian accounts despite the fact that it could have offered the same service to other national groups. The "real" Americans, naturally, did not buy their insurance from a company only identified with the Lithuanian community. That meant that there was no purpose in walking around from house to house without first having selected specific addresses. I had to learn where the Lithuanian families lived and then make my calls at their homes. What made my job harder was that I didn't have a car and didn't know my way around all the little towns where Lithuanians, who had immigrated before World War I, were long settled.

The company had client listings only for existing and former clients. I would start with these listings then check the telephone directories in their towns to see if any of their family members or others with Lithuanian surnames lived there as well. Again, the names were not always easy to recognize – many of our country folk had changed their surnames to make them more American sounding.

In a while, I caught on that I could find addresses of Lithuanians from the parish priest. I'd come into some small town and first pay a call on the monsignor of the local Lithuanian church. We'd engage in pleasant conversation about Lithuania, and sometimes I'd be invited to have lunch or dinner at his residence. By the end of our encounter, the priest would not only provide me with addresses of Lithuanians but also advise me on which ones to call first and the best way to approach them for a sale.

Learning where Lithuanians lived was merely the beginning of my work. Next a more difficult task faced me. I had to know how to start a conversation that would not provoke a household member to slam the door in my face as soon as I said that I was an insurance agent. If I was lucky enough to be allowed inside, it meant that I had an opportunity to enlist a new client. Usually I was able to interest a householder merely by mentioning that I had recently arrived from Lithuania. Since my Lithuanian pronunciation was much different from that of the older generation, I didn't even have to tell people I was a new immigrant. They would catch on to my accent right away and ask, "Young fellow, where did you come from?" When I told them, the man of the house would usually call out to another room, "Hey, ma, come on out. We have a man here from Lithuania." Then my chances for success really increased.

The mass emigration from Germany had not started yet, so my story was enough to interest the old-timers instantly. Most of them had left Lithuania before World War I; some had been born in the United States. All of them were curious about the goings-on in the country which had once been their homeland, one they had not seen with their own eyes for many decades.

We'd start talking about the war. I'd tell them that I had lived in Lithuania during the years of the first Soviet occupation, and what went on in our country after the Germans took over. It would seem as though we had entirely forgotten why I had originally knocked on their door. However, my host would eventually inquire how I had ended up in the United States and what I was doing here.

Most of the people in all those little towns were coal miners. They had worked very hard their entire lives but had not acquired much wealth. Therefore it was not easy to convince them to part with several dollars to buy insurance for their families. Still, I was able to do it in many instances. After our heartfelt conversations, even very old folk would sign up for insurance along with the younger ones. I started earning a decent income for those times. One month I earned about $200 and the next – $300! Even more importantly, this job taught me a lot about the psychology of social interaction, something every businessman needs to know.

The money that I brought home made a huge difference for my family. After I received my first paycheck, I decided that it was no longer necessary for Alexandra to work at the sewing facility in New York. The family could survive on my income alone. By April of 1947, Jurate and Alexandra moved to Wilkes-Barre to be with me.

At first we all lived together in my attic room. As luck would have it, that summer was extremely hot, and our room became unbearably stuffy. But on balance, we felt as though we were living very well. We were able to buy all sorts of food and clothing, so much more than we had as refugees.

We decided to send Jurate to a nursery school run by a convent of nuns so that she could play with children of her own age, get accustomed to the new location and learn English. I still remember the first time that we took our child to the school. The nuns spoke kindly to her, and she began dancing merrily. However, as soon as we turned around to go, leaving her alone with her teacher, Jurate started to wail mournfully. We felt so sorry for our little baby; she was only four years old. But what else could we do? We had to get her used to a new life in America. In no time at all, Jurate felt comfortable in her new surroundings and was chatting away easily in English.

Wilkes-Barre, Pennsylvania, 1947

Changes were taking place in my work as well. I decided to recruit one or two other Lithuanians to help out. More and more were trickling in from Germany and looking for jobs. I invited one fellow with whom I had studied at Vilnius University to work as an insurance agent with me. A while later I took on another colleague, Vytautas Dambrava, who was to become a future Ambassador of Lithuania to Spain. I remember that he was especially good at this job.

It didn't take long to form a small organization of insurance agents, something that the Catholic company had never had before. I had been their first agent and, by the end of that first summer, there were already seven agents, and I was their manager. The company also paid me a certain percentage of their income. At long last, I was able to stop walking from house to house on my own. I devoted my time to locating target addresses and distributing sales territories for our new agents.

Yale University – A Gift of Fate

September was approaching, and I had to get ready for my studies at Yale. The Board of Directors wanted me to commit to working for their insurance company after my doctoral studies; in exchange the company would pay me a monthly stipend of $200. That amount of money permitted a comfortable life style in those times. I did not have to think long about the offer; I went ahead and signed the agreement.

Only later, after I was living in New Haven and studying at Yale, did I comprehend that once I had a doctorate degree from such a prestigious university, I would not want to manage a small office of insurance agents. From the day that I arrived at Yale, I found myself in an environment that was at an entirely different social and intellectual level. Clearly, after my studies, I would be able to look for a much better position than the one the Lithuanian insurance company would be able to offer.

I informed the Board of Directors in November that I would not be able to fulfill my obligation to return to work for them after graduation. Of course that meant that I lost the stipend though I still received some money for the contracts I had brought in previously. Those commissions were not large, however, and it was not easy for us to live on that income alone.

The five hundred dollar stipend from Yale, which was provided by a private foundation, was a one time gift. Thus, during the early months of my studies, I continued with my insurance work in New Haven, New Britain and other small nearby towns where sizeable Lithuanian communities resided.

Alexandra also found employment right away at the Gilbert Toy Factory. Her job was to clean the screws for the toys. The work was grueling; the poor woman would come home with bleeding fingers and her nails all torn. The pay was very modest – only $25 per week – but even that small sum came in very handy for us.

While it stretched our budget, we were looking ahead. At the end of 1947, a great many more Lithuanians, including some of our friends and relatives, were trying to get to the United States from Germany. Our intention was to provide them with living quarters when they first arrived. While waiting for them, we sublet several rooms in our attic to other Yale students.

At first we were not able to provide our relatives and friends with the sort of documentation required by the Government of the United States of anyone requesting a visa. We had to find American citizens who either owned property or had steady sources of good income and would agree to sign the appropriate papers. Such a guarantor undertook a great financial responsibility. Naturally only a few of the older Lithuanian émigrés could be persuaded to do this. We promised them that they would never actually have to provide any sort of support for the immigrants we were inviting. In terms of the law, however, these people had to take on a serious financial obligation on behalf of someone they had never met and knew nothing about.

Despite such difficulties, I managed to provide official invitations for a rather large group of friends. It helped considerably that I had made contacts with a great many of the earlier generation of immigrants in the course of my work as an insurance agent. I would bring my fellow Lithuanians to tears, telling them about the hardships of life in a refugee camp. Then, frequently, one of the wealthier members of the community would agree to help someone come to America. Their confidence in me was greatly strengthened by the fact that I had the honor of studying at Yale University.

New Haven, 1948

My first concern was for my sister Victoria's family. Afterwards I arranged immigration for Professor Juozas Pažemeckis, a distinguished public activist; Česlovas Januša, an artist; Romas Samulis, my wife's cousin, and his family and my friend Kęstutis Valiūnas along with his wife, mother and two brothers. Over time I managed to arrange invitations for quite a few other Lithuanians. In all I must have helped several dozen people reach the United States. Most of them would stay with me upon their arrival, and I would try to find jobs for them as well. My sister, Victoria, and her family stayed with us for probably the longest time. I was very happy that I was also able to arrange a job for Joseph Gruodis, her husband, in New Haven.

All these concerns took a great deal of time. Meanwhile the requirements of the study program at Yale were very demanding. During the first few weeks there, I was still working as an insurance agent. I realized that I was unable to prepare for my seminars adequately. A great deal of literature had to be read since the discussions in each class were based on required readings. All the other students were active participants. But I didn't know what to say. For a while, I could get by with the excuse that I had just come from Europe and I was not very good in English. These excuses, however, were no help when it came time to take the exams. When I realized that I would have to concentrate entirely on my studies, I resigned as an insurance agent. I tried to spend as little time as possible on other matters but I obviously could not entirely ignore all the relatives and acquaintances who were still stuck in Germany and anxious to come to America.

I still don't know how I was able to pass all my exams relatively successfully at the end of the first session. Whenever I had to answer questions on unfamiliar topics, I would try to fill in the gaps with my own ideas. I had no clue if those thoughts were all that original or worthy of attention, but Yale was known to encourage independent thinking. Professors apparently liked this type of approach on my part. Four years later, I think I was one of the first in my group to defend his doctoral thesis.

Unquestionably I did read a tremendous amount of academic literature. Day in and day out, I spent hours on end, sitting in the university library. I was competing with the best American students who had already graduated with master's degrees. My level of English fluency was an obstacle for some time. Though I could speak and understand rather well, writing was still difficult.

In addition to my studies, I wanted to enjoy the incredibly interesting and varied cultural life at Yale. World-renowned musicians played concerts every week on campus. Nobel Prize winning scholars and authors read public lectures. Besides all that, Alexandra and I loved films. We weren't able to go to the movies very often due to a lack of time and money but, nonetheless, we did not deny ourselves this pleasure whenever a spare Friday appeared.

We were also drawn to the evenings and festivities at the Lithuanian Community Center. Attending mass on Sundays was a tradition, steeped in our blood since childhood which we always upheld. We frequented the nearest Lithuanian parish, *Švento Kazimiero* 'St. Casmir' Church, whose monsignor became a good friend of ours. Alexandra, meanwhile, enjoyed singing in the church choir and joined the Lithuanian drama group as well.

During my second year of studies, a Yale professor wrote me a recommendation for a job teaching economics at the nearby Albertus Magnus College for Women. Although attending the lectures for my doctoral program and preparing for the various seminars took up a lot of time, I had to earn more money somehow. The college paid me about $200, which helped us lead a rather normal lifestyle. Alexandra no longer had to work at the toy factory where the job was hard and the pay was meager. I was even able to support our relatives who were coming in from Germany by that time.

Teaching at the college also helped me improve my English skills. Naturally I spoke English with an accent. I would tell my students who I was and where I had come from. I sensed that the young women were sympathetic and forgave me for any rough spots in my speech. It probably also helped that I was still young myself, barely 30 years old.

There were some amusing incidents in my job. Once, during my lecture, I mentioned the name of William Faulkner, the American writer who had left a marked impression on me. I noticed that my students were giggling. I did not understand what was going on. When I repeated the author's name once more, open laughter broke out in class. I asked, "What is going on? Did I say something wrong?" They kept on laughing. No one said a word. Finally, one young woman, blushing wildly, corrected me, "You are not pronouncing the name correctly. You have to say "Falkner" not "Fukner". Now I was blushing. I had heard Americans using a word like that in the streets; however, I did not know exactly what it meant though I sensed it was not to be used in polite company.

I taught at Albertus Magnus College for the rest of the three years of my doctoral studies. This took considerable moving around. I would read a lecture and then run off to listen to a lecture at Yale – and I mean literally run. To save money, I avoided using the bus. Since the distance between the college and the university was considerable, I would often have to jog to class so as not to be late.

Attendance at doctoral lectures was not required, but exams had to be passed to accumulate the needed number of credits for the degree. My studies were economic theory and the history of economic evolution. Needless to say, I had a tremendous amount of reading. I would get to the university library at its opening hour and sit with my books until the librarian ushered me out at closing time. I also spent many long nights with my books. Happily, reading was something I had enjoyed since childhood.

Of greatest interest to me were the studies in world industry and international trade. The subject that was hardest for me was the mathematics of economics; I had a rough time passing those exams. It was a completely new field for me, one that I had never come in contact with at Kaunas or Vilnius or Tübingen Universities. At first, when the professors would start writing all the different formulas on the board and proceed to derive their equivalencies, I was totally lost. Fortunately I was able to get help from a good friend who understood the application of mathematical methods in economics. I got along well with all the students in my classes; several of them would often offer to help me with my studies.

I also enjoyed good relations with everyone on the staff of Yale. Professor Edward W. Bakke, a man of Norwegian descent, who taught a course in labor relations in the Department of Economics, took an interest in my progress. Other experts in their fields – John Perry Miller, the professor of the history of economy, and Professors Lloyd G. Reynolds and Charles E. Lindblom, two renowned scholars – were always glad to help. All I had to say was, "Professor, I don't quite understand this," and they never refused to meet with me. They would take any length of time to explain the complex theories in their disciplines.

With certain instructors, personal friendships also developed. Professors Bakke and Miller were guests at our home several times. They also invited us to visit them. A special relationship evolved with John Miller who went on to become the dean of the Graduate School. We stayed in touch with him until his death.

I passed all my exams successfully. My final year was spent writing my doctoral dissertation on the Sovietization of the Czechoslovakian economy. I selected this topic because it was a continuation of my thesis on the collectivization of Lithuanian agriculture which I had defended at Vilnius University. This one, of course, covered the topic in a broader and more complex scope. Even at Yale I was still keenly interested in the manner in which the Soviet Union was transferring its economic principles into the lands which it had vanquished in Eastern and Central Europe. I was convinced that the Soviet system for managing the economy was no more than a historical experiment, doomed to become an unavoidable failure. I could not believe that the command economy in which private ownership and business initiative did not exist could compete in the long run with the free market, or that people would work well in a system where the motivational stimulus of making money did not exist.

The Czechoslovakian economy, well developed and modern for the times up to the Second World War, had been managed on the basis of private capital for a long time. I wanted to investigate the reactions to Soviet influence there. Czechoslovakia also had been distinguished in the region for the high educational level and excellent managerial skills of its population. I was eager to discover an explanation of what happens to a strong economy after the nationalization of private ownership and the entrenchment of the Soviet ruling system.

In theory one might assume that a communist system had no advantage in a backward Soviet Union. However, Czechoslovakia had operated on a well-developed system. If the new communist ways proved completely ineffective there, it would prove that command methods could not possibly succeed in any economy. In the end, I reached such a conclusion in my dissertation. Thus I was convinced that the Soviet system would ultimately wear out all its capabilities in all countries and slowly begin to deteriorate. Free market elements would have to be incorporated. This would then hasten the decline of communism and, in the end, it was bound to fail, politically as well as economically. This analysis strengthened my conviction that Lithuania would again eventually become a free country. However, looking at this from another point of view, it may have been my own unyielding faith in the liberation of my homeland that drove me to the conclusion of my dissertation – the inevitable breakdown of communism.

Essentially I wrote my dissertation during the final year of my doctoral studies. The first three years were spent attending classes and taking exams. It was not easy to earn a doctorate degree in this amount of time. Once I had passed my exams, I was permitted to defend my dissertation at any time over the next four years. This, however, was far too great a luxury for me. I had to work to support my family. Therefore I was determined to complete all my requirements during the years of my doctoral studies.

Writing my paper demanded a huge amount of effort. I first had to gather a great deal of information and data and then systematize all the empirical work. I remember that my card catalogue of all the citations I had gathered barely fit into a large box. The research on the state of the economy in Czechoslovakia during those times was based on earlier reviews of its economic development. I also discussed the political situation of the country and analyzed Marxist economic theories. There was a plethora of resources on which my work was based. All sorts of publications could be found in the bountiful stacks of the Yale Library along with press and statistical summaries that had somehow been brought in from Czechoslovakia. All I needed to do was ask for any book or report and, in a few weeks, I would receive it. To this day, I don't know through what channels that information came to me. I did meet the person who provided me with all the resources I needed, but he was discretely silent when I asked how he received data which was held secret in communist countries. I can only guess that the statistics I requested came either from the United States Embassy in Prague or the CIA. It seemed that the capabilities of Yale University were nearly limitless.

I had no particular problems with English during the final years of my doctoral studies. By participating in discussions and reading books, I had gained nearly total fluency in English. I also managed to write quite accurately. But the fact that I was able to finish my dissertation in such a short time was actually due to all the sacrifices my wife made for me.

I would write my drafts by hand; Alexandra would type them up. This was quite a feat since she hardly knew any English at the time. She learned to touch type and, letter by letter, she transcribed all the long drafts I had written. She spent hours hunched over the typewriter, working late into the night. The final manuscript was nearly 600 pages long!

My dissertation was finished in April of 1951. By this time I was 33 years old. In early June, I was called to defend it before the members of the academic council who issued the doctorate degree. They overwhelmed me with numerous questions. Having to explain one claim after another to the panel was excruciatingly difficult. All the while, this responsibility was like a vise, pressing against my temples. When I returned home in the evening, I had a tremendous headache, but the heavy weight on my shoulders had lifted.

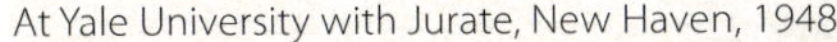

At Yale University with Jurate, New Haven, 1948

Juozas (now Joseph), a Yale University Ph.D. with Alexandra; (from the left) his high school teacher, Vladas Kulbokas; sister, Victoria; Mrs. Kęstutis Valiūnas and his daughter, Jurate, May 15, 1951

Professor Robert A. Dahl, an expert in comparative analyses of economic systems who was the head of my doctoral committee, and Dr. John Miller, the Dean of our school who had assisted me a great deal, proposed that I publish a book on my work. Reluctantly I rejected their offer. Traditionally doctoral candidates had to pay for the publication of a book out of their own pockets; the university did not contribute any funding for this. I had no money for such a matter. Later on there was no sense in publishing a book because the statistical data on which my work had been based was already out-of-date. Thus my dissertation can only be found today in the Yale library.

In fact copies of dissertations and abstracts from all over the world can be found at the library of Yale University. Once I took my business partner, Dr. Ellshoff, the President of Dortmund Steel Alliance, and another German businessman, also with a doctorate degree, to the library. Just for fun, they looked up their own names in the catalogue of academic work. The Germans were stunned to discover that Yale had copies of their dissertations, which they had written before the Second World War.

Enticing Offers and Decisions

No more than a few days had passed after the defense of my dissertation when I received an invitation addressed to Joseph Kazickas from Georgetown University in Washington. (I was now using the English version of my name, Juozas.) I realized that I might be offered work there. In the meantime, I had already sent copies of my resume and letters of application to the Department of Defense and the State Department.

I took a trip to Washington. My plan was to visit not only Georgetown but also the federal divisions to which I had applied. I had learned that government administrators were assigned positions in accordance with their work experience, level of education and success in a chosen career. My doctorate degree was in and of itself a basis for placement at a high level.

During my interview at the State Department, I was told that the office was indeed interested in my education and experience, but I was offered only a part-time consultancy with a monthly salary. Though I had a green card, I did not yet have my citizenship. That most likely prevented me from getting a more stable position in a government office that was engaged in foreign relations. (Actually I did become a full-fledged citizen the following year in 1952.)

Two very pleasant officers met with me at the Department of Defense, where I was also offered a job as a consultant. I would have had to perform fairly regular special assignments for the Pentagon, but the job did not involve my being in the office for any determined number of hours. "You would be able to hold down another fulltime job while performing this additional work for us," explained the officers. "You will not have any problems should you decide that you want to work concurrently as a consultant for us and the State Department."

Next I paid a visit to Georgetown University. Here I was offered a fulltime position as an assistant professor of economics at once. The annual salary was set at $7,800 which, in 1951, was a good income for a comfortable life style for a family. Other Lithuanians who had settled in the United States had to work very hard as blue-collar laborers in factories for a much lower salaries. Still, they were very happy that they were able to live much better in the United States than they had in Germany.

New Haven, 1950

I calculated what my earnings would be. Along with my Georgetown salary, I had the opportunity to make another $3,000 annually as a consultant for the Pentagon and the State Department. This meant an income of nearly $11,000 each year. Although my after-tax income would be less, I still felt that with that amount I could live like a truly rich person.

Such conditions were exceptionally enticing. I talked it over with Alexandra. It seemed virtually impossible to reject such offers. It was not only the income that delighted me. I was also attracted to the opportunity for an academic career at the university.

Shortly thereafter I informed Georgetown University that I was seriously considering accepting the position of assistant professor. I rented a small, brand new house and brought Alexandra and Jurate down from New Haven. I decided that I could allow myself such luxury in anticipation of my salary come September even if I had not yet actually signed an agreement with Georgetown University.

But fate intervened. As I was organizing my affairs, my friend, Kęstutis Valiūnas, who had relocated from Germany, came by to visit me and asked, "So, when are we going to go into business together?"

Several years ago, when I was getting ready to come to the United States, I had promised Kęstutis that we would go into business together once we were in America. Kęstutis may have been five years younger than I was, but he influenced me a good deal while we were both studying at Tübingen University. He was an extremely energetic and self-confident young man. Even in Germany, Kęstutis had some business dealings and had even managed to buy himself an automobile. I had not heard of any other Lithuanian refugee who had been able to do that.

He arrived in the United States in 1950 by virtue of the documents which I had arranged for him. He wanted to talk about doing business together, but I had to tell him that I would not be able to engage in any other activity until I completed my doctoral degree. At the time he still didn't know how to speak English and had no idea what he could do in the United States. Thus he left his wife and child to live with us and returned to Germany. There he again went into business, working with a Lithuanian politician, Dr. Petras Karvelis.

I felt somewhat responsible for the situation in which Kęstutis found himself. He was, in a sense, forced to return to Germany. One day, when

I was close to defending my dissertation, I received a letter from him asking me to purchase a large number of typewriters. I sent him the goods via American Express to Germany. This was a very small trading operation, but it was the first time that I had actually gotten involved in a business deal.

The visit from Kęstutis was not exactly unexpected. In a way, I had been waiting for such a talk with him. I wanted to have a heart-to-heart discussion regarding my own future plans. "Now, you did promise me that as soon as you finished your doctorate you would go into business with me," Kęstutis reminded me after hearing about my offer from Georgetown. By this time he also had his doctorate degree from Tübingen University. But, unlike me, he was not interested in an academic career. All he wanted was a business venture.

Our talk was not an easy one. At that time a university position seemed loftier and more prestigious than some kind of business. Being a professor in Lithuania meant a great deal more than being a businessman. Over the long run of my life in the United States, I have come to realize that academic work does not carry as much of an aura of respect as it had in prewar Lithuania. It is just one form of employment among numerous other endeavors. A successful businessperson can rise to a much higher public status than a professor might, not to mention the financial opportunities that are available to him.

However, at that time, I had no idea about the advantages of a business career. Alexandra had also worked at Vilnius University and she had high respect for our instructors. She also dreamed about my becoming a professor. The status of a professor's wife was much more attractive in her eyes than that of a businessman's wife.

It was not only the prestige of working at a university that appealed to me. I was truly interested in such work and felt it suited me. I also believed that I had the ability to advance to the position of a full professorship in time. The entire sphere of business, on the other hand, was totally new and unknown to me.

At the same time I felt a moral commitment to Kęstutis. I was in a quandary, trying to come to a decision. But as matters turned out, our first serious venture into business was fateful, and it changed the rest of my life.

Becoming A Businessman

It so happened that, when I was packing up my family to move to Washington, I ran into a friend, John Gilmore, who asked me if by chance I knew anyone in Europe who could supply some cement. Apparently a mass construction boom had taken off in Florida and cement was in short supply. Prices were escalating. Gilmore had a client in Florida who desperately needed cement and he wondered if it were possible to buy some in Germany at a lower price than was available in the United States. Construction had not yet taken off in Europe at the time. He had made some calculations and believed that one could earn a fair profit, even after adding in the transportation expenses.

When he told me he needed 45,000 tons, which would fill three average-size freighters, I was stunned. To me that seemed like an incredibly large-scale operation. In no time at all, I told Kęstutis about this conversation and asked him to look around in Germany for some cement. "I'll handle the order from my end in the United States," I proposed excitedly.

Kęstutis immediately called a large cement manufacturer and trading company in Germany. I remember that we sat and planned our talk with the factory in advance so that we would not waste any minutes on the telephone. There was simply no money for a lengthy overseas call.

When we learned that this company could indeed supply the cement, we were thrilled. But our excitement was short-lived. ATT – American Telephone and Telegraph – called me back immediately and asked how I intended to pay for the call – by cash or by bank transfer?

My usual telephone bill was about $20 a month. Suddenly I was being told that the charge for the call to Germany was $270! Everything went dark before my eyes. What a catastrophe! I had no idea where we could find that kind of money nor did I know if anything would actually come of our plan to trade in cement.

Kęstutis left immediately for Germany. By then we had managed to sign a contract with the Florida buyer for the cement as well as an agreement with the manufacturer of these building materials. With these guarantees in hand, we were able to charter three freighters. The ships sailed in, the buyer got his cement and Kęstutis Valiūnas and I earned several thousand dollars each.

That kind of profit made a deep impact on me. I considered the number of lectures I would have to deliver before I'd be able to earn this sort of money and here I did it in with one deal! By now my family was packed and ready to move to Washington. I had already paid the rent for three months in advance. But suddenly I was smitten with a great temptation not to sign with the university but to continue in the business which had gotten off to such a successful start.

At this point in time, I was in debt for a few thousand dollars. I calculated how many months it would take me to be free of debt on an assistant professor's salary. With all the money that I got for the cement sale, I realized I could pay off everyone I owed and still have a thousand dollars or so left over.

I kept thinking about this; I discussed it with Alexandra. She was pregnant with our second child – Joseph Mindaugas. (He was born on November 14, 1951.) I had to evaluate our situation very carefully.

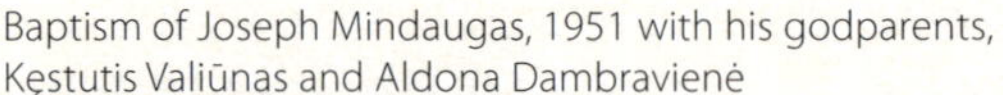
Baptism of Joseph Mindaugas, 1951 with his godparents, Kęstutis Valiūnas and Aldona Dambravienė

I finally came to a most difficult decision. I went to the university and from there to the State Department and the Department of Defense. I told them that my circumstances had changed and I had to reject their job offers. We decided to move to the New York suburb of New Rochelle. We rented a comfortable three bedroom house there and furnished it nicely with my first earnings in business.

September, 1951

I was a bit downhearted when Joseph decided to give up a job at the university and take up business. It annoyed me to think that some American Lithuanian acquaintances of mine might have been right. When Joseph started his doctoral studies, more than one of them would say to me, "What does he need that schooling for? Wouldn't you be better off if he just went to work?" Some even tried to scare me, trying to convince me that he would leave me as soon as he got well educated. Over and over, I heard the story about some Lithuanian woman who had worked very hard to put her husband through the university until he graduated and became a doctor. Then he left his wife and went off to live with another woman.

I was not worried that something like that would happen to me. But it was also true that Joseph had already started earning rather good money from the insurance company. Besides he has always been very good at coming up with new ideas. He has a knack for being quick-witted and getting along well with people. Finding a different sort of job would have also been easy for him.

When he started his studies, we really had to scrimp and count every penny. I was completely prepared to live under difficult conditions for a certain time since I imagined he was going to have an academic career. Professors in Lithuania and Germany always had prestigious positions in society. The hope I had of becoming the wife of a professor carried me through those very tough and uncertain times.

Those first months of life in the United States, while Juozas was still waiting to start his studies at Yale, were the most difficult for me. That was when I had to work for Mr. Diržys at his sewing plant. He paid a half dollar for every hundred sewn on buttons. The Italian women working with me had a system. They would bring a whole bunch of already threaded needles to work with them. Then they would sew on those buttons at lightning speed.

At first doing the job that quickly was impossible for me. I would get exhausted, and my fingers bled from poking them with my needle. In time, however, I got used to the work. Mrs. Diržienė, the wife of Diržys, also taught me to thread my needles at home, so I could work without any breaks on the job. In time I could also finish just as many buttons as the other women did.

I noticed that the women always took a lot of breaks. I knew that they could have sewn on far more buttons than the standard that was set for us, but they seemed satisfied to complete a minimum number in an hour's work. Then my Italian colleagues told me that it was not worth the effort to go over the quota. Once Diržys noticed how fast we worked, he would simply lower the price of the piecework. They explained that we would be ordered to sew on more buttons but we'd still get the same pay. They were probably right about that.

There was also a group of Lithuanian women of the older immigrant generation working at the factory. I just didn't want to get all that friendly with them. These women would brag that they believed in communism. I'd hear some remarks aimed in my direction from time to time. "This high-standing lady decided to come over here. Let her have a taste of our worker's bread too."

Sometimes I could not contain myself and I'd snap back at them, "It's easy for you to gab about communism, living in America. You never saw it with your own eyes. All of you have a house and even a car, even though you are ordinary unskilled workers. Go live in Lithuania and you can find out the real meaning of communism. We'll see how fast all your sympathies for communism evaporate then."

Of course, these women didn't want to listen to me. They knew my husband was traveling around to all the Lithuanian communities, speaking about the evils of communism. These worshippers of Antanas Bimba were convinced that we were serving capitalist propaganda, and that's why we were making every effort to compromise the ideas of communism. It was easier just to avoid talking to them. I tried to stay wrapped up in my own thoughts and did my sewing in silence every day, believing all the time that this was just a temporary stage in our destiny.

That's exactly all it was. After a few months, we left for New Haven. I changed my job at the Diržys Sewing Factory for a job in a toy factory, which was sadly not much better. I was relieved when, a while later, Joseph said that, if we carefully curtailed our expenses, we could manage without my meager earnings. He had started teaching at Albertus Magnus College by then. His salary of a few hundred dollars per month was enough to pay for our apartment, food, clothing and occasional tickets to a movie.

The class in economics which Joseph taught was an elective, not a required course. At first only five girls registered for his class. Soon afterwards, though, everyone at the college seemed to develop an interest in economic theory. By mid-year, a few dozen girls were attending his class. I had to endure my husband's popularity with the young students. At the year's end party, one after another walked up to us and barely acknowledged my presence before whisking my husband off to dance with them. I admit I was a little jealous but consoled myself that at least there was no threat of unemployment due to low attendance in his classes.

The four years at Yale flew by. Those were years of studies for me as well. I tried as best as I could to help my husband. With barely any knowledge of English, I typed hundreds of pages of his dissertation. And then, just when the goal has been reached, my Joseph, a doctor of philosophy in economics, suddenly changed his mind, gave up a potential professorship and decided to go into business. I did not argue with his decision but, at first, it was hard for me to understand why he was doing this. After all he could have become a businessman without a doctorate degree from Yale. It seemed as though those four years of studies were now meaningless.

Calmly and patiently, Joseph started explaining why he had decided to do this. I understood that a professor's position is not a highly paid one. Maybe that is why the position does not have as much prestige in the United States as it does in Europe. We have debts after his studies. And there are still relatives in Germany waiting for us to help them get resettled. I thought that maybe it isn't so awful after all for Joseph to engage in business for a while to earn more money than he might at the university. Besides an academic career demands spending long hours in a library. While Joseph was able to sit through his academic studies with incredible perseverance, I know he is primarily a man of action.

[Right away we started to live in a style that we never would have been able to dream of on a professor's salary. All I can do now is smile, remembering my ambition to be the wife of a professor. I have to admit that Joseph was absolutely right in his determination to choose a different road in life. Business offered him much better opportunities to make use of his personality traits, talents, drive and energy.]

Business Whirlwinds

Kęstutis Valiūnas and I both firmly believed that we would get more orders from Florida for cement. But that never happened. Apparently those clients only wanted to use our services that one time because they were late in fulfilling their obligations and were under the threat of incurring fines. Once conditions stabilized, they went back to their original American suppliers.

We had no idea what to try next. Unexpectedly a perfect way out of the situation materialized. One of my fellow classmates from Yale introduced me to a government official who had worked in different programs of the Marshall Plan for rebuilding Europe. I learned from him that Americans were rapidly building huge military bases in North Africa. A severe shortage of steel had developed. "Go talk to people. You might land some sort of contract," he suggested.

Kęstutis was back in Germany at the time. We agreed that I should fly to Libya to try to negotiate with the Americans, and he would use his contacts in Germany at Ferrostahl, a huge construction and trading company, to arrange for steel. Our plan was actually quite risky. A trip to Tripoli, the capital of Libya, was quite expensive. There was no guarantee that we would get anything out of it. Fortunately the Ferrostahl office in New York gave us money for my expenses.

I went to Libya and met with U.S. military officials. I then flew to Germany to discuss with Ferrostahl executives the necessary steel specifications, the desired quantities and delivery deadlines. They said they needed some time to study our proposals.

In the meanwhile, Kęstutis and I started scouting other companies which also might be able to supply steel for the military base constructions. At a subsidiary of Hamburg's Reunert Company, we learned that they could make timely deliveries for the American orders but they lacked sufficient coal for steel production. "Get that for us and we'll be able to smelt that steel for you in time," the company director told us.

A chance occurrence helped us once again. Through some contacts, I met Ray Maust, the owner of several coal mines in Virginia and Kentucky. He was a gruff, ill-tempered man who walked around his mines with two revolvers hooked on his belt but a smart businessman, direct and to the point.

Kęstutis Valiūnas and Joseph Kazickas

Once we assured him that we could provide guarantees from Reunert, he suggested we go to his export company, named Salljoan for his daughters, to discuss all the specifics regarding the terms of contract.

Salljoan first had to deliver a trial shipment of 10,000 tons of cocking coal for the Germans. If the quality was suitable for smelting steel, the next order from Germany would be for 100,000 tons. We agreed that each ton would be priced at $20 and thirty cents of this was to be our commission. Our first shipment of coal gave us an income of $3,000 without our having to invest a single cent. Our initial successes made us feel like rich men. We even bought ourselves brand new automobiles. My first car was an aqua colored Buick Roadmaster.

The strangest thing was that nothing ever came of our initial idea to supply steel for the construction of American military bases. The steel needed in Libya must have been purchased elsewhere while we were concerned with getting the coal for the Reunert Company. This experience convinced us of one thing – nothing bad happens that doesn't turn out for the best. By working through the entire process, we unearthed a much more profitable business niche – trade in coal.

The Kazickas' Buick Roadmaster, 1951

Early in 1952 we registered our own coal export company, naming it after the river that ran across Vilnius – Neris Coal and Carbon Corporation. Kęstutis and I divided the stock ownership equally.

Reunert had plenty of work even without the American orders. The economy of Germany was just starting to recover at that time. Our business grew as the Germans placed several more large orders for coal. We began to get more involved in the transport of goods, an operation which also increased our earnings. We added new companies to our list of clients and also made contacts with other steel mills in Western Europe.

It seemed as though our business would keep on growing but, towards the end of 1952, we ran into some big problems. Competition from a dozen or so American companies combined with the recovery of coal mining in Germany brought our business to a complete standstill. We did not have a single order.

Meanwhile I had just built myself a huge five-bedroom house in New Rochelle. As is usually the case, the building ended up costing approximately twice what I had expected. Additionally I had taken a sizeable loan from the bank since I was confident that our business and profits were destined to expand. At the same time, another child was on the way. In March 1953, my son Alexander Kestutis was born.

Our house still smelled of fresh paint when we moved in. We hadn't even bought drapes for the windows when reality struck. I had no income at all. I did not know how I could meet the interest payments on my bank loan. Losing our new home was a real risk that loomed before me. Suddenly we had to count every penny. Just when the end was near, one friend from Yale, Barbara Fine, who worked for Chase Manhattan Bank at the time, helped me avoid total ruin. As soon as she heard about my precarious situation, Barbara took out a bank loan in her own name and lent me several thousand dollars.

Of course I was not sitting around on my hands. Through many a sleepless night, I tossed and turned, wondering what I should do. I tried to meet as many people as possible from the local New Rochelle business community. I went out of my way to learn what they were involved in to find possibilities for deals. But the situation seemed hopeless – simply nothing came up.

We had to christen Kestutis, but I didn't even have money for this important family celebration. Then I remembered my piggy bank. When I first went into business and everything was going smoothly, I played a little game. Every evening when I came home, I would take all the coins and bills out of my pockets and put them into a tin can. All these months, I had never taken out a single cent.

When Alexandra and I opened up our tin bank and started counting, we couldn't believe our eyes. We had saved around $600! That gave us enough money to have a real christening party. We invited our relatives and some Lithuanian friends and had a very good time. But I could not stop worrying – how on earth are we going to live tomorrow?

By a stroke of good fortune, our business crisis only lasted about six months. That year, 1953, was the worst year of my life as a businessman, but by December we again managed to sign a contract for supplying coal, even if it wasn't an especially large one. The following year our business completely recovered and was larger than before.

Economic stagnation ended in Germany. The industry of this country hit a rapid level of growth. German coal mines were no longer able to satisfy the needs of a booming economy, and the government did away with all protectionist regulations. We were able to negotiate five and ten year contracts with favorable prices. These contracts provided our company with stability and guaranteed our survival even during crisis periods.

We eventually got involved in selling coal to France, the Netherlands, Belgium and Italy, where we became one of the most active suppliers to the steel industry.

Competition in the coal business intensified more and more over the years. Quite a bit of psychological know-how was needed to retain our old clients because our competitors tried to woo them away more than once. Sometimes we had to sign contracts that required a great deal of work but brought very little profit. At one point, our own cut per ton was no more than a mere five cents. Nonetheless, we did have some profitable agreements which paid off the less successful contracts and resulted in a tidy overage. Our company was supplying over a million tons of coal each year by the late 1960s. On average each ton brought us forty to fifty cents in profit.

During the 1970s our revenues again increased. Nevertheless, we kept our company small with only five employees and worked long hours. Our goal was always to retain and strengthen our good reputation. Thus we were always careful to uphold every contract term. On-time delivery of coal was a key factor in our business operations, and we were never late on a delivery.

At the end of the 1960s, we located our office to 530 Fifth Avenue in Manhattan. Eventually we moved to Madison Avenue, renting an entire floor of a skyscraper.

Then, all of a sudden, another economic recession hit Western Europe early in the 1980s. The demand for coal dropped sharply. Because our company was primarily working long-term supply contracts by then, the freight ships we hired continued to deliver coal in the agreed quantities to Europe. Tons of it were piling up over there. Our situation was better than that of the German companies who did not hold long-term supply contracts. As matters stood, German companies were forced to continue buying from us, and no one was ordering from the local coal mines anymore.

The cost of warehousing the coal created a huge loss for the Germans because they could no longer utilize all the coal we were supplying to them. We met with our German buyers to discuss a way out of the situation that would be equally acceptable to us both. We determined it would cost them less to pay us for a breach of contract. Then we could stop transporting shiploads of coal to Germany.

It was incredibly beneficial to us to terminate the contract. We got paid $3.75 for every ton of coal that would not get delivered. The Germans paid nearly $10 million for terminating the contracts. Naturally we had to share this money with our mining partners, but approximately half of it went to our company. We never realized a profit like this in the business of shipping coal under our contracts.

We were the first coal company to sign such an agreement. Later on other companies also rushed to offer a similar deal to their partners. However, nobody got this kind of money for canceling contracts. Thereafter the Germans agreed to pay only fifty cents per ton of undelivered coal.

Our coal business with Germany never did recover again after this particular crisis. Construction of a major natural gas supply pipeline from Russia to West Germany was completed soon after. Gas producers in Europe lost the market, and one after another ceased their operations. They had been our primary buyers for the coal we delivered.

But by another stroke of luck, we discovered a new market – Japan. During the 1980s, Japanese industry was booming, ultimately causing a sharp coal deficit for its energy suppliers. I started to make contacts with Japanese businesspeople. Once again, influential acquaintances opened the doors of opportunity for me.

Just before Alexandra and I left for the 1964 Olympics in Tokyo, we developed a friendship with Admiral Arthur Redford. During the Second World War, he had been in charge of the Far East headquarters of the United States Armed Forces, led by General Douglas MacArthur. Later on he had headed the occupational army headquarters in Japan. When we told Admiral Redford that we were going to the Olympics, he gave me a letter of introduction to an important Japanese industrialist, a certain Mr. Aso, who was the son-in-law of the Japanese Prime Minister as well as a member of the Japanese Olympic Games Committee.

In Tokyo we delivered the letter but did not get to meet Mr. Aso personally. However, to my surprise, one evening just as the Games were coming to a close, we received an invitation from Mr. Aso to dinner. The note did not say where the dinner was to take place; it only gave the time when the limousine would pick us up.

We drove through a gate which encircled a garden, tastefully landscaped in flowers and decorative trees. A mansion in an old style of Japanese architecture, which was flooded in lights, turned out to be Mr. Aso's home.

There were about twenty people in the house, mingling and sipping cocktails. Most of them were members of the International Olympics Committee. For some reason, our hosts were not rushing to invite us to be seated for supper. Mr. Aso explained, "We are awaiting the arrival of the heir to the Japanese throne – the honorary chairman of the Olympic Games Committee of Japan."

Soon Crown Prince Akihito came in with his wife, Michiko. He was a very young, attractive man who spoke excellent English. We had the opportunity to talk at length with him and his wife, the future Empress, about sports and the successful Olympic Games. That evening I also met several other influential Japanese guests.

Years later, after we began doing business with Japan, these acquaintanceships proved very beneficial. I realized that the mere fact that I had been invited to that dinner and spoke with the heir to the throne and his wife – now their Imperial Highnesses – made a tremendous impression on the Japanese. Traditions and rituals have exceptional significance in Japan, and simply being seated at the same table with the Emperor meant that one was an honorable person and worthy of respect.

I appreciated even more the immeasurable loyalty that Japanese people have for their Emperor, a symbol of Japan's power, when I heard the following story related to me by my friend, Nat Wakamura, an executive with the Nippon Steel Corporation, Japan's largest steel company. Wakamura's wife, Tako, was a descendent of an aristocratic family in Japan; her grandfather had been the Chancellor of Emperor Hirohito's Palace. She introduced me to her father, Mr. Kabajama, who later on visited our home in East Hampton.

This gentleman was the same age as Emperor Hirohito and had grown up with him in the Royal Palace. When the Emperor took ill, Mr. Kabajama also became very ill. Wakamura told me that, when his father-in-law was in his sick bed, he constantly inquired about the health of His

Highness. When he heard that the Emperor was still holding his own, he said, "I have no right to leave sooner than our ruler does." However, once he got the announcement, "Japan is in mourning. The Emperor has died," Mr. Kabajama also quietly died the same evening.

My contacts in Japan were very helpful in business, which developed rather fast and successfully. We signed coal supply contracts with the Japanese at profitable terms. They would pay a good price provided they were assured of getting their fuel supplies on time. The business that Neris Coal and Carbon Corporation enjoyed with Japan until the mid-1990s was enjoyable and lucrative. The demand for coal there was much greater than it had been during the best of times in Germany. The only difficulty that we experienced was being able to supply the quantities that Japanese companies wanted. We had to hire extra brokers to help us find additional sources at the most beneficial prices.

With Nat Wakamura, Tokyo, 1976

My own work in this business was far more creative than administrative. It was extremely important to study the course of the economy in various countries. Although I did analyze economic indicators, conversations with friends and acquaintances from the business world served me all the more. The most important premise for my business was making contacts with a variety of influential people which often led to new opportunities.

In 1970 our company entered the oil business in addition to supplying coal. We bought petroleum in Venezuela and transported it to Germany. On a few occasions, we chartered tankers from Aristotle Onassis. Through him I also had the opportunity to meet Jacqueline, the widow of John Kennedy, after her marriage to this renowned Greek shipping magnate.

Interestingly, many people assume that I am Greek because Lithuanians and Greeks have common sounding last names that often end in – is or – as. I could not resist having a little fun with this when I tried to get through to Onassis one day. When I gave my name to his secretary, she immediately asked, "Are you Greek?"

Without hesitating I replied, "Isn't that clear from my name?" So the secretary started speaking to me in Greek while I answered her in Lithuanian. A very bewildered young woman at the other end of the line said, "I'm sorry, sir. I don't understand you."

"Ah, madam, where are you from?" I asked.

"I'm from Brooklyn," she said.

"Oh it's no wonder then," I calmly explained. "I'm speaking the ancient Hellenic Greek. You speak Brooklyn Greek." Before I could say I was only joking, the secretary put me right through to Onassis.

On My Own

At the end of the 1970s, Neris became involved in manufacturing operations in the Philippines where we established a steel pipe production plant. Imelda Marcos came to the grand opening of our company. This project was interesting although not very lucrative and lasted nearly ten years until it was taken over by our Filipino partners.

But in 1975 I decided to part company with Kęstutis Valiūnas. I bought out his share in Neris Carbon and Oil, the name of our company at that time, and continued in the coal business on my own.

We went our separate ways honorably and without conflicts. Even after we no longer had any common links in business, we still stayed in contact with one another and remained good friends. I consider our nearly 25 years of working together to have been my great good fortune.

Kęstutis Valiūnas successfully allotted all his time to engage in Lithuanian activities. He was elected the Chairman of VLIK, the 'Supreme Committee for Liberation of Lithuania'. Since the occupation of Lithuania, this organization had taken on an important role, acting as the provisional government of Lithuania in exile. It was involved in the struggle for the liberation of Lithuania and helped maintain our national culture in a wide spectrum of activities. Furthermore, Valiūnas, later authored a book on the activities of this organization.

In the meantime, I focused on my business dealings. Along with the coal trade, I was becoming more attracted to investments in other fields of economic activity. Energy projects were always of great interest to me. The oil crisis hit in the 1970s when petroleum prices leaped from $10 to $50 in a very short time. I invested quite a lot of money into the development of alternative energy sources, including a geothermal project in California.

In the early 1980s, I got involved in the development of a 4,000-acre citrus plantation in Florida. We acquired land near West Palm Beach which was excellently suited for raising citrus fruit. Our orchard never had a problem with frost even during the coldest winters.

Since our orchards matured, every year we have been selling more than a million boxes of oranges, mandarins, grapefruit and lemons domestically and also for export, mostly to Japan. This business has proved to be quite profitable with a generous return on my investment. Perhaps more money might be earned in other business areas but, as far as I was concerned, this was about more than profit. It was also a joy for me to enjoy the excellent fruit that was delivered to us from this grove all year round.

Unfortunately I have a melancholy feeling that our citrus garden will probably be liquidated soon. Over the past three decades, Palm Beach has greatly expanded and the city boundary has begun to push up against our land. Real estate development companies are now offering much more than the value of our fruit trees for our land. I am sad to think that the grove will have to go, but business is business. Sooner or later, a decision will probably be made to sell and, instead of orange trees, new luxurious homes will spring up for more retirees to enjoy in Florida.

Once I started getting sizeable earnings from coal trade, I was able to keep my promise to Alexandra to go on a trip to Europe. I had sworn to do that when the ship that was carrying us to the United States pulled away from the shores of Germany, and she lamented that she would never see Europe again.

We decided to go to the 1952 Olympic Games in Helsinki and visit a few other countries. (Since then, we have attended a great many summer Olympic Games, including the most recent ones in Sydney in 2000 and Athens in 2004.)

In early November of 1951, we moved from New Haven into our New Rochelle home to be closer to New York City. Two weeks later, on November 14, our first son was born. We gave him the name of Joseph with the middle name of Mindaugas after our king who had forged the nation of Lithuania with his crowning in 1253. Jurate, now nearly nine years old, was doing well in school. The children gave us endless joy.

The following year, Joseph announced that he wanted to keep his promise to take me to Europe. This was my first trip since we landed on these shores. We drove all over Germany, Italy and Switzerland on our way to the Olympic Games in Helsinki.

When we arrived in St. Moritz, Joseph was suddenly stricken with an attack of appendicitis and had to undergo emergency surgery. His recovery was sufficiently rapid, but his wound had not completely healed when we were supposed to leave for Milan and fly to Helsinki. Joseph was still unable to drive, so I was the one who had to sit behind the wheel. I'll never forget the nerve-wracking, narrow, winding roadways over the Alps and through numerous tunnels. By some stroke of good luck, we managed to get to Milan.

On March 18, 1953, our second son was born. We officially named him Alexander Kestutis and thought we would call him by his middle name – Kestutis – after our Lithuanian Grand Duke who safeguarded our borders from the ravaging Crusaders during the late 1300s. [But since we were in the United States, the nickname of Alex quickly caught on.]

Three years later on October 13, 1956, Michael Vytautas was born. His middle name is for our Grand Duke, known as Vytautas the Great, who ruled from 1392 to 1429 when Lithuania was at its height of power.

Exactly one day less than a year later, on October 12, 1957, we were blessed with another son, John Algirdas, whose mid-namesake was the Grand Duke who ruled our old country jointly with his brother Kęstutis.

Since the boys were all born in the United States, we knew they would grow up totally American but we liked the idea of giving them nationalistic middle names to remind them of their Lithuanian heritage.

St. Moritz, 1953

So it came to be that seemingly overnight, we were raising five children. With four boys under the age of six, we decided that we wanted a place out of the city to spend our summers. Joseph bought a spacious, old-style house in East Hampton which he remodeled. On the property he added a large swimming pool, an orchard and flower gardens. We became members of the Maidstone Club where our sons made their mark in golf, swimming and tennis. But golf was the family passion. The four Kazickas brothers each won the Club championship over the years – a feat that had never been accomplished at that time at any other high-ranking golf club and was written up by Golf Digest *magazine.*

The years went by, and our children grew quickly. We began traveling all over the world a great deal. We rarely felt like tourists though because Joseph had friends and acquaintances nearly everywhere we went who would always take us under their wings with pleasure.

One of my greatest impressions was a trip to India where we met with the Maharajas of Bikaner and Udaipur whom Joseph knew from a hunting trip. They invited us to stay with them in their luxurious palaces where dozens of servants waited on us hand and foot. I felt as though I had been magically transported into a storybook land.

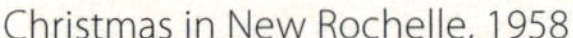

Christmas in New Rochelle, 1958

Upon meeting us, nearly everyone, especially an American, is always intrigued with our national origin. Many people had never heard of Lithuania. Indeed, during the terrible years of the Soviet occupation, our country was not even on any maps. I never hesitate to explain our heritage and our culture. My homeland was and always has been very dear to me.

March 13, 1959

Alex lost his first tooth today. He'll be five in a few days. The little ones, John and Michael, are playing so nicely. They are like twins. But they are so jealous of me. They clamor for my attention and shout for my help. They are like frisky little lambs.

I could write so much about the boys – about every one of their naughty moments, their conversations, their first steps – everything! I'll never end this diary that Joseph gave me when Jurate was born.

But these days I write so seldom. There is simply no time. But I know I will carry all these precious memories forever in my heart.

Cat Cay Island, Bahamas

Less than sixty miles from the shores of Florida is a place we call heaven on earth, our very own little paradise – Cat Cay.

This tiny island in the Bahamas, with a shoreline of coral reefs, is encircled by sugar-white sandy beaches, endlessly washed by turquoise-colored waves. Palms and pines, redwood and guaiacum trees, tamarind pods and a multitude of tropical trees grow in lush abundance over the tiny island. Intoxicating scents from flowering bushes, red rose mallows, bougainvillea and an array of other blossoms waft through the air.

Cat Cay became a part of our lives quite by accident. It was Christmas of 1967. Wilfred F. Rockwell, the head of Rockwell Corporation, one of the largest aviation and space technology companies in the world, invited us to visit his winter retreat on Bimini Island in the Bahamas. Rockwell had a home and a guest house along with a private dock on some 1,000 acres of land.

One evening, as we sat sipping cocktails and watching the sunset, our conversation turned to Hurricane Betsy which, in 1965, had devastated a small nearby island – Cat Cay. Once the exclusive destination of the rich and famous, Cat Cay was now rundown and abandoned.

Long ago Cat Cay had been a citadel of pirates. Its masters had been Morgan, Blackbeard and other seafaring robbers. Queen Victoria of England gifted this island to Captain William Henry Stuart in 1874. Over time it passed into the hands of Captain Haigh, a member of one of England's aristocratic families. An aristocratic gentleman, named Louis Wasey, bought the island from Haigh's descendants in 1931, built a home for himself and his guests and later turned the island into an exclusive private club.

A peak of prosperity for the island came after World War II when Edward VIII, the Duke of Windsor and former King of England, visited often. The Duke, who also held the post of Governor of the Bahamas, would come to Cat Cay to fish and play golf with his wife, Wally Simpson, for whom he had relinquished his rights to the throne.

The island flourished during those times. Cat Cay Club was considered one of the most prestigious in the world. Only the most influential American families, such as the Pews, Sloans, Vanderbilts and others were members of this exclusive club. However, social change, starting slowly after World War II, affected these people as well. This Anglo-Saxon club of high society became more democratic and opened its doors to successful Americans of other descents.

Nonetheless, Cat Cay Club upheld its image as a place of exclusive membership for the exceptional, the cream of society. Louis Wasey, the owner of the island, was in the public relations and advertising business. He made sure that club members included only owners of large-scale businesses and representatives of the old landed gentry in finance and industry. He made shrewd use of these contacts to expand his own business dealings.

Wasey always generated an atmosphere that was exceptionally majestic and ceremonial at his club. All arrivals, sailing into the island, were greeted by a native band. The owner of the island always personally came out to welcome each visitor and arranged a reception in honor of the newly arrived guest that same evening. If by chance some person, invited by another member, was considered unworthy of the Cat Cay Club community, Wasey would wait until that guest had departed. Then he'd

Cat Cay, 1970

Cat Cay

clap his hands together indicating that no way would that person ever again set foot on his island.

"All this is nothing more than a faded vision of the past," Rockwell reminisced about the glory of the Cat Cay Club. "Wasey's daughter, Jane, is now selling the island." Then an idea came to him and he added, "Maybe we should go over there and have a look around. Let's see if that island is worth buying."

I was pleased with such an invitation. I wanted to see with my own eyes what was left of the most prestigious club in the Bahamas after the hurricane. That very same day, Rockwell and I got into a boat and sailed off for Cat Cay, which was only a dozen miles from Bimini.

Abandoned and unkempt for the past three years, the island had again become a wild scrubland of palms, bushes and vines. Not a hint remained that this had once been a vacation haven for the rich. I was struck by an eerie sense of desolation and mystery. We could barely find a place to walk. All the pathways and sandy roads had been blown over by debris and plants sprouted through their cracks. Tropical bushes that grow exceedingly fast in the wild had overtaken the entire island. Their dizzying fragrances overwhelmed us as we forced our way through this jungle.

We searched for the golf course. It was engulfed with branches from broken trees and overgrown with shrubs and tangled vines. I spotted one house through the brush which seemed to have escaped serious damage from the hurricane, although a nearby swimming pool was in pitiful ruins.

On our way back to Bimini, all we could talk about was the enchanting place we had just visited. Though the Cat Cay of its former days of glory was no more, the abundance of natural beauty had left a powerful impression. That same evening, Rockwell began to talk seriously about buying the island. "This place is incredibly beautiful. Sure it's been damaged, but that's not so terrible. We can always rebuild the harbor and fix the golf course. In fact we can equip everything in the place better than it had been before," he said, inviting me to join him in this venture.

I thought long and hard, knowing that the cost of developing the island would be much more than either Rockwell or I calculated. But something about Cat Cay gripped my heart. Financially it did not make sense to buy an island in the Bahamas. Yet I kept dreaming about those placid crystalline waters, the soothing warm breezes, the utter peace I felt there.

About a month later, after some negotiation with Jane Wasey, Rockwell and I became the new owners of Cat Cay Island.

It did not take long for us to establish an enlarged owners' partnership and a club. Twenty of us – mostly our acquaintances and a few members of the old club – became partner owners. Each one took on a financial obligation to redevelop the island.

The first job was to equip and increase the capacity of the power station that had previously existed. Then the harbor was reconstructed and the golf course put back in order. A little later we built a desalinization

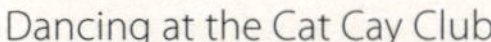

Dancing at the Cat Cay Club

plant for the seawater and repaired an old storage unit to collect rainwater. Prior to that, fresh water had to be hauled in from the mainland.

Then we took on the job of enlarging our membership to bring more life to the island. Little by little the island began to thrive, as new members bought houses and rebuilt them. I bought a house on the beach that had not been badly damaged by the hurricane. The renovations were completed in time for a family Christmas vacation in 1970, though we were still without furniture. Alexandra and I had to sleep stretched out on the floor.

This was Alexandra's first visit to the island. We had already traveled all over the world and had seen many beautiful places. Nevertheless, we had never before experienced such a peaceful aura and such a strong link between human life and nature. The sunsets are spectacular. On December evenings, as you watch the reddish disk of a waning sun slip into the ocean in the west, you can see the rounded silvery moon rising in the east as if it were emerging from the sea.

Over three decades have passed since our first night on Cat Cay Island. After all this time, one thing is perfectly clear. Here we truly feel as if we are in paradise.

The Joys of Gardening

That first Christmas, Alexandra and I walked arm in arm all over the island, telling each other again and again – this is indeed a paradise. But in spite of my happiness, I had a nagging sense that there was still something lacking in all this beauty. Then it finally hit me. In paradise there has to be at least one apple tree. Not only did we not see a single apple tree but no fruit trees of any kind existed (except for some tamarinds whose pods are not really suitable for eating).

One evening I asked Fred Crawford, one of the few members of the club who had been on the island in the days of Louis Wasey, why there were no fruit trees.

"You know, some people had tried to plant orchards on their lots but they never had any success with them. The soil is too sandy and alkaline, and it rarely rains here. We get some rainfall in July and August, but that's not enough moisture for the trees to bear fruit."

In the orchard, Cat Cay

Nevertheless, I became obsessed with creating my own tropical orchard on the island. I wanted all kinds of unknown trees, so our visitors could sample fruit they have never tasted before. I began reading all sorts of literature on exotic plants to get a grasp of tropical plant life theory and even joined the International Rare Tropical Fruit Association based in Miami.

My very first fruit tree was a papaya. I had noticed one growing in a distant corner of the island near a garbage dump. I dug it out and transplanted it on my own lot. The tree was watered and fertilized consistently, and it finally took root, producing very tasty fruit.

I decided to grow more papayas, experimenting with the best way to develop the most flavorful fruit. Each tree was numbered; and after it bore fruit, I would offer my family and guests a taste. They would evaluate the flavor on a five point scale. On the basis of such a survey, I pin-pointed the trees which produced the most delicious papaya and used those seeds to plant new trees. I do believe that there is no other place, at least in Florida, where a papaya more delicious than mine can be found.

Consulting with a tropical fruit expert from Miami, I then went on to plant grapefruit, oranges, lemons, mandarins and limes. I installed an underground watering system on my land. Presently the earth is moisturized regularly with water, liquid fertilizer and other vital nutrients by this system.

Once my citrus trees blossomed, I was successful in raising the rarest of plants from tropical lands like Thailand, Costa Rica and the Amazon River basin. Eventually I had 55 varieties of fruit trees growing in my orchard including the dovyalis, rambutan, black sapote (which has the flavor of melted chocolate), Malaysia apple, Chinese lychee, breadfruit tree, Barbados cherry, calamondin, canistel, kumquat, guava, icarambola, carrisa, loquats and many, many more. Few people had ever even heard of these exotic fruits that I cultivated in my little garden.

Hurricane Andrew

Hurricane Andrew swept over Cat Cay Island on August 23, 1992. As the storm approached the Bahamas and Florida, we were in New York, nervously listening to the weather forecasts every day. Warnings were issued that Cat Cay could end up being in the eye of the hurricane, and that's exactly what happened.

At the time, there were about fifty people on the island, mostly service staff. For a while everyone stood staring out at the ocean where, several miles away, the waters were being literally lifted up to the sky by the horrendous winds. Suddenly the wind completely subsided. There was practically no air to breathe – the whirl of the hurricane had sucked it all up. A frightening weird calm descended over the island. And then, at around four o'clock in the morning, the silence literally exploded.

The hurricane winds reached speeds over 160 miles per hour. Andrew was one of the strongest hurricanes ever. It devastated not only Cat Cay but Southern Florida as well. Damages from the hurricane reached some $12 billion.

Several months after the hurricane, I visited the island. I could not believe my eyes when I saw the destruction. The winds of the tornado were so powerful that a boat, anchored at the pier by Bebe Rebozo's home, had been tossed into the swimming pool upside down. Another yacht had ended up on a small hill.

Our house was badly damaged. The roof, doors and windows were missing. Only the walls still stood. Splinters of our furnishings were scattered all over our property. The strangest thing was that one of our sofas from the first floor had been thrown up the stairs to the second floor. Everything that had not been blown out of our roofless house was thoroughly drenched by the rains and now reeked of mildew.

But I was not prepared for what was left of my once beautifully maintained orchard. Many of the trees were completely broken in pieces and some had been ripped out of the ground with their roots. Even a great many palm trees had also been uprooted. Not a single tree that had been in the path of the tornado-like whirlwinds remained. All my beloved rare fruit trees, with the exception of some kumquats and avocados, were gone.

After Hurricane Andrew some of the owners decided to sell their homes and their shares in the island. The number of our members dropped and fewer people came to spend their vacations here. But Alexandra and I did not abandon Cat Cay. We rebuilt our house and continued to spend our winters on the island. And over time the Club was revitalized. (And I'm happy to say that, little by little, my garden of exotic fruits has been resurrected and today is flourishing albeit with only a few fruit trees.)

Today there are many owners of companies and executives of major corporations who are part of the Cat Cay Club. In addition to our family members, many distinguished guests have come to our home. A memorable event was a visit by the astronauts who flew a space rocket to the moon for the very first time in history. When they came to our home, Alexandra gave them some marmalade made from my kumquats. A few years later, I ran into one of the astronauts in California, who remembered the visit to our home, and jokingly told me that he was still smacking his lips over our marmalade.

Another vacationer on Cat Cay was Richard Nixon, the President of the United States although, at the time, he had already resigned his post. Nixon was a friend of Bebe Rebozo, one of our club members, and stayed at his home during his visits. Richard Nixon spent many a day on the island, writing his book of memoirs. There was no better place on earth to accomplish such a job.

Nixon loved to play golf. I saw him on the course, pushing his own golf cart and putting away without any security people around him. Even the Secret Service believed Cat Cay to be so safe that they saw no reason to follow the President around on the golf course.

Former President Lyndon Johnson also spent a few days relaxing on Cat Cay as a guest of Augustine Bush, the owner of the Budweiser beer brewery, who kept his luxurious yacht in the harbor.

Our Odyssey Continues

Ever since childhood, I had been dreaming about seeing the world. This everlasting dream of mine could finally come true after I became a businessman.

Alexandra and I tried to visit all the most interesting places in the world where miracles of nature and architecture were displayed. We marveled at Angkor Wat in Cambodia, Machu Picchu in Peru, the Taj Mahal in Agra and the pyramids of Egypt. We trekked through the surroundings of Buddha's birthplace in India and walked the Stations of the Cross of Jesus Christ in Jerusalem. We watched the funeral ceremonies on the Ganges River and sailed down the Yangtze River on the Mao Tse-Tung ship from Tibet to Shanghai. We traveled from the vast plains of Africa to the heights of the Himalayas.

Travel was something more than a source of pleasure for me. I valued the experiences as the best means to understand how varied life can be and to delve into the very essence of mankind. I wanted very much to impart such a sense of learning and adventure to my children as well. We made every effort to include them in our travels, so long as the trips did not interfere with their schoolwork.

Heartbreak

When our eldest son, Joseph, graduated from the university, we decided to give him an extraordinary gift – a trip around the world of several months in duration. He selected the route on his own, wanting to learn more about the religious and spiritual evolvement of mankind through the shrines and monasteries of Jerusalem, Angkor Wat and Japan. Joseph returned aglow in the joy of the impressions that he had experienced.

Our second-born son, Alexander (whom we always called by his Lithuanian name, Kestutis), graduated from the university in 1976. I also offered him a three month trip around the world before he was to start a job with a large shipping company. I felt such an experience would be valuable since Kestutis would be working in the area of international business.

Our son left early in October traveling alone. Wherever he landed, he would send us a postcard and call home regularly. I will never forget his call from Tehran. We talked for a full half hour. Kestutis enthusiastically described all the places he had seen celebrating ancient Persian culture. From there Kestutis flew to India and Nepal. We could hardly wait to get his next phone call.

The day was the 10th of December, a Sunday; the spirit of Christmas was enveloping the entire United States. Alexandra was peacefully reading a book while listening to music. Unexpectedly a telegram arrived from the United States Ambassador in Nepal. It read: "With great regret, we

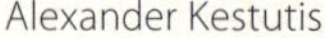
Alexander Kestutis

must inform you that your son, Alexander Kazickas, was found dead in his hotel room in Katmandu. Kindly contact our Embassy right away regarding the transport of his remains."

Everything went black before my eyes. I went into the next room where Alexandra was reading. "Alytė, I have to tell you some horrible news," I managed to stutter out.

I began reading the telegram. She raised her eyes up from her book and stared at me. I choked. I could not complete the sentence.

She noticed that I was squeezing the telegram in my hand. "What happened? What are you holding?" she insisted.

I held the letter out to her, telling her, "Kestutis has died."

Alexandra did not cry out. I could see that she had closed her eyes; she sat, frozen in her chair. The music was still playing, but it seemed as though an ominous silence overtook the entire room. We did not speak a single word to one another. Both of us felt crushed into nothingness. Kestutis had always seemed the child who was closest to me. Not only did he resemble me the most by his looks but also by his character. He had distinguished himself as a terrific athlete – he had won several prizes in swimming and several golf championships. The whole family was immensely proud of him.

Now, without warning, we were being told that our son was gone. We simply could not believe it.

Once I had composed myself, the first thing I did on that sad, sad Sunday – the most tragic day of our lives – was to telephone Jurate

and Joseph. Then I had to break the terrible news to Michael, who was fourteen, and our youngest son, John, then thirteen. Every time I told one of them what had happened, I felt a fresh, hard blow to my being. In another way, it helped me through those most difficult hours because we were sharing our common pain.

All of us were so shaken on that day that we were unable to worry about how to bring Kestutis' body back home. We just could not rush into doing anything. Neither Alexandra nor I had the strength to fly to Katmandu. We decided that our oldest children, Jurate and Joseph, would go to handle all the arrangements. By sheer coincidence, the son of our neighbors in New Rochelle worked at the embassy in Katmandu and was able to help them.

The day after they arrived, Kestutis was cremated. Only his ashes would return to New York.

Naturally an autopsy had been done in Nepal before the cremation to determine why someone in the bloom of his youth had suddenly met with death. For some reason, no cause of death could be established.

On the table in his hotel room, there were two, still unmailed letters – one to us and one to his girlfriend. Reading the letter that was addressed to us, and knowing that our beloved Kestutis was no longer with us, we were deeply shaken by his last sentence: "No matter what might ever happen to me in life, I will always love and honor you."

Some time later, I recalled a strange sort of omen which I had experienced. The night on which Kestutis died, I had seen him in a prophetic dream. He seemed to be approaching me, walking on some sort of grass. I remember that I was amazed at how translucent the light around him seemed to be. The nearer Kestutis came towards me, the smaller he became. From the figure of a grown man, Kestutis suddenly turned into a shadow. When it seemed that he was about to reach me, he disappeared entirely. At that moment, I awoke, awash in some inexplicable anxiety. However, by the morning, this bad sense of foreboding quickly dissipated. It was only after I had received the telegram about this tragedy did I realize that the dream must have come to me during those moments in which Kestutis met his death.

Nothing was left but to uphold our final obligations to Kestutis – never to forget him and never to stop loving him. I was so deeply moved by his expression of love for us in the last unmailed letter of his life. We knew we had to immortalize his memory in some way at Katmandu.

Several thousand Catholics live in Nepal, where they are a religious minority; they feel discriminated against and are not entirely free to express the teachings of their religion. Even as late as the 1980s, there was no Catholic Church in Katmandu. When we learned this, we wrote to the Jesuits, telling them that we would like to build a shrine in memory of our son, Kestutis. That was a start. The entire Catholic community of the country pooled their resources, other sponsors came forth and the walls of an actual church, not just a shrine, went up. Eventually the beautiful Church of the Assumption was built.

In 1998 Alexandra and I, accompanied by Jurate, Joseph and his wife, Lucy, traveled to Katmandu for a special mass in memory of Kestutis. His name is inscribed in gold on the main altar of the church.

As the private mass was ending, several women came into church, one holding an infant in her arms. They were there for a christening but, for some unknown reason, neither the father nor the godfather had arrived. They asked if we would stand in for the missing participants and my son, Joe, and I happily obliged. We were all deeply moved by the symbolism of this occurrence. We had just finished the prayers in remembrance of our son who had left this earth at a very young age. And here we were, christening a newly born life.

Via Dolorosa

For some, the loss of a child might shake their faith to the core. I must admit that many times in my deep pain I could only ask God, "Why? " But it seemed futile to me to rage in anger at the injustice of it all. In a way, the pain that I suffered over the loss of my beloved son strengthened my religion.

When I was invited to get involved in the restoration of the Via Dolorosa where Jesus suffered before his death, I was grateful for the opportunity.

Alexandra and I had already visited Jerusalem several times in our earlier days of travel. Each time, as I followed the Stations of the Cross, I felt a great sense of despair. I could not understand how Golgotha Road, a place visited by Christians from all over the world, could be so neglected. All along that sacred path were shacks in sad disrepair and piles of trash everywhere. It actually took a good deal of effort to find the locations of the blessed Stations because there were few signs or memorial plaques. There was not even adequate lighting so that once it got dark, it was quite dangerous for any pilgrims of prayer to visit.

I tried hard to come up with an explanation for the lack of attention to such a place of holiness. The world capital for Catholics had become Rome. Neither the Protestant nor the Orthodox Churches considered Jerusalem to be a center of their religions either. The end result was that most Christians took too little care of the holy city. As far as Jews and Arabs were concerned, Jesus Christ was simply a prophet of another foreign religion. Besides, their frequent wars with one another gave them different worries that took priority over other matters.

For me Jerusalem is the only true religious center for all Christians. The origins of our faith came from this city. The place where Christ had to carry his cross to provide salvation for all human beings had to be more important to us than Rome. Rome, after all, was merely the capital of popes.

A very well maintained, huge Muslim Mosque stood in the center of Jerusalem and it was considered one of the most important shrines in the city. For Jews the holy place in the city was the Wailing Wall, where thousands could be seen praying daily. The Eastern Orthodox also had their own church in the center. The overall impression was that Roman Catholic places of worship in Jerusalem were the most poorly maintained.

My son-in-law, Roger Altman, told me about the initiative to repair and restore the Stations of the Cross. It was sponsored by The Jerusalem Foundation with the support of John Whitehead, a prominent New Yorker who was a former Deputy Secretary of State and Chairman of Goldman Sachs. I was eager to get involved.

All of our children traveled with us to attend the celebration, marking the completion of the restoration of the Stations of the Cross in March of 2000. The first thing that our family did was to kneel in prayer for the soul of Kestutis, our beloved son and brother.

The celebration lasted three days. A very intensive program for visiting Palestine was offered to the special guests and other representatives of the Jerusalem Foundation. Shimon Peres, who was the former Prime Minister and, at that time, the Minister of Regional Cooperation of Israel, arranged a lunch for us. Our host for dinner was the Minister of Tourism, Amnon Lipkin Shahak. We also met with top officials of the autonomous government of Palestine, leaders of Palestine's Christian communities and the patriarch of Jerusalem, Michael Sabaha.

I had another reason for helping with the restoration of the Stations of the Cross. I also wanted to contribute in my own way to continue the dialogue of reconciliation between Lithuanians and Jews, a relationship that was often strained as a result of World War II. The new democratically elected government in Lithuania had acknowledged the terrible atrocities that had been committed by some Lithuanians during the war. I felt fortunate to be able to make a philanthropic gesture in Jerusalem. The city was not only a holy place for Christians, it was also a significant monument of culture for the nation of Israel. During the ceremony, I sensed that the Israelis were appreciative of our efforts. They were people who knew how to show their gratitude whenever someone does a good deed for them.

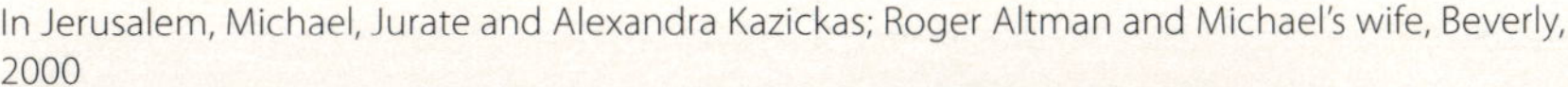

In Jerusalem, Michael, Jurate and Alexandra Kazickas; Roger Altman and Michael's wife, Beverly, 2000

Jurate and little Joseph, 1952

My Children

Family life has always been important to me. I grew up in a loving, supportive home and learned so much from my parents. The loss of my father at an early age was devastating. I knew that in my life I wanted a big family – children and grandchildren – to fill a house with love and laughter.

All my children are precious to me. Jurate has a special place in my heart, being the only girl and the only child who lived through the tempestuous war years, when our lives were so unsettled. But I longed for a son and could not have been happier when our first boy, Joseph Mindaugas, was born on November 14, 1951. After so many years of waiting and expectation, it was a thrilling moment to welcome him into this world. Alexandra and I had difficulty agreeing whether he looked more like a Kazickas or a Kalvėnas (her family) but, already at birth, we knew that he was going to be tall and handsome.

And then it seemed, in a blink of an eye, in less than five years, three more sons came into our lives. Faster than we ever expected, our home in New Rochelle was brimming with warmth, boisterous play and mischief-making. I was a strict parent, that I know, but I felt it was very important to teach the children how to behave properly.

Our summers in East Hampton were the happiest of times. We enrolled the boys in lessons for swimming, sailing, tennis and golf. I myself did not really have the opportunity to play sports when I was young and felt that was missing in my life. So I took special pleasure in seeing my boys become such superb athletes.

And they were all fantastic sportsmen. Kestutis was such a strong swimmer, he could have been a junior Olympian. Every weekend we would travel together to meets all over the East coast. Those were precious times for me and him. John too was an excellent competitive swimmer.

Jurate with Joseph and Alexander, 1953

But it was golf that became the Kazickas boys' passion. Each one of them won the Maidstone Club golf championship – some even several times – earning a mention for this unusual family feat in a popular sports magazine.

But what I cared about most of all was giving my children the best education I could afford. The decision to send Joe at age eleven to Switzerland to attend Le Rosey was not an easy one. I felt that attending a European school was the best way for him to learn several languages. Being an international businessman, I knew how important it was to be able to converse in someone's native tongue. I also felt he would make friendships with a cross section of European society that would last a lifetime. We missed him terribly, but luckily I was able to visit him during my frequent business trips abroad. We sent the other boys, however, to schools closer to home. All the boys went to excellent prep schools and graduated from good colleges.

I delight in what makes each of my children unique and special. Jurate was independent and adventurous. She went to Kenya after college as a volunteer teacher, was a photo journalist in Vietnam (where she was wounded covering the battle of Khe sanh in 1968), went on a Mt. Everest expedition and had an interesting career as a reporter and author of several books.

Joe has an adventurous streak too. For a while, living in a trailer, he worked for a coal company in Kentucky. Then he started a hot tub business and eventually moved on to real estate. Unlike me he is extremely handy around the house, seemingly able to build or fix anything.

Alex (as we called Kestutis) was outgoing, handsome and friendly but deeply insecure, despite his many gifts. He kept so much to himself. We had no idea he was a hero until a woman wrote us after his death that he had saved her son's life from drowning. It was just another day at the beach for him.

Michael was a worrier when he was little but became a strong, disciplined and determined adult. He has a fierce competitive streak which makes him a good winner but an unhappy loser, especially in golf. But those qualities stand him in good stead in his job as a commodities trader.

As a child John had an unending interest in building model airplanes. His need to know why they too often crashed may have motivated him to study engineering in college. Now he works with me on various business

Jurate with her four brothers, 1958

projects, and I could not manage without him. He is sensitive, compassionate and always ready to help anyone in need.

I remember so many happy family times – the boys frolicking like little puppies on the lawn in East Hampton, our skiing trips to Europe, an African safari, the long snowy winters in New Rochelle and Christmas vacations in Cat Cay.

And yet certain bitter sweet moments rise to the surface when I think of my sons. Joe must have been six or seven when he entered his first swimming race. He had trained very hard for it. I watched my dear little boy paddle furiously only to come in last. When he got out of the water, he gave me a hug and said with a big smile, "Dad, we made it!" And then he hung his head down and cried.

And then there was a moment that Alexandra can never forget. One day, exasperated with the unruly behavior of the boys, she remarked that she was sure none of them would take care of her when she was old and grey. The boys scampered out to play but, a few minutes later, Michael slipped into the room. He took Alexandra's hand and looked somberly into her eyes. "Mommy," he said, "I will always take care of you."

New Years in St. Moritz with the family, 1964

Some memories just stay in our hearts forever and fill us with such deep sentiment.

Now the boys are doing well in their careers and more importantly, they are happily married and fathers themselves. Alexandra and I have eleven grandchildren whom we treasure. When we all get together for Thanksgiving or a special birthday, I cannot contain my joy thinking how very blessed I am.

My mother always used to say that the only thing that matters in a person is goodness. It is not material wealth or professional success or public accolade that determines someone's worth. I can honestly say all my children are good people.

And I am very proud of them.

A Passion for Hunting

One of the great passions of my life is hunting which, I think, I inherited from my father and my ancestors. They, like nearly all the Lithuanians who had been exiled to Chornaya Padina, liked to hunt. After the family moved to Lithuania, my father continued this pastime that he so enjoyed and taught me as well. I must have been about ten years old when I began shooting sparrows which were so plentiful that farmers were intent on reducing their numbers. In the winter, my father and I trudged through the snow in the forest looking for rabbits. Unfortunately I was only able to pursue this sport with him for a few winter seasons because he died soon after. The joys of a hunt were forgotten for many years after that.

Hunting in Somalia

A chance occurrence helped me to rediscover this sport. In the mid-1960s, I met the editor of *Fields and Streams* magazine. He asked me if I happened to be a hunter. I told

On a tiger hunt in India

him how I had hunted rabbits as a child. "Why not give it a try again?" he suggested. He told me that during the hunting season, deer could be shot at several locations around New York State. "But, if you'd like to get involved in some more serious hunting, go to Alaska! That is absolutely the best."

After a few seasons of deer hunting in the Catskills and Maine, where I had bought some property, I decided to go to Alaska. The magazine editor helped me meet some of the best guides in the area.

I spent three incredibly fascinating weeks in Alaska. During that trip, I saw moose, decked out in their gigantic horns, deer and black and brown bears. I didn't come home with too many trophies, but that was not so important. It was the wonders of nature itself that brought the greatest pleasure.

My most exciting hunting adventure was in India in February of 1962. A close friend of mine, Bhagvata Singh, the Great Maharana of Udaipur, invited me to go on a tiger hunt. Alexandra and I stayed in the Maharana's huge palace in Udaipur, which is in the state of Rajasthan. It was the most fantastic place I had ever seen. Elaborate carvings graced the columns to the entrance of the grand, palatial building; its rooftop contained dozens of multifaceted towers and peaks. A fountain with pools in the center of the courtyards contributed to a refreshing coolness. The marble floors were inlaid with intricate mosaics. The walls and ceilings were covered in colorful decor while silks and muslins graced the hallways.

We were provided with the special bedroom that Queen Elizabeth II and her husband, Prince Phillip of Great Britain, had stayed in during their hunting trip just a few days earlier. I liked to joke later that I had had the honor of sharing a bed with the Queen of England. My wife would always snap right back that fortune had smiled on her too because she had been able to share the same bed as Prince Phillip.

In the morning servants brought us breakfast that was served on a huge balcony, overlooking the private zoo of the Maharana. The sounds of screeching monkeys and the clamor of exotic birds among a setting of lush, tropical plants provided the entertainment for this, our most unusual meal. Amidst this splendor, we suddenly remembered that it was February 18th, and what this date meant to us. Exactly fifteen years ago, we had sailed into New York harbor. It seemed like only yesterday that we had been just like all the other ill-fated war refugees, ragged immigrants entering the United States. I looked over at Alexandra and I understood that she was thinking exactly the same thing. I said to her, "Can you imagine how strangely the fate of a person can turn? A terrible misfortune becomes a stroke of great luck. We have certainly traveled down a long road over those years, haven't we? We started from that little shoemaker's room in Pasvalys and today we have reached a Maharaja's palace in India."

After breakfast we set out on a day long trip into the jungle for the hunt. Tigers were generally hunted from one of two positions, either sitting atop an elephant or aiming from a special fixture in a tree called a machan. About a thousand people get involved in a hunt like this. A wide passageway of twenty to thirty yards is cleared in the jungle. From a distance of about five miles away, animal drivers create a bellow of all sorts of noises to frighten the animals and make them run down this passageway towards us.

As you lay in wait for a slowly approaching tiger, you first hear the shriek of monkeys and anxious birds. The sounds of fear from the jungle

Hunting in India with the Maharaja of Bikaner, Karni Singh

inhabitants heighten the tension in the atmosphere. The hunter has to wait without so much as moving a muscle because tigers are noted for their unusually keen sight. They notice the least out-of-the-ordinary movement in their surroundings. The hunter has to keep a sharp eye on the clearing since a tiger will always try to get past any open space as fast as possible and can jump across it in a blink of an eye with no more than two leaps. The only chance a hunter has to shoot the animal is while it is within the clearing. On that day, as soon as the tiger came into view, I aimed carefully and pulled the trigger. The mighty beast fell instantly. It turned out I had shot a record size tigress – the largest one in more than fifty years.

I tried out both types of tiger hunting – the treetop machan as well as the more dangerous method of sitting in a special basket on top of an elephant as the tigers are driven in our direction. A machan is affixed to a tree at a height of some seven yards, and a tiger is capable of actually jumping up into it. The greater threat of an attack by a tiger, however, is when the hunter is sitting on an elephant.

Today, of course, tiger hunting is completely prohibited and rightly so because their numbers have dwindled and they are now an endangered species.

For many years, my hunting trips brought me from Alaska to Africa and from India to New Zealand. I have accumulated more than a hundred trophies and was fortunate enough to shoot several prize quality trophies. One was the biggest she-tiger which had been terrorizing all the villagers in the surrounding areas of Rajasthan. Other trophies of mine are also very rare, including gigantic elephant tusks which decorate my home in Vilnius.

Now, of course, my hunting career is over. I know that today the sport is controversial. But back in the 50s and 60s, game was plentiful, and the wildlife conservation movement was not as active as it is now. While I have no regrets about my hunting, I doubt that I could participate in the sport today. Lions and leopards, tigers and elephants and even the ugly and menacing Cape buffalo should be enjoyed as God's creatures. Now I'd rather go out into the jungle armed with a camera instead of a gun.

The Art of Friendship

I have to admit that hunting was also important to me because of the opportunities it provided for business contacts. Hunting makes for close relationships. People who barely know one another readily become friends when forced to face danger and live in extreme circumstances. It's an understandable process. Even those who are accustomed to palatial residences find themselves in entirely natural surroundings, climbing mountains, wading through swamps, crawling through gnarled bushes and sleeping in tents without any of the usual comforts. This makes for a special bonding. Sitting together at night by a campfire and sharing our adventures make all the members of the hunting party feel like brothers and sisters.

What greatly fostered the success of my business ventures was that I had a great many friends over my lifetime. Fate brought me together with a variety of different people, and these casual acquaintances grew into friendships. The men and women who became my friends were simply interesting to me in many different ways. A relationship would develop on its own accord, sometimes just by playing golf or chatting at different receptions.

For some reason, conversations always flowed easily for me. Somehow I was always able to engage in discussions on a variety of topics of interest with prominent people including those who were considerably older than I was.

One such person was the distinguished American industrialist, Fred Crawford, who created TRW, the gigantic electronics and space industry company. He was a member of the old Cat Cay Club founded by Louis R. Wasey and spent several months a year on the island until his death at age 103. Crawford was also a member of the boards of many corporations and knew the influential political and financial elite of the world. He even once met Stalin himself during the years of WWII, when Fred was in charge of American military supply operations in the Soviet Union.

The man was charming and a natural conversationalist, able to interact readily and elegantly with the most eminent people. I learned many social arts from Fred. Thanks to his admirable political insights, humor and tremendous life experiences, he was able to make gracious speeches and lively toasts.

For many years, Fred Crawford was a widower. He used to wear a pin on his jacket which read "BOW – Beware of Widowers." However, when he was 85 years of age, he finally married his long-time secretary, Kay.

Fred and Alexandra, who would often be the only two members on the island, became great golfing buddies over the years in Cat Cay. They took their golf very seriously, playing fiercely for a dollar a game.

To celebrate his 100-year birthday, Fred arranged an unforgettable and very merry party called the "Crawford Circus." Some 400 guests came to pay their respects to this wonderful man. The amazing thing was that despite his many years, he managed to remember the name of each arriving guest. As we crept up the long line of well-wishers, we watched Fred personally greet every guest. He joked with each one and remembered some past encounter they had shared.

During dinner Fred delivered a lengthy, wise and humor-filled speech that reviewed his entire life. He never so much as glanced at a single

Alexandra with Helmut Horten and friends in Düsseldorf, 1963

note. At the end of his talk, he said that he wanted to express his special gratitude to all the guests who had come to his party from seventeen different countries of the world. Without missing a single beat, this centenarian proceeded to name every country along with the names of the people from each place. After he named the sixteenth country, he fell silent. A long pause hung in the air. Could he have forgotten the last country? Certainly not! At last he added, "It gives me great pleasure to tell you that here with me today are my closest friends from one other country – Alexandra and Joseph Kazickas from Lithuania. Only truthfully speaking, they did not come to America today or yesterday. They actually got here several decades ago." Alexandra and I were immensely flattered by his gracious reference to us.

I also received some exceptionally important lessons in life from my close friend Helmut Horten, a prominent and wealthy German businessman who owned a chain of department stores. I believe it was in 1965 when I was introduced to Horten by the Henkels, one of Germany's prominent families in finance and industry. After the Second World War, the Henkels managed a chemical concern and also owned many other companies.

The Henkels invited me to a reception in their home which was attended by a great many of the German elite in society and business. When I met Horten, a conversation began flowing easily between us at once. I told him that I was an enthusiastic hunter and proceeded to recount stories of my favorite hunts in Alaska. Horten came alive and, out of the blue, he said to me, "I'm leaving for a hunt to Austria tomorrow. Let's go together!"

I was stunned to get such an unexpected invitation. (As I got to know him over the years, I became accustomed to his mercurial and impetuous personality.) I tried to tell him that I couldn't go, but he was insistent. "I don't want to hear another word. Be ready tomorrow morning. I'll send a car over to your hotel, and it will drive you directly to my plane."

The offer was very tempting, but I had an important business meeting the next day and was simply unable to accept. Horten made me promise we would go hunting together one day. We made a deal that he'd arrange a hunt for me in Austria and I'd reciprocate in Alaska.

Later I learned that Horten had rented the hunting palace which had once belonged to the former Austrian Emperor, Franz Josef I, in the eastern Alps relatively near to Vienna. This estate included close to 100,000 acres of woodland together with the Hapsburg Castle, complete with all its rich paintings and tapestries. Horten was obligated to maintain the castle at his own expense, upholding all the strict State requirements for monument protection.

The next time I was in Germany, I called Horten, and he invited me for lunch in his starkly modern home in Düsseldorf. The house was very large with dozens of servants taking care of it and the beautiful gardens. In the middle of the meal, Horten invited me to fly with him in his private plane to Cap d'Antibes on the French Riviera, where he was remodeling his villa.

The villa, which had belonged to the famous French winemaker, Andre Dubone, overlooked the Mediterranean Sea. Within it an entire recreational complex had been erected. The house had a spectacular pool set into the rocks, a sports field, a guesthouse and a building for servants' quarters which contained a tunnel under the main road leading into the owner's villa. It was hard to imagine how such a spectacular place could be improved, but a few ideas came up as we looked over everything. I had a few suggestions myself. That was the beginning of my friendship with Horten, one that lasted for three decades.

A year went by during which we found the time for a number of pleasant interludes and hunting trips. Several times I organized trips to Alaska, but Horten was never able to come, once because of an earthquake that damaged the airport at Anchorage. We did hunt together a number of times in Europe though. I remember vividly our visits to the hunting territories of Yugoslavia, arranged for Horten by invitation from Marshall Tito, the country's dictator. I have no idea how Horten managed to meet Tito, but he even got the right to rent facilities at two of the Marshall's hunting lodges. One was in a park near Belgrade and the other, in the boundless forests of East Croatia.

It was early wintertime. Over the crackling snow, we rode on sleighs drawn by white horses that were covered in frost from the cold. We had hoped to meet Tito but, at the last minute, he was not able to join us in the hunt. The organizers had been planning for Tito to shoot a bear – their winter hibernation had not yet begun. The drivers tracked one bear and watched it, saving it especially for the Marshall. Though our goal had been to hunt down a mountain sheep – a true beauty with powerful horns – once it was clear that Tito was not coming, we were given the honor of going after that bear. I was the lucky one who got the trophy.

During our time together, I noticed that Horten was frequently concerned with his health. His personal physician accompanied him everywhere. I found out that Horten was disabled. His left leg had been paralyzed from the waist since his childhood as result of polio. Nevertheless, he had learned to walk in an elegant gait, holding a stance, taut like a violin string, never bending his leg at the knee. In truth it wasn't all that obvious that he had a limp. But, naturally, this handicap caused him a lot of problems. His leg was as hard as a rock and every morning, it would have to be massaged for nearly an hour.

Understandably Horten was unable to serve in the military. Despite this he was arrested for a time after the Second World War. During the years of Nazi rule, he owned several department stores. Although he had nothing in common with the Nazis, he was unable to evade interrogations, simply because he was one of the wealthiest people in Germany under Hitler. In the early weeks following the war, even the Allied Special

Services were suspicious of his affluence. Horten spent several months in jail but was never tried in court.

All of the stores that Horten owned wound up in the East German Zone. Naturally the East German government immediately nationalized all of them. He was forced to rebuild his sales empire from scratch.

One evening over dinner, Horten told me his story. It seems that after he came out of jail, he went to a banker that he knew and asked for some kind of a job. He had been left with little money to start a business. This banker said, "I don't have a suitable job for you but I can give you a loan. Buy yourself a store and try to get by on that."

Horten took that loan from Commerzbank and bought a department store in Düsselberg. He refurbished it so that the store was more modern than any other that existed during postwar times. Sales went well for him and, in a short time, he got credit again, this time from Deutsche Bank. With this money, he acquired several other stores. By the time I met Horten, he already owned sixty-six gigantic department stores.

I was intrigued by his business success. After all, he had started from ground zero to create an entire network of shopping centers. One day, relaxing by his pool at the Cap d'Antibes villa, I had a thought.

"Helmut," I said to him, "when it comes to money, you are a miracle worker. I wonder – is it really worthwhile, spending your time handling the management of your company, now that your retail operations have grown to such a size? You've already given up all the direct administration of your business. You're just handling the flow of finances now. Wouldn't you be better off selling all your property and devoting yourself to capital management? That way, you'd be free to invest in a variety of projects that are the most interesting to you. I'm certain that with your financial talents, you'd be making a much greater profit doing that."

Horten was quiet for a time and then he said to me, "You know, that's a very interesting idea. I'll think about it."

Our conversation on this topic came to an end. However, after some time, I got a call from him in New York. "The last time we were together, you brought up quite a good idea. Maybe you know somebody in America who would be interested in buying my retail outlets?" he asked me.

At the time Alexandra and I had decided to buy a house in Florida at the private Hobe Sound Club Resort. To buy property, a person first had to be accepted into the local community which was dominated by one family. A friend promised to ask Senator Prescott Bush (father of the former President of the United States, George Bush, and grandfather of President George W. Bush) to recommend me for membership in the club. I got an invitation to attend a cocktail party that the Senator was holding.

That evening I happened to meet the chief financial officer of the massive Sears Roebuck store chain. We had exchanged business cards. So, when Helmut Horten asked me if I knew of anyone who might be interested in his stores, I immediately remembered this person. I picked up the phone and called him to ask if Sears Roebuck would be interested in entering the German market.

"What a great offer! We just moved into Spain and we intend to expand in Europe. I'll introduce you to head of our international development company. You can discuss this matter with him," he said.

I called the gentleman and he was eager to meet Mr. Horten. Within weeks negotiations began between the two parties. I was empowered to be the intermediary for the transactions. All the necessary data was gathered; the terms were agreeable to both sides, and it seemed that a contract between Sears and the Germans would be signed quickly

I had not made any arrangements for a commission for my own mediation but I believed that Horten would offer me some compensation for my assistance, assuming the deal was successfully closed.

Then, at the last minute, the deal fell through. Horten told me he had decided to sell his shares of his company to Deutsche Bank and the British Tobacco Company. Under the circumstances, I did not expect to get any sort of payment. So I simply tossed the entire affair out of my mind.

Several months went by. One day, a mail courier delivered a registered letter from Helmut Horten to me at my office. I opened the envelope and started reading. "Thanks for the great idea. You helped me tremendously. Everything worked out in the best possible way – my stores have been successfully sold."

There was a check, made out in my name, in that envelope. I looked at it and looked at it again. I could not believe my eyes – it was made out for two million dollars!

Undoubtedly Horten's negotiations with Sears Roebuck, the company that I had brought in, prompted Deutsche Bank to get seriously involved.

Such a competitive situation helped Horten in making a highly advantageous sale. Nonetheless, this certainly did not obligate him to me in any way. Despite that he most generously extended his gratitude to me for my intermediary services. This man enjoyed making those kinds of grand gestures in the style of the old aristocracy.

After this our friendship became all the more solid. I invited Horten to visit us on Cat Cay. He loved the place so much that he decided to buy himself a home on the island as well. One thing led to another, and suddenly Horten announced he wanted to buy the entire island. His architects designed an incredible vision for the project, including a park on uninhabited South Cat with a dining room and a bar, part of which would be underwater with a glass wall separating it from the ocean.

Horten declared that he was prepared to invest $15 million in this venture. Besides he promised that, should he purchase all of Cat Cay from us, he could put everything in order on the island much more quickly than the club could because, needless to say, he was able to put up all the money required immediately for the reconstruction of the island.

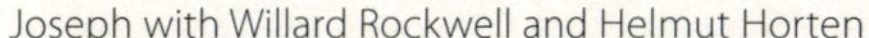
Joseph with Willard Rockwell and Helmut Horten

After long discussions with other property owners, who clearly did not like the idea of one man controlling their beautiful island, I told Horten that, in my opinion, his offer would not be acceptable to the members of the club. I sensed that this greatly disappointed him.

A while later, I received a letter from Horten. He wrote to me that he had decided not to settle on Cat Cay but in Nassau, the capital city of the Bahamas. And that's exactly what he did. He bought a huge, luxurious villa at Lyford Club from a Greek shipping tycoon and never returned to Cat Cay again.

Our relationship was never the same after that. It wasn't just that he was annoyed about not being able to become the owner of Cat Cay. The break in our friendship was probably due more to the fact that Horten fell under the spell of one woman. He had been a bachelor all this time. Then a very pretty Austrian woman, named Heidi, who was a good deal younger than he was, came into his life. Helmut was totally enamored and decided to marry her. All of us who were his friends suspected that this young lady loved Helmut's money more than she loved Helmut. We all felt the marriage was a mistake and tried to sway him from taking the step. Nevertheless, he married Heidi. Now that she was Helmut's wife, she did everything in her power to keep him at a distance from his old friends.

Of course our relationship did not break off entirely. I still visited him at his home in Switzerland. I tried to be friendly and respectful with Heidi but I could not escape her intrigues, and eventually my meetings with Horten became more and more infrequent.

Horten was not fated to enjoy married life for long. After his death, I read in the newspaper that he left an estate of 4.5 billion German marks. Presumably Heidi inherited his fortune.

It saddened me to hear of his passing. Though we had drifted apart during the last years of his life, I still considered him one of my closest friends and one who had had a tremendous influence on my life. I would have liked to stay on close terms with him forever.

No less important to me was my friendship with a prominent American statesman and public activist, John McCloy. During World War II, John McCloy served as the Deputy Secretary of the United States Department of Defense. After the war, he took command as the High

Commissioner for Occupied Germany. He knew all the great politicians of the world, including Winston Churchill, Charles de Gaulle and Joseph Stalin. Later McCloy went into law. He also held the post of Chairman of the Board of the gigantic Chase Manhattan Bank and was the personal advisor to several presidents of the United States. Moreover he managed the Ford Foundation, one of the most important philanthropic institutions in the world.

Most importantly, however, he was the Chairman of the Presidential Advisory Committee on Arms Control and Disarmament, known in Washington simply as the McCloy Committee. This man's work has been studied in several monographs and biographies. He was considered one of the five most influential people in the United States in his day.

John McCloy was about ten years older than I was. I met him quite by chance when Ludwig Erhard, the Minister of the Economy of Germany (later Chancellor), arrived in the United States. The Council on Foreign Affairs, headed by John McCloy, arranged a dinner in honor of Mr. Erhard.

Joseph celebrates his 50th birthday with friends in New York, 1968

With Mr. and Mrs. John McCloy and their daughter, Ellen, at the Taj Mahal

At the time I was involved in trading coal with Germany. I was acquainted with the son of the former German Chancellor, G. Stresemann, who was working for Chase Manhattan Bank. He arranged an invitation for me to attend the dinner for Erhard.

After dinner I had an opportunity to speak with McCloy. I told him that I was living in Germany in a war refugee camp during the time that he was the High Commissioner for Occupied Germany. Then I added, "Now I'm supplying Germans with coal and that way I'm contributing somewhat to the reconstruction of Germany – the work that you started so successfully."

This man was very reserved; he had a closed, formal nature. Still, I sensed that my words had interested him. At that point in our conversation, other people came up to him, and there was no chance to continue our talk. Nevertheless, as we were bidding our farewells, he said to me, "Give me a call whenever it's convenient for you."

There was no way I was going to miss this opportunity to meet personally with such a formidable man. When I called him two weeks later, I was pleased that he had not forgotten our little chat. He invited me for lunch.

That was an extremely important meeting for me. McCloy was sincerely interested in how we Lithuanians had lived in the refugee camps. He inquired about the events in occupied Lithuania. I noticed his intent and intelligent eyes observing me. McCloy usually maintained a certain distance in his relationships. He did not rush to make personal contacts. But I had a feeling that he enjoyed our talk as much as I did.

Not long after this first lunch of ours, I got an invitation to attend a cocktail party at his home. Our acquaintanceship grew stronger and, over the long term, it grew into a friendship. Among other matters, a passion for hunting also brought us together. There was a time that I had the opportunity to invite him in the name of the Maharana of Udaipur for a hunt in India. Later on I asked Helmut Horten to arrange an invitation for him to hunt in Yugoslavia. I was not seeking some sort of special advantages from this friendship. I treasured our time together and was always humbled that I had the unique opportunity of knowing such a great man and learning from him.

PART V

Bridges Back to the Homeland

During the years of the Cold War, there was considerable debate within the émigré community on whether or not to have contact with visitors from Soviet Lithuania. The Lithuanian Activist Front, a leader of the resistance movement against Bolshevik and Nazi rule of which I was a member in Vilnius during the war, continued pursuing its goal for the liberation of Lithuania from abroad. *Santara-Šviesa* , the "Unity-Light," in the meantime, was a liberal political organization formed after the war in the United States by Lithuanian refugees, students and young people. Its primary focus was to make non-political contacts, such as in the area of culture and sports, with individuals from Soviet Lithuania.

Most émigré organizations and my friends from Lithuania who were members and supporters of the Activist Front did not agree with the policies of *Santara-Šviesa*. We felt that the Soviets should not be provided the slightest opportunity to use any contacts with émigrés for their own propaganda purposes. The Soviets were always ready to boast that any sort of interactions with the émigré community was evidence of a favorable view of the regime. They would exaggerate this notion that many Lithuanians from capitalistic America were yearning to return to Lithuania because now, they claimed, the communists had instituted an enlightened progressive political system in the country. Furthermore, we were well aware that the KGB employed the most cunning methods in their efforts to recruit the émigrés who were visiting their land of birth to become their agents.

Lithuanian Activist Front, 1953

Although I was aware of the prevailing opinions in the community and agreed with the official policy of the Activist Front, I would still occasionally meet with people from Lithuania privately whenever such an opportunity presented itself. First of all, I was anxious to get any kind of news about the current situation in Lithuania. Second, I wanted to do a bit of propagandizing myself about America. I knew that people living under the Soviet regime were presented with a distorted picture of life in a capitalist system. I felt I could score some points for democracy and freedom from my own experiences.

As early as 1953, I had the first chance to interact with someone who had arrived in the West from my occupied homeland. Such contacts were incredibly rare back then. I had flown to Italy to attend to some business matters and stopped in Milan where I called an old friend of mine, Monsignor Tulaba, who was living in Rome. He told me that a delegation of scientists from the Soviet Union was in Rome and heading to Milan. The group included a Lithuanian doctor.

"You could try to meet him," said Monsignor Tulaba. "He won't be afraid to talk with you."

It was after 9:00 o'clock at night when I rang up the hotel where the delegation was staying and asked for the last name of the man the monsignor had provided.

Nobody picked up the phone. Every half hour or so, I called again but still nobody answered. By now, it was nearly 11:00 p.m. Finally, a man answered the phone. I spoke in Russian, "Please, may I talk to Doctor…" adding the Lithuanian surname.

Another voice came on the line in a few seconds. "Doctor, this is Juozas Kazickas calling to welcome you in Milan," I said in Lithuanian. "It would be a great pleasure if we could actually meet one another."

"Unfortunately, it is impossible because tomorrow morning at six we are flying to Moscow," he said.

I didn't want to give up so I said, "Perhaps you could come visit me for an hour? Or, I could even come to your hotel right now."

"Give me your phone number, and I'll call you in a little while," the scientist told me. That was the end of that conversation.

When he finally called, it was after midnight. "I might be able to visit you for a short while but I don't have any money," he told me. I explained that I would meet him outside my hotel and pay for the taxi.

I waited in the hotel lobby. One half hour passed, then another and still my guest did not show up. I stood outside in the rain, watching for a car. The hotel was deserted except for an elderly porter snoozing in one of the lobby chairs. I was about to lose all hope that a fellow from my Soviet-occupied homeland would ever keep his promise. Then, all of a sudden, a taxi appeared in front of the hotel. By this time, it was three o'clock in the morning.

I invited my guest to come up to my room. He was clearly nervous. He kept tapping one foot and then the other while standing in place. Then, he glanced over at the porter and said, "Maybe we could just have a talk right here?"

We sat down in some wide armchairs in a corner of the lobby. I told him that I had left Lithuania in July of 1944 and, since that time on, I had not had a single chance to meet anyone still living in our country. My wife, Alexandra, and I had tried to contact the Lithuanian basketball players on the USSR team during the 1952 Olympic Games in Helsinki but without success.

As I talked, my guest seemed to gather his wits. Slowly, he began telling me about the earth shattering events taking place in Lithuania – massive deportations to Siberia, patriotic battles waged by partisans against the Russian occupiers and the ways in which the *stribai* – 'quislings' – degraded their victims by tossing their twisted corpses out in town squares. I had heard about all of this before but only third-hand. I knew about *stribai*, a demeaning Lithuanian term for local inhabitants who were aiding the Soviets and whom the Communist Party called "defenders of the people." The man and I sat in that lobby chatting until the hotel slowly awakened at about 5:00 a.m.

I never did find out what sort of position my mysterious guest from Soviet Lithuania held. I assumed he was a member of the Communist Party. How else could he have been allowed to travel to the West in 1953, only a few months after the death of Stalin? But I felt that he was a man of patriotic convictions, no matter how deeply he had to hide them. After many years, when I visited Lithuania for the first time, I tried to find this man. I never did learn anything about him except that he had been sent somewhere to Russia.

After I returned to New York, I told my friends in the Lithuanian Activist Front about this meeting. Monsignor Balkūnas assured me that I had come back with very interesting news. He persuaded me to talk about the meeting at the Lithuanian parish after mass and distributed a printed announcement that I would share news from the homeland based on my conversation with a scientist from Lithuania. An entirely unexpected thing happened. An assistant to the consul of the Lithuanian diplomatic office for the area stood at the gates to the church, warning people not to go listen to Kazickas because I had been influenced by the Communists. Luckily, no one paid much attention to him and people filled the auditorium. Clearly, they all wanted to hear what little I had learned about life in occupied Lithuania.

Years later, there were other encounters with fellow countrymen from Lithuania who came to the West, not all of them pleasant.

Once, when I was in Paris during the mid 1980s, an old friend of mine, artist Vytautas Kasiulis, called to tell me that a well-known Lithuanian film producer, Vytautas Žalakevičius, had arrived in the city with a Soviet delegation. He asked if I would like to meet him. Though the surname of Žalakevičius meant nothing to me, and I had never seen or heard of a single one of his films, I thought it would be useful to talk to him.

I suggested to Kasiulis that he come with the guest to my hotel. I already knew that people coming from Soviet Lithuania generally had no Western currency. Thus, I thought I would invite the movie director for supper and talk with him about events in my homeland. I figured the director would find it interesting to look around a five-star Western hotel. Instead, Kasiulis told me the guest would rather invite me to visit him.

Kasiulis and I went to some third-rate hotel where the Soviet delegation was housed. The director's room was rather dingy, but he greeted us with dignity and, I might add, with some pride. He immediately pulled a bottle of cognac from his suitcase and showed us the label which was marked with several stars. Then he offered us a drink, boasting that this was a cognac of the highest quality from Georgia.

We all had a sip of the cognac. To be polite, I praised the drink, although it actually seemed to me of questionable quality. We sat for a while in the hotel room, and then I suggested that we go to a good restaurant in Paris.

By now Žalakevičius had enjoyed several shots of his Georgian brandy and was most agreeable to my invitation. Figuring that he would feel more comfortable in a familiar environment, I took him to a fancy Russian restaurant where a gypsy band was playing romantic folk music in the elegant room.

To start our enjoyment of the evening, I ordered some French cognac and traditional Russian dishes – *blini* (thin pancakes) with caviar. The conversation, however, was not connecting readily. The director seemed stuffy in some ways and quite uninhibited in others. When he was asked about life in Lithuania, he praised the Soviet order and boasted about how much he had achieved. It took a while but it seemed that we were finally relating on a more personal level, speaking more freely and sincerely. I lost track of how many toasts we had raised to the prosperity of Lithuania. Finally I said, "Vytautas, fly over to visit me in New York. We will take a tour around America. You can see with your own eyes the real life in the United States."

I could see his jaws freeze as he chewed his food. Suddenly he yelled out, "This is a provocation! You can't buy me – no way!!!!"

His outburst stunned the room. The music actually quieted down, and all the people in the restaurant turned to stare at us. At this point, the director leaped up and grabbed the tablecloth with both hands. With a terrible crash, he flung everything on the table down on the ground. I barely managed to jump out of the way to avoid the bottles of wine from splashing all over me. Everything was still except for the sounds of breaking plates and glass. A sickly silence hung over the restaurant. The other patrons stared at us in dumbfounded shock. I wanted to sink into the ground. The Lithuanian director was running through the restaurant towards the door by this time. Kasiulis was chasing after him, crying out, "Vytautas! Vytautas, what has come over you? Stop!"

Stupefied, I was left standing at the overturned table by myself. The restaurant owner came rushing over. I explained to him that my guest had had too much to drink. The music started playing again. I paid the bill, not only for dinner but for all the broken china as well. Then I ducked out of the place as fast as I could. Curious glances followed me all the way out the door.

Much later I learned the upshot of this event. It seems that Žalakevičius wrote an article in some Soviet newspaper. He claimed that a representative of a nationalistic Lithuanian organization had tried to convince him to betray his Soviet homeland but he had delivered a very staunch rebuff to such a provocation.

Trips to Lithuania

As much as I longed to see my homeland again, I did not yet feel it was safe for me to go back. However, my daughter, Jurate, decided to go to Lithuania in 1968. She had been working as a reporter covering the Vietnam War and got a visa through Intourist to travel across Siberia on the Trans-Siberian Railroad. After ten days in November on the train across the vast frozen countryside, she finally reached Moscow. Then from Leningrad (as St. Petersburg was named during the Soviet period), she flew to Vilnius where she spent three interesting, if somewhat depressing days. It broke her heart to see how miserably people were living, in constant fear of the KGB and spying neighbors.

Alexandra also visited Lithuania earlier than I did in the 1970s. I decided not to go with her at that time because I felt that I could cause problems to any people who might meet me. Back in those days, very few émigrés went to Lithuania. In the meantime, people who were politically active in opposition to Moscow – the types that Soviet propaganda had named anti-Soviet – would not set foot into Lithuania at all. Our policy not to have any relations with the Soviet government caused us to hold fast to such a position. Alexandra, however, was burning with a passion to go home and see her old friends there. I did not try to dissuade her.

I arranged a going away party for her. We toasted Alexandra as though she were going off to war. A veteran of United States politics, John McCloy, was at our dinner. In my toast I said that he had liberated Europe. Now, however, I just might have to plead with him, "Liberate Alexandra from the Soviet gulag."

With the same sort of humor, he shot right back at me, "Well, look out! America just might have to declare a war against the Soviets to bring your wife home."

Of course we were just joking around. I did not really believe that a trip to occupied Lithuania would prove to be dangerous to Alexandra in any way. Alexandra ended up making three or four more trips during Soviet times. Once she stayed an entire month with her friend Stasė. Nevertheless, I could not go with her because of my political principles.

However, in 1979, the situation was different. Vilnius University was celebrating its 400-year anniversary. I thought that this might be a perfect opportunity to visit Lithuania without violating my principles. I was a graduate of this university. The celebration was relevant not only to Lithuania. It reflected on the ancient roots of our culture and the traditions that had come from Western countries. I was actually surprised that the Russian government would permit commemoration of this date. After all, this highlighted the fact that Lithuania had a university much earlier than Russia did.

We flew to Vilnius via Prague and Leningrad. We were obligated to spend several days in the city although I just wanted to get to Lithuania as fast as possible. Rules were rules. All Lithuanians, traveling to the Soviet Union from the United States, had to have a stopover in Moscow or Leningrad.

Upon arrival in Leningrad, we first had to stand in a long, slow-moving line through the border control station and customs checkpoint. There, walking up and down and in and around the line of a teeming mass of several hundred people, were two men, probably border control officers, looking over every face. Unexpectedly, they stopped right next to me and stated, "*Vash pasport pozhalsta* 'Your passport, please.'" They stood there, flipping the pages of my passport, carefully examining every stamp.

When they took my passport away for further inspection – mine was the only one they seemed to be interested in – I started kidding around, "Well, Alytė (as I endearingly called Alexandra), you see the sort of fate that we have come to. It seems that you're going to be a widow." In a while, though, my passport was returned to me without a word of explanation.

We passed through border control and stood in the line waiting for the customs check. I was bringing in a huge stack of books - all published in the United States in the Lithuanian language. Naturally the contents of all of them tended to be anti-Soviet. The customs officers opened my suitcase. The books were the first things they grabbed. They unpacked all of them and carried them off into a nearby office. We waited and waited; minutes passed but the customs officers didn't show up. At long last, one appeared with another officer who, as it turned out, was his boss.

"Are you intending to read these books yourself?" asked the senior officer in English.

I answered, "Yes, of course I am. If I have nothing else to do, I will enjoy reading them."

"All right," he said to me and then turned to the customs officer. I heard him say, "*Vsë khorosho, propusti* 'Everything is fine. Let him pass.'"

There were more books and magazines in our other suitcases, but the officer did not go through any more of our things. He closed our baggage, and we were permitted to enter the Soviet Union with all our anti-Soviet literature.

Once in the airport lobby, we noticed a hotel driver holding a sign that read, "Mrs. and Mr. Kazickas." He had arrived to meet us in the most luxurious Russian car there was – a "Chaika" limousine. Such a car was used mostly by members of the Soviet government and the highest Party officials.

Pribaltijskij Hotel had been constructed very recently in preparation for the 1980 Olympics Games. We were provided apartments over two floors which included seven rooms – a couple of bedrooms, a living room and dining room, an office and a separate room containing a piano. Nevertheless, the standards of service were a far cry from that of a five-star hotel in the West. One minor detail gave us a good laugh. The bathroom was huge and its floor and walls were impressively laid in marble. All of it looked very beautiful except that hanging in line on the towel rack were these tiny towels that looked more like rags for polishing shoes.

That evening we went downstairs to the restaurant for supper. The decor literally glittered in luxury – marble, mirrors and chandeliers. The menu contained forty pages of a vast array of dishes, described in English, German and Russian. Alexandra and I began reading the offerings – red and black caviar, several varieties of salmon and sturgeon and even snails. What a fabulous selection, I marveled.

Our official waiter approached. He had that pungent smell of someone who did not bathe often. I glanced at his hands. There was dirt under his untrimmed fingernails. Well, what else could we do but order? I started naming our selections. "The salmon appetizer, please..."

The waiter interrupted me with a cough and stated, "*Netu*." He repeated this in English, "No."

I asked for sturgeon – again *netu*. How about black caviar? The retort was the usual no. Astonished, I finally asked him, "What is it that you do have?"

With this, he finally offered an explanation, "You can only order those dishes that have a price listed." I looked in the menu again. About one in every ten items had a price. In reality, there was practically nothing to order!

Later we were given one explanation for this situation. The hotel was owned by a Swedish company, so most of the hotel guests were Scandinavians. Apparently the only purpose for their "tourism" was to come to Leningrad for the weekend, drink Russian vodka all day with no holds barred and maybe have an encounter with some Russian woman at night. The hotel cuisine did not seem of much interest to them.

A personal guide escorted us on a tour of the museums in Leningrad. We visited the Hermitage, Russian, and Peterhof State Museums. The array of artwork was tremendous, all displayed in the deluxe palaces of the Czar. But surrounding the museums were rundown residential buildings and streets filled with weary, sullen people.

One evening, we decided to go to the Kirov Theater, one that was well known in the West. Misunderstandings started from the start when I tried to order tickets at our hotel. Behind the window of the Guest Service stand were two ladies, chatting and totally oblivious to us. I stood waiting for them to notice me. They continued with their gossip, never turning their heads in my direction. Finally one of them glanced over at me. "What do you want?" she said menacingly.

When I said I would like tickets to the Kirov Theater, she snapped, "No tickets." Then she turned back to talk with her friend.

"Why are there no tickets?" I asked her. "I was told that I could buy them at your desk," I added before she had a chance to get involved in her own conversation again.

"The only ones left are very expensive," she retorted.

"My dear madam," I said to her, "I did not ask you for cheap tickets. I am only interested in the most expensive seating."

This seemed to impress her, and she telephoned the theater. Tickets appeared. While this transaction was going on, an elegant woman came behind me. As I stepped away from the window, I heard her very pleasant voice pleading in Russian for tickets to the theater. "How pathetic," I thought to myself. "A person of good manners has to beg some surly woman just to gain entrance to the ballet."

The driver took us to the Kirov Theater in the Chaika limousine that had been assigned to us. We told him the time he was to return to pick us up. But after the performance, when we went out into the street, the car was not there. We watched other people rushing past to the bus stops while we just stood there, stomping our feet from the cold in the dark. It was already after midnight, and I had no idea how to telephone the hotel. The only choice I had left was to try to hail a taxi.

No taxi was in sight, but some private automobile finally stopped and drove us to the hotel. I had no rubles so I gave the driver a ten dollar bill. The man became visibly shaken; he was afraid to take the money. He seemed to want to take it but did not dare. Somehow I persuaded him to accept the bill.

Naturally I tried to get an explanation the following morning about why no one had arrived to pick us up from the theater. Apparently our driver finished his shift and neglected to let his replacement know what he was supposed to do.

Finally our tourist program in Leningrad ended, and we were able to fly to Vilnius, the capital of Lithuania. I observed the passengers in the plane; nearly all were Russians. A sense of sadness came over me. Here I was, returning to my homeland, and all I could hear was Russian being spoken all around me.

After checking in at the *Lietuva* 'Lithuania' Hotel, we did not stop to rest. Right away we went out for a stroll around town. It was hard to believe that we were finally walking on those same streets where we had walked – thirty-five years ago! We rode over to our old Žvėrynas neighborhood to have a look at the house in which we had lived before the war. Time seemed to have stopped in this district. Very little had changed over all those years.

Unlike most other arriving émigrés who tended to travel in groups, we had selected the individualized sightseeing program. That way we were not obligated to go on planned excursions. We could walk around Vilnius at our own will. Thus we had some entirely unexpected meetings on several occasions. Some of our more distant relatives had heard about our arrival and they came out to meet us. The first thing we noticed was how restrained people were when they interacted with us.

Once we were visiting the home of a famous heart surgeon, Professor Marcinkevičius. He lived in the best furnished apartment that we saw on that visit. When we discussed some controversial issues, our hosts silently pointed to the walls to alert us that the KGB could very well be listening. Even our relatives, particularly when they came to see us at our hotel, clearly avoided any candid heart-to-heart talks. They assumed, as did I, that our hotel rooms were bugged to record all of our conversations.

I had no doubt that we were being watched and followed the entire time. Nonetheless, I did have an opportunity to hear stories from our relatives about life in postwar occupied Lithuania that shook my soul. They told me about the corpses tossed in the town squares after the war, about the collective atmosphere of fear and the terrible level of poverty. One of my aunts said that after her husband and son had died just days apart, she was unable to bury them because she had no money for the coffins. She had been left alone in her one room apartment for a week with several very young children and the two bodies.

The Vice Chancellor of Vilnius University, Jonas Grigonis, with whom I had been exchanging letters some time earlier, invited me to the celebrations for the anniversary commemoration. Grigonis devoted himself to our service. He introduced us to Chancellor Jonas Kubilius and made sure that we could attend each anniversary event. One that we did not attend was a formal unveiling of the statues of Lenin and Vincas Kapsukas, another Communist "hero." He was in effect a traitor to his own country because, in 1919, he worked for the Bolsheviks, controlling Lithuanian territories. We realized that this was no more than an ideological formality being forced on the professorial staff, but we wanted no part of it.

The smell of fresh paint was all over Vilnius University. Repairs were still underway in some areas. It thrilled me to walk through those old hallways and poke my nose into the classroom auditoriums where Alytė and I had once sat for our lectures. The courtyards were all spruced up, looking even more romantic than we remembered them during our youth. However, the farther I walked into the Old Town, the more it became apparent that other buildings and homes had been completely neglected over all those decades.

The event that I probably liked the best of all the Vilnius University celebrations was the student procession that led from the university facilities across town all the way to Vingis Park. We felt the spontaneity, the spirit of youth which was unrestrained and free of Soviet dogma.

The anniversary reception, held in the oldest building of the university, was also impressive. After the ceremonies, we met with our old friend, Petras Katilius, a renowned mathematics professor. He had been my sister Victoria's neighbor before and during the war. Alexandra had met him even earlier while working at the university. Up until we left Lithuania in the summer of 1944, we stayed in touch with him. And now – 35 years later – we ran into Katilius once again, this time with his new wife. We walked together from Vilnius University to their home in the Antakalnis area, a good five kilometers.

Petras started telling me about the situation in Lithuania. He talked about the denationalization policy, the way it was being implemented and the kind of propaganda being issued to accomplish it. He explained that, although people were no longer being deported since Stalin's death, the Soviet system itself had not changed by much. Petras always considered that the occupation of Lithuania was the most horrible tragedy that could have happened to our country. I felt the same way.

I noticed that as he was talking, Petras kept looking over his shoulder to check if anyone was following us. Our wives were walking ahead of us a bit. To my overwhelming surprise, when we walked into their apartment, Mrs. Katilienė (she was Petras' second wife after his first wife had died) began chatting to an entirely different tune. Immediately she began praising what a good life they had in Soviet Lithuania, and how this government took great care of the sciences and education. Petras, in the meantime, sat there as though he had no tongue. It was hard for Alexandra and me to stay quiet. We were tactful at first but then we began contradicting her somewhat. She actually got red in the face as she leaped to explain excitedly that under Smetona (the President of the country before the war), people had had hard lives in Lithuania and now they were all ecstatic under Soviet rule. I kept wondering – what on earth is she bragging about? Here she was, the wife of a professor, which meant she and her husband were in the category of people who were better taken care of than most. Yet they were living in a shabby apartment; in the United States, only the newest immigrants who were still trying to find their fortune in the country would live in such poor conditions.

What confused me even more was that I happened to know Mrs. Katilienė's sister who lived in the United States. She was a member of the Lithuanian Activist Front and always energetically participated in all of our activities directed against the USSR. After I returned to the United State, I told her about this particular discussion during our visit. She simply waved her hand and stated, "Her brains have gotten scrambled."

Our visa only permitted us to stay in Lithuania for five days. However, at the end of this time, we were given a ten day extension for our stay. We moved from the *Lietuva* 'Lithuania' Hotel to *Draugystė* 'Friendship' Hotel. There we were provided with a better apartment of several rooms.

Tėviškė 'Homeland' Society took over the responsibility for our care from Intourist. We had a long talk with Soviet General Pranas Petronis, Chairman of the Society, who welcomed us. He formulated his thoughts very diplomatically but, nonetheless, he let us know cautiously that the situation of Lithuania was not an easy one. I thought that this man was trying to let me know by insinuation that he was not pleased with the Soviet occupation. The General mentioned that they – I understood that to mean the Lithuanian Communist administration – were trying to uphold the Lithuanian language and a sense of nationality, and that was why contacts with Lithuanian émigrés were so important. I got the impression that he knew quite a bit about my activities and my social standing in the American-Lithuanian community.

After our conversation, I kept trying to figure out what it all meant. Here was a Soviet general who was responsible for looking after émigrés. Yet he seemed not to be a loyal servant of the occupiers.

At the time that I had been attending military school in Panemunė, Pranas Petronis had been a Senior Lieutenant, an instructor of the young cadre of soldiers. I remembered him because I would always salute him. He didn't seem to recognize me and, for some reason, I didn't mention that we had known one another in the past. I also knew his younger brother who had worked for me during the war. Later I was sorry that I had kept that information to myself.

The fact that our caretakers from the *Tėviškė* 'Homeland' Society were so service-oriented actually surprised me. They allowed us to travel anywhere we wanted, whereas other visitors to Lithuania frequently complained that the Soviets seriously curtailed their freedom of movement. We were able to visit the cities of Kaunas, Panevėžys, Palanga, Zarasai and Rokiškis. I met with some of the friends from my youth. In Kaunas I saw Juozas Juodišius who had participated in the anti-Soviet and anti-Nazi undergrounds with me. He had been released from a ten-year term of imprisonment in Siberia during the times of Nikita Khrushchev, whereupon he returned to Lithuania.

With an aching heart, I listened to his remembrances about these experiences. He was not afraid to speak openly about his past. He talked about his uncle, who had once served as a general and ended up in a Soviet prison camp. His crime was that he had written a letter of complaint to Stalin. During his interrogations, both of his legs were broken. He did not survive these tortures – he died very shortly afterwards. The strength of my friend's spirit amazed me. He recounted the most horrifying events in a calm voice, devoid of a single note of regret or bitterness about his ruined life. Such was the history of our country – a destruction of the destinies of its people.

Another friend I was able to locate was Jonas Šimukonis who had been my assistant at the Municipality. He was the one who had once tried to warn me about the fact that the NKVD had their eyes on me. Though I was not able to see him in person, we did speak on the telephone.

Before our return to the United States, Intourist required that we stopover again in Moscow. After my visit to Lithuania, I had no desire for any excursions in Russia. We were housed in the most pompous Nacional Hotel. Our apartments, we were informed, were the same where Richard Nixon, the President of the United States, had once stayed. Again we got seven rooms that included a winter garden. All this was quite costly, but I think that as a Lithuanian refugee, forced to flee to the West from the Russians, I had the satisfaction of being able to stay in the best facilities of their capital city.

Something very strange occurred while we were dining at the Nacional Hotel restaurant. The maitre d' sat us at a small table where two other ladies had already been seated. Although we noticed several empty tables, he explained that there were no other places available. It turned out that both of these Russian ladies spoke good English. One told us that her husband was the captain of a freighter and that he sailed all over the world. Before long this woman began making very negative comments about life in the Soviet Union, constantly comparing local conditions with all the opportunities that people had in the West. She said that existence in her country was simply pitiful.

Struck by her candor, I asked how it was that she had no fear discussing such things with foreigners, strangers to her, and in a public restaurant no less. The woman was somewhat taken aback; she said rather indignantly that she had nothing to fear. Her husband had many influential friends and even in the worst event, he could always find some way out of the situation. Afterwards our conversation took a more politically neutral course. I suspected that these women may have been planted by the KGB to pump some information out of us about our meetings with people in Lithuania and their moods about the country.

The next day, we had to visit the Kremlin Square and some museums with our guide. After the intensity of my emotional visit to Lithuania, all I wanted to do was to get back to the United States as soon as possible. I decided to shorten our stay in Moscow by two days. Intourist, the organizers of our tour, took advantage of this and virtually robbed me. They refused to change the date of our plane tickets to London and demanded that I buy another set of tickets. I finally agreed to pay an exorbitant sum just to avoid wasting any more time in Russia.

The next time that I visited Lithuania was in 1990 during the exhilarating days before the declaration of independence when Mikhail Gorbachev was making a historical visit to our country. My wife, Alytė, did not wait that long, however. Over a period of ten years, she managed to make three more trips to see the land of her birth.

The Spectre of the KGB

An opinion had formed in the Lithuanian émigré community of the United States, true or not, that I was an affluent man of high standing in the social strata of the United States with a great many professional and personal contacts. At the same time, by the 1970s, my daughter Jurate was working as a journalist with the Associated Press in New York and Washington. Apparently all this interested the United States branch of the Soviet Secret Service, which was "looking after" the émigré community from the Baltic countries. On several occasions, I sensed that their people were trying to find a way to meet me.

Some people associated with the KGB were actually quite pleasant. We were aware back then that the *Tėviškė* Society, which had been formed to maintain contacts with émigrés, also frequently cooperated with the KGB. When Jurate visited Lithuania in 1968, a most likeable woman from the Society, Monika Ravinskienė, began handling her itinerary and travel needs. (Some time later, she also visited us in the United States.) Again, when we flew in for the 400-year anniversary of Vilnius University in 1979, this same woman was at our beck and call, making every effort to service all our requirements.

When our five-day visa for staying in Lithuania expired, Mrs. Ravinskienė helped us to extend it for another 10 days. We also got a permit to travel all over the country without any restrictions. Naturally she would go everywhere with us but she was always sufficiently tactful. Whenever her presence clearly interfered in our interactions with relatives or friends, she understood perfectly that she needed to step aside and leave us alone. That way we could calmly continue our conversations without the ever-present ears of the KGB.

Ravinskas, this woman's husband, worked as some sort of a manager for a Lithuanian film organization. One day he drove us to the Palanga seaside resort and introduced us to the director of the local movie theater. The man always spoke to us "correctly" in a way deemed appropriate for a Soviet citizen to talk with an American Lithuanian. Things changed when we were left alone with the Palanga theater director. He looked around the place and immediately said to us, "Don't listen to all that nonsense that he's blabbing to you over here." With that the man proceeded to explain to us exactly how difficult it was for Lithuanians to live in the country since it was occupied by Russians. I recall his gallows humor as he talked about day-to-day matters. During the summers, the residents of this resort would actually move into doghouses to live, just so they could rent out their apartments to earn a spare ruble or so to add to their miserable wages. And this man was certainly not the only one who dared to speak entirely openly to us about the reality of matters in Lithuania.

Meanwhile agents of the KGB did follow us over to the United States. A certain Dr. Gintautas, who somehow emigrated from Lithuania to the United States, tried very hard to make friends with us. Gintautas was an accommodating fellow who was always offering to assist us at any sign of illness. He was a decent physician. After our country reestablished its independence, Gintautas organized a shipment of medicine to Lithuania. However, it later became clear that he had been recruited by the KGB. The man admitted to having worked with Soviet Security but insisted he had never informed on anyone, nor had he ever caused anyone any harm. I can believe that that might have been true.

However, it was hard for me to imagine how the KGB had been able to persuade Gintautas to become an agent. I felt very uncomfortable when Lietuvos Aidas '*Echo of Lithuania*' newspaper published an article about him in their series *Voratinklis* 'Spider Web,' which chronicled the extent of KGB infiltration. Gintautas had not only visited us in East Hampton but he had also tried to make friends with numerous other émigrés. Our good feelings about him changed when we suspected that all his overtures had been according to KGB instructions. After the article on him appeared, Gintautas disappeared, and I never ran into him again.

Actually Gintautas had already seemed suspicious to me during the first visit to the United States by the Prime Minister of newly independent Lithuania, Kazimiera Prunskienė in 1990. Gintautas showed up in Washington immediately, coming from his residence in New Jersey. Right away he forced himself on the Prime Minister as though they might have been long-time friends. They went shopping together, and he rushed to buy her all sorts of clothing. That sort of generosity on the part of Gintautas seemed strange. He must have spent several thousand dollars although I had never noticed him throwing his money around before.

More shady characters appeared, all wanting to interact with the Prime Minister. One Swede, who said he was from Oregon, offered to make a personal contribution to Prunskienė to the tune of $300,000. After some suspicious conversations, he suddenly disappeared.

At one event I was attending, a man walked up to me and introduced himself. He was Juozapas Grigutis, an advisor for the Permanent Mission of the USSR to the United Nations. His was the highest diplomatic position of any Lithuanian working abroad. Some time had passed after our initial meeting when Mr. Grigutis telephoned me. I invited him to be a guest in our home.

By this time, the *Sąjūdis* movement (described later in greater detail), which had stimulated a massive national reawakening in the people of Lithuania, was already well-entrenched. Mr. Grigutis arrived at our home and proceeded to tell us that the Soviet government was extremely disturbed about the activities in Lithuania. "An entire array of information from Moscow passes through my hands. If it interests you, I could make copies of certain material to show you," he offered.

"That would certainly be extremely interesting," I answered. "I would be most grateful."

He kept his word. For our next meetings, he brought copies of various instructional news items from Moscow. He translated the Russian into

Lithuanian for me. There were no great secrets in this material. Most outlined the sorts of rules to which the representatives from the Soviet Union at the United Nations had to adhere regarding issues of the Baltic countries. The instructions were to defend steadfastly the Moscow position that Lithuania, Latvia and Estonia were not occupied in 1940, but rather had joined the USSR on their own free will.

Mikhail Gorbachev, the head of the USSR at the time, was singing exactly that same tune. It was interesting to learn that Moscow was instructing their diplomatic service to be on the alert. The danger was possible "outbursts" by American immigrants from Baltic countries. Soviet diplomats were told to reject decisively any such statements. Furthermore, they had to maintain that any nationalistic activities aiming to reinstate their own statehood were detrimental to the policies for *glasnost* and *perestroika*.

Mr. Grigutis always acted in a conspiratorial manner in his interactions with me. For example, he never called me from his own office – only from a phone booth on the street. From there he would only tell me that he had some information for me; then we'd arrange when and where to meet.

By this time, I was in frequent contact with Vytautas Landsbergis, leader of the *Sąjūdis* movement. I would share with him pieces of the more interesting data which I received from Grigutis.

One day two men walked into my office. They pulled out their identification badges and introduced themselves as officials of the FBI. "We are aware that you've been meeting with Mr. Grigutis, a Soviet employee at the United Nations. We would like to know what kind of relationship you have with him," one of them asked me very directly.

I answered, "This connection is very interesting to me. Grigutis is providing me with all sorts of information about how Moscow views what is happening in my homeland. He asks me no questions about the United States. Even if he did, I have no secret information to give him. But why is the FBI interested in our relationship?"

At that point, the man explained that the bureau was aware of my work to benefit Lithuania, and they simply wanted to clarify what it was that Mr. Grigutis wanted to achieve by meeting with me. They left me their business cards and asked me to call them if I should have any information of interest to them.

It turned out that I needed those phone numbers a while later. When Lithuania declared the reestablishment of its Independence on March 11 of 1990, I began considering how it might be possible to establish a direct telephone connection between Vilnius and the West, circumventing Moscow. Thus I called those federal agents and asked if their office might be able to recommend ways in which this could be done. I wanted to provide the government of Lithuania with a telecommunications line which could not be controlled by the Soviet Union.

Both of them came over to talk to me. I explained to them the difficulty of the situation in which the Lithuanian government found itself because Moscow was able to track all of their discussions. "Would it be possible to lay a direct telephone line with Vilnius by means of some sort of station that could be erected on a boat sailing on the Baltic Sea?" I inquired.

At first they said nothing except to promise they'd discuss this with their superiors and let me know later whether or not they'd be able to assist me. In no time at all, they called me back, but the answer was negative. The government was not able to get involved in matters of this nature.

The FBI was also interested in another Lithuanian of my acquaintance – Valdemaras Kančas, who worked for the USSR embassy in Washington D.C. He was in charge of handling visas to Lithuania and was always very helpful. I happened to learn several days in advance about the upcoming declaration of the Act of Independence, which was to be announced on March 11, 1990. Jurate and I wanted to fly to Lithuania immediately, and I asked this man for assistance in getting rush visas. Kančas organized our visas in a single day – an unheard of feat. Thanks to him, we were both sitting in the Parliament chambers in Vilnius for those historical moments.

However, prior to my departure, once again two men came into my office and introduced themselves as officials of the CIA. Their questions were typical: "What sorts of matters are you involved in? What do you and Kančas talk about?" Once again the CIA agents explained that they were not interested in me but in Valdemaras Kančas. They already knew about my views and efforts to aid Lithuania. That man, however, was serving another power. Nonetheless, I was still not convinced that they had not investigated me as well, just to make sure.

After the Soviet Union fell apart, Mr. Kančas' employment at the Russian Consulate was terminated. He received permission to reside in the United States and went to work for a small company. In other words, the CIA must not have had any serious claims against him. Once he invited me to an art opening and introduced me to his new employer. He called a few more times after that, proposing some sort of business venture in which I had no interest. Eventually our contacts broke off.

Neither did I avoid interactions with gentlemen such as Albertas Laurinčiukas, a former editor of *Tiesa 'Truth'*, a communist newspaper for Lithuania during the Soviet period. But I never had any illusions about such people. Any time that Moscow sent any Lithuanian to the United States for several years, there was no question about the true nature of their employment. For one they had to write Soviet propaganda for the local press. Then they were also obligated to report on their discussions with the émigré community. I was comfortable relating to these people because they could not trick me into giving up some secrets about America. I simply didn't know anything of intelligence value. Furthermore, I never discussed any of the ongoing political and public matters of the Lithuanian émigrés. The visitors, on the other hand, would sometimes accidentally let something of interest slip during our talks, even though they were Soviet government envoys.

Once Laurinčiukas visited our home with his wife and young daughter. I knew that this man was especially spiteful in his attacks on the American system in the Lithuanian press. His daughter began running around our house. She spotted our sons' playroom, filled with all sorts of toys and games to entertain children. There was a moan in the little girl's voice as she tried to show her parents what she had seen. "Mother, look over here at this. And look at that!"

Albertas' wife sighed deeply and said to us, "Maybe the time will come, when we'll be able to live at least a little more like you do in America."

I didn't hesitate with my retort, "Definitely. As soon as Lithuania becomes free, you'll be able to live this way too."

Albertas Laurinčiukas pretended not to hear my words.

Undying Hope

In the 1960s and 70s, I was immersed in family and business matters. I also traveled a great deal and had many social obligations. This left me little time to be especially active in Lithuanian affairs. Despite this I remained a member of the organization which I had revived in the United States – the Lithuanian Activist Front – and also financially supported the Lithuanian World Community, which still has chapter communities in approximately thirty countries of the world and focuses on the preservation of Lithuanian national identity.

I also tried to contribute as much as I could to various political actions planned by the émigré community and provide financial support for several other Lithuanian organizations. Once, together with Father Dabušis, a Roman Catholic priest, I was able to convince a bachelor with no relatives to leave all his property to Lithuanian foundations. The man had lived modestly but, when his will was read, our cause was enriched by $170,000.

I had many opportunities to speak at various émigré functions where I would lay out my views about the future of Soviet occupied Lithuania. After the end of World War II, I was convinced that the Russians would be in Lithuania for a long period. I never had illusions like some of my fellow countrymen did that the West would quickly liberate our homeland; they kept waiting and waiting for such a moment.

However, it seemed that over time, I turned out to be the greater optimist as compared to many of my acquaintances. I did not believe that the Soviet Union could survive forever. In my speeches, I always said that we must never lose hope. The time will arrive, I predicted, when the Soviet Union will begin falling apart. Our job was to remind the world consistently about the case for the liberation of Lithuania.

One day, going through my old papers, I ran across some 1960 clippings from the émigré press. One article was about a speech I had made during a February 16th Independence Day celebration. The reporter wrote that I had been trying to dispel the generally pessimistic view of the audience about the hopeless future of our country. It was true that an ever-greater part of the émigré community had been getting disheartened and disillusioned, believing that the USSR would never withdraw from

Joseph with Jonas Krukonis who donated all his property to the Lithuanian Fund

Lithuania and that our land was doomed to disappear from the political maps of the world. I had staunchly argued that I believed I would live to see Lithuania become free once again. It seemed to me that the Soviet system had begun slowly to disintegrate from the time of Stalin's death. In my view, the reforms that Nikita Khrushchev (who instituted an official policy for peaceful coexistence with capitalism during the Cold War) was undertaking indicated that the Stalinist regime was undergoing a crisis. Economically it was becoming less and less effective. The so-called "thawing" period, in my opinion, was nothing more than a hopeless effort to rejuvenate the fading viability of the Soviet system without making essential changes.

After Nikita Khrushchev condemned the policies that Stalin had implemented, it became somewhat easier to maintain contacts with people in Lithuania. More liberal tourist travel to the USSR provided an opportunity to visit the home country. Under such circumstances, the non-recognition policy of the occupation of Lithuania, officially held by the United States, became all the more relevant.

Émigrés began writing letters to their relatives in Lithuania and sending them care packages. Under Stalin, having close relatives who had ended up in the West after the war posed serious danger. During the years of Khrushchev, no one was deported to Siberia any longer just for getting a letter or package from America. So we became braver about writing and sending gifts to our relatives. Nonetheless, we wrote very infrequently and very carefully. The Catholic Aid Organization was in a better position to send charity to Lithuania. Their work helped many more residents in Lithuania than any of us could do individually. Thus I made monetary donations to this organization as well. Besides Catholic Aid also provided a channel of support for the publication of the famous *Lithuanian Catholic Church Chronicles* in Lithuania which was a major source of information about the underground activities of dissidents during the Soviet occupation.

Supportive Friends

During the Cuban Crisis of 1962, when the USSR dislocated atomic armament missiles in Cuba, humankind found itself on the edge of yet another World War. The United States had declared a blockade on Cuba. The navies of the two superpowers of the world were on the alert. President John Kennedy issued an ultimatum to the Soviet Union to remove its missiles; the threat of an atomic war became frighteningly real. Heated diplomatic negotiations got going between Washington and Moscow. Nikita Khrushchev quickly sent one of his best diplomats to the United States – Vasili Kuznetsov, USSR Deputy Minister of Foreign Affairs. In the meantime, President Kennedy delegated my old friend, John McCloy, to represent the United States in negotiations with the Russians. He invited me to be an informal advisor to him.

One day McCloy's secretary called me to say that John wanted me to come to his home in Manhattan at 5:00 p.m. Upon arrival, I was escorted into his library.

"Joe, I want to talk something over with you," McCloy said. "You know the Soviet Union well; you have been studying the events over there for many years. At this point in our negotiations, the Russians have agreed to remove their missiles from Cuba. However, they are demanding concessions from our side. They insist on an agreement to let them maintain a military base over there. Our delegation for the negotiations is inclined to concede on this issue. What would your opinion be on this?"

I told him that if it were up to me, I would hold a stricter stance. "Cuba – it's virtually at the shores of the United States. Even if nuclear weapon disarmament is achieved, Russian military units would be a constant source of tension," I said. "Besides, a military base would greatly strengthen the regime of Fidel Castro. So, since the Soviet Union is backing down on the issue of their missiles, it would be worthwhile to hold to a hard line position. Pressure them to rescind on having their military base as well." That was the crux of my opinion on the matter.

John McCloy heard me out and then began laying out another viewpoint. In his opinion, the paltry number of Russian Army units would not pose any serious danger to the United States from a military standpoint. In fact the opposite was true. Supporting and maintaining the Army would be a heavy economic burden on the Soviet Union due to the great distance from their home base. Furthermore, the USSR would be forced to help Cuba in all sorts of ways. Regarding the stability of Castro's regime, the presence of military bases could prove to be a double-edged sword. On one hand, this would demonstrate that the Soviet Union is defending Cuba. On the other hand, the presence of a foreign army over the long term could well cause unrest amongst local citizens. "The most important aspect," McCloy continued his argument, "is that by conceding on the issue of the military bases, the United States would let Moscow 'save face'. That would show that Moscow had not surrendered, but that a mutual compromise had been reached."

We continued to debate one argument after another. Apparently the U.S. negotiating team had already decided on the position described by McCloy. I think by discussing the matter with me, he wanted to test the substance of such arguments. History has proved that his position was partially but not entirely correct. Indeed the support of its own military base along with all of Cuba under a total economic blockade cost the USSR an unusually heavy price. This might well have hastened the demise of the Soviet Union. The downside was that with Soviet assistance, the regime of Fidel Castro became stronger, and he was able to retain power all the longer.

Somewhat later I was able to offer more significant assistance to McCloy when President Lyndon Johnson entrusted him with an exceptionally delicate diplomatic mission.

During the mid-1960s, the United States faced some serious problems in its relations with France which was headed by President Charles de Gaulle at the time. In 1966 France had pulled out of NATO's integrated military structure. It then attempted to pressure the Federal Republic of Germany to enter into a national defense treaty thereby weakening the influence of the United States in Europe.

President Lyndon Johnson asked McCloy to go to Germany. There he was to meet unofficially with influential German politicians and confidentially relay the extremely negative view of the United States on the political initiative of Charles de Gaulle, which was raising a threat to the unity of Western countries and even to their own security.

John McCloy knew that I had many years of experience in doing business with Germany and I had acquaintances at influential levels in business and politics. He invited me over and told me about the diplomatic mission with which he had been entrusted. "I'm rather well known in Germany. If I appear somewhere publicly, it could attract the attention of the press. Public attention would not be desirable. Maybe you could help me find some out-of-the-way private place where I could meet with certain German politicians?" John asked me.

I told him I could always ask Helmut Horten to arrange a gathering at his estate. He would be able to invite persons of interest to McCloy to arrive privately. I called Horten. He needed no explanations; he understood the confidentiality of my request. Horten promised to guarantee absolute privacy for our meetings.

I joined McCloy on this trip to Germany. We flew into the Cologne Airport early in the morning. After we passed through customs control, Horten's driver arrived to bring us to Düsseldorf. The first threat to the confidentiality of our trip arose right there. Horten had sent us his Rolls-Royce limousine – it always attracted attention. "Well, it seems like he sure went overboard in this case," was all that McCloy had to say about his misgivings. Fortunately no one recognized him this time.

That same evening, Franz Josef Strauss arrived at Horten's manor. Strauss was the leader of the Christian Social Union of Germany and a member of the Government of the Federal Republic of Germany under Chancellor Kurt Georg Kiesinger. McCloy had a lengthy talk with him after which he received staunch endorsement of the United States position on the matter. Over the next three days, dignitaries of the coalition and the opposition in the government, even including the Social Democrats, came to Horten's home. In addition to politicians, talks were also held with highly influential business people and financial supporters of different political parties in Germany. I was present at these discussions and met all of the people who attended them.

Three days later, we were ready to return to the United States, but first McCloy said he absolutely had to stop over in Bonn to meet with the United States Ambassador for Germany. At that time, the Ambassador was George McGhee, a multimillionaire from Oklahoma and a man of great ambition. We went to visit the Ambassador together. McGhee had known McCloy from earlier times and he met us most graciously. We were invited to join him for lunch.

McCloy started his conversation cautiously, saying that he had met some of his acquaintances and representatives from various political parties in Germany. The Ambassador listened carefully but showed no emotion. When McCloy finally mentioned that it was President Lyndon Johnson, who had requested that he meet with German politicians, I noticed an instant reaction from McGhee – his cheeks flashed red for a second. Clearly the Ambassador felt greatly slighted by this.

Subtly McCloy tried to find a way out of this rather awkward situation. He proceeded to explain that at this time, the objective had been to speak with these people on a strictly private basis. Because he knew all these people since the days he had served as High Commissioner for Occupied Germany, the President had asked him to hold such talks discretely. "Your active assistance in this matter will no doubt be required as well in due time. For now the signal to the Germans had to be entirely unofficial. That's the only reason that you were not involved. My assignment was only to lay the groundwork for your further endeavors," McCloy tactfully reassured the Ambassador.

Tensions eased as the conversation continued. McGhee listened intensely, as McCloy related the various viewpoints of Germans regarding the French initiative.

During our entire flight back to the United States, John McCloy wrote his report about his meetings in Germany. I was honored and flattered that the report, which would go to President Johnson and was more than sixty pages in length, included my participation in these important events.

Another opportunity came up for me to be a special sort of intermediary for McCloy in Germany. This time I was involved in handling his personal rather than governmental matters.

A certain symbol of Germany's industrial might from old times was the Krupp Conglomerate which was engaged in smelting steel, mining and manufacturing armaments. The Allies arrested Alfred Krupp, the head of the family business, after World War II and sentenced him to ten years in prison. In reality, he had nothing to do with Hitler but he was the owner of a factory producing weapons. The Nazis actually governed everything in Germany during the war years. John McCloy felt that such a sentence was unjust. While he served as Commissioner for Germany, McCloy made efforts to assure that Alfred Krupp be released from prison in a few years under amnesty provisions.

I had an opportunity to meet the Krupp family. Alfred's younger brother, Berthold, had once invited me to Germany to hunt in 1968. To my surprise, the invitation instructed me to come wearing a tuxedo. Upon arrival I learned that a concert and gala dinner had been arranged at the Krupp mansion in Essen. During the hunt my position was right alongside Alfred Krupp. Thus we were able to exchange a few words with one another.

I asked him if he was acquainted with John McCloy. "I've never met him," answered Krupp, "but I've certainly heard a great deal about this person. I am very grateful to him for shortening my imprisonment. "

I suggested perhaps Krupp would like to meet McCloy. Alfred mulled over the idea. "That would provide me an opportunity to thank him for my early release. But how could such a meeting be arranged?'

I had an idea. I would coordinate a time convenient for both him and McCloy and arrange a hunt in Alaska for a couple of weeks. Krupp liked the idea.

When I told McCloy about my conversation with Krupp, he said he wouldn't decline a chance to make Krupp's acquaintance during a hunt, but he'd want assurance of full confidentiality for such a meeting. It seems that his wife, Ellen Zinser, was an American of German descent. Speculation could easily arise that amnesty had been arranged for Alfred Krupp as a result of McCloy's family ties in Germany. Also, some critics had accused McCloy of releasing Krupp in order to ease the path of German rearmament, a charge that McCloy had vehemently denied. The public is always quick to interpret all sorts of objectionable connections in such cases. I assured McCloy I would guarantee absolute privacy during our hunting trip. A while later McCloy informed me that he could take a week or so from work to go to Alaska. Krupp agreed to accommodate his own schedule to ours.

Everything was all arranged when an unexpected obstacle arose. Because Alfred Krupp had been convicted of a war crime, he had to get a special visa to enter the United States. The U.S. Ambassador to Germany could not issue this visa; documents had to be submitted directly to Washington. This meant that Alfred Krupp would not be able to avoid public attention to this trip. Under the circumstances, a hunt in Alaska was impossible.

Nonetheless, this did not daunt my efforts to introduce the two men. I suggested to McCloy that perhaps we could arrange a meeting with Krupp when he would be in Europe on other matters. It did not take long for such an opportunity to arise. A major conference of world leaders was being held in Milan, and McCloy was delegated to be one of the U.S. representatives. After the Milan conference, he would be able to fly to Germany to meet Alfred Krupp.

I made the arrangements with Krupp's brother, Berthold von Bohlen und Halbach (the surname of Krupp only applied to the oldest son, the inheritor of the family's industrial empire). McCloy was to be a guest in their home, and I would escort him.

We flew from Milan to Essen and drove by automobile to the gigantic Krupp palace where the entire family was gathered. Lunch had been arranged in our honor at the palace and then supper was to be held at the manor of von Bohlen und Halbach.

I can't say that this trip was particularly successful. Alfred Krupp was a tall man with a stiff, military carriage. His face was angular with aristocratic features; he never smiled. When interacting with anyone, Krupp was markedly courteous. And while he was very formal, he was also modest. He spoke English quite well, so there was no language barrier between him and McCloy. But like McCloy, he was a man of few words, and I had to make a supreme effort to keep the conversation from dying between the two men. Upon our meeting, Krupp's opening words were, "Thank you for the amnesty." With that, he shut down. There they were, McCloy and Krupp, sitting next to each other with nothing to say.

My saving grace in such rare cases was to launch into the subject of hunting. Alfred's brother, Berthold, and his wife, an American, had been to Alaska at my invitation. Thus, for a time, we were able to talk about how interesting it was to hunt in Alaska. Our host listened quietly and rarely made any comments. I remember that the lunch arrangements were exceptionally celebratory. A group of smartly dressed waiters served us a fabulous meal. The atmosphere, however, totally lacked ease and comfort.

Of course, this encounter with Alfred Krupp could not have much pleased John McCloy, but he was gracious as usual and never uttered a word of complaint to me. That was the last time I saw Alfred Krupp. I did meet often, however, with his brother, Berthold. Not only did he visit my home on many occasions but so did both of his children.

I never had any direct business relationships with the Krupps. My acquaintance with this family was strictly a personal one. Indirectly we did supply coal to one German company which sold it to Krupp factories.

The family dynasty ended with the demise of Alfred Krupp. He divorced his wife, and then their son was disenfranchised from the family due to his unacceptable, fast life style. He received an annuity and spent his days as a playboy until his untimely death. After Alfred Krupp resigned from the company, the new general director, who was hired from outside the family circle, was Berthold Baitz. I had known him for many years, and we enjoyed a solid friendship.

Sometime later I had another opportunity to connect McCloy with a prominent German family. I was friendly with Baron von Thyssen, an enormously wealthy man who was the owner of probably the most valuable private art collection in the world. Our paths often crossed socially. He had been married twice and was now divorced. I told him I wanted to introduce him to a very pretty young woman who was outgoing, charming and intelligent. As soon as he heard that it was John McCloy's daughter, Ellen, he was eager to meet her.

The next time the Baron was visiting New York, I invited him and Ellen to Caravel, a popular restaurant at the time. As if purposely arranged, the most unusual thing occurred that night. The city had a complete electrical blackout. We dined by candlelight until midnight. Afterwards, the two of them met on their own. For a while it seemed that a romance was successfully blossoming between the Baron and Ellen. But it was not meant to be and eventually, they drifted apart.

Encounters with United States Presidents

I had a chance to raise the issue of Lithuania's occupation to all of the postwar Presidents of the United States, from Dwight D. Eisenhower to George Bush Senior. Put into perspective, these encounters were modest and no doubt totally forgettable for the luminaries involved. But they meant a great deal to me. If only for a few minutes, I was able to make a case for the independence of my beloved homeland with the most powerful people in the world. And, of course, I could never help thinking how a poor refugee like me could end up having a private conversation with a former President of the United States on a topic so dear to my heart.

My first presidential encounter was with General Eisenhower who had been the Supreme Commander of the Allied Expeditionary Forces during the Second World War. After the war he was Commander of the United States Occupational Army in Germany. Since those times, he remained in my mind as one of the most distinguished persons who had had a role in influencing my own destiny as well.

Here's the story. I was acquainted with one of Eisenhower's friends, Robert Anderson, who was the Secretary of the Navy and later Secretary of the Treasury in the Eisenhower administration. Anderson had promised to arrange a meeting for me with the President, but the opportunity did not arise until 1961, after Eisenhower had completed both of his terms in office.

Visiting me in New York at that time was the Maharana of Udaipur who also wanted very much to meet President Eisenhower. Anderson transmitted the President's invitation for us to join him for dinner at the Waldorf Astoria Hotel where he was staying. Only the four of us dined together – the Maharana, Dwight Eisenhower, Robert Anderson and I. Thus we were able to engage in a more meaningful conversation. The President recalled visiting the refugee camps after the war when he was the General of the Occupational Army in Germany. He remarked that Lithuanians had organized their lives better than any of the other national groups living in refugee colonies over there. During our talk, Eisenhower did not disguise his extremely negative opinion about the Soviet Empire. He said that we must not lose hope – such an inhumane political system was bound to crumble sooner or later.

At the time that this conversation was taking place with Eisenhower, John Kennedy was the President of the United States. I had had a chance to interact with him during the 1960s. Kennedy was still a Senator then but he had already decided to run for President. I was acquainted with Karmel Offey, an American of Italian descent, who had worked for the United States Embassy in Moscow and was Kennedy's friend. Offey was well informed about the situation in Lithuania, and he knew that there was a rather extensive Lithuanian community in the United States. He asked me to meet with Senator Kennedy to explain the situation in Lithuania to him. Of course I was pleased to have such an opportunity.

I went to Washington to the Senate offices and spoke with Kennedy. The talk lasted a good half hour. I was able to tell him about the occupation of Lithuania, the sort of terror that the Soviet government had instituted to quell the country's resistance and what the American-Lithuanian community expected from the government of the United States. Kennedy told me that he was an impassioned supporter of human rights and freedom in the whole world. Therefore, he would not be merely a disinterested observer of historical injustice; he would make all possible efforts to assist the destiny of Lithuania. Naturally Kennedy did not hesitate to encourage me to go out and organize Lithuanians to vote for him because he was the best candidate for defending the ideals of democracy.

After the assassination of President Kennedy, I met President Lyndon Johnson in 1969 when he came to Cat Cay to visit his friend, Augustus Bush. A sailor arrived at my house and invited me to come out to Bush's

With former President, Dwight D. Eisenhower, and Bhagvata Singh, Maharana of Udaipur, New York, 1963

yacht which was anchored off shore. Of course I went, knowing that President Johnson, who had recently completed his term in office a half year ago, and his wife, Lady Bird, were staying on the boat. Bush said to me, "The President is looking for a golf partner. Would you like to play with him?"

I was delighted to have such an opportunity. This was a perfect chance for me to speak with a person of great influence in the Democratic Party, even if he was no longer the President.

Johnson went out to the golf course, escorted by two personal bodyguards. These men proved to be very useful to us; they helped us find our golf balls which kept disappearing into the bushes. We had a good laugh about all this later, claiming that nobody could ever say our game was less than a grand success. After all we had found more golf balls in the thick brush than we had lost. After our round of golf, Johnson joined me for a drink at the Club bar.

As we were sipping whiskey, he turned to me and said, "You speak with an unusual accent. Where are you from?"

Upon hearing my nationality, Lyndon Johnson virtually shouted out in surprise, "Lithuanian?!" With that, he began praising my fellow nationals, saying they were hard-working, persistent and cultured people. He even added that Lithuanians were the best-looking people on earth.

I had to laugh at that statement. "Mr. President, you probably don't have me in mind saying that."

"Naturally I don't mean you," Johnson retorted back. "I mean my grandson."

It turned out that President Johnson's daughter, Luci Baines, was married to Patrick Nugent, who was of Lithuanian descent. He had been born in the United States, but his parents had emigrated from Lithuania. (Luci eventually ended up divorcing Nugent, but at the time that I was conversing with Lyndon Johnson, they were still married. Johnson may not have praised Lithuanians so much had the divorce already taken place.)

This gave me the perfect opportunity to discuss matters closest to my heart. "Mr. President, your son-in-law is a Lithuanian; your grandson is a Lithuanian too. In other words, you have a family connection to my country. While you were holding office, you made several public statements that the United States does not recognize the occupation of Lithuania. Your predecessors did the same; however, words are not enough. Lithuania's situation has not changed one iota although several decades have passed. Perhaps now that you have finished your term in office, could you could make use of your authority and support Lithuania more openly?"

Lyndon Johnson nodded in agreement. "You are absolutely correct," he said. "I have to think this over. What would I be able to do?"

I said I hoped we could get together at some time in the future. I wanted Johnson to sign some declarations, initiated by the émigré community, urging reestablishment of Lithuania's independence. Unfortunately nothing came of my intention. I did not meet with Johnson again, and three years later, he died.

Richard Nixon also visited Cat Cay. I saw him several times playing golf after he had resigned the Presidency due to the Watergate scandal in 1974. Once I exchanged a few words with him. I reminded him that we had met before he had been elected President. He said he remembered me and graciously invited me to visit him at Bebe Rebozo's house where he was staying. The President promised to give me his book of memoirs with his autograph. However, I never did drop over because Rebozo had asked all club members to leave Nixon in peace.

Of course it was quite probable that Richard Nixon, a man who had spoken to thousands of people in his lifetime, had merely claimed to have remembered me out of courtesy. But for me, our meeting years earlier had been very memorable. At that time I had persuaded him to sign a declaration demanding that the Soviet Union terminate its occupation of Lithuania.

Early in the 1960s, the Lithuanian émigré community considered that its most important mission was to remind the world consistently about the plight of Lithuania. The Latvian and Estonian communities in the United States were planning a mass demonstration at the United Nations headquarters in New York when the General Assembly was in session. That provided the perfect opportunity for raising the issue of the occupation of the Baltic countries. Community organizers passed a decision to give this event some publicity and clout. Thus a half page ad was purchased in *The New York Times* for a declaration of support for our countries' independence movements.

I was able to gain agreements from several renowned Americans to sign our demand for the reestablishment of Lithuania's independence. Working with Admiral Redford, who signed the document himself, we were able to get Richard Nixon, then in private law practice, to add his name. Over all the decades that Lithuania was occupied, I believe that Richard Nixon, the chief executive of the United States for six years, was the President who was the most helpful towards our country.

After Nixon resigned, Vice President Gerald Ford took office. I was also able to talk with him briefly at a Bohemian Club outing in California.

The Bohemian Club is an unusual institution for the financial and social elite that can probably only be found in America. Its members include many corporate executives, celebrities and famous personages from various levels of society – a good percentage of the people listed in *Who's Who*. The Club acquired a 2,700-acre retreat in a California forest of gigantic redwoods named the Bohemian Grove. Invitations to the annual festivities were sent to prominent politicians and country leaders from all over the world. If invited by a club member, an outsider was able to attend the gatherings but no more than three times in a lifetime. I managed to make full use of this opportunity since I was invited three times by my friends, Fred Crawford and Willard Rockwell. Once, German Chancellor Helmut Schmidt was a guest. In perfect English, he read a most interesting lecture on international politics.

At such Bohemian Club functions, people walked from one camp to another, interacted and made new contacts. I visited with President Gerald Ford and, during our chat, I mentioned that I had been born in Lithuania. For some reason the President said that he had Latvian friends who were fine fellows. I first thought that he might have confused our nationalities. However, he actually had met with some Latvians, although there were few of them living in the United States. As far as Lithuanians were concerned, he mentioned that he was aware that we had sizeable and politically active communities, particularly in Chicago.

As usual I immediately directed the conversation about Lithuania's existing situation as an occupied country. Maybe because Ford was the president, he merely listened to my words reservedly, making no comments himself. Before long Secretary of State Henry Kissinger walked up to Ford, and our talk about the Baltic countries came to an end.

Meeting President Ronald Reagan and Nancy Reagan at the White House

Another time I saw Ronald Reagan at a Bohemian Grove retreat. However, he was surrounded by other people the entire time. All I could do was introduce myself but I was unable to speak with him personally. My chance to interact with Ronald Reagan came later. Since I had been a financial supporter of the Republican Party for many years, I was invited to a reception at the White House when Ronald Reagan was President.

I was able to speak with him for several minutes. At the time Gorbachev had just come into power. Reagan upheld a very hard line, one of absolutely no concessions to the Soviet Union. I praised Reagan for his position, telling him that most American-Lithuanians, including me, supported such a policy, believing it to be sound. Our opinion was that in the long run, this stand would assist the liberation of all the USSR republics. Reagan listened to me intently. Then he asked me what sort of news was forthcoming from the Baltic countries about the mood of the public. I answered that although Gorbachev's *perestroika* policy had just barely been launched, I was already hearing from people about rising hopes in Lithuania. They believed that the Soviet Union was going to be forced to change and downscale the communist dictatorship. Under such circumstances, the ability of the United States to increase pressure on the Soviets was especially relevant. Unfortunately our conversation was cut short when First Lady Nancy Reagan approached and steered the President away.

Prior to Ronald Reagan, I was able to meet President Jimmy Carter through my daughter, Jurate, who was working as an Associated Press reporter in Washington at the time. She invited me to escort her to a Christmas reception for accredited journalists at the White House. Not only did I get a chance to speak with Jimmy Carter but also to enjoy a dance with his wife, Rosalynn.

Jurate had had numerous interactions with Jimmy Carter so she introduced me to him. We struck up an effortless conversation; the tone was not the least bit official. It was easy to be casual right from the start. I said that while my Lithuanian-born daughter and I were incredibly happy in the United States, there was only one thing lacking for our complete bliss – we needed more activity by the United States to liberate our homeland. Carter listened and smiled but made no comment.

That was not the only talk that I was able to have with Jimmy Carter. Ten years later, in January of 1991, at the height of tensions between the Soviets and Lithuania over the independence movement, Russian tanks brutally attacked unarmed Lithuanian citizens who were holding vigils at key institutions – the Parliament and Government buildings, TV and radio transmitters, utility companies and such in Vilnius. The world watched in horror at this display of Stalinist-like tactics to crush peaceful demonstrations to retain control over the territory.

Carter had already been out of office for a considerable time and had gained a reputation for his activities as a peace mediator around the world. I wanted to ask him to get involved in the negotiations between Lithuania and Russia for the recognition of our independence. Again Jurate helped me contact him. (By then she was married to Roger Altman who had served as Assistant Secretary of the Treasury in the Carter administration.)

Over the phone, Carter and I discussed at great length the international situation and Lithuania's case. We also deliberated possible diplomatic steps that could be taken. The former President was greatly impressed by

With President George Bush, Sr., May 3, 1990

the peaceful, unarmed resistance of Lithuanians in their fight for freedom. The movement for independence was called the "singing revolution" in the United States as well as back in Lithuania. Carter said that he had been upset by the brutal violence with which Soviets had attacked the people of our country.

Several weeks later, I received a letter from Jimmy Carter. He informed me that he had offered his assistance to Gorbachev to begin a dialogue with the government of Lithuania. However, the Soviet leader had rejected his offer for mediating such talks. At the same time, I kept the leader of Lithuania, Vytautas Landsbergis, Chairman of the (then) Supreme Council, informed about President Carter's initiatives.

The first time I met George Bush, Sr. was at a private cocktail party when he was Vice President. I told him that I was grateful to his father for recommending me to the Hobe Sound Club. I also made mention of another, rather comical circumstance. Once I had been visiting my friends, Robert and Paula Timmerman, at their home which was right on the Atlantic Coast in Kennebunkport, Maine. Bush had his own residence next door at Walker Cove. I told him that I used to see him walking around his swimming pool. Bush laughed. "Hopefully, I had my towel around me."

The next time I met George Bush, he was President, and Lithuania had made the decisive step of separating itself from the Soviet Union. It was the spring of 1990 when the first Prime Minister of Lithuania, Kazimiera Prunskienė, arrived in Washington and set into motion a string of historic events I will never forget.

At the Dawn of Independence

Mikhail Gorbachev came into power in the USSR, instituting his *perestroika* policy, which was favorably received by the West. Observing these events, my hopes rose that this empire would collapse from internal struggles. I felt that the introduction of certain free market elements into the economy by the new Soviet government which were in direct contradiction to the fundamentals of the communist system would destabilize the dictatorially based political order of the country. The *glasnost* policy which followed *perestroika* allowed the press to disclose the historical aspects of the Soviet Union publicly along with problems existing in the country. The Communist Party was now incapable of retaining its usual vacuum of information by which it would only issue propaganda through all media channels. Freedom of speech has always been a deadly threat to any totalitarian regime that rests on a foundation of untruths to justify its right to rule.

Well before the *Sąjūdis* movement had formed in Lithuania, I was convinced that the Soviet Union would implode. There was only one relevant question – how soon would that occur? In discussions with my friends, as Gorbachev waged his reforms, I forecast that the USSR would come to its demise in two or three years. Some argued with me, saying that a superpower could not fall apart in such lightening speed. As events unfolded, it turned out that I was quite accurate in guessing when the Soviet empire would fall apart.

That did not really please me. Actually I became very anxious about the future of Lithuania. No one could be certain that the disintegration of the USSR would occur without bloodshed. The dissolution of such a huge country was likely to result in final convulsions and potentially instigate a tremendous wave of terror. I was afraid that the old Communist guard might use violent means to save their empire. In such a case, chaos was unavoidable, possibly bringing enormous tragedy. I was never able to forget the frightening visions, carved in my mind since early childhood, of the Russian Revolution and the civil war that ensued. I kept mulling over in my mind – God forbid, could something similar happen, as the old system falls apart? Although this time the old system was communism, could the same kinds of upheavals occur? I tried to cling to the hope that such a cataclysm could be avoided. In retrospect it was highly likely that the well-balanced policies of the West served to avert such a tragedy.

The dialogue that Gorbachev initiated with the West was met with extraordinary approval. Most analysts believed that it was of the utmost importance to help Gorbachev strengthen his position within the USSR. The issue of the Baltic countries was not a high priority in the minds of many American politicians. Foreign policy revolved around the issue of world stability.

The hopes of the émigré community flared up again in the belief that Gorbachev's *perestroika* and *glasnost* policies would positively alter the situation of our country. One event that took place was significant enough to draw national press attention and brought unspeakable joy to the hearts of American-Lithuanians.

By this time, the secret addendum to the Molotov-Ribbentrop Pact of August 23, 1939 had come to light. Just prior to its attack upon Poland, Germany had signed an agreement with the USSR on the division of territorial spheres of influence. Initially Lithuania was relegated to the German sphere of influence; however, when Lithuania refused to act as a German ally and attack Poland, it was shifted to the Soviet sphere in a second secret pact addendum, signed in Moscow on September 27th of that same year. That meant that the occupation of Lithuania had been planned in advance by two presumably enemy forces.

A massive demonstration denouncing the Molotov-Ribbentrop Pact took place in Vilnius on August 23, 1987, by the statue of Adomas Mickevičius, a beloved poet of Lithuania and Poland. When I heard this news, I thought to myself, "What we have been waiting for so long has finally ignited Lithuania. Gorbachev offered a taste of freedom; now he won't be able to stem the flood of desire for more."

A film of the demonstration was brought to New York from Vilnius. We sat and watched footage of a meeting attended by a number of Communist government activists. Heatedly they were complaining that it was only the upstarts and criminals who had gathered by the statue of Mickevičius. They claimed that the society at large in Lithuania was roundly condemning their actions. The film gave me a hearty laugh. I thought, "Go ahead and keep on explaining and pretending. You're going to have to do a whole lot of that now."

All sorts of discussions among Lithuanian Americans ensued about the situation and the potential for further actions. I still had certain apprehensions. The Soviet Union had improved to some extent its image on human rights. Gaining endorsement for the reestablishment of our country's independence could prove more difficult under the circumstances. My guess was that Gorbachev would offer some form of autonomy within the USSR. I doubted that he would allow the Baltic countries to regain the statehood which had been wrested away from them by force. The West, which feared an unpredictable and rapid fall of the Soviet Union, just might agree to autonomy as an entirely suitable resolution to the problem.

In the meantime, the *Sąjūdis* movement had become very active in Lithuania. *Sąjūdis* was established on June 3, 1988, at a meeting of intellectuals in Vilnius, as a Lithuanian citizens' movement calling for greater political, economic and cultural autonomy in response to Gorbachev's policy of perestroika. A few weeks later, a rally of 50,000 people demonstrated support for *Sąjūdis* and demanded that delegates to the 19th Communist Party Conference press for greater freedom in the country's economic and cultural matters, including reinstatement of the prewar flag and anthem. The movement, which was essentially one of national rebirth, gained massive public support, and the lives of Lithuanians changed irreversibly.

I had some apprehensions when the *Sąjūdis* movement was first formed. Algirdas Brazauskas (who eventually became the first elected President of postwar independent Lithuania from 1993 to 1998), was then the First Secretary of the Lithuanian Communist Party. He and the Communists under his leadership brought up a murky idea on autonomy. I was afraid that this sort of concession to the Soviet government would prove to be a kind of opiate, satisfying a good portion of Lithuanian society but not achieving the primary objective – an independent State of Lithuania opting for a Western, democratic orientation. The longed-for reality would thus be postponed to an undesignated and far off future.

Early on it seemed as though the *Sąjūdis* movement was still afraid to discuss the reestablishment of independence head-on and might concede to some undefined form of autonomy while remaining under USSR jurisdiction. As a temporary tactic, such a stance could be considered understandable and justifiable. It could serve to calm Moscow down a bit over the course of the political battle. However, such a tactic could only work for the short term. The critical factor was that it might lead to the loss of the primary aim – independent statehood.

Nevertheless, *Sąjūdis* took root, rapidly becoming even stronger. Certainly I was overjoyed at such a turn of events but, at the same time, I still harbored certain fears. This movement attracted the public's support and trust at a level that had never before been witnessed. Nevertheless, its leadership was still in the hands of former Communists. It made me nervous to think that they could succumb to Gorbachev's proposal of purported autonomy and lead Lithuania down such a dead-end byway.

Cautious cries for the reestablishment of Lithuanian statehood rang out during another demonstration at Vingis Park in Vilnius, also organized by *Sąjūdis* on August 23, 1988, marking the dark day that the Molotov-Ribbentrop Act was signed. I first learned about this political action when it was reported in a brief news clip over national television in the United States. Shortly thereafter acquaintances from Lithuania began telephoning me. They enthusiastically related the happenings at Vingis Park. Now I realized that our country was approaching independence in unexpectedly broad steps. I also understood that it was incredibly important that neither Lithuania nor the West make any serious mistakes, which might jeopardize our life-long dream of freedom.

Sąjūdis representatives began traveling to the United States right after that. They must have all visited my home at some point. Several of them stayed in the two apartments in my Manhattan office building, including such distinguished Rebirth movement activists as Vytautas

Landsbergis and his wife Gražina. Their visits were a source of great pleasure for me. For one our interactions were always most invigorating. At the same time, I felt that I was supporting the *Sąjūdis* movement by offering a domicile in New York. All these people were carrying out a vitally important mission by publicizing to Americans what was happening in Lithuania. Vytautas Landsbergis once actually arranged a press conference in my office; a group of reporters from all the major national television stations of the United States arrived with their TV cameras in hand.

Jurate, a reporter for many years, retained good relations with distinguished mass media representatives in the United States. She never missed an opportunity to impress upon such people the obligation of the United States to support the political pursuits of Lithuania. One of her good acquaintances was Jack Rosenthal, who was at that time Editorial Page Editor of *The New York Times*. Rosenthal always made time to meet with *Sąjūdis* movement representatives or the political leaders of a still unrecognized Lithuania, like Kazimiera Prunskienė. He'd also invite other members of *The Times* editorial staff to these meetings. All of them considerably influenced the position taken by the newspaper.

Initially United States newspapers took a rather cold stance on Lithuanian pursuits to reestablish statehood. In time the view changed. Editorials began to express approval of Lithuania's split from the Soviet Union. When Lithuania announced its Act for the Reestablishment of Independence on March 11, 1990, *The New York Times* printed the news on its front page under a huge banner headline. Not long thereafter it took an editorial position in favor of international recognition of Lithuania's independence.

I noticed one aspect to the meetings with Lithuanian politicians at *The Times* office. Jack Rosenthal would listen sincerely to their talks, asking a great many questions in the meantime. The other editors at a meeting would simply sit there, indifferent and seemingly bored. I thanked Rosenthal for his interest in my homeland.

"Don't be surprised, Joe," he told me. "The roots of both our families come from Lithuania. My grandparents lived in Kaunas." Apparently Jack Rosenthal's maternal grandfather, Henzel Kaplan, had been a respected lumber merchant in Lithuania. He had actually been awarded a medal of honor and was well acquainted with prewar President Antanas Smetona. Tragically he and his wife, Cipe, along with six of her nine siblings, perished during the war.

One day Jack Rosenthal told me that he very much wanted to visit Lithuania with his wife, Holly, and walk around the areas where his grandparents had lived. There was one stipulation. He wanted no public attention, from either politicians or the press. "Would it be possible to arrange such a visit for us – incognito?" he asked me. I told him it was indeed entirely possible.

Jack Rosenthal visited Lithuania in the fall of 1990. Although the country had declared its independence, realistically it was still a Soviet environment. Nevertheless, Jack returned from his trip very pleased. He told me all about it and later wrote me a letter of gratitude. Then he threw a party at his home for his friends just to share his experiences in Lithuania. Enthralled he talked about the beauty of the Old Towns in Vilnius and Kaunas. He said he had walked through all the courtyards of our old university, stopping in cafes there. Just as he had requested, his trip to Lithuania was a quiet one; there was no attention from the press. Still, this man of much influence over public opinion in the United States found time to meet with a few local politicians, including Vytautas Landsbergis, the actual leader of Lithuania at the time and Emanuelis Zingeris, a Jewish member of Parliament. He also had some talks with Arvydas Juozaitis, a philosopher and an activist in the early days of the *Sąjūdis* movement, and Česlovas Juršėnas, the Senior Editor of *Vakarinės naujienos 'Evening News'* (and later a signatory of the Act of Independence).

Rosenthal's interest in Lithuania did not stop even after international recognition. I had the honor of arranging receptions for Lithuania's Presidents – Algirdas Brazauskas and his successor Valdas Adamkus – and the Chairman of the *Seimas*, Vytautas Landsbergis, when they visited the States. I always invited Jack and Holly to these functions, and he always accepted with pleasure. His stance was always very modest at these functions. He never talked about his influence on *The New York Times*, which continuously took an evermore encouraging position on Lithuania.

Back in 1989, as Christmas approached, news broke that the Lithuanian Communist Party intended to split from the centralized USSR Party. Though my convictions were vehemently anti-communist my entire life, I considered this to be an exceptionally meaningful decision, a step in advancing independence for the country. Undoubtedly Algirdas Brazauskas and his command were astute politicians, attempting to retain their authority in the minds of the public-at-large, as the *Sąjūdis* movement became the dominant and most popular political force. Their move did indeed strike a strong blow against the Soviet government. Western media also paid quite a bit of attention to this event.

None of the communists from any other Soviet republic had dared to deliver such a slap in the face to Moscow. The breakaway of the Lithuanian Communist Party clearly showed that even Party members had patriotic aspirations. In the meantime, the Soviet system was completely losing support in the country.

At that time I frequently spoke with *Sąjūdis* movement leader, Vytautas Landsbergis, by telephone. I would pass on any information I was able to learn about the United States government position on the issue of the Baltic countries. Naturally I would also hear his thoughts about the situation in Lithuania, which filled me with mixed feelings of hope and anxiety.

A realistic threat arose that the infuriated orthodox-minded Communists of the USSR could demand of the KGB to incite some sort of provocation in Lithuania, thereby clearing the way for outright repressions. For a time I had calmed myself, believing that Gorbachev would not undertake a fight with the entire country but now I was concerned.

At the same time, I believed that Lithuania should start thinking about its economic reorganization. Lithuania was unable to manage its own economy independently while the occupational Soviet Army was still in the country, but I felt that the foundations of a free market system had to be laid as quickly as possible.

I approached my son-in-law, Roger Altman. Would he be able to help in pulling together a program, transferring the economy of Lithuania from centralized planning to a free market system? Roger said he knew one of the leading experts in economics in America – Harvard University Professor Lawrence Summers – and would try to persuade him to undertake this job.

Professor Summers was keenly interested in such a proposal when I met with him in Boston to explain the political situation in Lithuania.

Jurate and Roger Altman on their wedding day, Cat Cay, December, 1981

Then I asked how he thought he might be able to help our country. Professor Summers agreed to formulate a plan for reorganizing the centrally planned economic system. "I can ask my university to give me a couple of weeks vacation time," he said as he considered the assignment. "I'd request another colleague, Andrei Schleifer, from the University of Chicago to help me on this. We could go to Lithuania together. That would give us enough time to pull together an outline for reorganizing certain aspects of the economy."

The two economists and I decided to go to Vilnius in January at the same time, as it turned out, that Gorbachev would make a historic visit to Lithuania (the first time that a head of the USSR had ever visited the country). I realized that the events in our country were approaching a climax. Gorbachev was coming to appeal to Lithuanians not to press for independence in exchange for a promise that the Supreme Soviet would consider laws for secession, including more decentralization and democratization.

On an impulse Jurate arranged to go with me. She was also very sensitive to all the events taking place during the "Rebirth" of Lithuania, following them with deep interest and sensitivity. So, early in January, we flew into Riga and drove to Vilnius, past the locales of my childhood in the Pasvalys Region. On the way we stopped in Saločiai. There I walked into a store to buy something to drink. I knew that even the most common goods were frequently unavailable in the Soviet Union; nonetheless, the bareness of those store shelves shocked me. There were a few rows of Russian vodka and a few bottles of soft drinks. Atop the ice chest lay a couple of smelly frozen fish along with some stale slabs of black bread. I wondered how on earth people here managed to live at all. Only by raising a pig or a cow themselves were small town residents able to survive. Such was the life which Soviet socialism offered its citizens.

When Mikhail Gorbachev met with the intelligentsia of our country, I sat alongside Romualdas Sikorskis, a supporter of independence and the Minister of Finance since 1957 (holding this position for the first independent Government under Prime Minister Kazimiera Prunskienė from 1990 to 1991). The demagogic speech by the Soviet leader was very emotional for both of us. It was difficult to surmise what Gorbachev actually expected to gain. It appeared as though he was beginning to understand what the predominate mood was in Lithuania but apparently he still had hopes that by issuing threats and some vague promises, he would be able to put the brakes on the process of secession from the Soviet Union.

Gorbachev went into the streets of Vilnius, where he was surrounded by ordinary citizens, who shook their fists and shouted at the Soviet leader to give them their freedom. I was so proud to hear the people of Lithuania tell Gorbachev to his face that our country had only one non-negotiable goal – independence. The Soviet leader appeared dejected at such a unanimous expression of an incredibly tough position.

Meanwhile I arranged for Summers and Shleifer to meet with key economists, bankers and heads of various enterprises in Lithuania to help organize a transition from planned management to an economy that is regulated by free market forces.

During that week in January, I was convinced that soon a very decisive step would be taken towards the reestablishment of independence. Bear in mind that this realization came without a single *Sąjūdis* movement politician saying anything of the like to me.

A few weeks passed. Early in March, Vytautas Landsbergis called and invited me to come to Lithuania as soon as possible. He didn't tell me over the phone what was supposed to happen, but I suspected that the Act for the Reestablishment of Independence was about to be declared. I yearned to be in my homeland during such a historical moment. I had to fly out to Vilnius without delay. Again Jurate wanted to join me. I telephoned Valdemaras Kančas at the Soviet Embassy, and he promised to do his best to get us a visa in 24 hours. He succeeded, and the following day Jurate and I boarded the plane, flying to Europe then once again, landing in Riga.

We arrived in the capital of Latvia in the morning. The border control allowed Jurate to pass but detained me without an explanation for nearly an hour. Finally we boarded a plane to Kaunas. When we landed at the airport, Rimas Stankevičius, the brother of *Sąjūdis* activist (and soon to be Prime Minister) Kazimiera Prunskienė, met us for the drive to Vilnius. We simply dropped our things at the *Draugystė* 'Friendship' Hotel and rushed off to the Supreme Council building.

We arrived just as the session was starting and stayed there until late that night. The whole time I was very excited, waiting for the historical moment – the declaration of the Reestablishment of Independence Act. To think that I had been waiting fifty years for this moment! One by one the delegates announced their votes. The tension was almost unbearable. In the end, of the 130 deputies in the chambers, 124 voted in favor, six had abstained – and no one was against an independent state of Lithuania.

Everyone in the hall took hold of each other's hands. Unexpectedly a massive yellow, green and red flag rolled up from the floor at the front of the room to cover up the giant bronze hammer and sickle on the wall. For decades our national flag had been outlawed and now it reappeared to obliterate that despised symbol of Soviet power which had loomed over the chamber for so long.

Tears flooded my eyes; the pent up sorrow in the depth of my heart broke loose. I thought I was in some fabulous dream. It was one of the strongest emotional moments of my entire life.

Later that same night, we witnessed another dramatic moment when the Soviet coat of arms was ripped off the face of the Supreme Council building by an exuberant crowd, celebrating their freedom.

We left the Supreme Council at about one o'clock in the morning in a light chilly drizzle. My eyes beheld a wondrous sight as we walked out the door. A huge crowd waving the tri-color flags and singing filled the square in front of the building. As I was making my way through the sea of people, they knelt on the ground before me and grabbed my hands, trying to kiss them. I think these ordinary citizens thought that I was one of the signatories of the Act of Independence. Even though my body was shaking from the cold dampness, I did not want to leave this place. I wanted to savor the moment forever.

Jurate went back to the States a few days later, while I remained for another few weeks to assist Kazimiera Prunskienė, who had been elected Prime Minister immediately after the declaration, in organizing the work of the new Government. She provided me with a separate office, where I tried to coordinate her demanding schedule. Everyone, it seemed, wanted to meet with the Prime Minister. During those heady days, I worked day and night and hardly ever left the Government building.

The Cabinet was in the process of formation; a tremendous pressure hovered over all governmental officials. The old Soviet ministers still worked for a certain time. They walked around, looking worried and glum. It was obvious that most of them would have to be replaced. Once

I tried to joke about it in the cafeteria. I asked several ministers dining there, why they didn't seem to be in a good mood – after all the fact that Lithuania had declared its independence was cause for happiness. There was no response. My question simply hung in the air in an uncomfortable silence.

Prunskienė formed her Cabinet of Ministers in a matter of a few days. Meanwhile threats rumbled in from Moscow. The economic blockade was instituted shortly thereafter. Still, the Government did not panic. The predominate thinking was that the economy of Lithuania was sufficiently strong to withstand Soviet pressure and after all, the blockade could not last forever. The most important factor in our optimism was that the people of Lithuania seemed prepared to adjust to the upcoming difficulties. Freedom was worth any price.

Doors of the West Open for Lithuania

The excitement of history unfolding back in Lithuania faded after my return to the States. My anxiety level started rising again. The West showed no desire to recognize the independence of Lithuania, not even by some cautious step. The paradox of the situation amazed me. The United States and the Western European countries consistently retained official policies of non-recognition of USSR occupation over the entire 45 years of Moscow control. While this sort of national policy may have been no more than a formality, nevertheless, it seemed that under current circumstances, the West could logically do nothing else than to recognize independence. After all a democratically elected body of representatives had taken the mandate of the majority to reinstate Lithuania's statehood. All American Lithuanians were waiting for the West to initiate diplomatic relations with the Government under Prime Minister Kazimiera Prunskienė at some level, even if it was not their highest priority. More than a month had passed since the March 11th declaration of independence. There was still no sign that the United States intended to recognize the reestablished statehood of Lithuania.

Then one day Prunskienė called me and said she was preparing for a trip to Canada. From there she intended to go to Washington D.C. She asked if Jurate and I could arrange a press conference for her with reporters from the leading American newspapers. While her planned visit was primarily private, at the same time, the Prime Minister wanted to take the opportunity to contact media outlets. Her goal was to spotlight Lithuania's precarious situation.

I happened to know a very influential director of the United States Information Agency, Frank Shakespeare, who had worked there during Ronald Reagan's administration. I might never have thought of calling him except that he was in East Hampton right at the time that Prunskienė contacted me about her intentions to visit Washington. This confluence of events must have been fate.

An idea flashed in my mind. Shakespeare knew all the top people in the media of the United States. I thought he just might agree to organize some press conferences with the representatives of leading newspapers and television stations for the Prime Minister.

I invited Shakespeare for lunch, and we had a long talk. I explained that the land of my ancestry maintained its independent status, the existence of which the United States and numerous other Western countries had formally recognized during all the years of Soviet occupation. But now the situation had hit a perplexing dead end. The democratic world seemed to agree that the Independence Act was legal – to wit, *de jure* recognition was granted. But by the same token, all the democratic countries were avoiding actual diplomatic recognition of a free and independent Lithuania and its government. Shakespeare clearly understood that the Prime Minister had to get the attention of American politicians; I did not have to go into detail about the importance of this for the country. My only request was for Shakespeare to help us publicize Dr. Prunskienė's visit to Washington with the national press corps.

Shakespeare listened to me intently. He asked me many questions, taking a keen interest in the historical facts of the occupation of the Baltic countries. Our luncheon stretched out into a long and productive afternoon. His opinion of Lithuania was positive; he was ready to assist as best he could. At that point, I suddenly had an idea. One overriding principle of my life came to bear – always pursue the maximum possible outcome in a situation. So I went ahead and asked Shakespeare, if perhaps he could use his contacts to arrange an audience for our Prime Minister with President Bush at the White House.

At that time Shakespeare was retired and had withdrawn from active political life. However, there was not a doubt in my mind that he still had excellent contacts at the top government levels.

Shakespeare did not answer my question specifically. All he said was, "I understand your concern. I have great sympathies for your country. Still, I can't make any promises, especially regarding a meeting with the President. I've had some conflicts with George Bush. My relationship with him is not so good that I can simply call him up on the phone. However, I'll see what I can do. At the very least, it might be possible to arrange a meeting with Vice President Quayle."

When Shakespeare left, he did make one promise. Since there was little time left before the Prime Minister's arrival, he said he would talk to William Kristol, Chief of Staff to Vice President Quayle, the next day about the possibility of a White House visit.

Shakespeare kept his promise. He called me in the afternoon to inform me that he had spoken with Mr. Kristol. Apparently Quayle would not object to a meeting with Dr. Prunskienė. However, the issue still had to be brought up with the National Security Council. That seemed positive enough, but then another obstacle came up. The Vice President was scheduled to be out of town during the same days that Dr. Prunskienė would be in Washington.

Dr. Prunskienė could not adjust her schedule for the United States. She had an appointment to meet with the Canadian Minister of Foreign Affairs prior to leaving. The situation seemed hopeless. As though he were comforting me, Shakespeare mentioned that he'd try to discuss the matter with Kristol again. Possibly a meeting with President Bush was not out of the question. Besides, this proposal still had to be discussed with Lawrence Eagleburger, Deputy Secretary of State, and Condoleezza Rice, Special Assistant to the National Security Affairs Advisor on the USSR and Eastern Europe. (She would go on to become the National Security Adviser and then Secretary of State in the George W. Bush's administration.)

There really was little hope that anything would come to pass. That same evening Shakespeare called me again, saying he had done all that he could. All that was left was to await a reply from the White House. I didn't have to wait long. The next day, the telephone rang. A woman's

In Washington with Prime Minister Prunskienė and her brother, Rimas Stankevičius, May, 1990

voice informed me that Bill Kristol wanted to speak to me. When I finally hung up the phone, I still could not believe what I had just heard. President George Bush agreed to meet with Prime Minister Prunskienė on May 3, 1990.

My heart was thumping with joy in my chest. Immediately I called Jurate, who flew to Washington to help oversee all the details for Dr. Prunskienė's visit to the White House. In addition to the overall thrill of the moment, I was extremely gratified that my daughter took upon herself all the organizational matters for the Prime Minister's affairs in the United States. Jurate spared neither time nor money and worked tirelessly with experts in handling special functions for visiting dignitaries.

We organized a precise schedule for Dr. Prunskienė in Washington. Planning was down to a minute's accuracy – sitting down in the limousine, driving time, disembarking time, arriving at one function or another and traveling to the next destination. The calendar for meetings kept growing longer by the day. As soon as word spread through the halls of United States governmental institutions that the Prime Minister of Lithuania was meeting the President, calls started coming in. The White House Chief of Staff and the Congress minority leader wanted meetings with her. The next thing we knew, the Senate got involved. Senators Jesse Helms, the Chairman of the Foreign Relations Committee, and Bob Dole also wanted to see Dr. Prunskienė.

I had a chance to speak with Senator Bob Dole before the Prime Minister's arrival. He encouraged me by saying, "Don't be afraid to demand recognition of Lithuania during the meeting with President Bush. We'll take it upon ourselves here in the Senate to pressure him as needed."

Arrival day came. Jurate and I flew to the Canadian border in a chartered private plane to meet Prunskienė. She was escorted by local Lithuanians, who had arranged a ceremonial departure from Canada for her. The Prime Minister finally crossed the border and passed into our hands.

Jurate and I took responsibility for financing all the costs of the Prime Minister's historical visit – luxurious hotel accommodations, limousines and receptions held in her name. There was a delightful turnaround in this situation. The émigré community also wanted to contribute in some way. Once news hit that President George Bush would be receiving Dr. Prunskienė, even the World Lithuanian Community wanted to take part.

Vytautas Bieliauskas, Chairman of the World Community, was anxious to be in the Prime Minister's entourage, escorting her to the meeting with the President. Naturally the Lithuanian Ambassador in Washington, Stasys Lozoraitis, also expected to be included. However, the final decision on who would escort the Prime Minister was in the hands of the White House. In the end these two individuals were not invited to participate in the meeting between Bush and Prunskienė. I know that must have been difficult for Ambassador Lozoraitis, the official representative of Lithuania. Matters unfolded in such a way that he remained on the sidelines, not only in organizing the visit but during the actual meeting at the White House as well.

Press attention to the Prime Minister's schedule grew by the minute. Prunskienė was invited to speak to the National Press Club. National television outlets, including the *Today Show*, began clamoring to put her on the air; all the leading newspapers, *The New York Times, The Washington Post* and *The Wall St. Journal,* requested interviews.

The public relations company that we had hired prepared massive briefing books and wrote speeches for Prunskienė for each of her meetings with government officials in Washington. She rifled through them and then set them aside, saying "I won't need any prepared texts. I know what to say."

Such self-assurance was a bit surprising, coming from a woman with comparatively little political experience who did not speak English and was on her first trip abroad to the West. But Dr. Prunskienė proved to be absolutely right. By speaking about Lithuania's matters in a simple and straightforward manner, the Prime Minister left an impression of sincerity and openness; she was a woman deeply concerned about her country's future. Those speeches written by the public relations people were geared to American audiences, but her own choice of words probably carried more weight. American journalists appreciated that she boldly replied to every question at the National Press Club. Unlike the average politicians, she didn't blow smokescreens on an issue. Lithuania was different; it had just regained independence from a 50-year occupation. Hers was a fresh and entirely appropriate style. The sincerity and passion exhibited by Prunskienė added a special charm to her entire United States visit. Americans generously complimented her at every public appearance.

The White House informed us that only two designated people could accompany the Prime Minister – translator Viktoras Nakas and me. Even Prunskienė's brother, Rimas Stankevičius, who accompanied her everywhere on this trip, had to wait in the reception area of the White House. President Bush had his own translator – a Lithuanian – American.

As could be expected, the meeting did not proceed without some translating glitches. President Bush was obviously accustomed to having his words second-guessed and instantly translated. He felt that he could simply talk on without stopping for any pauses for the translator. It takes a top-level translator to handle that kind of situation. Nakas was up to the job, but the other man lagged behind, particularly when the conversation started rolling rather dynamically.

In spite of these difficulties, the atmosphere was very friendly from the first few minutes. All the tension due to the official nature of the meeting was instantly dissipated when Bush took Prunskienė by the arm and led her to her chair.

The meeting with the President took longer than had been scheduled. Bush listened calmly to Prunskienė's words. She told him that Lithuania had the right to re-declare, and the West had the obligation to recognize the statehood of the country. Bush replied that, although he understood and supported our position, the United States had an exceptional global responsibility to assure world stability. That hinged on relations with the Soviet Union. Bush emphasized that the United States wanted the reforms undertaken by Mikhail Gorbachev to succeed. In the meantime, the pursuit of independence by Lithuania and the other Baltic countries was in effect undermining Gorbachev's position. For this reason the United States was keenly observing the state of affairs; however, no risky steps were being taken for the time being.

The President made some comments at the end of the talk that drew our attention. As though it were an afterthought, he stated that it would be best if the countries of Western Europe were to get more involved in the recognition of Lithuania. He, on the other hand, would make use of his confidential contacts with Gorbachev to support the goals of the Baltic Republics. In bidding farewell, the President said that he would be pleased to continue this meeting but, unfortunately, others were already waiting for him. "Where will you be heading after this

Washington visit?" Bush asked unexpectedly, as he extended his hand to bid me goodbye.

"We intend to fly to London. The Lithuanian Community there is arranging a reception for our Prime Minister," I replied.

"Aren't you planning to meet with Margaret Thatcher?" Bush asked. This question took me aback. There had been no discussion about such a high-level meeting in London.

"Naturally, that would be great," I commented.

"You need to use the opportunity," Bush added and our conversation ended.

We found the television and newspaper reporters out on the lawn waiting for us as we left the White House. Dr. Prunskienė proceeded to answer their questions. Suddenly one of the aides from Bush's office approached me and said, "I have an urgent message for you."

She handed me a piece of paper. I read it. At first I didn't catch on to the meaning of the words. "Mr. Kazickas. The Ambassador of Great Britain in Washington has the honor to request your call." A telephone number was indicated.

I put the note in my pocket. The press conference on the lawn of the White House lasted a good half hour, and it took another half hour to get back to the hotel. Only then did I telephone the Ambassador. He had already left the Embassy premises, so the call was transferred to one of his assistants.

I was stunned at what I heard on the other end of the line. "We've been waiting for your call. We have been informed that the Lithuanian Prime Minister would like to meet with Margaret Thatcher," he said.

I wanted to shout with joy but I had to control myself. In as calm a voice as I could muster, I said, "Oh yes. Certainly, our Prime Minister wishes to meet your Prime Minister."

"Then, we'd ask you to please hurry and bring in Dr. Prunskienė's passport along with the passports of her entourage as quickly as you can," the British official said. "We need to process their visas for travel to Great Britain."

I did not waste a single minute. I took those passports by taxi to the Embassy of Great Britain myself. There I met the assistant to the Ambassador. He asked how long the meeting with President Bush had lasted, who had participated and what issues had been raised during the talk. He also wanted to hear our arguments as to why the West should recognize the independence of Lithuania. Apparently he had to write a report to the Foreign Affairs Ministry of Great Britain without delay.

Even as the visas were being stamped into all the Lithuanian passports, I learned that Margaret Thatcher would receive Dr. Prunskienė in a few days. In the highest spirits, I went back to the hotel.

Then I learned that an official from the German Embassy in Washington had left a message, asking me to call him back as soon as I returned. Suspecting that the Germans might be considering some even higher-level meeting with Dr. Prunskienė, I requested a meeting with Chairman Kohl. I went to the German embassy where two diplomats received me. They too proceeded to ask me about the meeting with President Bush. This conversation was very similar to the one at the British Embassy. The Germans seemed rather surprised that she had been received at the White House. Finally they said, "We heard that your Prime Minister will shortly be meeting with Margaret Thatcher in London. If Dr. Prunskienė could fly to Bonn, German Chancellor Helmut Kohl would be able to receive her."

Soon after Lithuanian Ambassador, Richard Bačkis, called us from Paris, and we learned that French President Francois Mitterrand was also interested in seeing Kazimiera Prunskienė.

I am convinced that all these meetings became possible due to the fact that President Bush had agreed to receive Dr. Prunskienė. He may well have urged the leaders of the allied countries – Great Britain, France and Germany – to meet with the Lithuanian Prime Minister. Obviously it was not a chance comment by George Bush that the countries of Western Europe needed to interact more with Lithuania. In the meantime, the United States was inclined to uphold a policy of silent diplomacy. Receiving Kazimiera Prunskienė in effect meant applying pressure on USSR President Mikhail Gorbachev, who was strongly supported by the West. Such a tactic was clearly beneficial to Lithuania.

As soon as Prunskienė arrived in the United States, Lithuanian Ambassador Lozoraitis left Washington. It's unlikely that this was simply a diplomatic misunderstanding. I tend to think that in this way, Lozoraitis displayed his displeasure regarding the arrangements for this historic visit. He must have felt slighted that I was the one who had managed to reach an agreement with the White House for the Prime Minister's meeting with the President.

He was even more upset that he was not invited to participate in the meeting with George Bush. But I think the White House wanted the talk to appear more private than official because the mere fact that attention was being paid to Prunskienė was enough of an annoyance to Moscow. Independent Lithuania was not recognized by the Soviet Union; therefore, attendance by an official Lithuanian diplomat was not desirable. This same protocol was observed during all the other visits by the Lithuanian Prime Minister to the West European capitals.

Kazimiera Prunskienė was very displeased, not only that Lozoraitis was away from Washington during her stay in the United States but also that he may have left deliberately. I telephoned him in Italy and urged him to return to the States. He began explaining that he had to resolve some important issues at the Vatican. Sparing no words I told Lozoraitis, "This is all going to look very strange to everyone – here the Prime Minister of Lithuania is about to meet the President of the United States, and the Ambassador representing her country is abroad to handle 'more important' matters."

Lozoraitis flew back to Washington the next day. That evening I invited Prunskienė and her brother for dinner with Lozoraitis at the Jockey Club. From the start a tension hung over all the interactions between the Prime Minister and the Ambassador. While dining an open argument flared between them. Angrily Prunskienė declared that Lozoraitis was not adequately representing the Government of Lithuania in Washington, and overall it was not clear what he was doing at all. Both proceeded to talk in raised voices; this made me feel most uncomfortable. Prunskienė did not have the slightest desire to hear his explanations about why it had been so important for him to go to Rome. Furthermore, she was very critical about all of his work as the Lithuanian Ambassador in Washington. I got the impression that the Prime Minister's self-confidence had grown considerably since her reception at the White House. She derided Lozoraitis as though he were a common subordinate.

Nonetheless, my relationship with Lozoraitis remained quite matter-of-fact and proper, even after this unpleasant episode. At a later time, I invited him to join *Seimas* Chairman Vytautas Landsbergis for a visit to our home in East Hampton.

After the White House meeting, Dr. Prunskienė spent a few more days in Washington and then flew to London. I accompanied her because I had taken responsibility for financing this leg of her trip as well, including hotel and transportation expenses.

Representatives of the British-Lithuanian Community met us at Heathrow. However, not a single government official was present. The same thing happened in the other capitals of Western Europe where we were invited. This was obviously meant to demonstrate that the visit was private, not at an official level.

It was peak traffic time in the morning. We drove into the city at a snail's pace following a seemingly endless line of automobiles. Though Prunskienė's driver broke all traffic regulations to get into London, we were a half hour late to our first meeting with a member of the opposition party in Parliament

The car in which I sat lagged far behind. By the time I got to the hotel, the Lithuanian Prime Minister was already in the assembly hall, speaking with a leader of the Labor Party and then with the head of the opposition party in Parliament. He was explaining the official position in London in respect to Lithuania and warning Dr. Prunskienė that Margaret Thatcher was very taken with Gorbachev and she ardently supported him. Hearing this, I was afraid that the talk with the Prime Minister of Great Britain would prove cold and formal.

The next morning on May 9th, we left for 10 Downing Street, the famous residence of the Prime Minister of Great Britain. The meeting with Margaret Thatcher was scheduled for 10:00 a.m. When I booked a limousine for the occasion, I carefully asked how long it would take to drive from our hotel to Downing Street. To make sure that we would not be delayed by morning traffic, we arrived a half hour early. We drove around in circles and then approached the gates to the residence at 9:45. The guards checked our documents and permitted us to enter the courtyard.

Personally I had never had an opportunity to visit the offices of the British Prime Minister. However, I was struck with a strange sense of *déjà vu* when we climbed to the second floor and I saw an old-fashioned clock there. I suddenly remembered from long ago a lecture by my professor,

Dr. Jurgutis. He had told us about his visit to a reception here before the war and described the clock. A sense of epochs, a connection of eras suddenly hit me. Here I was escorting the Prime Minister of Lithuania in May of 1990 for a meeting with the Prime Minister of Great Britain. I had seen that clock before in my mind's eye, listening to tales about World War II. It was as though I had already been there.

We walked into the reception area of the Prime Minister's office. Mrs. Thatcher's Secretary, Mr. Powell, greeted us and asked us to wait a few minutes. At precisely 10:00 a.m., as scheduled, the door to the Prime Minister's office opened, and we were beckoned to come in.

Margaret Thatcher looked striking, wearing a tasteful classic suit, set off by a string of pearls. This most dignified lady clearly exhibited great self-confidence and a certain aristocratic air from the very start. She sat straight and tall and calmly held her hands, never making a gesture, even as the tension of the discussion grew.

We had been told in advance that our talk was scheduled for exactly one half hour to 10:30 a.m. From the first few moments, Thatcher took firm control of the direction of the talk. She began discussing the global situation. Similarly to President Bush, she also emphasized that, although the pursuits of Lithuania were understandable and she was sympathetic, we had to appreciate that international recognition of our state was too complicated at this time. We should not expect any fast resolution to the issue.

Early in the talk Thatcher began praising Gorbachev, claiming that this politician was the first leader of the Soviet Union with whom the West was able to find a common dialogue. She said that no one had ever expected that the democratic reforms he was undertaking would be so extensive; these were opening up a new era in international relations. She went on to urge Lithuania and the other Baltic countries to consider global interests and make every effort not to hinder Gorbachev's policies.

We were led to understand that it would still take some time before the West would be able to recognize the independence of our country. That would be too strong a blow to the positions taken by the Soviet leader. By the same token, Margaret Thatcher seemed to console us that the time would come for international recognition. We had to have patience for conditions to ripen appropriately. She said that we would not have too long a wait – presumably no more than three to five years before Lithuania would be granted full recognition of its independence and, consequently, diplomatic relations. In the opinion of the British Prime Minister, events were unfolding in a direction favorable to the Baltic countries. All that was needed was to assure that Gorbachev's reforms would not be curtailed.

I glanced very discretely at my watch. It was eighteen minutes after ten. The meeting was to end at 10:30, but Thatcher continued her speech, never pausing for our Prime Minister to interject a single statement. How could this monologue be interrupted? Getting anxious, I glanced over at Prunskienė. Right then Margaret Thatcher suddenly stopped, virtually in mid-sentence, and said, "Your reaction perplexes me somewhat. Don't you agree with my viewpoint?"

At that point Prunskienė took over the discussion. Logically and clearly, she stated what the absolute majority of the Lithuanian population stood for. She explained that our country also has its rights, ones which should not raise any doubts anywhere in the world. The nation of Lithuania had firmly declared that it was reestablishing its statehood. If Western countries were sincere about democratic values, they were obligated to recognize our country and cease indulging the desires of the occupying country.

The quiet ticking of the clock was a reminder that it was already 10:30. The British Prime Minister's Secretary Powell turned towards his superior, but Thatcher did not indicate a single sign of impatience. Nearly unnoticeably he rose from his chair and left the office. He must have gone out to inform the Prime Minister's Secretariat that the talk was extended and any other meeting would begin late.

Unbelievably, our planned half hour visit with Margaret Thatcher continued for over an hour. The British Prime Minister took a serious interest in this discussion and extended the time of our talk several times more. The ending of our visit was absolutely astounding. Unexpectedly Margaret Thatcher stated that she endorsed most of the ideas she had just heard. She said that she intended to telephone Mikhail Gorbachev in support of Lithuania's position. And that was not all. She went on to say that she would sign a letter to the leader of the Soviet Union in which the goals of our country were to be defended.

I got the impression that, although Thatcher was considered an ardent admirer of Gorbachev, after this meeting with Prunskienė, she was prepared to support Lithuania more openly than President George Bush would. On the other hand, this might have been a joint tactic by the West: the United States wanted to stay back in the shadows in the deliberations about recognition of the Baltic counties. In the meantime, it encouraged its allies in Europe to take the initiative on the issue. (Perhaps this also explains why the first country which dared to recognize Lithuanian independence in 1991 was tiny Iceland.)

Kazimiera Prunskienė and the members of her entourage, as well as myself, considered the meeting with Margaret Thatcher incredibly successful. The goodwill of Margaret Thatcher had been won. This was critical because the British Prime Minister, nicknamed the Iron Lady, always decided on all issues relevant to foreign affairs on her own, paying little heed to the opinions of others.

That same day the Lithuanian Prime Minister met with several more members of Parliament. She also had supper with two Parliamentarians who strongly supported our drive for independence. This was also very encouraging.

The following day, we flew to Paris, knowing the exact time that French President Francois Mitterrand would be receiving us. The protocol of French diplomacy is renowned for it exceptional ceremony. The most minute detail for receiving a representative from a foreign country is ascribed special meaning. The sign of greatest respect is when the President comes down the stairs himself to meet the limousine delivering the guests into the Presidential courtyard. A somewhat lesser sign of hospitality is shown when the French leader remains atop the stairs for the guest to climb up to him. A much lower level of reception is indicated when the President simply receives the guest in his office without coming forth with any greeting.

The visit of Kazimiera Prunskienė was apparently assigned an even lower status. We were not escorted through the front door into the receiving area of the President's office. Instead we were led in through a side door and had to walk past some sort of secretarial offices. As we passed, the workers barely looked up from their papers. When we reached the entrance to the reception area of the President's office, we were told to wait. (Actually we had not entered the White House through the main entrance either, but at least President Bush did not make us go through any service offices.) Paris sent a clear signal of our true status. In the eyes of the French Government, the Prime Minister of an unrecognized Lithuania was a lady of low importance.

The talk with President Francois Mitterrand, attended by the French Minister of Foreign Affairs, Mr. Dumas, proceeded in a chilly atmosphere. Ambassador Bačkis translated for us. Mitterrand seemed to listen to Kazimiera Prunskienė with indifference. He sat with a rather proud bearing, never showing the least sign of interest on his face. Occasionally Prunskienė would end her statement, and an uncomfortable pause would ensue. The Foreign Affairs Minister helped out during such instances. He seemed to be much more favorably inclined towards Lithuania. From time to time, he'd make a comment to the President that seemed to favor our position.

Prunskienė had already decided beforehand that during her talk with President Mitterrand, she would request that France return the (prewar) Lithuanian Embassy building in Paris which had been illegally appropriated by the Soviet Union long ago. Our visit was probably the first to raise this issue. Mitterrand would not discuss the return of our embassy building at all. He merely stated in a cold voice that it was much too early to bring up this topic. (Indeed, the matter was not resolved for another eleven years when French President Jacques Chirac visited Vilnius.)

Our meetings with George Bush and especially with Margaret Thatcher had lasted considerably longer than originally anticipated. In Paris the talk ended to the precise minute scheduled. In exactly a half hour, Mitterrand, who had asked hardly any questions, rose from his chair and bid farewell.

One more important and, I'd say, considerably more successful meeting took place with the Mayor of Paris, the current President Jacques Chirac, who agreed to see Dr. Prunskienė. The difference was like night and day, starting from the location of the talk. With President Mitterrand, we had met in comparatively modest facilities, probably his work office. The Mayor, on the other hand, welcomed us in an elaborate hall, glittering in the luxury of past times. This naturally formed an entirely different atmosphere for the discussion. Chirac complimented Dr. Prunskienė and spoke about his feelings of friendship for Lithuania. His warm comments mitigated our disappointment about our meeting with President Mitterrand.

The trip to Germany awaited us the next morning. We flew directly to Bonn where Chancellor Helmut Kohl received us the same day. Once again we experienced a rather friendly meeting. Much as Margaret Thatcher had, Kohl also believed that the course of Soviet events would generate realistic conditions for the international recognition of Lithuania's independence. He offered his opinion on the best tactics for retaining relations with Gorbachev. The Chancellor was in a gracious mood. He told us that he'd love to have lunch with us but unfortunately he had to leave Bonn very soon. In his stead, he requested lunch to be arranged for us with Germany's Foreign Affairs Minister, Hans Genscher.

The Government of Germany was unique in its hospitality to Prunskienė. Lunch with a Foreign Affairs Minister had not been offered to her and her entourage in any other country. Hans Genscher arrived, escorted by several aides. No translator was needed because Dr. Prunskienė spoke German well. My early lessons in the German language served me enough to understand what was being discussed. Lunch passed most enjoyably. Genscher was most charming and in an excellent mood. He wished Lithuania international recognition as quickly as possible. He also mentioned that Germany would open an embassy in Lithuania which would undertake the development of economic relations. There was one stipulation though – we simply had to wait some undetermined time longer.

Several years later, I happened to meet Hans Genscher at a reception when he was in Washington. By that time, he was no longer Germany's Foreign Affairs Minister, so no official duties constrained him. We were both happy to recount that Lithuania had indeed become realistically independent in such a comparatively short time. Remembering the lunch with Prunskienė and our delegation, Genscher said, "So, you see. I was right after all. You did not have to wait long at all. Germany has had its embassy in Vilnius and you have had yours in Bonn for already a considerable time."

Quirks of Diplomacy

After our lunch with Genscher, Prunskienė's historic trip through five countries, including Canada, the United States, England, France and Germany was over. The diplomatic blockade around Lithuania was now effectively cracked. The Prime Minister and her entourage had to return to Lithuania the next day. An unexpected idea crossed my mind during a reception with the German Lithuanian Community. I suggested to the Prime Minister that she call the Soviet Ambassador in Germany upon her return to her hotel and suggest a meeting. I explained my thinking: "It would be worthwhile to provide him with some information about all your discussions with the leaders of the Western countries who spoke favorably about diplomatic recognition of Lithuania. An act of goodwill like that would show Moscow that you are willing to talk, to negotiate."

Prunskienė liked the idea. She invited me to participate in the talk with the Soviet Ambassador, but I declined. I did not believe my presence would be helpful. "I think you'd be better off speaking with him alone," I told her. "The Ambassador could harbor some suspicions about me, an American, someone he doesn't know. We don't need that. He just might be apprehensive about speaking his mind, worrying that I might have something to do with the American government. I think he'll be much more open if the talk is just between the two of you, eye to eye."

The USSR Ambassador in Germany, escorted by one other person, arrived that evening at the hotel to see Prunskienė. My room was right next to hers, so I heard her guests arrive. Their conversation lasted a full hour before both men left. She immediately came over to share her impressions with me.

The Soviet Ambassador knew the entire itinerary of the Lithuanian Prime Minister – not only about the meeting in Bonn, but about the meetings in every other capital city. According to Prunskienė, though, he wasn't inclined to believe that all the Western leaders had assured her that international recognition of Lithuania was essentially decided, that it was simply a matter of time for the proper conditions to unfold. The Soviet diplomat went so far as to say that based on their information, nothing had been promised to Prunskienė. Furthermore, her meetings with the leaders of the world powers had no political significance whatsoever; they had been designated the meaningless status of a private audience. Apparently this entire talk had been very tense and unpleasant.

I had to decide whether I should fly with Prunskienė to Vilnius in the morning or leave for Rome. After the exchange between the Prime Minister and the Soviet Ambassador, I had no further illusions about a positive dialogue with Moscow, at least not in the near future. The opposite was possible – all sorts of provocations, attacks, or actual use of military strength might be expected.

When I was back in Washington, I called a representative of the Vatican Nuncio to see whether I could be granted an audience with the Pope's Secretary of State at the Vatican after the Lithuanian Prime Minister's trip. He assured me that could be arranged, so I resolved to fly to Rome to keep this meeting. I could not pass up such an opportunity under the circumstances. It was important to inform the Vatican about the Prime Minister's talks with the various heads of state. At the same time, I intended to ask for more active assistance on the part of the Catholic Church for the current situation in Lithuania which is predominately a Catholic country.

I notified Lithuanian Ambassador Stasys Lozoraitis, who again was in Rome, about my intent to visit the Vatican. He was the first person I called as soon as I arrived in Rome. We got together right away to have supper and discuss the political situation. I delivered quite a thorough account to him about this entire diplomatic mission. Finally I inquired if he had learned the time that I was to arrive at the Pope's Secretariat.

I was stunned at his answer. He announced, "I called the office but I was told that no one had heard about any visit being planned by you with the Secretary of State."

I could not believe it. The Nuncio for the United States was far too serious an institution to have made such a mistake. It would not offer such a meeting on its initiative alone without confirming it with the Vatican. Lozoraitis promised to try once more to clarify the matter with the Secretariat.

The following day Lozoraitis informed me that, although no audience with the Secretary of State was possible because he was with the Pope in Mexico, I would be able to meet with a Monsignor who worked in diplomatic services for the Pope.

At the appointed time, I arrived at the Vatican. The diplomatic service facilities alone left a tremendous impression. The place was an endless labyrinth of ancient art. The corridor was bedecked in pictures, paintings on the walls and ceilings; an array of sculptures graced its path. This vision of wealth and grandeur was augmented by the Swiss guards standing at attention in ceremonial uniforms, as though they had stepped straight out of the Middle Ages.

The Monsignor who received me was an assistant to the Vatican's Secretary of State. As it turned out, he spoke good English. He first inquired if Lozoraitis would be participating in our talk. All I could say was that I didn't know. In truth Lozoraitis had merely let me know the time that I was to arrive at the Vatican; he never mentioned anything about his joining me.

The Monsignor said that he had heard about my efforts in arranging the meeting for the Lithuanian Prime Minister with President Bush. He also added that he was well acquainted with Frank Shakespeare, who once was United States Ambassador to Italy. To open our conversation, the Vatican diplomat said, "We have been informed about the meetings of the Lithuanian Prime Minister in the United States and Europe. However, we'd like to hear about them in greater detail and get your opinion about the talks."

"I think that Prime Minister Prunskienė accomplished more than we expected," I said. "Not only did the most influential statesmen in the West meet with her, they also confirmed that the issue regarding Lithuania's recognition is now on the agenda of world politics. In fact I got the impression that they were making certain excuses to explain why they were unable to enter into official diplomatic relations with our country right away. They promised that we would not have long to wait."

Once I offered my opinion about the success of this diplomatic mission, I apologized to the Monsignor that I might tell him a few things in a manner that was more straightforward than was the custom. "I am not a diplomat. I'm speaking with you as a private individual who is well familiar with the injustices committed against Lithuania. Please, don't take this in a wrong way, but I do want to ask you one thing. Why is it that the Vatican has not made any effort to help our country win international recognition, even though it has a great deal of information about the struggle by the Catholic Church for religious freedom in occupied Lithuania? This is not pleasant to say, but I know that Lithuanian Catholics are astonished by such passive behavior on the part of the Vatican. The Holy Father John Paul II, more than any other previous pope, perfectly understands that the Communist regime is opposed to human rights and he knows the situation of Lithuania very well."

It was true that many American Lithuanians thought that the Vatican would be the first to recognize the independence of Lithuania, a Catholic country, thereby encouraging other countries to follow its example. I could not forget that the Pope never appointed a Cardinal for Lithuania during the entire Soviet period. It wasn't until Gorbachev's reforms were in full swing and *Sąjūdis* was active that Archbishop Vincentas Sladkevičius was at long last granted this title.

Hearing this, the Monsignor interrupted me. He said that a cardinal had been appointed for Lithuania earlier, but it had never been publicly announced. The man's name now remains in the Pope's heart. All I could say was that it was regretful that no one ever knows about that person to this day. During all the years of Soviet repressions, the appointment of a cardinal would have lifted the spirits of the Lithuanian people.

The Monsignor listened quietly and made some notes. Then he set down his pen and assured me that the Holy Father was firm in his support of Lithuanian independence. However, when it came to official diplomatic recognition, the Vatican was forced to consider all the potential negative consequences for taking such a step. He reminded me that, in addition to Lithuanians, there were many other Catholics living within the Soviet Union. Should the Vatican recognize the independence of Lithuania, a wave of repressions against these people could arise.

Undaunted I spent the entire hour of our talk repeating one statement: Lithuanians were loyal to the Catholic Church even during the hardest years of the occupation. I also noted that disappointment with Vatican policies could grow. "You associate with Lithuanian priests, but I bet not a single one would dare to tell you this. As a lay person, I feel I must express these views," I said to the Vatican diplomat.

As soon as I returned to the hotel, I called Lozoraitis and offered to write a comprehensive report, not only on the talk with the Monsignor but also on all the meetings in the United States and Europe by Prunskienė. I thought this kind of information would assist him, the Lithuanian Ambassador, to stay abreast of the political situation. This job took an entire day; I left my room only to eat supper. My writings filled an entire notebook. I placed it into an envelope and gave $20 to the hotel doorman to mail it to the indicated address.

A couple of months went by. I happened to run into Lozoraitis and I told him that I'd like to make a copy of my report on the diplomatic mission which I had sent him. "What report?" Lozoraitis asked me. "I never got anything from you."

I was at a loss for words. This was a huge blow to me. I had written that report right after the trip with Prunskienė while the all the impressions were still fresh in my mind. I had included a great deal of details on the meetings and documented the ideas expressed. It was distressing to think that a document such as this, which could have assisted scholars in understanding the events of the times, was lost. I could not comprehend how this could have happened. I telephoned the hotel, but they said that they had mailed the envelope. The only thing I could think of was that the doorman took my money but didn't actually bother to mail the packet of material.

Months of Anxiety

When my trip with Kazimiera Prunskienė through the capitals of Western Europe ended, I returned to New York. I would telephone her frequently in Vilnius to learn about the changes in the political situation in Lithuania. Moscow was tightening the economic blockade around Lithuania. The blockade, which was imposed on April 17, 1990 and lasted for three months, was a source of considerable anxiety to me and the rest of the country.

Dr. Prunskienė empowered me in the name of the Government of Lithuania to negotiate on various issues with representatives from the United States and other countries. I was even permitted to sign contracts of an economic nature involving the Government. I had not asked for this job. However, Lithuania did not yet have a single commercial attaché abroad at the time. Therefore the Prime Minister asked me to be on the lookout for American companies that might be interested in an opportunity to do business in Lithuania. Her hopes were that such companies might at least send their representatives to review the situation in Vilnius.

Of course these preliminary actions could not ease the Russian economic blockade. Nonetheless, this work was essential for the future. Additionally it would demonstrate to Moscow that business contacts could be developed in Lithuania independently. So I started looking around for possible sources of business. With the government's permission, I was able to speak officially on its behalf; my discussions were not merely on private matters. Mostly I approached my own acquaintances in an effort to get some attention for Lithuania. My friends never doubted my word that I had the right to represent the Government and never asked for proof. Two later Prime Ministers – Gediminas Vagnorius and Adolfas Šleževičius – also issued such credentials to me.

Most importantly I began to think about the economic situation in Lithuania. I believed that it was essential to start the reorganization of the economy without delay. The foundations of a free market system had to be laid as quickly as possible. The economic blockade clearly showed that only the private business sector, largely undeveloped at the time, was able to supply the country with at least part of vitally needed raw materials.

I asked Larry Summers and Andrei Shleifer to come back to Lithuania which they graciously did. Working out of office facilities provided by Prunskienė in the Government building, every day they met with the most important economists, businessmen and bankers. They lectured and explained all sorts of methods that could be used for the transition to a free market economy. Furthermore, during their stay, they managed to write a thorough memorandum to the Government, laying out a plan for reorganizing the economy.

These people were more than excellent theoreticians. They also had practical experience. When my son-in-law, Roger, took the position of Deputy Secretary of the Treasury Department in President Clinton's first administration, he invited Professor Summers, who had also worked at the World Bank, to serve as Undersecretary. In 1996, Larry Summers became Secretary of the Treasury. After his government service, he was named President of Harvard University.

Right at the time that I arrived in Lithuania with the American professors, Prunskienė had just been to Moscow, meeting with Gorbachev. She had reached an agreement to have the blockade lifted, but that was in exchange for calling a moratorium on the Act of Independence. These terms worried me. Weighing the potential political harm that such a step might cause was no easy matter. A heated controversy flared over this move in Parliament. There was a conflict of opinion between Prime Minister Prunskienė and *Seimas* Chairman Landsbergis though, at the time, it was still undercover. To me it was clear that Moscow had raised some sort of a threatening ultimatum. While I often thought that certain political compromises may be expedient, in this case, however, I felt that the Independence Act itself must not be conceded to any degree.

Prunskienė and I had a good relationship based on mutual trust. However, not only did she neglect to tell me that an effort at a political compromise with Gorbachev was being considered, she never spoke to me about the matter in any way at all. The news I heard was that an ill-defined moratorium on the validity of the Independence Act had been bargained. And this news came from the lips of Chairman Landsbergis, not Prime Minister Prunskienė.

Over time the in-fighting among *Sąjūdis* movement leaders calmed down. It seemed as though Moscow was getting accustomed to the special status of Lithuania. Although the USSR did not recognize its independence, it did not dare take military action. The economic blockade eased. (In fact some studies found that, ultimately, the blockade on Lithuania caused greater economic losses to Moscow than it did to Lithuania.) Then, like a bolt of lightning from a clear blue sky, came a political crisis and the tragic events of January 1991.

Prunskienė's brother, Rimas Stankevičius, called me one day in January from Germany. He informed me that his sister's Government had been pressured into resigning. I had already heard news about a wave of disturbances fomenting in Vilnius, probably incited by the Communist Party and the KGB. And now I was overwhelmed to hear that Prunskienė had resigned and that she had quickly left for Germany.

I did have a talk with Prunskienė personally. I could hardly contain my exasperation, listening to her blaming Landsbergis for all the troubles in Vilnius. The loss of the Prime Minister's post appeared to worry her more than did all the trials awaiting Lithuania. I admired Dr. Prunskienė for all she had accomplished on behalf of Lithuania but, during this conversation, I could not shake the feeling that through her own erratic behavior, she was dissipating all her earlier accomplishments.

My response to her was blunt. I told her what I thought about her dramatic resignation, her public display of suffering great insult and, not the least, her leaving behind all the work that was so needed for Lithuania. Further I said she had an obligation during the country's difficult times to find the energy to work jointly with Landsbergis. Stepping down from all her duties was undignified. As could be expected, Prunskienė leaped to defend herself, telling me about all sorts of horrid intrigues. It greatly saddened me to listen to all that.

Landsbergis later commented on this conflict to me. He spoke about it much more calmly in a reserved manner; he showed no personal emotions on the matter. He simply told me that there was no other choice in the matter. The Government had to be changed because its leader had resigned from office and had refused to reconsider her decision. I was aware that there had been certain discord between him and Prunskienė even before this latest crisis. However, Landsbergis was not inclined to discuss this.

The situation was nerve-wracking in Lithuania at the time. Much unrest revolved around the price reforms that Prime Minister Prunskienė had recently instituted. News reached us in the States that, although these reforms had been recalled after the Government resigned, the KGB and Communist Party structures were agitating Russian and Polish minority groups, pitting them against an independent Lithuanian government. Demonstrations ensued in the capital. Overall the number of people attracted to anti-Lithuania protests was comparatively low, and they were not causing any actual danger to the government. But the potential of civic unrest and disturbances was the real threat, because that could provide a pretext for Russia to use military force in Lithuania.

"It has begun," I thought with an aching heart when I heard the news over television. Starting the night of January 12 and continuing into the early morning hours of January 13, the Soviet Army attacked civil buildings and the television station and transmission tower in Vilnius. Newspapers around the world ran more detailed coverage of events in Lithuania the following morning. Unarmed civilians held watch around these buildings all night to prevent pro-Soviet forces from disrupting their normal flow of work. Soviet tanks drove directly into masses of people at the Vilnius television tower in a display of brute force. Thirteen people were killed and many hundreds more were seriously injured.

The entire émigré community was shaken to the core. We had all been so thrilled with the declaration of independence. We had begun to believe that independence would be won without the shedding of a single drop of blood. Now we knew that Moscow was capable of using indiscriminate military force against a still very fragile Lithuania and its newly born statehood. Our country seemed to be teetering on the edge of a bottomless pit.

The situation prompted all American Lithuanians into action immediately to help the homeland. Basically I never got off the telephone during those days. I called all my friends and acquaintances who had influential political contacts and asked for their support to help my country. "Call the White House. Call your congressmen," I begged. "Put pressure on our politicians. We can't let them sit by passively. We need them to deliver decisive protests against such actions by Moscow."

Jurate and her husband, Roger Altman, who knew everyone at the top level of the Democrat Party (though the Party was out of power at the time), rallied to help. We used all our contacts in the national media to publicize our contention that Moscow had stepped over the bounds of civilized behavior. Americans had to be persuaded not to believe Gorbachev's claims that he had known nothing about the military action to be taken in Vilnius.

I contacted Landsbergis on the telephone. Even though he was overwhelmed with urgent matters, he always took the time to talk to me about the latest events in Lithuania, so I could inform the media and the politicians of the United States.

My respect for Vytautas Landsbergis grew tremendously during those days. I admired his determination, courage and energy in undertaking a multitude of activities. He was the true leader of Lithuania at that time. Even we American Lithuanians, living far away, keenly sensed this.

Jurate and her daughter, Alexandra, demonstrating in New York, 1989

The dramatic events prompted me to call a Cat Cay Club member, Charles Cobb, the United States Ambassador in Iceland. Once, on a visit to the Bahamas, his guest had been the Foreign Affairs Minister of Iceland. News had reached me that this country was especially sympathetic towards Lithuania and that it might even enter into diplomatic relations at some sort of official level with Vilnius. Thus I decided to discuss this with Ambassador Cobb.

When I called, Cobb still did not know about any contacts between Lithuania and Iceland. However, he told me that such an idea was worthy of serious consideration. A small country could accomplish this more easily than a large country could without serious repercussion from Moscow. The Ambassador asked me to inform him in greater detail about the political situation, legal aspects and history of Lithuania. At the conclusion of our conversation, Cobb told me that he intended to find out if the United States State Department would be in favor of a decision by Iceland to recognize Lithuania. "I can assure you that I will support your efforts for the diplomatic recognition of Lithuania as best I can."

Cobb discussed the matter with State Department Deputy Secretary Lawrence Eagleburger, who was one of the most favorably disposed activists in President Bush's administration. Furthermore, he had participated in the talks with Prime Minister Prunskienė at the White House. Afterwards I asked another good friend, Bill Simon, who had been Secretary of the Treasury under President Reagan, to call Eagleburger. Simon also confirmed that the Deputy Secretary supported more active diplomatic support for our country. Apparently Eagleburger favored the idea that Iceland be the first country to recognize Lithuania.

Well after the end of his career as ambassador, Cobb told me that back in early 1991, the State Department had authorized him to inform the Government of Iceland in Reykjavik that it held a positive view on plans to recognize Lithuania; he had been directed to do this in as persuasive a manner as possible. It's hard to know the actual results of his efforts. Nonetheless, I don't doubt that the Government of Iceland, which on April 16th 1991 became the first country in the world to recognize Lithuanian independence, did not take its decisive step until it had received a behind-the-scenes blessing from the United States and, most likely, Great Britain.

In August of 1991, hard-line Russian Communists, seeking to safeguard the Soviet empire, organized a governmental overthrow in their own country. The *putsch* or 'coup' in Moscow, the success of which would have been the death knell for any independence for Lithuania and the other two Baltic Republics, failed so fast that we American Lithuanians barely had time to be frightened. Instead we were filled with tremendous joy that Boris Yeltsin, soon to become the Russian President, was the victor in a matter of days. I realized at once that the Soviet Union had already come to its demise. Lithuania had to move immediately to win realistic independence and international recognition in the event that chaos might erupt in the ruins of the former empire.

That's exactly what happened. Within days after the failed Moscow *putsch*, the world began recognizing the independence of the Baltic countries. With trembling hearts, we listened as one Western European country after another declared diplomatic relations with Lithuania. The United States, however, seemed in no rush to recognize our homeland. Washington did not announce formal recognition until September 2,

1991, after most Western countries had already done so. This fact did not trouble me as much as it did other American Lithuanians, who were highly insulted. It was a political tactic of the Bush Administration, one the President relayed to us during our meeting with the Prime Minister. The United States had consistently held to this line, urging its allies to take the first steps in support of the Baltic countries, ahead of Washington. In the meantime, the United States remained in the background, upholding the best possible relations with Mikhail Gorbachev.

On September 16, 1991, Lithuania joined the United Nations. I sat in the magnificent hall of the General Assembly, as Vytautas Landsbergis addressed the delegates. The booming ovation by representatives from nations all over the world, as Lithuania was accepted into this august body, is a sound I shall never forget. Even more emotional for me and my family was the raising of the yellow, green and red Lithuanian flag outside the UN, as it joined the panoply of colors representing all the other member nations.

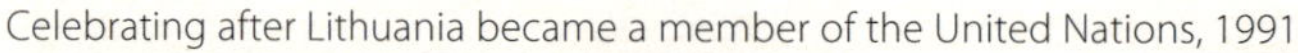
Celebrating after Lithuania became a member of the United Nations, 1991

The World Discovers Lithuania

Lithuania, having regained its self-determination after 50 years, was an entirely unknown land to the world. In the minds of many, it was nothing more than some backwoods of Eastern Europe, which had splintered off from the former Soviet empire. I was determined to introduce my homeland to as many people as I could, especially those who were in a position to help Lithuania with its pressing social and economic needs.

During the historic session at the United Nations, I happened to meet Maria Pia Fanfani, the wife of Amintore Fanfani, one of the most distinguished Italian politicians who had served several times as Prime Minister and later as Senate Chairman. We struck up a conversation about Lithuania. As so often has happened in my life, this serendipitous encounter led to wonderful things. Fanfani was the head of "Together for Peace," a foundation that she had founded, and in no time at all, at my behest, she organized a shipment of medicine, clothing and toys for the children of Lithuania.

Mrs. Fanfani came to Vilnius where she was received by the Ministry of Health Care and attended a luncheon with Prime Minister Gediminas Vagnorius. Later she and I visited children's homes and hospitals to distribute her gifts. (I was somewhat surprised that much of the clothing sent as humanitarian aid carried labels of distinguished Italian designers and fashion houses and was clearly not second rate. Apparently Mrs. Fanfani had solicited contributions from the heads of famous companies who pulled the same apparel from their warehouses that went to very expensive retail outlets.)

At one hospital, we saw a ten-year old girl with a severe case of leukemia. This poor child could hardly speak from the pain. When Mrs. Fanfani asked her what sort of gift she would like, the little girl said in a weak, barely audible voice, "A Barbie doll." But there were no Barbies in the delivery from Italy. Mrs. Fanfani demanded that this kind of doll be found somewhere in Lithuania, no matter the cost. A Barbie doll surfaced rather quickly but at an astronomical price - $500. We paid it without haggling. The next time we visited the hospital, Mrs. Fanfani gave the girl this doll. We were so moved when the child, who had barely spoken, suddenly began talking to her new friend, Barbie.

We also went to the Antakalnis District of Vilnius to a home for disabled children, some of whom had been born crippled as a result of the Chernobyl nuclear power plant accident in 1989. The administrators of the place obviously tried to take care of the facilities and the children as best as they could. Everything was clean and the linen was laundered. Still, the visions there were heart breaking. One child was without a leg, another without an arm and a third was so twisted by illness that he could not move. Mrs. Fanfani sat down next to the children on the floor, showing them the toys that she brought and playing with them for nearly an hour.

With Mrs. Maria Pia Fanfani, 1992

Mrs. Fanfani left Lithuania filled with emotion and empathy for our land. My contacts with her continued well after this trip. I was delighted when she later invited me to the 1992 Together for Peace awards ceremony under the tutelage of Queen Sophia of Spain in Madrid. When I called to thank her for the invitation, I had an idea. Many of Europe's leading personages in society were to attend the awards ceremony. Maybe Lithuania could somehow be represented at this event. I suggested to Mrs. Fanfani that she include our young musical prodigy, violinist Vilhelmas Čepinskis, as part of the entertainment.

But Mrs. Fanfani was hesitant. She asked, "Is he truly a sufficiently accomplished violinist to play at such a gathering? After all the Queens of both Spain and Jordan will be attending as well as the Aga Khan, Baron Thyssen, Mr. Agnelli and numerous other famous people with sophisticated tastes in music."

"You will definitely not be disappointed with our young star," I guaranteed her.

Finally she confirmed that Čepinskis would be able to play at the reception at the Royal Palace of Spain. However, his appearance was to last no longer than five minutes, and he would have to play the violin without accompaniment.

I was a bit worried about this. Vilhelmas was only 15 years old. He would have to play alone in front of the bejeweled European aristocracy. But when I spoke with Vilhelmas, he said he was prepared. I was probably more nervous than he was about his appearance. When he got ready to climb on stage, he seemed neither frightened nor stressed.

I shot a look over to him, indicating, "You've got to succeed!" He truly performed beautifully. On stage this young man looked as dignified and aristocratic as a young prince. He played a composition by Paganini *a cappela* with excellent style. Queen Sophia rose from her seat, went up on stage and kissed him, as ovations thundered from the audience. I noticed that she was trying to say something to Vilhelmas but, since he did not understand a word of English, he simply stood stricken. I had to rush over to help him with a translation.

With Queen Noor Al Hussein of Jordan, 1996

"Please tell him that he is a fabulous violinist," said the Queen. "I was overjoyed hearing his performance. Ask him if he would agree to play at our palace for a special private reception."

I translated this and, of course, Vilhelmas agreed to perform for Spain's royal family and their guests. There really wasn't even any need to ask. But I wanted to leave an impression that this was a serious impresario. So I said that we would definitely try to find time in our intensive concert schedule to appear at Escorial Palace.

I don't think Vilhelmas ever played again at the Royal Palace of Spain. Nevertheless, I am sure that Queen Sophia was very moved by his performance and her invitation at the time was sincere.

Even before Mrs. Fanfani came to Vilnius, I had started looking for ways to receive aid from similar organizations in the United States. Her foundation was actually quite small in comparison with the giants in philanthropy like the Rockefeller Brothers Fund, the Pew Charitable Trust, the Heritage Foundation, the Soros Open Society Fund and other foundations established by the financial magnates of the United States.

While Lithuania was still seeking independence and had not yet attained international recognition in the late 1980s, I talked to my dear friend, Colin Campbell, the President of the Rockefeller Brothers Fund, about visiting Vilnius. He had been the Provost of Wesleyan University, which my sons, Joseph and Michael, had attended. Campbell agreed immediately and said he would invite his friend along, a man who was one of the heads of the Pew Trust, one of the largest charitable institutions in the United States.

After visits to Estonia and Latvia, the two men and I were met at the border by Prime Minister Prunskienė's brother, Rimas.The Government had sent over three cars for us, so we drove off separately. As we were heading towards Vilnius, I noticed that we had turned off the main road near Saločiai Town and were traveling over a small bridge. The next thing I knew, our car stopped. I looked out the window – we were right at the gates of a cemetery. The other two cars also stopped by us. Rimas got out first and opened the trunk of the car. He pulled out a beautiful wreath of fresh flowers. Rimas turned to me and said, "Mr. Joseph, we'd like to place this wreath on your father's grave."

The last time I had visited my father's grave was during a trip to Lithuania in 1979. Although I had been to Lithuania several times since, I never found time to get over to Saločiai Town. Emotions flooded over me to think that now I finally had a chance to bow my head for a few moments at my father's place of eternal rest. The group of us walked inside the cemetery. It was quite late by then, and there wasn't a single light installed on the premises. Rimas had a small flashlight with him but, in the dark, I still got lost. I seemed to be walking in circles and all the headstones looked alike. My father's grave was nowhere to be seen.

Father's grave in Saločiai Town

In the meantime, the representatives of the Rockefeller and Pew Foundations were stumbling around, trying to keep up with me. With an aching heart, I realized that this rather ghostly search had to be cut short. The wan light from the flashlight illuminated an old bent cross in an area of long-neglected gravesites, overgrown with grass.

I stopped and said, "Let's place the wreath on the grave of this person whom I don't know and who is probably forgotten by all." I knelt down and we all said a prayer for my father and all the other people for whom Saločiai Cemetery had become their final place of rest.

When we got back to our cars, I noticed an unusually somber look on my guests' faces. Years later Campbell told me that our prayer together in the darkness by a neglected grave with its crooked cross had affected him deeply. An inexplicable sense of the mystery of life and eternity had permeated his soul. This experience, he said, was the most lasting impression of his entire trip through the Baltic countries.

After several days visiting educational institutions, both of my guests thought that their foundations might support a program for computer technology in Lithuania. We agreed that Vytautas Magnus University in Kaunas would send a list of the technology, books and equipment needed to set up a computer class facility. That would be their official request for aid from the Rockefeller and Pew Foundations.

Unfortunately officials at the University never followed through with a list of requested items. Whether it was apathy or disorganization, I was never sure. The application deadline came and went. To make matters worse, this plan for financial assistance was to extend for several years; it was not a one-time allocation. The requirement had been spelled out at our meeting, and all had agreed. All they needed to do was to send a letter with their own priority needs. For some reason, the university was not capable of accomplishing this most elementary task. I'm convinced that Vytautas Magnus University, and Lithuania for that matter, lost grant money to the tune of several hundred thousand dollars for such unwarranted neglect.

I also participated to some extent in getting the George Soros Fund to Lithuania. This famous philanthropist was someone I had known from long ago. We had been introduced by a Hungarian Countess who had a home in East Hampton near our summerhouse.

At the end of 1990, I went to see Soros who was setting up a Fund to support young democracies and stimulate openness in their politics. He explained that for the moment, the priority of the Fund was Russia. This country greatly impacted the entire region of post-communist countries. Nevertheless, activities were to expand to other countries as well, including Lithuania, Latvia and Estonia.

Then, he proceeded to discuss his plans for the Baltic region. His intention was to establish a College of Business Administration, offering a master's degree program in common for the three countries. I wholeheartedly agreed that training for work under free market conditions was essential. My suggestion was to establish such a school in Lithuania, which was the largest of the Baltic Republics and had centuries of traditions in higher education. Mulling that over, he said he probably would do just that.

Further Soros told me that environmental protection issues also worried him greatly. He was convinced that Russia has neglected this sphere to a threatening degree. I told him that, in my opinion, the situation in the Baltic countries should be somewhat better but also required his funding. We proceeded to discuss avenues for such work in all three countries.

Talking about the Baltics, though, Soros grumbled that this region was largely unfamiliar to him. He said he had no contacts there and didn't know people he could trust. After telling me this, Soros asked me if I would agree to be his representative in the Baltic Republics.

I graciously thanked him for the offer and said I was keenly interested in having the Soros Fund enter Lithuania. Unfortunately I'd be unable to represent him. I had just started organizing the Litcom Company in Lithuania. By this time, I was also in my 70s; I had to save my energy. I didn't want to be a representative in name only, one who didn't really accomplish much.

Soros said he could understand my situation but wondered if I could organize a trip throughout the Baltic countries for him and possibly accompany him. Unfortunately, I had to attend to important business matters during that time and could not possibly travel with him. What I did agree to do, though, was to arrange his program in Lithuania and schedule meetings with high-level government officials and other persons of interest to his fund.

Soros took that trip quite soon thereafter. After visiting all three Baltic countries, he called me and said how pleased he was with his trip. But he had decided to establish the College of Business Administration in Tallinn and not Vilnius, as we had discussed earlier. In Lithuania he intended to establish an environmental protection office, serving all three countries. I asked why he had chosen Tallinn over Vilnius for the college. "It seemed to me that more people in Estonia than in Lithuania can speak English," he explained. "You know, all the subjects at the college will be taught in English."

I wasn't sure if it was actually true that more Estonians spoke better English than Lithuanians did. Nevertheless, I understood from our conversation that Soros had simply taken a greater interest in Estonia for implementing his idea for a college. That indicated that once again, Lithuanians had only themselves to blame. Estonia beat them in this game.

However, the Soros Open Society Fund did start actively operating in Lithuania. Unquestionably this organization contributed so much to our country by its endeavors to develop democratic societies and stimulate culture and education.

Jurate and I also established the Kazickas Family Foundation with offices in Vilnius and New York. On an American scale, our fund is very small. We realize that the need for charity in Lithuania exceeds our capabilities by a hundred or maybe, a thousand times over. We have decided to give priority for funding to educational programs.

Our most important charitable work in Lithuania today is to help computerize all the secondary schools in the country. I had noticed that the rural areas of Lithuania were socially and economically hardest hit. There is a huge gap in development between the small towns and the much better off major cities – Vilnius, Klaipėda and Kaunas. The question often comes up – why do we buy computers instead of food? The answer is straightforward. The tremendous wave of poverty in the rural areas is too deep to solve with only a few million *litas*, the currency of Lithuania. Were such a sum of money allocated to social welfare, it would be instantly consumed, leaving nothing for the future. It's much more meaningful to contribute to the learning of young people from outlying areas by providing them access to modern informational technology. This satisfies the innate curiosity of young people while, at the same time, gives them skills to compete better in the job market. Now they'll have the opportunity to form the kind of goals that might save them from the downfall of part of the older generation – the desperation of poverty and the curse of alcoholism.

Of course simply buying computers for schools will not eliminate computer illiteracy. There is a real shortage of teachers capable of instructing children to use computers. I remember a case at one of the schools that we visited. A young student was introduced to us with great pride because he was the only one at the school who actually knew how to look for information on the Internet. There are probably quite a few schools at which no one knows how to operate a computer. Our foundation is unable to resolve this problem. This is a matter for the government to undertake. However, an available computer in class can at least be a stimulus for young, enterprising teachers to begin learning its use.

Ominitel, the cellular phone company I helped found in 1992, joined our family fund in this project. With an allocation of several million *litas*, we now have an impressive sum of money to start up computer classes, as well as to link them to the Internet. We intend to look for more donations from corporations and other foundations to expand this project. Naturally the government is also involved. My hope is that over the next five years, Lithuania might catch up with the average level of computerization in the European Union. For the time being, this gap seems only to be widening. Lithuania must race with all its might to catch up with the West.

The future plans for our family fund are to expand our activities in Lithuania. In addition to supporting educational programs, we hope to back projects with potential in the sciences, cultural activities, health care, child welfare and even sports.

Bringing in Business

Since I had so many business acquaintances in the Western world from various countries, I was able to introduce many of them to Lithuania and its economic and cultural opportunities. It was clear to me that the only way poverty and backwardness in Lithuania could be overcome was with an injection of foreign capital. The most powerful multinational companies with modern production capabilities had to be wooed to enter Lithuania. With luck and perseverance, I participated in attracting some large-scale companies from the United States to do business there.

Back when Prunskienė was still Prime Minister, I had already started looking around for opportunities to introduce Lithuania to large companies. I never missed a chance to attend receptions for their presidents and owners. In our conversations, I would always bring up Lithuania, a country which had just reestablished statehood. It was like tossing out a fishing line. The idea was to find someone who might bite. Once interested they would send their experts to analyze business potentials in our country.

Such a tactic ultimately led to my first success which was the Phillip Morris Company. One of the largest companies in the United States, it was engaged in the production not only of cigarettes but also food products. I met with Mr. Gembler, the head of Phillip Morris Europe Division in Lausanne, who said the company's first intention was to build a tobacco factory in Lithuania to serve the Baltic region. "That's why we'd like your help." He quickly added that all they expected from me were recommendations for resolving problems that came up. They were not requesting full representation in Lithuania.

I answered that I considered it my personal obligation to help business development in my country. For that reason alone, I agreed to be of service. At that point, Mr. Gembler inquired what compensation I would like for my assistance.

"It's really not at all important to me how much you might pay for my help. You can even pay me nothing," I responded. "Let's agree to this. Don't take on any financial obligations right now. At the end of the year, you can assess if I have been of any value to you. Then you can decide if you'd like to award me some sort of compensation."

The Phillip Morris representatives were taken back by my offer. They actually asked if they could discuss my proposition with someone else in the company. After huddling together, they accepted it.

That was not all however; I had another condition for my involvement. I told them that their associates in Lithuania must never pay a single bribe to anyone. If any officials were to try to shake down the company, they must inform me immediately. I noticed that my words confused my listeners. Thus I explained to them that in all post-Soviet countries, including Lithuania, some people were accustomed to bettering their personal well-being by taking bribes. There was always a chance that, while resolving pressing matters, they might be led to understand that everything could be handled more simply and quickly by some greasing of the palms.

"That doesn't mean that it's not possible to work in Lithuania without giving bribes," I explained. "It's very important to me that serious-minded foreign concerns work in my country in an above board manner from the start. My country needs to start slowly learning about transparency in business dealings. This way foreign companies can contribute to opening up our society."

The Phillip Morris people were very pleased to hear this. They had been harboring suspicions that corruption could be one of the most serious obstacles to their operations in post-communist countries.

With that I got to work, meeting with influential government and opposition officials. No favoritism was requested on the company's behalf. All I wanted to do was to help the leading politicians of the country understand the sort of long-term benefit that this company would bring by its operations. This was essential in order to develop a political atmosphere that was conducive to future investments. Additionally all means for possible selfish and willful actions on the part of governmental officials had to be blocked.

Naturally I was not much in favor of promoting more smoking in Lithuania. One thing was clear, though: it was better for a smoker to have access to good-quality tobacco, which was less harmful to health than all the awful Soviet brands. Besides Phillip Morris also intended to invest in the confectionary business, making candy and snack foods, and develop exports of these products through their Kraft Foods division. This promised new jobs in Lithuania, the presence of a modern manufacturing plant and honest payment of taxes to the national budget.

All this actually occurred. Phillip Morris first bought out the old tobacco factories in the country and later built a new plant. Ultimately Kraft Foods invested in the Kaunas Confectionary Factory and proceeded to make chocolates and a variety of other sweets. A year passed after my initial talk with Mr. Gembler. One fine day, I was surprised to receive a generous check from the company's headquarters in Lausanne, even though I had not requested any specific compensation.

Coca Cola was the second company from the United States which I helped to get started in Lithuania.

Actually I first had a meeting with the head of the European division of Pepsi Cola, which enjoyed considerable success in Russia and was considering the Lithuanian market. But since he did not request my help, I turned my attention towards their competitor, Coca Cola.

One of our Cat Cay Island Club members was a Norwegian, Tore Bu, the head of Coca Cola's European division, whom I had known for quite some time. I told him, "Pepsi Cola is just getting ready to start their operations in Lithuania but, for some reason, they're not in any rush. Why not get a firm foothold in this market while they are taking their time?"

Tore Bu took an interest in my proposal at once. He asked me to organize a trip to Lithuania to look over the business situation. The trip came about very quickly. After negotiations with one brewery fell through, Coca Cola made a deal to partner with Alita, a sparkling wine maker. Before long the Americans invested sizeable funds and launched production in Lithuania.

Another U.S. company, which I brought to Lithuania, was Williams. Although this company's operations could not exactly be called successful, I have never had any regrets for my role. Williams simply did not handle well the wave of propaganda that accompanied them from their first steps in Lithuania. They were never able to overcome the whirlwind of lies and rumors that swept around them the entire time. Likewise there were many falsehoods said about me and my son-in-law in the course of events. However, the story needs to be told from the beginning.

Granting of an honorary doctorate by Kaunas University of Technology. 1989

Back during the times of the Government under Prunskienė, I began searching for means to insure a supply of energy for Lithuania that would be independent of Russia. Landsbergis in particular was extremely concerned about this. Lithuania had one state-owned oil refinery plant, Mažeikių Nafta. An oil terminal at the seacoast was still in the planning stages. Clearly only one alternative was available – to get a powerful Western oil company interested in buying an interest in this strategically important plant.

My first discussion on this was with the representative in the United States for Agip, an Italian company. My daughter and son-in-law were personally acquainted with the man; he had attended various receptions held in their home. The idea of working in Lithuania intrigued him. He contacted his superiors in Italy and, before long, the company sent experts to research the situation in Lithuania. Upon the conclusion of their trip, I flew to Rome to speak with Agip directors. There I learned the actual situation. Agip wanted to start operations in Lithuania but only in conjunction with Lukoil, the Russian oil company. It was apparent that the real intention of Agip was to engage in business with Russia. Our country was of interest merely as an extension of their Russian business. In other words, they would not guarantee any sort of independent energy supply for Lithuania.

Another aspect repulsed me even more. They suggested that five per cent of their investment sum be set aside as commission payments for other people whenever the need arose. To me this implied that they were ready to handle their business by distributing bribes; such behavior was not uncommon in Russia. Conditions of this nature made me nervous. I severed any further interactions with them. I have no idea of the steps that Agip took later, but they never did anything serious in Lithuania.

By this time, the Lithuanian Democratic Labor Party dominated the Government. Algirdas Brazauskas took office as President. He asked me to search for American companies which might want to become partners in the Mažeikių Nafta Refinery and oil terminal, now in the process of construction at Būtingė Town.

One time I was playing golf when I ran into a close friend, Ken Jamieson, the Chairman of the Board of Directors of Exxon Corporation, the largest oil concern in the United States and probably the world. I told him that Lithuania was looking for a strategic partner for its oil industry. He promised to have a talk with the Vice President in charge of their European Division to request a review of such an opportunity. Shortly after a representative of Exxon called me to let me know that their European Division was sending a large group of experts to Lithuania. The group was to examine the situation in the oil market and offer recommendations for possible business prospects.

The experts arrived in Lithuania, visited Mažeikiai (the town where the refinery is located), held many meetings in Vilnius and gathered a variety of information. I had high hopes that matters would start moving and the oil industry of the country would land in reliable hands. However, weeks rolled by without any news from Exxon. Finally President Brazauskas asked me to find out what happened.

I telephoned Ken Jamieson and asked if Exxon had come to any decisions regarding Lithuania. What I heard certainly did not give me any cause for joy. It seems that the European Division experts completed a situational analysis of the country's market and the refinery and had concluded that acquisition of Mažeikių Nafta was not worthwhile. Exxon probably decided they did not want to risk their relations with the Russians. They would have to put their money into Lithuania, which promised a very hazy future business perspective because of problems getting a supply of crude oil to the refinery. Furthermore, the market in Lithuania was no more than a drop in the ocean to such a gigantic multinational company.

Later a myth grew in Lithuania that Mažeikių Nafta could have been easily sold to some other Western company and much more profitably than the results of the later sale to Williams. Due to my experience, I knew that such thinking was erroneous. It was nonsense to presume that a line of companies was standing outside the door of the refinery, dreaming about a chance to invest their money into Mažeikių Nafta as quickly as possible. Realistically, the Lithuanian oil refinery was simply of no interest to major Western oil companies.

Just as my spirits were sinking, I heard that a large and reputable American company was indeed interested in the oil conglomerate in Lithuania. My son-in-law, Roger Altman, who ran an investment company, told me one day that one of his clients, Williams Companies, was looking into the Lithuanian oil market and had requested financial expertise on Mažeikių Nafta. Roger invited me to join in their next meeting as an individual well versed on the situation in Lithuania. At that time I primarily listened to what was being said. I offered a bit of advice but I was not planning to get further involved in this investment plan.

Later I found out that Roger's company had performed an ordered financial report on the refinery on behalf of Williams and the conclusions were not positive. My son-in-law had great sympathy for Lithuania, however, he valued his good name too well to submit a client some embellished analysis on an actual situation. He recommended against the acquisition of Mažeikių Nafta by Williams due to its high business risk which pertained to limited sources of crude supplies.

Nevertheless, Williams continued scouting in Lithuania. Slowly the company entered into negotiations for the purchase of Mažeikių Nafta stock. At that point, I was invited to help reach an agreement between the American company and the Government of Lithuania. I dove right into matters with great enthusiasm, believing that Williams Company would be able to secure independent supplies of crude oil. There was not a doubt in my mind that an investment of this scope would be highly beneficial to the country economically. I had already heard talk about mismanagement and large-scale embezzlements going on at Mažeikių Nafta. It seemed to me that there was only one way to rescue Lithuania's oil refinery from a threatening bankruptcy – involvement by a reputable American company.

The negotiations proceeded with difficulty. Williams bargained hard, aiming to win as many concessions as possible to their interests. Although I did not participate directly in the negotiations, I was constantly informed of the progress of the talks. I didn't try to get to the bottom of all the legal and financial intricacies contained in the terms of contract. However, when differences of opinion arose, I would try to mediate without directly representing either side. The goal was to keep the dialogue going between Williams and the Government of Lithuania. American national interests were also involved. The United States Ambassador in Vilnius was keenly observing the course of negotiations; he was eager for an agreement to culminate. The Ambassador himself asked me on a number of occasions to assist in the deliberations on one issue or another.

This position on the part of the American government was a clear indication that the acquisition of Mažeikių Nafta had great political as well as strategic importance. Lithuania was already knocking on the doors of NATO by this time. Apparently Americans were also concerned about guarantees of energy supplies, independent of Russia, for their upcoming new member in the North Atlantic Treaty Organization.

Meanwhile the local political situation resulted in a new Cabinet of Ministers. Now Rolandas Paksas was named Prime Minister. I heard complaints from Williams representatives that they were unable to find common points for discussion with the new Prime Minister and the new Minister of the Economy, Eugenijus Maldeikis. The Americans harbored suspicions that Maldeikis was favoring the Russian company, Lukoil. There was much grumbling that negotiations dragged on needlessly, deliberating meaningless points.

Indeed much time was wasted in the process. The lack of clarity in the interminable discussions was a great disadvantage to all – Mažeikių Nafta, Lithuania and Williams. Negotiations stalled but, at long last, a mutual agreement appeared to have been reached. I was very pleased that this most complicating problem for the country had finally been resolved. I looked forward to attending the upcoming ceremonial signing of the agreement, expecting that it would be an enjoyable event, a culmination of the grueling work of negotiations. The last thing I expected was that the agreement on different points of the contract would result in a huge political scandal that hit like a thunderclap. Prime Minister Paksas publicly refused to sign the agreement with Williams, claiming it was detrimental to Lithuania. He and two of his ministers made a great display of resigning from office over this issue. The situation now was critical. At the last minute, the United States Embassy and some Lithuanian politicians moved in to soothe over matters.

The agreement was saved. The signing took place (an Interim Prime Minister was quickly delegated). Unfortunately all the negative press greatly influenced anti-American public opinion. Outside the *Seimas* building, demonstrators gathered, shouting that Lithuania was being sold to foreigners. Holding a brick in his outstretched hand and waving it threateningly before an agitated crowd was Arvydas Juozaitis, the one-time philosopher whom I had befriended during the early days of the *Sąjūdis* movement.

The press wrote all sorts of inaccurate articles about my son-in-law and me which were very disheartening. After all of this, I no longer got involved in the relations between Williams and the Government of Lithuania. I never analyzed all the terms of the agreement for Mažeikių Nafta either. Maybe the negotiators on the Lithuanian side did make mistakes, providing Williams too much insurance against their own business risk as was claimed. Even so that sort of position on the American side should not be overly condemned. They were determined to start a business in an unfamiliar market. They had already encountered opposition from the Russian oil company, Lukoil, which was accustomed to dictating conditions in this region.

All in all, I expected now that the agreement with Williams was closed and that every future Government of the country would try to work hand-in-hand with the American managers of Mažeikių Nafta. It was now in the interests of Lithuania to assure the company's success. However, I heard complaints that Williams had to work in an extremely unfavorable political atmosphere. Apparently certain politicians could not care less about the consequences to Lithuania. They wanted matters at Mažeikių Nafta to run as badly as possible. Such ill will could indeed interfere with the ability of Williams to reach positive business results.

On the other hand, Williams might have made more efforts to improve their image in Lithuania. Early on, well before the signing of the agreement, when only a few publications had issued negative opinions on the American company, I advised the members of top management to become more active and publicly explain their intentions. Further I suggested that they should not spare funds for charity, sports and advertising. They neglected to do this for a long time, probably believing that it was best to maintain a distance from the controversy raging in Lithuania. In the meantime, their opponents worked the propaganda with all their might. While the Americans stood by quietly, an image of Williams as an enemy of Lithuania effectively formed.

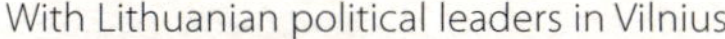
With Lithuanian political leaders in Vilnius

Williams concluded the acquisition of Mažeikių Nafta in 1999. The acquisition became a football in Lithuanian politics. Opposition to Williams was seemingly well financed because it never abated in the media. It was even a key topic in the Presidential election campaign debate in 2003. In August 2002, Williams sold its interests and management rights to the Russian privately owned company, Yukos Oil.

Omnitel – A Child of Fortune

My oldest son, Joseph, came to work for my company, Neris, in 1980. The scope of coal exports had started shrinking, and I decided to turn the business over to my son. Joe continued exporting coal for about another five years, but the amount of business was declining. Major oil and coal corporations have taken over the world market in coal trading. Average-sized companies, such as mine, had a hard time surviving.

While Joe was engaged in the coal business, I would help him handle certain matters. However, I spent most of my time on other investment projects. I got interested in exploring business possibilities in Lithuania. Even before the declaration of the Independence Act on March 11, 1990, I was already considering ways in which I could get involved in the economy of the country.

The idea for forming a cellular (mobile) telephone company unexpectedly came to me back then for political reasons. My initial efforts were to find ways to provide the *Sąjūdis* movement, later on, the government officials of Lithuania with a communications channel that was free of Moscow control.

Calling from New York to Vilnius was a terrible headache in those early days. I'd have to muster up all my patience while dialing a number in Vilnius over and over again. This would sometimes take an entire hour. The Moscow code had to be dialed first. Generally a busy signal would start beeping. If you succeeded in connecting, then Vilnius was always busy. This process could go on endlessly.

During the *perestroika* period, it was clear that the old and inefficient telephone lines were incapable of handling the increasing numbers of international calls between the Soviet Union and the West. But after independence, since all calls were still routed through Moscow, I believe there was a conscious effort to hinder international communications. We could sense that someone was listening to our conversations, especially when the contact was with important politicians of the country. We'd hear strange sounds and, when the line would start breaking up, we'd joke around, saying we had to wait until the tape of the outside listener was replaced.

I became obsessed with the notion that something had to be done to overcome this reliance on Moscow for our phone lines. An idea was forming in my mind to find a way to lay a wireless channel of communications between Lithuania and the West.

Cellular telephone communications were expanding in the West. The United States was in the early stages of laying the groundwork for such linking channels. I began considering different means for generating a satellite connection whose signal could be directed towards any area on earth for contacts between Lithuania and the West. Such telephones were already being used in areas where cable connections were impossible, particularly on ships. Personally I did not have a satellite telephone; however, I had seen them on the yachts of some of my friends. Otherwise I really didn't know anything about this technology. First I needed specialists who could advise me on the possibilities for launching this sort of telecommunications in Lithuania.

I decided to ask officials at the CIA about this. They declined to help, arguing that the CIA could not get involved in such matters, but I did not give up. I asked my stockbroker to direct me to companies engaged in satellite communications. One sent over their specialist to talk to me. By coincidence this man, Bob Wilson, was an American of Lithuanian descent. He promised to introduce me to two experts who had previously worked for International Telephone and Telegraph (ITT), one of the leading telecommunications companies in the world.

When we got together, I was somewhat surprised that the experts spoke very little themselves; they mostly listened to what Bob Wilson and I had to say. But they promised to analyze the situation and provide us with specific answers to the questions I had raised. (It wasn't until later that I learned from Wilson that both of these men were communications engineers working for the FBI.)

After a few weeks, we met again with these men who told me that they were unable to get involved in such a project themselves. Nonetheless, they introduced me to a highly qualified specialist in satellite communications systems. He was also an American of Lithuanian descent who had participated in setting up the so-called "hot line" between Washington and Moscow. His job had been to work with Soviet telephone specialists. In other words, he was very familiar with the technical aspects of Lithuania's trunk lines and other sorts of local communication conditions.

His name was Algimantas Prekeris. After I called him, I learned that he had been a postwar immigrant, the same as I. Having been born in Lithuania, he had not forgotten his native language.

Prekeris enthusiastically approved of my idea. The Government of Lithuania, at the very least, had to have a satellite link installed. However, he could not give me an immediate answer about how this could be accomplished from a technical standpoint nor how much such a project might cost.

Prekeris and I met again after a week. He explained, "There are several means for installing satellite communications for the government of Lithuania, but a number of problems come up. The first is an international problem. The link has to be officially registered. However, will Moscow agree to this? Probably not. If we set it up without registering it, in a sense, we would be operating illegally. We'd be more or less telephone pirates."

Nevertheless, he recommended some other means for such a connection that seemed quite realistic. One was to hire or acquire a ship, sailing on the neutral waters of the Baltic Sea, and install a satellite station on it. A low-power station of sufficient strength to send telephone signals over to the ship would then be erected in Lithuania. Unfortunately, this method had many drawbacks. The capacity for communications would be very low and could be used only by a few people – *Seimas* Chairman Landsbergis and Prime Minister Vagnorius. The expenses were considerable, and there would be serious legal difficulties.

Another means of installing a satellite link, according to Prekeris, was to build a fairly powerful earth station in Lithuania which could transmit signals directly to one of the satellites. No ship on the Baltic Sea would be needed in this case. The capacities for telephone service were also considerably greater. The Government of Lithuania would need to issue an official permit for such a station, and Prekeris would see to the registration with the Federal Communications Commission. At that point, an agreement could be drawn up with ITT, Sprint or some other company which would be able to receive signals from Lithuania via their own networks and supply services for the desired number of telephone calls. However, the potential success of this plan was not clear either. No one could firmly assure that the huge Western companies would supply services to clients in Lithuania, particularly if Russia were to threaten some sort of sanctions.

Prekeris said he knew where to acquire a satellite station. I asked what the possible price for such technology might be. Apparently a sum of some two to three million dollars was needed. Delivery of station equipment and its installation in Lithuania could be handled in three months. "If it's really possible to acquire satellite communications this quickly, then let's push this project forward," I said.

Not long after, Landsbergis flew to Washington for a reception and met Prekeris. When we told Landsbergis about our idea, he was enthusiastic. "Get this done as fast as possible! You will be provided with all the necessary permits and any other conditions for this work."

Prekeris wasted no time and received his company's permit for erecting an earth satellite station in Lithuania. He took on this work energetically. He flew to Vilnius a number of times, handled all the necessary documentations and drafted the specifications for erecting the station. At that point, the necessary equipment was purchased and delivered, and a satellite station was assembled. But Prekeris was too much of an optimist in predicting three months for the project's completion. Despite the fact that we spared neither our forces nor our money, it took about twice as long to finish the job.

When I started this project, Lithuania had not yet recovered from the bloody January 13th attack. By the time we surmounted all our difficulties and installed the station in the Nemenčinė area, not far from Vilnius, the political situation had changed. The Soviet Union began crumbling after the attempted overthrow of Gorbachev in August of 1991. Lithuania won true independence and action for international recognition immediately thereafter. Even with these new conditions and the fact that much of the direct control from Moscow had been severed, an adequate communications channel was still vitally needed.

New Omnitel office in Kaunas

I named my newly registered telecommunications company, Litcom. The giant multinational, ITT, agreed to work with us. This permitted telephone calls to and from Lithuania from any area in the world, circumventing Moscow entirely. Neither Latvia nor Estonia had such a system at the time. Naturally orders for telecommunications services soon starting coming in from these countries, as well as the Ukraine. This greatly increased the number of Litcom users. The satellite station was able to operate at a profit from the start although profits, of course, were still insignificant.

But soon there was a problem. Quite quickly we noticed that the number of subscribers from the Ukraine was quickly increasing. For some reason, they would limit all their calls to a very short duration, lasting only seconds. Our engineers caught on to the situation. The Ukrainians had built their own station and were only using Litcom to connect into ITT networks with their own subscribers. In essence they were cheating us. We had no use for clients like those.

Satellite stations were built in both Latvia and Estonia in about a year. Litcom was now limited to the Lithuanian market alone. However, by that time, the number of users had grown in our own country, permitting us to operate at a profit. This was icing on the cake. Earnings were not my prime consideration when I decided to undertake the project. My entire motive was to help Lithuania break away from the dangerous, absolute dependence on Moscow in one critical area – international telephone communications.

However, during 1992, it became clear that telecommunications service was not merely a political necessity but a serious business with high demand in Lithuania that would require development and new investments. I decided that the time had come for wireless, not satellite, connections. The future was in mobile communications – cell phones. My nephew, Gediminas Gruodis, came to work for Litcom. Eventually he took over the management of the new mobile telecommunications company that we named Omnitel.

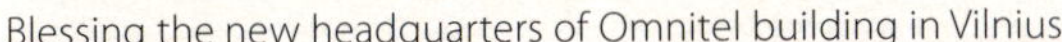

Blessing the new headquarters of Omnitel building in Vilnius

After researching the possibilities for supplying mobile phone service in Lithuania and preparing a business plan in 1993, we met with the Prime Minister, Adolfas Šleževičius. He had an idea. "Could you interest some leading cellular company like Motorola to enter into a joint business venture with you?" he asked us. Laying out his reasoning, he said, "This company is already selling their products here, and it has made a good name for itself. Your request for a license to operate cellular communications would gain in stature; plus greater financial opportunities would open up."

Šleževičius remembered one thing more. A Lithuanian by the name of Jonas Šalčius worked for Motorola in Chicago and came to Lithuania on business quite often. I phoned him in Chicago. He reminded me that we had met at various functions of the American Lithuanian Community. Without having to go into any long introduction, I told him about my desire to establish a mobile cellular phone company in Lithuania. This company, I said, could significantly contribute to the modernization of our country. "Perhaps Motorola might want to get involved in this business. What do you think?" I asked Jonas.

He explained that his work was not related to Motorola's investment projects but promised to speak with his colleagues who were responsible for this sphere of operations. I didn't need to wait long for an answer. "My company is keenly interested in your proposal," Jonas said when he called back.

I asked him to forward my invitation to the appropriate Motorola representatives to come to New York where we could discuss the matter. During our first meeting, we agreed that I would sell Motorola 38% of the shares in Litcom, leaving 62% in the hands of my family, which was exactly what I had offered them. At the time Motorola would have been satisfied with 25% of the company. However, I wanted this powerful company to get involved in our project on a greater scale. That would make Motorola all the more committed to its success.

The situation of Litcom was pressing us to find a strategic partner as fast as possible. We were operating solely in the market of one country. We clearly understood that, should someone else form a mobile phone company, we would have to pull out of the business because profitability would become impossible. We'd be holding a reasonably powerful satellite station, but one that was doomed to becoming entirely unnecessary. This did happen over time. As the business in cellular phone service expanded, the station in Nemenčinė had to be dismantled.

As early as 1993, I understood that we would have to operate on the basis of modern wireless connection technologies. We still couldn't quite imagine what sort of an investment was necessary; however, our calculations showed that we wouldn't get by without some $10 million. Later we learned that the investment would require 10 times that of the initial projection. Even our original estimate had appeared overwhelming to us. We didn't want to risk such a huge amount of money in an entirely new business alone.

Naturally we had no idea in 1993 that the use of cellular telephones in Lithuania would grow in leaps and bounds at a maddening speed. Our initial forecast was to serve 16,000 subscribers by the year 2000. But when the year 2000 arrived, Omnitel had 308,000 clients! Such growth, twenty times greater than anticipated, also required investments several times greater than planned.

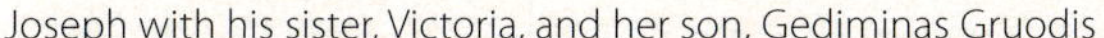
Joseph with his sister, Victoria, and her son, Gediminas Gruodis

The initial, modest idea grew into a serious business venture, demanding tremendous investments. At the start, I was simply pleased to be creating something entirely new in Lithuania. I had little concept of the ultimate demand for mobile phone services. All I knew was that I was risking my own money.

Once Motorola became the new stockholder in Omnitel, it was easier to obtain the investments we needed for the development and growth of Omnitel and the telecommunications system – about $150 million. With the participation of Motorola, a giant multinational in telecommunications technology, we received bank loans at favorable terms and a credit from a special support program of the United States for developing countries.

Omnitel grew at a rate that was much more rapid and successful than we would have ever dared to dream. All I had wanted in the beginning was independence from Moscow. Later I wanted to contribute to the modernization of my country. Modern, reliable communications have tremendous influence on the entire evolvement of the economy. In the end business success had clearly followed me once again. Omnitel became one of the most profitable companies in Lithuania. I was actually glad when Bitė Company and, later, Tele-2 began competing with us. My forecast of this situation proved correct. The appearance of competitors only enlivened the market in Lithuania. Cellular telephones became extremely popular. The number of Omnitel clients grew even more rapidly than during the early years when we were the only operators. Now there's an Internet boom in Lithuania. Since Omnitel is the largest mobile telecommunications company in all three Baltic Republics, I expect that it will be playing first violin once again.

I was proud of Omnitel's success. Nevertheless, the time came for me to think about finding another powerful strategic partner to take over the control of the company which I had built. Telecommunications is a rapidly developing sphere of business. New technology is discovered constantly, expanding the use of its services. Omnitel may have been the largest operator of mobile telephone services in the Baltic Republics; on a world scale, it was a comparatively small venture.

Gigantic global corporations have become entrenched in the telecommunications business; they have divided up virtually all world markets among themselves. This is a business of limitless opportunities. The capital of different telecommunications corporations is often intertwined. They own each other's stocks and form joint venture companies. By combining their forces, these giant multinationals are rapidly able to introduce innovations and acquire inventions.

Omnitel reached a peak in 1997; we had to decide anew on growth plans for our company. Geographic expansion was one option. Omnitel could begin operating in telecommunications markets of other countries. New clients were still available in Lithuania and could be attracted. A launch of new, related telecommunications technology was also possible. Either one of these three choices required large capital investments and organizational experience.

Our greatest asset was that we had a powerful partner in Motorola which controlled over a third of the share in Omnitel. Its top management valued the growth and profitability of our company. However, Motorola did not have particularly strategic interests in Lithuania. Since it was primarily a manufacturer of telecommunications technology, the supply of mobile phone services was a business that was in second or third place of importance to them.

I also had personal reasons for considering the transfer of Omnitel management to a strategic partner. I was approaching the eighth decade of my life. I sensed that my active participation in business was coming to an end. It was time for me to give up the difficult obligations as Chairman of the Omnitel Board of Directors. I knew that the only way I could withdraw with a clear conscience was to find a solid, powerful partner for the company I had created.

Yet I had another reason to look for a strategic partner. The proposed Law on Telecommunications of Lithuania included provisions for certain monopolistic rights for Lithuanian Telecom. Furthermore, the Government awarded Telecom a license for providing Internet services without opening bidding procedures on tenders. I understood that this could raise a threat to our company in the future. Should Lithuanian Telecom purchase a powerful company – exactly what it did indeed do – it would be a tough competitor due to the amount of available capital and tremendous experience it had in this field.

We hired two investment consultants from the United States, Lehman Brothers and Evercore Partners. They performed situational analyses on the Lithuanian economy and growth trends and made future projections on the telecommunications business perspectives. They also assessed our competition and arrived at the same conclusion as I had – we had to find a strategic partner.

In 1998, we made a very favorable deal with the consortium of Finnish Sonera and Swedish Telia, both highly experienced mobile communications operators who were also the new owners of Lithuanian Telecom. I sold my family's controlling stock package in Omnitel but retained about 10% in our own hands. This was at the request of the Swedish and Finnish sides. They persuaded me not to resign from the company which I had formed. I agreed to stay on for a time as the Honorary Chairman of the Omnitel Board of Directors.

Acquaintances in the World of Politics

I became acquainted with probably all the most important politicians during the Rebirth period of Lithuania. That was a very intense time in our country's history, and there were frequent, harsh disagreements between the different parties. Some politicians felt an absolute aversion for one another. However, I always tried to interact with all naturally, paying no attention to their interrelationships. Nobody ever found fault with me for this.

For example, I always did and do consider Vytautas Landsbergis to be my friend. By the same token, I also consider leftist leader Algirdas Brazauskas, who won the Presidency in the summer of 1993, a friend as well. These two distinguished men in Lithuanian politics were diametrically opposed to one another ideologically. Both knew that I interacted with each of them and each one respectfully tolerated this. They never indicated the least bit of annoyance with me for this.

I have never stopped respecting Landsbergis for his unwavering principles in defending Lithuania from any sort of encroachment on its sovereignty. Naturally he always first perceived such schemes in Russian politics, which he vigilantly watched, probably with a good dose of suspicion. The outlook of Brazauskas was considerably different in this aspect.

It was easy for me to understand the certain distrust that Landsbergis had towards Russia due to my own experience when the ultimate

With Professor and Parliamentarian Landsbergis and his wife, Gražina in East Hampton

Russian occupation caused me to flee my own homeland. Every large country, particularly one with centuries of imperialistic traditions, at least attempts to dominate its own region. I am convinced that Russia is changing, becoming more democratic. However, that doesn't mean that its pursuit for domination has entirely disappeared, especially in regard to the Baltic Republics, which Russia has always considered within its own sphere of influence. Thus I essentially endorse the views of Landsbergis that danger from Russia continues to exist and that vigilance is necessary, operating under the principle of "hoping for the best but preparing for the worst."

Of course I wouldn't approve of a somewhat hysterical reaction to every political step that Russia takes. I don't think it's appropriate always to perceive guile from Russia and an effort to harm Lithuania. It's simply necessary to uphold a calm and deliberate political stance in respect to Russia without falling into its hands. In most cases, it seemed to me that Landsbergis was attempting to execute politics of this specific sort.

I met Brazauskas back when he served as the second in command to Prime Minister Prunskienė. His decision to accept this position after first turning down the offer to serve as Assistant to the Chairman of the Parliament (then the Supreme Council), Landsbergis, had somewhat surprised me. Back then Brazauskas was Secretary of the Communist Party for Lithuania. I have been a staunch opponent of this political force all my life. Regardless I felt a personal sense of respect for Brazauskas for his determination to serve Prunskienė in the first Government. Such a move was testimony that to this politician, responsibility for his country took precedence over his personal ambitions.

When I was visiting Vilnius in January 1990 with Larry Summers and his colleague, Andrei Shleifer, who were helping to reorganize the economy of Lithuania, I decided to call on the leaders of the Communist Party. I thought it would be well worth the while to explain the possible means for transition from a centralized command to a market economy. Brazauskas invited us to the Party headquarters, located in the building that was transferred to the newly independent Government. All the predecessors of Brazauskas had also occupied this same office.

At the start off our discussion, I said in jest, "We have come to tell you how to introduce material inequality in Lithuania – if socialism was equality in poverty, then capitalism is inequality in wealth."

Brazauskas laughed heartily at my little joke. From our very first meeting, my impression of Brazauskas was that he was definitely not imprisoned in the petrified dogma of communism. He displayed a sharp-witted and healthy mind; he was able to interact with people easily. The American professors also formed a positive opinion about Brazauskas.

A few months later, Prime Minister Prunskienė called to ask if I would be able to host Brazauskas during his visit to the United States. The American Lithuanian Community made it a point to keep him at a distance as a Communist Party leader (notwithstanding that, by that time, his political party was the Lithuanian Democratic Labor Party). Actually Brazauskas did not force himself on the community. Instead he met only with his acquaintances. I invited him for lunch at the Yale University Club in New York with three affluent Americans of Lithuanian descent. These men had not retained any contacts with our ethnic community; therefore they were able to speak with Brazauskas solely as the Vice Prime Minister of Lithuania, devoid of negative emotions towards him as a former communist.

With the President Algirdas Brazauskas on the occasion of receiving the Order of Gediminas award, 1995

The Kazickas family with President Brazauskas

It turned out to be easy to get along with Brazauskas. Over lunch he said that he was tasting oysters for the first time in his life. He had a good time, laughing about this. "Here I am," he joked, "I've lived nearly six decades and never knew before that shellfish is edible and an entirely delicious food."

Without question we also discussed the political situation of Lithuania but more in terms of international aspects. That time Brazauskas did not mention a word about any internal disagreements.

Brazauskas was elected President in February of 1993. I called on him at the Presidency, which, at the time, was still in the *Seimas* building, to congratulate him on his victory. We wound up having a lengthy discussion. I told him about my plans for developing wireless phone connections in Lithuania. He listened to me with great interest and promised his help should any bureaucratic obstacles interfere with my plans.

From that time forth, I developed very friendly relations with Brazauskas. The transition in his political biography did not stand in our way at all. We had many pleasant talks while he was in office and after his term had ended. The fact that I did not approve of his return into the political arena in 2000 and told him so, looking straight in his eyes, had no negative influence on our relationship either. I had given him all my arguments why I thought he was making a mistake by stepping back in as the leader of the leftists, representing them by taking on the duties of Prime Minister. My being so straightforward with him did not cause Brazauskas any discomfort. It seemed the opposite happened. A while later, I received a letter from him in which he thanked me for speaking so openly with him.

In 1997 the President elected for a five year term was Valdas Adamkus, who was born in Lithuania and immigrated to the United States in 1949. Although, during his campaign, questions were raised whether an émigré could understand the depth of national emotion – from the suffering and despair of people during the Soviet occupation to the struggle for freedom and independence – I soon became convinced that he was outstandingly capable of defending Lithuania's interests in the international arena, particularly since Lithuania was knocking on the doors of NATO and the European Union. Furthermore, he displayed an elegant political style. As his first campaign progressed, Adamkus proved that he could gain the respect of the country and guide it into its integration with the wider world.

When Adamkus ran for a second term in office in 2002, I was very supportive. I felt it was exceedingly important under existing local condition that no special interest groups would have undue influence over a politician of this stature. In my opinion, Lithuania needed a president who was not a member of any party to bring better balance to the political forces operating in the country.

But that time Adamkus lost unexpectedly by a thin margin to populist Rolandas Paksas, who was later impeached by a Parliamentary vote on April 6, 2004. Soon afterwards, when the new election was announced, Adamkus ran for president and was elected once again, defeating Kazimiera Prunskienė in a close race.

For me his victory was an especially happy and satisfying one. Despite nail-biting tension as the polls were closing, I had no doubt that he would win especially after the scandalous tenure of Paksas and the revelations of machinations by unsavory Russian characters to control the presidency. (Adamkus finally won with 52 per cent of the vote.) But the tightness of the race revealed a great deal to me about the mood of the Lithuanian

At the golden wedding anniversary of President Valdas Adamkus and his wife, Alma, in Vilnius, September 1, 2001

people. I sensed that people were concerned about his age (he was 77 at the time) and were looking for someone different who would bring unity, hope and leadership that was much needed after Paksas. Prunskienė was indeed younger and a well-known personality who was associated in people's minds with Sąjūdis and the March 11 Declaration of Independence and had served as Lithuania's first Prime Minister.

But I think that President Adamkus is the right man at the right time for Lithuania. He has excellent relationships with foreign leaders like George Bush, Jacques Chirac and Tony Blair as well as European royalty. In many instances the protocol rules were broken, and he has been treated like a leader from a country of much larger size and importance than our humble homeland.

I only regret that the Lithuania media rarely writes about these kinds of details. I presume journalists are concerned that such reports might be seen as promotion of a personality cult. They had enough of that under the Soviet system.

Over the years our friendship has developed into a very meaningful and mutually respectful relationship. Such a relationship is possible only between people whose moral and ethical standards are very similar. To me he is a man of the highest standards and also my friend with whom I can exchange ideas, opinions and suggestions without reservations. President Adamkus in his position, as courteous as he is with many people, does not have the same luxury of openness in human interactions as I do. Thus having me as sounding board in difficult times, I feel, may be a comfort to him and, needless to say, being able to talk to him frankly is a great honor and privilege for me.

All my life I have respected people with whom it's possible to speak one's mind openly, even though opinions may sometimes vary. I have befriended a great number of individuals; naturally some hold convictions that are different from my own. Despite this, I am usually able to maintain excellent personal relationships with a broad variety of people.

I think I have several advantages. For one, I am older than most of my friends in Lithuanian politics. Further, my life's experiences are significantly different from theirs because I am not directly involved in politics. Thus everyone understands that I am entirely independent. I'm not looking for any sort of privileges or support from my interactions with them. Only one aspect binds our relationships – we all have a mutual and keen desire that whatever affects Lithuania should be for the best.

June 23, 2000

I have not written a word in 41 years! So much has happened in my life. I have been sad and happy. I have traveled around the world, seen the most beautiful sights, and met with famous and important people. It's been an exciting life.

The children are grown, married and with children themselves. They live happily and well. But I cannot get over the loss of Alex. That was the greatest tragedy of my life.

And yet, how blessed I am to have this wonderful husband in my life. He has embraced me, cared for me and showered me with many worldly gifts.

But his enduring love is the greatest gift of all.

A Special Anniversary

Alexandra's and my 60th wedding anniversary on August 15, 2001 was approaching. I thought how wonderful it would be to celebrate our diamond anniversary at our home in Vilnius next to *Šv. Jonų* 'Sts. Johns''

Church – the spot where I had won my beloved's heart for life, way back during Christmas of 1940.

The thought of making a home on *Šv. Jono* 'St. John's' Street a gift for Alexandra did not come to me at once. Initially I was just looking for a place to display my hunting trophies. There were well over a hundred of them, scattered over my several homes; some were very rare and valuable. I thought my collection would make quite a nice gift for Lithuania if I were to arrange an exposition of hunting trophies, supplementing them with some art pieces.

The idea first came to Alexandra. She said to me, "Why don't you buy a house in Vilnius and make it into a small hunting museum? It could include a movie theater for educational purposes. We could show films on nature, for example the National Geographic series, to children and young people." Alexandra began tossing out all sorts of proposals.

I thought that was a great idea. All I had to do was bring it to life. I started looking around the center of Vilnius for a suitable place. After taking a look at a building on *Šv. Jono* Street in the Old Town, I knew I wanted to buy it right away. Its location held many memories. Nearby were the buildings of Vilnius University where we had received our educations. I was also reminded of my Christmas date with Alexandra, which took place so long ago next to this house. It seemed very symbolic to return to the dawning of our lives together after six decades.

After I bought the building, I hired architects to design a museum in it. But it turned out that these facilities were not especially suitable for displaying hunting trophies. I had to give up on the idea. Brazauskas suggested that I donate my collection to the historical museum at Trakai which is a reconstruction of an ancient castle, the capital of Lithuania during the 1400s, prior to Vilnius, situated on five lakes. It is a popular destination for tourists. I saw a similar exhibit there, and that convinced me that this would be a suitable home for my trophies. When I arrived in Vilnius for our anniversary celebration, I donated part of my collection to the Trakai museum.

Since I no longer needed such a space, I had to figure out what to do with my acquisition on *Šv. Jono* Street. It seemed best to develop it into a representational residence, adapted to the historical look of the site which is surrounded by monuments of ancient architecture. A small plot

60th wedding anniversary, August 15, 2001

The house on Šv. Jono Street

of land belonged to the house. I decided that I would clean up the yard and the surroundings and develop a cozy garden.

I proceeded to build a home. Although I would have little use for it, I felt as though I were repaying an old debt to Vilnius, the city of my studies, my youth and my love. In a way, it was also a repayment of a debt to Lithuania. I wanted the house to harmonize with the rest of the historic Old Town and upgrade the somewhat neglected territory where the manor of Cardinal Jurgis Radvila had once stood. This desire to beautify the Vilnius Old Town prompted me to spare no effort in fixing up the exterior of the house and creating an elegant interior.

Naturally reconstruction and decorative work took some time but, by the spring of 2001, it was near completion. I could see that the house suited my aesthetic taste and I felt comfortable in it. I thought it would be an ideal place for Alexandra and me to celebrate our 60th anniversary.

That August our family of twenty-one-members gathered together in Vilnius – eleven grandchildren, our daughter and three sons with their spouses and, of course, Alytė and I, the diamond-honed newlyweds. Over a hundred of our friends came from the United States, several European countries and even Australia. The eve of our anniversary was spent with our guests, listening to a wondrous concert held especially for our occasion at *Šv. Kazimiero* 'St. Casmir's' Church. Running through my mind was how very good it felt to be back in the land of my birthright.

The 15th of August arrived. Alytė and I were just as nervous as we were sixty years ago, awaiting the blessing of our union from the priest at Šv. *Mikalojaus* 'St. Michael's' Church, back in 1941. The only difference was that this time, we were blessed by a member of the American émigré community, Bishop Paulius Baltakis.

It seemed that we landed back in time to 1941. Our marriage might have taken place only yesterday. Again a party awaited the public declaration of our love. Only this time, the party was not around an impoverished wartime table in an apartment with darkened windows. We celebrated at an elegant restaurant with 300 guests.

A group of friends met us with flowers as we walked out of church. I looked over at my Alytė, who was aglow in happiness. It gave me pause for wonder. I have no idea how long God intends for us to live, but we shall never stop greeting each God-given day with joy.

EPILOGUE

President George W. Bush with Lithuanian dignitaries, 2004

I thought that Lithuania becoming truly independent again would be the ultimate achievement for all of us who worked so hard and so long to make it possible. It was then beyond thrilling to join the community of the United Nations and finally to be admitted to NATO, the capstone of Lithuania's reentry into the free world. Now we are also members of the European Union.

In all my conversations with Presidents over the years, starting with Dwight Eisenhower to George Bush, when I was promoting the cause of an independent Lithuania, I always hoped that some day, an American President would come and visit.

With Presidents Adamkus of Lithuania and George Bush of the United States, 2004

In November 2002, the White House announced that President George W. Bush would travel to Lithuania after a meeting of NATO in Prague. For me it was beyond a dream come true, and I hastily arranged a trip to Vilnius so I could be there.

At a reception for Bush in the City Hall, it just so happened that I was standing close to the podium when I saw Secretary of State Colin Powell and National Security Adviser, Condoleeza Rice.

"Miss Rice, I don't know if you remember me, but I am very grateful for what you did for Lithuania. May I kiss you?" She looked at me with a bemused expression. I said I hoped my humorous attempt at gallantry was not too forward and she would be reminded of the meeting in the Oval Office in 1990 with Prime Minister Prunskienė and President George Bush.

Rice smiled. "Yes, yes, I remember you very well."

And I said, "Thank you very much. You see what happened as a result of that meeting. Lithuania is free, about to enter NATO, and you had a lot to do with that. I love you. I really do. "

Sadly I did not get to kiss her but I did grab an opportunity to speak with the President later at a photo session.

As he was shaking hands with well-wishers and saying good-bye on his way out of the room, I approached him and said, "President Bush, I just want you to know that I am indebted to three generations of the Bush family."

"Fine, fine. That's very nice," he mumbled as he started to walk away. Suddenly he turned around and said, "What do you mean by three generations?"

"Your grandfather, your father and you."

"How come?" he said, looking puzzled.

"Your grandfather was one of my sponsors to the Hobe Sound Club. Your father met with me and Prime Minister Prunskienė and was responsible for our meetings with Mrs. Thatcher and the heads of state of France and Germany and now you have helped Lithuania be admitted to NATO. I am so grateful."

And that was that. It was another one of my small, serendipitous encounters with a U.S. president. But at least I was able to say thank-you for what America has done for my beloved Lithuania.

But the true end of this odyssey, when my life came full circle, happened a few years earlier when I saw the place that I once assumed was lost to me forever.

All my life, I had a tremendous longing and desire to go back to Chornaya Padina and see the village where I was born, my parents were born and the tragedy of the deportation of my ancestors took place. That deportation of 1863 was, in a sense, a prelude to what happened when the Soviets took over in 1940 and hundreds of thousands of people were exiled to Siberia. When I heard that a group of students had gone there to do research on the remains of the Lithuanian community and I saw the video of their visit, I knew I had to go see my birthplace and say a prayer at the graves of my ancestors.

And then, in a most fortuitous way through John Mroz of the East West Institute, I was introduced to the Russian billionaire, Mikhail Khodorkofsky, the founder of Yukos Oil. He was the most prominent of the infamous Russian oligarchs who amassed huge fortunes in the years after the collapse of the Soviet empire in smart and fast dealings. (In 2005, as it would happen, he was sentenced to prison for eight years on charges of fraud and tax evasion.)

But, at the time I met him in the spring of 2001, I saw a modest, unassuming young man who was looking for advice on how to make the most of his substantial financial investment in Lithuania. We went for dinner at 21 Club and had an interesting discussion about the local economy and the political situation.

In the course of our long conversation, I told Khodorkofsky of my dream to visit Chornaya Padina. Out of the blue, he offered me the use of his private plane for the journey and insisted I call his chief aide when I wanted to make the trip.

About a year later, in June of 2002, there I was, sitting on a luxurious G5, feasting on champagne and caviar, with my wife and my four children on our way to Saratov, the closest airport to Chornaya Padina. Upon our arrival, the local dignitaries welcomed us and entertained us with a tour of the city and a festive dinner on the Volga. Staring at the wide, grey waters, I remembered my first glimpse of the fabled river in 1923 when my parents, my sister, Victoria, and I were returning to Lithuania. The Volga looked enormous to me then, as if we would never get to the other side and continue the long journey home.

I could hardly sleep that night in anticipation of the bus trip to Chornaya Padina, a distance of about 100 kilometers that took us nearly four hours over a rutted country road. Gazing at the vast expanse of green fields with nary a house or a horse or a farmer in sight, I felt even more deeply the sad plight of my ancestors. How bleak everything must have looked to them – those open steppes and nothing but uncertainty ahead of them.

The emotional tension kept building until, at last, we turned off the main road past clumps of wooden houses, and then I saw the one dirt road of my birthplace. I was barely five years old when my family left, but somewhere in my distant memory, it all came back to me.

The whole village had turned out to welcome us – more than a hundred strong. They stood on the steps of the local school with flowers. A young girl in our national costume extended the traditional greeting with a plate of bread and salt. I was surrounded by smiling, welcoming people who reached out to grab my hand. Some even had the Kazickas name and insisted they were my cousins. Perhaps they were since some of my relatives had stayed behind in 1923. Amazingly a few in the village could still speak Lithuanian.

I was unprepared for the intensity of my own emotions. I don't think anyone – my family or the people there – realized what I was going through. I suddenly felt as if I was in communion with the spirit of my ancestors. I felt such a deep connection and understanding that within us is the heritage of our parents and grandparents and that life is everlasting. We are transmitting to our own children our very being, our essence. I will continue to be alive in their persons long after I am gone from this earth as the spirit of my parents lives on in me.

In Chornaya Padina, 2002

I barely had time to collect myself when we were treated to a sumptuous lunch of soups, meats and salads and, of course, plenty of vodka. We sang some traditional Lithuanian songs, made toasts and exchanged gifts. I received a silver flask and my children were given pieces of wood painted with forest scenes. On my part, I had brought a dozen boxes of Lithuanian products including bread, cheese, honey, chocolates and spirits. I also presented the community with a computer for the school.

When I rose to speak, it was difficult for me to control my emotions. I felt as if they were all my relatives. Spiritually we were indeed family, linked together by our common heritage. In a profound way, I felt that I was home. I spoke of the beauty of Lithuania, the vitality in the country now that we were at last free and my hope that they could see the land whose soul ran through their blood. Some of the old ladies with weathered faces, their heads covered in scarves, wept.

I realized with sadness that very few of the people there would ever have the opportunity to travel the thousand miles to Lithuania. And maybe, for the young ones who had grown up in Russia, my sentimental outpouring had no relevance. But, nevertheless, I wanted them to feel the depth of my love for our mutual homeland.

After lunch we walked along the one main street through the village which, of course, was nothing more than a rutted, dusty dirt road.

Chornaya Padina, 2002

The old, rickety wooden houses with decoratively carved shutters and splashes of blue paint looked exactly as they did 80 years ago. But where was my house? Apparently it had burned down years ago, and now on the site was what looked like an auto repair shop with men at work on a broken down, rusty truck.

And where was the church that used to be right across from our house? The church was no more, replaced by a cultural center with a larger-than-life white plaster statue of Lenin in front.

We were invited to enter inside some of the houses. I always remembered that in my family's house, everything was clean and bright. I remembered how the beds were made with huge pillows. The floors were always shiny, gleaming in the sun that poured through lace-covered windows. When we went into the home of Mrs. Kazickas, the former principal of the school, those images of my childhood were reflected in the coziness of her home. There were rugs on the floors, little vases of plastic flowers and lace curtains on the windows. It was very shabby on the outside, but inside the family had made a real effort to create some beauty in their lives.

I think my children were shocked at the poverty of Chornaya Padina. But I was not surprised. I knew that those decades of Soviet oppression would take their toll. During the deportation, the Lithuanian community was able to create a standard of living that was much higher than that of the villages around it. Lithuanians exported grain, raised animals and built a school and church. This was something they were happy about – in spite of their forced eviction to the black hole of "Black Hollow."

But what I saw now was the brutal reality that there had been scant progress from the time my family left in 1923. The houses may have a black and white television now. But they looked exactly as they did a century ago. These people were living in a time warp, as if frozen in amber. I sensed there was no escape for them. They live there, they will die there. This was the end of their journey without hope.

Two old ladies, one on each of my arms, led me slowly to the cemetery. They could barely speak Lithuanian, but we conversed with great animation. I think all of us were pretending that we understood each other and remembered certain things, but the feelings were no less valid.

The cemetery was at the far end of the village enclosed by a rusty fence. Most of the gravestones were overgrown with tall grasses and weeds. Some mounds had no headstones or markings at all. I knew my great-grandfather and my grandfather were buried there somewhere, but it was impossible to find their graves.

In the middle of the cemetery stood a large cross draped with chains and two concrete slabs inscribed with the names of the original Lithuanian families who arrived in Chornaya Padina in 1863. The monument had been erected by Vladimir Kazarin, a Russian married to a Lithuanian deportee. He had been so moved by this story of the people who had suffered so much that he put up the memorial with his own hands. It was the only tangible evidence of any spirituality in that desolate, sad place, and I thought it was very beautiful.

After a few hours, it was time for us to head back to Vilnius. Just as we were leaving, a woman, named Albina, came up to me with a special request. With great urgency and whispering so no one else could hear, she asked if there was any way we could help to build a little chapel in the village. "We have no place to pray, no place to celebrate a baptism or a wedding. It would be so wonderful to have somewhere to go where we can find a few moments of spiritual peace."

I said I would do my best to help but put the thought aside as we bid our farewells and took the long trip back to Lithuania and then home to America. But the idea of building a chapel in Chornaya Padina kept haunting me. Seeing the statue of Lenin, where there once stood a church, bothered me. Wouldn't it be a wonderful thing, I decided, to contribute something to the spiritual life of this isolated community? This would be a much grander gift than a computer.

And so it was that less than a year later, I arranged for Mr. Kazarin to return to Chornaya Padina with a truck load of building supplies. The entire village pitched in to work on the construction. Now, near the cemetery, there is a beautiful red brick chapel with a simple stone slab altar, named St. Katerina, in memory of my mother. It is a welcome place for people to think about God in their lives.

To my great happiness, Albina told me there has been a profound religious rebirth in the village. People are asking to have their children baptized. There have been several weddings in the chapel. Every few weeks a priest comes from Saratov to conduct a mass. And now the residents of Chornaya Padina are talking about expanding the shrine since, some days, there is not enough room for all who want to come and pray.

I realize I will probably never see Chornaya Padina again. But I feel I fulfilled something for my parents. They would have been very happy that I went there to see where they were born, where they worked so hard and sweated in the fields on those long, hot summer days and where their relatives had died. Perhaps my children will go back one day and say a prayer in the little chapel for me and for all those who were not so fortunate to make it back to their beloved homeland, Lithuania, like I did with such joy and gratitude.

Palanga, 2001